Edited by Paul Bohannan

Law & warfare

Studies in the Anthropology of Conflict

Texas Press Sourcebooks in Anthropology

LAW AND WARFARE

Paul Bohannan

is professor of anthropology at the University of California, Santa Barbara. He previously taught at Northwestern University, where until 1963 he was also chairman of the Center for Social Science Research in African Affairs.

Born in Lincoln, Nebraska, he graduated from the University of Arizona and, a Rhodes scholar, attended Oxford University, where he received his B.Sc. and D.Phil. With his wife, Laura Bohannan, also an anthropologist, he spent a total of twenty-six months from 1949 to 1953 among the Tiv of central Nigeria, and in 1955 he spent nine months with the Wanga of Kenya.

Before going to Northwestern in 1959, he taught at Oxford University and Princeton University. He is the author of numerous monographs, articles, and books, including *Social Anthropology*, a textbook, and, with Philip Curtin, *Africa and Africans*. He has edited *African Homicide and Suicide* and, with George Dalton, a symposium, *Markets in Africa*. He wrote the *Encyclopedia Americana* article "Africa: Peoples and Cultures."

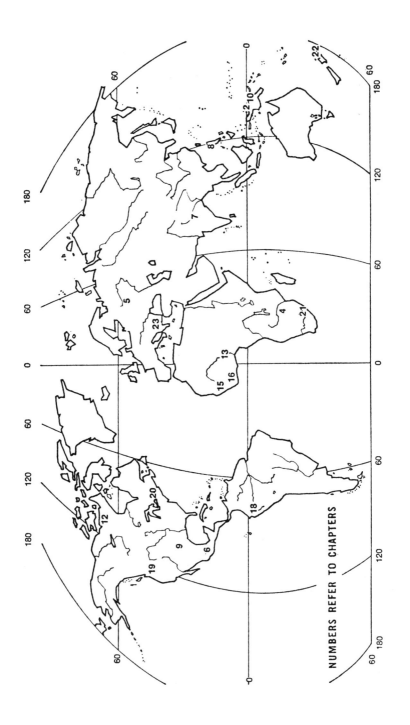

NUMBERS REFER TO CHAPTERS

Texas Press Sourcebooks in Anthropology
were originally published by the Natural History Press, a division
of Doubleday and Company, Inc. Responsibility for the series now
resides with the University of Texas Press, Box 7819, Austin, Texas
78713-7819. Whereas the series has been a joint effort between the
American Museum of Natural History and the Natural History
Press, future volumes in the series will be selected through the
auspices of the editorial offices of the University of Texas Press.

The purpose of the series will remain unchanged in its effort to
make available inexpensive, up-to-date, and authoritative volumes
for the student and the general reader in the field of anthropology.

Law
and
Warfare

Studies in the Anthropology of Conflict

Edited by Paul Bohannan

University of Texas Press

Austin

Published by arrangement with Doubleday & Company, Inc.
Previously published by the Natural History Press in cooperation
with Doubleday & Company, Inc.

Fourth Texas Printing, 1990

Requests for permission to reproduce material from this work
should be sent to Permissions, University of Texas Press, Box
7819, Austin, Texas 78713-7819.

∞ The paper used in this publication meets the minimum requirements
of American National Standard for Information Sciences—Perma-
nence of Paper for Printed Library Materials, ANSI Z39.48-1984.

Library of Congress Cataloging in Publication Data

Bohannan, Paul, ed.
    Law and warfare.

    (Texas Press sourcebooks in anthropology; 1)
    Reprint of the ed. published for the American Museum of
Natural History by the Natural History Press, Garden City, N.Y.,
in series: American Museum sourcebooks in anthropology.
Bibliography: p.
Includes index.
1. Law, Primitive—Addresses, essays, lectures. 2. Ethnological
jurisprudence—Addresses, essays, lectures. 3. War—Addresses,
essays, lectures. I. Title. II. Series. III. Series: American Museum
sourcebooks in anthropology.
Law   341.6   75-44033
ISBN 0-292-74617-2

CONTENTS

INTRODUCTION

Paul Bohannan

IN WESTERN society—and perhaps in most others, but that is beside our immediate point—conflict is unequivocally "a *bad* thing." It is typical that Western society tends to moralize about bad things—and, having salved its collective conscience, do nothing else. Westerners as a congeries of peoples do not like to think about or talk about cancer or hate or death—or conflict.

In the nineteenth century, we did it with sex—and are now putting up with the pendulum swing the while we congratulate ourselves on being "modern." In this mid-twentieth century, it is conflict and aggression that we have banished from polite society. And that is a tactical error, because conflict is just as basic an element as sex in the mammalian and cultural nature of man.

We shall never banish conflict. Indeed, it is wrongheaded and blind of us to think that we should. Rather, conflict must be controlled and must be utilized profitably in order to create more and better cultural means of living and working together—in short, conflict, whether it be marital or political, can, if it is adequately institutionalized, be used as the growing point of culture and of peace.

One of the important lessons to be gained from this book is the vision of how some societies of the world are racked by conflicts which other societies of the world have "solved." Head-hunting and feuding, wager of battle, ordeals and contests—all, in the West, have been replaced by the rule of law. And, indeed, to the lawyers and jurists of the world belongs a major part of the credit for the fact that some peoples of the world have managed to create institutions in which law and justice are on the same side, at least much of the time.

The West—and the world—need a new "code of aggression." We urgently need an institution that will control power institutions in which the power is inherent in two (or more) approximately equal political agents. In short, the next great step in legal institutions *must* be in the field of international law and other bicentric power situations. Bicentric power situations can be solved in some small-scale societies; but those which have developed the intricate national state have not yet solved the problems of the institutionalization of aggression.

The horizon is becoming clear. We know that mankind evolved to his present condition because he invented tools, and that one of the major types of tools to give him "survival value" was the weapon. We also know that every individual human creature must be "socialized"—which means that he must be taught the use of his society's tools, including weapons, and its concepts, including those about conflict. We are coming to know that conflict is not something to be "stopped," for that is merely wishful thinking of the blindest sort. Rather, society and individuals should be equipped to deal with it and profit from it.

Conflict is useful. In fact, society is impossible without conflict. But society is worse than impossible without control of conflict. The analogy to sex is relevant again: society is impossible without *regulated* sexuality: the degree of regulation differs among societies. But total repression leads to extinction; total lack of repression also leads to extinction. Total repression of conflict leads to anarchy just as surely as does total conflict.

We Westerners are afraid of conflict today because we no longer understand it. We see conflict in terms of divorce, rioting, war. And we reject them out of hand. And, when they happen, we have no "substitute institutions" to do the job that should have been done by the institution that failed. In the process— and to our cost—we do not allow ourselves to see that marriage, civil rights, and national states are all institutions built on conflict and its sensible, purposeful control.

This book examines conflict from the anthropological—which is to say, comparative—point of view. There are basically two forms of conflict resolution: administered rules and fighting. Law and war. Too much of either destroys what it is meant to protect or aggrandize.

I am interested, in this book, in bringing together good examples of various ways in which conflict is evaluated and handled. The book opens with three anthropological discussions of the nature of legal phenomena. Institutions and means of conflict resolution are then examined, most of them from several parts of the world: courts, middle men, self-help, wager of battle, contest, ordeal. Anyone can find gaps in either the geographical or the institutional coverage. Probably the biggest gap geographically is China and Russian Asia.

War—a word about which some purists make very restricted definitions (Turney-High 1949)—is represented by fewer articles, in part because there is so much smaller a literature from which to select. Here I have included articles on raids, either for heads or for livestock, and others on ways in which peoples organize for aggression in fairly large groups, and still others on tactics. I have also included an article on Albanian feuds, which are neither law nor war, but which rest uneasily—and most instructively—between the two.

Interestingly enough, warfare is seldom handled in the anthropological literature. With some noteworthy exceptions, the ethnography on it is of poorer quality than that on law, and the theoretical and comparative essays are comparatively rare. Turney-High's is probably the best book, but it runs to description and classification rather than to social and cultural analysis.

As in all American Museum Sourcebooks, an attempt has been made here to cover the phenomena in question as widely as possible, from as wide an ethnographic base as practical, and not to tout any particular area or any particular theoretical point of view. We recognize, of course, that mere arrangement presents a point of view, but this one seems minimally demanding. These articles are meant to present material for thought, discussion, and term papers. Most have been chosen from sources that are not readily available and certainly are scattered. I think they show how far we, as anthropologists and as Westerners, have come and how far we have to go.

PAUL BOHANNAN

Northwestern University
February 1966

Part I | THE NATURE OF LEGAL ANTHROPOLOGY

PRIMITIVE LAW

Robert Redfield

ONE WHO SETS out to talk about primitive law has a choice of three roads. The road to the right recognizes law to exist only where there are courts and codes supported by the fully politically organized state. This road quickly becomes a blind alley, for only a few preliterate societies have law in this sense, and these few are not characteristically primitive. Making this choice amounts to saying that there is no law in truly primitive society and that therefore there is nothing for one to talk about.

The road to the left has been recently opened with a great flourish by B. Malinowski (1926; 1934) and is apparently preferred by Julius Lips (1938). He who takes this road does not identify law with courts and codes. To Malinowski law consists of "the rules which curb human inclinations, passions or instinctive drives; rules which protect the rights of one citizen against the concupiscence, cupidity or malice of the other; rules which pertain to sex, property and safety." These rules are of course found everywhere, and in this sense law exists in the most primitive society. Malinowski (1938: lxii) notes that primitive people, like other people, are kept from doing what their neighbors do not want them to do chiefly not because of courts and policemen, but for many other personal and social reasons. In effect he bids us investigate the ways in which social control is brought about in the simpler societies, or at least the mechanisms whereby the individual is induced to do what people expect of him even

Reprinted by permission of the University of Cincinnati Law Review, from Vol. 33, No. 1, Winter 1964, pp. 1–22, and by permission of Dr. Margaret Park Redfield.

though through selfish interest he is tempted to do otherwise. This conception requires us to include under "law" any norm of conduct conformity to which is, as Malinowski puts it, "baited with inducements." If we take this road we find ourselves concerned with all the complicated and varying considerations of personal motivation and social advantage or disadvantage which are involved in deciding to do or not to do what people expect of us. Following him down this road, one has not too little to talk about but far too much.

There is no reason why one who wishes to do so should not study the mechanisms of social control. The effects of conventionalized relationships between members of a society in restricting the impulses of human nature and in bringing about established modes of conduct is an important subject. It is indeed highly desirable that we should study the functioning of law in its total social and personal setting, not only in primitive societies but in our own society. But to identify this subject matter with "law" has the great disadvantage of ignoring the special peculiarities of law as it is represented by what we know by that name in civilized societies. To us, who live under a developed system of law, law appears as something very different from the personal and cultural considerations which motivate our day-to-day choices of action. It appears as a system of principles and of restraints of action with accompanying paraphernalia of enforcement. The law is felt to be outside, independent, and coercive of us. Within its labyrinths we find our way as best we can.

This criticism, and others, of Malinowski's viewpoint with regard to primitive law have been effectively made by a lawyer, William Seagle (1937: 285). That writer also points out to students of the subject a middle road to follow. Along it at least one anthropologist, Radcliffe-Brown (1933: 202–6), is already going; it seems to me that this middle road is the wisest choice, so here I set out upon it.

I shall adhere to the idea of law that is derived from our acquaintance with the phenomenon as we know it in civilized societies: the systematic and formal application of force by the state in support of explicit rules of conduct. Like other institutions, law is represented on two sides, as Sumner (1906: 53) said: concept and structure. The concept consists of the principles and the rules restricting or requiring action; it is characteristic of law that these develop an explicitness and internal consistency, and that the maintenance and development of this internal organization becomes to the society, or at least to the lawyers, an objective in itself. The structure of the law is, of course, chiefly, process and court. Law is therefore recognizable in form: in formal statement of the rules, and in forms for securing compliance with the rules or satisfaction or punishment for their breach. The student of primitive law who follows the middle road will not expect to find among the simpler peoples a full development of something which he has first recognized in the complex and literate societies any more than he will expect to find double-entry bookkeeping there, or the outstanding examples of theology. But he may look for the modes of conduct in the simpler societies which in rudimentary form represent or anticipate law. He will not report as "primitive law" all socially or personally induced restraints upon human impulse to do something to the disadvantage of somebody else, but only such rules or procedures which, by their formal or systematic or coercive nature foreshadow our law and seem to illustrate the simpler modes of conduct out of which a law such as ours might develop. Our problem is, in Seagle's words, to determine "whether in the absence of full political organization and of specific juridical institutions such as courts and codes, certain modes of conduct may be segregated from the general body of conduct as at least incipiently legal" (Seagle 1937: 280).

There is, of course, no one "primitive law," any more than there is one primitive society. The preliterate societies vary greatly, and present us with many degrees and kinds of difference with regard to the presence of unwritten codes, of process, and of courts, and with many different forms and combinations of modes of conduct which foreshadow the juridical institutions of our own society. Here I may assemble and compare some of the rudiments of law as they are variously represented in very various societies. Only at the end of this paper shall I say something in general terms about what the rudimentary law found in primitive societies tends typically to be. The paper is chiefly devoted to pointing out that the beginnings of law are diverse, not unified, and to citing some instances of some of the principal elementary juridical, or proto-legal, institutions. The subject might be stated to be "rudimentary law as represented in some of the simpler societies." Rudimentary law might also be studied in such groups within the modern state as clubs, gangs and families. The highly developed state with its powerful law looms so large that perhaps we do not always see that within it are many little societies, each in some ways a little primitive society, enforcing its own special regulations with a little primitive law of its own. But here I stand as an anthropologist, and speak to the subject from what are sometimes called the "savage societies."

As the philosopher has been said to be able to begin any paper with Aristotle and the biologist with the amoeba, so the anthropologist is likely to start off with the Andaman Islanders; in the present instance this very primitive people is at hand to provide an instance of a society without even the most rudimentary elements of law, as I have just defined it. These natives have no means of composing disputes, and no specific sanctions which may be brought to bear on one who commits generally condemned acts. Apparently, quarrels are not infrequent, and may lead to considerable violence: a man may attack his adversary, or he may become so angry that he runs about ragefully destroying property, and not merely that of the immediate object of his anger, but any property that comes in his way. Yet a careful and critical student of the Andamanese (Radcliffe-Brown 1922: 48) tells us that there is no authority to intervene and no procedure to deal with the situation. The conventions of the society include no formal definition of appropriate compensation for the damage such a man may do, nor any specific procedure by which the injured party may secure revenge or damages, nor any way by which the group as a whole may punish the delinquent or secure itself against repetition of the act. A man who feels aggrieved may take whatever measures occur to him, acting for himself. If one man kills another, there are no consequences that are to be called "legal." A murderer will leave the camp and hide until he thinks he will be allowed to re-enter; or else the kinsmen of the dead man will take private vengeance. A man who makes himself generally disliked by violence or bad temper is visited by no specific sanction. Sorcery is recognized and is generally reprehensible, but no measures are taken against the sorcerer. In this particular society, therefore, the diffuse sanctions sometimes loosely lumped as "public opinion" (and the considerations of personal advantage and disadvantage which Malinowski is so interested in) are enough to keep the society running, and the people get along without any law at all.

There are other societies in which law is minimal not because conventional remedies are lacking but simply because controversy is strongly disapproved. This appears to be the case among the Zuni Indians. Here legal process is represented in simple form, for secular officials impose fines (Parsons 1917: 278–79), organizations of religious dancers may punish people who are delinquent in the performance of their ritual duties by ducking them (Parsons 1917), and cases of formal procedure against suspected witches are known (Stevenson 1901–2: 393–98). The Zuni constitute a more highly developed society than do the Andaman Islanders; there is a tribal organization, and certain functionaries are invested with authority on behalf of the tribe and may bring a formalized procedure to bear upon delinquents. Yet such occurrences are apparently rare, and this is so because of the strong dislike of controversy and indeed of any conspicuous behavior. Among the Zuni a man is not supposed to stand up for his rights; he is looked down upon if he gets into any sort of conflict or achieves notoriety. The best that one Zuni may say of another is that he "is a nice polite man. No one ever hears anything from him. He never gets into trouble. He's Badger clan and Muhekwe kiva and he always dances in the summer dances" (Bunzel 1929–30: 480).

The case of the Zuni Indians is probably more exceptional than typical. In a great many primitive societies one is supposed to stand up for one's rights and those of one's kinsmen, even if one makes a great disturbance doing so. There is probably a general human tendency to resent an injury and to strike back at the injurer. If a delict is regarded as an injury or a danger to the entire group, the demand of any specially injured party receives more general support. Yet I think it may be declared that in the primitive societies, on the whole, the specific secular sanctions that are likely to qualify as rudimentary law play a larger role in connection with private delicts, or torts, than they do in connection with public delicts, or crimes. What we so often find in the case of offenses against the entire group is that supernatural or ritual sanctions take care of these. Incest is typically regarded as a crime in primitive society. There are certainly plenty of cases where incest is punished by the society, but on the other hand the sometimes specified, sometimes vague results that are supposed automatically to follow, or to be inflicted by the supernaturals upon one who commits such a delinquency, are apt to be a very large part, or even all, of the sanctions which support the rule as to sex relations.

However this may be, the point to be made is that some of the most rudimentary legal institutions appear in connection with the systematization of the retaliative sanctions. *A* has done some injury to *B; B* is disposed to retaliate; the customs of the group say how he is to do it; and we have a very simple anticipation of law. If not curbed by convention a retaliation is likely to lead to a counter-retaliation, and so to public disorder. The Zuni tend to check the tendency at the outset by frowning upon controversy; it is probably commoner to allow the retaliation but to define its terms.

The conventionalization of the retaliative sanctions may involve the way in which the injured party may strike back at the injurer, or it may take the form of a scale of compensation to be paid and accepted in settlement of the claim. In the former case the principle involved is that of meeting force with force, but in so restricted a manner as to satisfy the injured person and yet bring the controversy to an end. The duel is an elementary juridical institution of this sort. In the case of payment of compensation the impulse to avenge the wrong is bought off with damages. Primitive societies provide abundant examples of both ways of conventionalizing the retaliative sanctions, and both ways occur in combination. So far as the manner of settlement, including the amounts to be paid, is fixed by custom for classes of cases, a sort of preliterate code results. So far as custom involves the way in which the injured person is to set about getting a settlement, whether by exercise of force in return or by collection of indemnity, there is a primitive anticipation of legal procedure.

The Yurok Indians of Northern California provide an instance of a society with a well-defined code of compensation yet without any formal procedure for punishing delinquents or for righting a wrong done an individual. Kroeber's account (Kroeber 1925) makes it clear that among these very primitive, food-collecting Indians it was well understood that "every possession and privilege, and every injury and offense" could "be exactly valued in terms of property"; and that "every invasion of privilege or property must be exactly compensated." The compensation took the form of handing over certain forms of wealth, including dentalium shells, woodpecker scalps, obsidian blades, and deerskins. The members of the society recognized many well-specified delicts, and the amount of compensation which it was appropriate to demand of one committing the corresponding wrong against another. For killing a man of social standing the indemnity was fifteen strings of dentalium, with perhaps a red obsidian, and a woodpecker scalp headband, besides handing over a daughter. A common man was worth only ten strings of dentalium. A seduction followed by a pregnancy cost five strings of dentalium or twenty woodpecker scalps. To utter the name of a dead man was an injury to his kin demanding a payment of two strings of thirteen shells each. If a couple with children separated, the woman could take them with her only on full repayment of her original purchase price. If a man beat his wife, she might go to her parents, who might keep her until the husband had paid them certain damages; then he might retake her. There were even obligations suggesting our laws of common carriers. A man able to take a traveler over a river had to provide free ferriage; if he refused to do so, the aggrieved traveler could claim three to six short strings of dentalia. A shaman who had declined to visit a patient was liable in the event of the latter's death, even after treatment by another shaman, for the full fee tendered her, or a little more.

In short, these Indians had a strong feeling for the definition of rights and obligations, and recognized certain appropriate damages for any private delicts. Nevertheless, this code was maintained not only without any court, but without any formal procedure at all. In this society there is no tribal organization whatsoever. Each little settlement is composed of men related by blood, and their wives. Property and rights pertain to the individual, or to this little hamlet of kinsmen. There are no clans, exogamic groups, or chiefs or governors. The satisfaction of claims is accomplished without any formal process. "Each side to an issue presses and resists vigorously, exacts all he can, yields where he has to, continues the controversy where continuance promises to be profitable or settlement suicidal, and usually ends in compromising more or less" (Kroeber 1925). An even more elaborate unwritten code of indemnity, with a sliding scale of payment depending on the social position of the injured party, is recognized by the Ifugao of Northern Luzon (Barton 1919). These people, like the Yurok, are also without tribal organization, and settlement of claims is effected simply by means of negotiations between the parties. But among the Ifugao the negotiations are carried on not by the parties themselves but by a compromiser, or go-between, selected for the purpose by the parties. The go-between has no authority and no force behind him; there is nothing to support his efforts to secure a settlement by acting for both parties except the fact that the only alternative to settlement is a long-drawn feud, which is wanted by neither party and nobody else.

It appears, therefore, that in certain societies entirely without legal proccss the disposition for an injured party to seek redress for a wrong not only is sanctioned, but appropriate compensation is socially recognized, and is, moreover, reduced to system. The rudiments of law may, on the other hand, also be recognized in the systematization of the forms and limits of retaliation by the injured party. In these cases there is a recognized procedure whereby the injured party may do a retaliative injury upon the man who has committed a wrong against him (or them). In many of these cases, the group does not treat the delict as a crime, conceding all interest in retaliation to the parties injured; but general opinion and custom hedge revenge with limitations which assure the termination of the dispute and the restoration of peace and public order. Among the aborigines of Australia there is a widespread pattern of custom whereby differences are composed and social equilibrium is restored by means of a regulated combat in which the blood of the offender is shed. A man charged with an offense meets his adversary, or his representatives, armed and painted in a way highly stylized by custom, and a certain number of weapons are thrown at him, which he attempts to ward off. Among the Gringai tribe individuals fought a personal quarrel with weapons nearest at hand, but in cases of serious offenses, the offender had to stand out, with a shield, while a number of spears, fixed according to the magnitude of his offense, were thrown at him. If he could defend himself, well and good; if he was injured or killed, the result was regarded by the group as concluding the affair. Among the Kurnai the relative of one supposed to have been killed by magic stood up opposite the person accused of the sorcery. The accused, aided by his wife and the women of the tribe, sang certain songs while the slain man's relative and the accused exchanged conventional feints and blows. Whatever was the outcome, the issue was regarded as closed (Howitt 1904: 343–45). In such cases apparently the older men of the tribe act as the agents of public opinion in enforcing these sanctions, requiring the parties to meet and direct-

ing the proceedings, although some of the instances reported involve leadership by the medicine man.

The practices just cited from Australia are not so much punishment as feuds shortened in the interests of the public. They are
interrupted and restrained killings. In this class of cases as well
as in the cases of simple societies with unwritten codes of damages, there is recognition of a sort of principle of equivalent retaliation. The principle is of course perfectly familiar in the law
of more complex societies. We know it in one form in the *lex
talionis*. The spirit of it is common in primitive societies which
do have recognizable juridical institutions. If a man of one clan
is killed, that clan may kill an equivalent man of another clan.
Among the Bageshu the one killed in retaliation must be exactly
equivalent; the wronged clan may wait until the son of the killer
is of the age of his father when the murder was done, and then
kill him (Roscoe: 1909). Among the Giriama the murderer must
be killed in just the same manner as that in which he killed his
victim. The principle of equivalence applies also to compensation
given in goods or wealth. Among East African Bantu tribes a
man pays less compensation for injuries to members of his own
clan than he pays to outsiders, because as a clan member he is
entitled to share in all compensations. This is certainly a legalistic
point of view.

The preceding remarks are made to direct attention to the importance of conventional treatment of the retaliative sanctions in
giving rise to proto-legal institutions. Custom restrains an injured party from unlimited revenge. Retaliative force is stylized
by custom into a sort of ritualistic revenge, and something like
legal process results. The claim is compounded by payment of
wealth equivalent to the loss incurred, and a code of damages
results. Either or both foreshadowing of full legal institutions
may take place without the development of a formal court to try
an issue. The few examples cited suggest that the development
of an unwritten code of indemnity is likely to occur in societies
where forms of wealth are recognized and much status attaches
to its possession. There is something that may be given up, that

people hate to give up, and that may be offered as equivalent to vengeance. It is also probably a favorable circumstance for the development of either unwritten codes of indemnity or of procedures for limited revenge that the public resentment of an injury be not too strongly disapproved by general social attitude. The Ifugao, a warlike man and a headhunter, certainly feels differently about contentiousness than does the Zuni Indian. It is expected of the Ifugao that he stand up for his rights. "Did he not do so he would become the prey of his fellows. No one would respect him . . . . he will hear himself accused of cowardice, and called a woman" (Barton 1919). It is notable that it is among some of the societies with the very simplest forms of organization that we encounter wealth and social status dependent thereon, together with the systematization of rules of indemnity.

The foregoing discussion has centered around the development of systems of compensation or of forms of socially approved retaliation in the development of what might be called a rudimentary law of torts. The beginnings of law may also be sought in the extent to which there is formal process in connection with delicts thought to be also, or only, wrongful acts committed against the society. It may be repeated that the commission of such a wrongful act is in many cases attended by several sanctions of different kinds: the diffuse sanctions of public contempt, dislike, withdrawal and the like; a supernatural sanction in the form of an unpleasant consequence to the body or spirit of the one who does the act; and some specific secular sanction imposed by the community or some part of it (Radcliffe-Brown 1933: 203). So far as any of these sanctions has a specific and formal aspect, it at least suggests law to us, although it is only the last of these—the impersonal application of force—that we are likely to think of as criminal law. Among the Chukchee (Hobley 1910: 80) a man who has become notoriously objectionable by bad conduct may be killed by his own clansmen. Such a man one day killed a reindeer by a careless blow. Whereupon his kinsmen stabbed him to death, saying, "Otherwise we shall have a feud on our hands." The other members of the community approved

the action. In such a case as this there was no court and no
sharply defined form of punishment; the case does not illustrate
law at all, in the sense in which the word is used in this paper.
Instances of customary punishment that amount to law are generally cases of societies with courts, as among the Akamba of
East Africa, where, after a council has deliberated over the case
of a notorious bad character, his clansmen will carry out the
punishment in a stereotyped manner, by slaying some of his
cattle or by dragging him from his hut and beating him.

The punishment of delicts by supernatural agencies plays a
great part in the system of controls of primitive societies; insofar
as the supposed consequences of committing the act are specific
and are thought surely to follow, they might be spoken of as a sort
of supernatural law. But to follow this line of thought with reference to the rudimentary legalism of primitive peoples would be
to carry the concept of law beyond the point where it is useful.
In some cases it is true that the commission of the interdicted
act is believed to bring about immediate consequences: to eat of
the chief's food is to bring death upon one's self; to profane the
sacred object is to cause one's hand to wither. But though there
are here rules with sanctions in connection, there is nothing procedural about the matter; there is no society or its representatives
to decide an issue or to measure a delict by a scale of punishment or of compensation. Indeed, what is characteristic of these
supernatural sanctions is that they are for the most part vague,
and for this very reason terrible; they are outside of the realm of
orderly process. We have the word "tabu" for those interdicts
which are attained by uncertain and perhaps awful consequences.
Nemesis is a kind of judgment, but it does not have the qualities
of judgment according to law.

A subject more relevant to the consideration of rudimentary
law is the conventionalization of the diffuse sanctions of public
contempt, criticism, and withdrawal. The systematic and impersonal application of force in the maintenance of individual rights
and in the public interest is the central substance of law, but it
must be recognized that sanctions other than force may be ap-

plied quite as formally and with the same social function. Indeed, to the man upon whom the sanction is applied there may not be much difference between the lash of the whip and the lash of the public's tongue. Moral force, if expressed in defined and open procedures, may fall upon a delinquent much as does physical force. Public ridicule may feel quite as coercive as imprisonment or destruction of property. In not a few primitive societies general disapproval is expressed not merely diffusely and casually, but in a sort of standardized collective gesture of disapproval. These modes of conduct we must recognize as closely related to law in that they are specific secular sanctions that have a public character and that assume a formal nature.

This sort of institution is still at a very low level of the juridical, where the injured party alone carries the sanction into effect. In the case of the Orokaiva of New Guinea, "when a man finds his coconuts stolen he may tie a fragment of husk to a stick and set it up on the track near his palms; then everyone will see that a theft has been committed, and the thief, even though his identity remains unknown, will feel a pang of shame whenever he passes the spot. Similarly, the owner of a ravaged garden will affix a taro leaf to a coconut palm in the midst of the village for all to see and for the special discomfort of the culprit" (Williams 1930: 329–30). But where the victim *is* known, and where the general public participate in application of a specific sanction rendering onerous the general disapproval, the approximation to a legal form is closer. An example of such an institution comes from the Sunda Islands, where a notorious liar receives his punishment in the following manner: Passers-by begin to make a heap of twigs near where the dishonesty occurred; the pile grows, making conspicuous and enduring the name and delinquency of the liar (Kennedy 1937: 363–64). Among the Hottentot an unpopular chief will be publicly lectured by the women (Hahn 1881: 28–29). Examples of the use of publicity in a formal manner without the exercise of force are to be found also in the case of delicts which are regarded chiefly or wholly as violations of the rights of individuals. Malinowski tells us how in the Trobriand

Islands parties to a dispute, "assisted by friends and relatives meet, harangue one another and hurl back recriminations" (Malinowski 1926: 60). This conventional name-calling has to some degree the effect of moving toward a solution of the conflict through the aid of publicity, because "such litigation allows people to give vent to their feelings and shows the trend of public opinion," although, Malinowski says, "sometimes it seems, however, only to harden the litigants." The best-reported instance of litigation by regulated abuse, to find a phrase for this class of institution, is the juridical drum songs of the Eskimo. In this case two men (or sometimes two women), having become enemies, encounter each other once a year in what they call a drum fight. Each party has a turn at singing a song, to the accompaniment of drums, in which he heaps abuse and mockery upon his adversary, reciting his version of the dispute, and seeking to bring shame upon the other. The songs are composed in advance, but follow traditional styles, and indeed apparently certain of these styles are belongings or appurtenances of family lines (Thalbitzer 1923: 166–68; 318–21).

These last cases, of the conventionalization of gestures of disapproval, suggest the importance of ceremonial in incipient law. Obligations and rights exist in custom in latency, so to speak, but very commonly there is some overt act which makes the relationship binding; ritual is the seal on the deed; it makes it effective. Two simple examples will stand for a large group of similar cases. In the Trobriand Islands the leader of an expedition, or the promoter of an industrial venture, gives a big ceremonial distribution of food. "Those who participate in it and benefit by the bounty are under an obligation to assist the leader throughout the enterprise" (Malinowski 1926: 61). So among the Maya Indians of present-day Yucatan, the obligation to take charge of the effigy of the patron saint and to assume the leadership of the annual festival is borne by one man, or a small group of men, for a year and is then passed on to a successor or successors. A man will make known his decision to accept the obligation in advance of the festival, but the matter is not irrevocable until at a certain moment in the course of the festivities he accepts certain pieces of ceremonial paraphernalia. This act, trifling as it may appear, is the solemnizing element; thereafter the volunteer may not withdraw. The sanctions that in these cases stand ready to come into operation if the one obligated fails to fulfill his promise may not be legal; the Maya Indian will not be put in jail if he decides not to go through with his obligation, and no one may collect damages for his failure to do so. He merely believes that the saint would punish him with some great misfortune, and he knows that his neighbors would look on him with contempt. We have now shifted the ground of inquiry; we are looking not at the proto-legal sanctions which attend the breach of an obligation or the commission of a wrong against the society, but are mentioning the role of ceremonial as a class of form by which rights and obligations are made less violable in advance of any possible breach. The subject is a very large one, and in a paper of the dimensions of this I can only mention it.

It will be noticed that so far in this discussion very little has been said about courts. The material brought forward has represented the systematization of indemnities so as to produce unwritten codes, and, more especially with rudimentary process in primitive societies. The Andaman Islanders are without either code or process. The Ifugao and the Yurok have explicit and systematic rules of indemnity; the Yurok carry out these rules without any formal procedure, while the Ifugao have only an arbitrator unaided by force. The conventionalized sanctions of retaliation, the exercise of force against a delinquent following the unformalized decisions of public opinion, and the ceremonial expressions of contempt or abuse, are all procedures which do not necessarily depend on courts for their application, and which, in fact, occur, in many of the instances cited, without the existence in the society represented of any court at all. The materials establish that process without courts is common in the simpler societies.

Inquiry as to the elementary forms of courts of law is naturally involved with inquiry as to the origins of the state. The society that is without tribal organization is a society without courts. Conversely, the courts in preliterate societies that do exist are courts maintained not by clans but by a council or a king who represents the entire tribe or local community. The case of the Chukchee, already mentioned, is one in which a conspicuous delinquent is killed by his own clansmen. There is no court to try him; informally expressed opinion results in the execution. In a great many societies the clans or other kinship groups deal with their delinquents directly, without any formal trial of an issue. The simple societies from which examples have been taken more than once in this paper, those of the Andaman Islanders, the Ifugao and the Yurok, are societies in which there is no state, unless we are to call the little settlement of kinsmen and their wives itself a state. Even among the Ifugao, where the settlement consists of a number of such groups of kinsmen, there is no political organization to hold the groups of kinsmen under a single superior authority. In societies that *do* have tribal, political organization, we recognize its existence just in the formal regulation of the conduct of the individual which is here our criterion of law. And the tribal law often has those elements of deliberation and procedure with regard to an issue which, institutionalized, we call a "court."

Some of the Plains Indian tribes provide instances of societies with a very simple tribal organization and a very simple tribal court. On the whole, the temper of these societies is individualistic. On the whole, the individual and the clan or the band or the soldier-society deals with other equivalent units in matters of dispute, without the exercise of any general tribal authority. On the other hand, a council meets to decide on matters of policy affecting the entire tribe, and legal and police functions are exercised on behalf of the entire tribe by special groups of warriors known in the literature as military societies. Lowie has made a special study of these military societies. They are the police and the law court, acting not simply for one clan but for a tribe made up of familial groups, in a very simple form. "Everywhere the basic idea is that during the hunt a group is vested with the power forcibly to prevent premature attacks on the herd and to punish offenders by corporal punishment, by confiscation of the game illegally secured, by destruction of property generally, and in extreme cases by killing them" (Lowie 1927: 103). On the whole, the authority of these associations lasted only during the emergency of the hunt. Yet a recent writer has shown (Hoebel 1936: 433–38) that they acted as a sort of court and as instruments of execution of judgment even on other occasions. Thus, among the Cheyenne the following incident occurred: An older Indian found his niece struggling through the snow and took her on his horse. They met with the young woman's husband, who became angry at the older Indian (although he was beyond the age of philandering) and wounded him with an arrow. The injury proved serious. The Fox Soldier society was convened by the old Indian's son-in-law. This military society decided to inflict a beating upon the offender. This it did, and also compelled him to remove the arrowhead from the injured man's arm. The delinquent became contrite and presented five horses to the military society in atonement. It should be emphasized that the old Indian, whose injury was made the basis of action both punitive and retributive, was not a member of the military society that acted as a court of law. The society acted on behalf of the total society. In the case of the Omaha, mentioned earlier, the council of chiefs of the tribe deliberated over the case of an evildoer, and if death was decreed, the council designated some trustworthy man to prick the convicted with the poisoned staff kept ready for the purpose (Fletcher and LaFlesche 1905–6: 213).

Among the North American Indians, and also among the aboriginal Australians, the exercise of tribal authority with respect to delicts is maintained with little formal procedure. In both continents power is distributed among the elder men, and councils of these discuss a case and come to a decision, but with little that could be called a rule of procedure or of evidence and without any strong sense of litigation as a contest within rules. The deliberative bodies here are perhaps to be called councils rather than fully developed courts. The case of a serious doer of wrong is considered with solemnity; speeches may be made on his behalf or against him; advice is given and weighed. The assemblies are courts in the sense that a body representative of the entire society deliberatively determines an issue of fact, reaches a decision in accordance with customary rules of justice, and puts into motion some instrument to carry into effect the remedy or punishment agreed upon. But if we demand of a court that it involve formalized procedures and rules by which an issue is to be presented, joined, and determined, then some of the societies in Africa most nearly meet the expectation. Among the Ashanti the procedures include the ordeal, the curse, and swearing on sacred objects. An accused person may demand as of right the procedure of ordeal so as to clear himself of the charge against him. Oaths are important not only in trials but in making obligations binding; everyone entering into any serious undertaking is required to drink a certain liquor accompanied by an imprecation that the supernatural may destroy him if he does not fulfill the obligation (Rattray 1929: 392–95). These African societies are strongly litigious; litigation is like a sport or an art in that it is an end in itself. Lindblom says of the Akamba that "to go into law is one of the most exquisite enjoyments . . . and in what a number of actions every old man has been a party!" (Lindblom 1920). The knowledge of the law is an important part of the lore of every elder person.

It is worth noting that in Africa the formal court does not everywhere function chiefly to defend the state, or the people, by punishing crimes, although this is very much the fact among the Ashanti, where delinquents are tried before the chief and many delicts are treated as public offenses. But among the natives southeast of Mount Kenya, the delicts of which the court takes cognizance are delicts against individuals. In this part of Africa, therefore, the court operates as a sort of commission of arbitration. When an Akamba court has decided as to the rights of a complaint, the judgment takes the form of a declaration that A has been wronged by B and B should atone or should receive a retaliative sanction at the hands of A's kinsmen. The court leaves the enforcement of the judgment to the kinship groups.

These pages have been devoted to a consideration, in the light of law as we know it in highly developed societies, of some comparable institutions in some primitive societies. The most obvious general conclusion about primitive law is that there is not much of it. Systematic and explicitly formulated rules of conduct and formal procedures for the enforcement of these rules by impersonal authority play a relatively small part in the maintenance of social control, and in some societies they are entirely lacking. On the whole, people do what they are expected to do because that is what they want to do and what (in the light of those inducements and customary advantages and disadvantages which Malinowski sometimes calls "law" and sometimes "effective custom") they find it expedient to do. This is what the old Indian was talking about when, after having been placed on a reservation, he said that in the old times "there was no law; everybody did what was right." On the reservation he found himself surrounded by compulsive regulations exterior to himself and independent of his conscience. It felt different from the good old days. In undisturbed primitive societies, as Durkheim put it, the consciences of individuals are uniform and strong. Human impulses are the same as everywhere else, but there is less need for a state-enforced legal system.

Nevertheless, as we have seen, rudimentary legal institutions are abundantly represented in many of the preliterate societies. The examples considered indicate that the rudiments of law are not to be found so distributed that any society examined will be found to have, in equal degree, the beginnings of code, process, and court. On the contrary, these aspects of the juridical appear singly or in varying combinations. In the case of certain societies that systematize indemnity in settlement of private delicts, a mere give-and-take within the limits set by custom is all that is needed to put these scales of damages into effect. Especially have we noted the frequent occurrences of formal procedure for the composition of disputes without any court to determine the matter at issue. The limited materials examined indicate that primitive law arises out of no single beginning but out of several. Emphasized here has been the formalization of terms of settlement of claims between parties and of procedure for securing satisfaction of claims, but we have also given examples of: the development of procedure for the expression of public condemnation, without force; the development of a formal quality in punitive sanctions imposed on those who commit delicts; the appearance of deliberative and consultive bodies (in at least the African cases with rules of procedure) to decide issues, make awards, and fix punishments; and, most generally, the role of ceremony in solemnizing and rendering more binding customary obligations.

On the whole, the more completely legal institutions are to be found in the most complex of the preliterate societies, while the least complex are without law, or have little of it. Nevertheless a systematization of indemnity may be highly developed in very simple societies. Legal institutions tend to appear, not merely where the society is complex, but also where contentiousness is favored by the mores. So, too, legalism may become a pattern of the culture; we should not hesitate to recognize its presence in the case of the Akamba, and its absence in the case of the Zuni Indians; the importance of law in the one case and its unimportance in the other is not to be explained as a simple function of different levels of social development. Some like litigation, and some don't; and this is true of peoples as of individuals.

In conclusion, two special points may be stated about primitive law, or about the social setting in which it lies, that have fallen through the mesh of the argument as it has been loosely woven here. I have said that, on the whole, primitive peoples get along with little law. One reason why this is so is to be found in the strength of supernatural sanctions in restraining socially disapproved conduct. It is probably not correct to say, as it has been said, that law has developed out of religion. But it is true that in the simple societies the sacred and supernatural sanctions play a large role as compared with the specific secular sanctions. We recognize something of the sort in the self-reproach or perhaps even horror we—or some of us—feel at the thought of committing perjury, but there is nothing in our society which in degree approaches the importance of what Radcliffe-Brown (1933: 203) calls the "ritual sanction." In many of these societies a delinquent brings about by his delinquency a condition of ritual uncleanness which is dangerous to him and to his entire group. This requires lustration or expiation, rather than punishment or compensation to an injured party. Incest, sacrilege, and witchcraft often bring about this result; these are the serious wrongful acts dangerous to the primitive man, above all others. On the other hand, murder and theft are often merely torts with him. The greater dread of the public delict behind which stands the sacred sanction may be illustrated by a simple example that comes from the Tlingit Indians (Oberg 1934: 145–46). If murder was committed, it was a matter for the clans to settle. But to prevent a general fight, a chief of high rank might intervene by stepping between the combatants with an important crest, symbolic of the clan status and of the supernaturals. It would be a desecration of the emblem if fighting occurred in these circumstances. In this way the reluctance to incur the supernatural sanction was deliberately utilized as an instrument of control.

The other special characterization of primitive law is the importance of bodies of kindred as parties to controversy and to legal action. The materials cited here have included many instances where the wrongs righted are wrongs against kinship groups, the claims are pressed by kinship groups, and the liability of the individual is to his kinship group. I have said that murder and theft are usually regarded as torts rather than as crimes, but the delict is not so much a wrong done an individual as a wrong done a familial group. Even where a tribal organization is fully developed, and a tribal council acts as a court of law, as among the Akamba, the killing of a member of one clan by a member of another is regarded simply as a wrong done to the clan of the man killed, to be settled by payment of indemnity to the relatives of the victim. Among the Australians, when a life is to be surrendered in payment for a life taken, it is not always the life of the slayer that is given up, but the life of any member of the slayer's group (Howitt 1904: 327–28). We may recognize that in a broad sense

Maine was right, when, in considering the early forms of the classic societies, he proposed that primitive society was to be regarded as an aggregation of families rather than of individuals. The prototype of law is to be found in largest part in procedures and standards by which custom regulates disputes between bodies of kin and assures the composition of these disputes in the interest of public peace.

THE ATTRIBUTES OF LAW

Leopold Pospisil

THE FOLLOWING proposition has been derived from cross-cultural research. If law is conceived as "rules or modes of conduct made obligatory by some sanction which is imposed and enforced for their violation by a controlling authority," then the analysis of such legal phenomena reveals a common pattern of attributes rather than one sweeping characteristic of law. These attributes, if considered in turn as criteria of law, separate it objectively from all other social phenomena.

Having discussed the form of law, we shall now analyze the legal phenomena and abstract attributes which they have in common. These attributes will also serve us as criteria for the more exact delimitation of the law's boundaries.

The decisions of an authority vary greatly and they embrace many facts that cannot be called law. In other words, we have to discover additional characteristics to differentiate legal decisions from political ones and from advice concerning nonsanctioned customs. We have also to distinguish law from purely religious phenomena and from the rest of culture. Social scientists have been searching for a single criterion of law which would constitute its essence. The most important early contributions in this respect have been made by Radcliffe-Brown and Malinowski.

Radcliffe-Brown (1952: 212) emphasized the physical sanction administered by a politically organized society as the basic

Extracted from Leopold Pospisil, *Kapauku Papuans and Their Law*. New Haven, Department of Anthropology, Yale University, Yale University Publications in Anthropology, Number 54, 1958, pp. 257–71, and reprinted by permission of the author.

criterion of law. Hoebel (1940: 47; 1954: 28) followed him in this respect. The emphasis upon the "politically organized society" led the former author to admit that there was an absence of law in some "more primitive cultures," and thus to limit the concept to cultures with a more formal political organization. The writer of this monograph agrees with the importance of the sanction criterion but is reluctant to accept the second proposition of "the politically organized society." This problem will be discussed later and an attempt will be made to show the universality of law and to refute the idea of a "lawless functioning group."

Malinowski selected as his main attribute of law the principle of obligation. The presence of obligation—that is, ties between two parties—defines a phenomenon as law, punishment being inessential because conformance is achieved through mutual service based on expectance of future reciprocal favors (Malinowski 1934: 30–42). This theory is much less workable than the one discussed in the previous paragraph, although it allows for the universality of law. N. S. Timasheff criticizes it by pointing out that although duels were obligatory in Europe, they were illegal (Timasheff 1938: 871).

The present writer objects to Malinowski's view because law is defined so broadly as to include most of the customs of a society. For this reason, the theory does not lend itself to being a workable tool for the ethnographer. Moreover, there are many kinds of obligations, like moral or religious ones, that have to be differentiated from the legal. Consequently, a "legal obligation" must be defined more exactly, and additional attributes are needed to set it aside from the other nonlegal cases.

We do not object to the above theories on the basis of their invalidity. Indeed, each of them elaborates a particular attribute which is important for our inquiry. The objection to these views lies in the fact that their attributes are insufficient for characterizing the essence of law. It is the contention of the writer, based upon the results of comparative research as well as upon the findings among the Kapauku, that not one attribute but rather a whole pattern of them which coexist in time form the core of the social phenomena which we call law. In the cultures studied, the writer has found four legal attributes which seem to be of importance: authority, true *obligatio,* intention of universal application, and sanction (see figure, page 34). In addition, a manifestation of a law has to have the form of a decision. This pattern of attributes, it is believed, constitutes the essence of law and may possibly provide an ethnographer with a workable tool.

THE ATTRIBUTE OF AUTHORITY

A decision to be legally relevant, or in other words to effect social control, has to be accepted by the parties to the dispute as a solution of the situation caused by the clash of their interests. An individual, or a subgroup, who possesses an influence which causes the majority of the members of the group to conform to his decisions, the writer calls an authority. We may ask whether we do not run the risk of making our legal concept nonuniversal by employing such an attribute. Many ethnographers have declared that there is genuine absence of authority in certain cultures. Some of them use expressions like "lateral social control" or "the group as a whole" (Yang 1945: 134) when referring to the agency of social control; such expressions are virtually identical with a statement of the absence of authority, if by authority we mean a specific individual (or individuals). Let us investigate one such case.

Gusinde says about the customary laws of the Yaghan ". . . that they are faithfully followed is looked after by the group as a whole" (Gusinde 1937: 628). Not being satisfied with the face value of the phrase "group as a whole" (*Allgemeinheit*), we may ask the question: who usually represents or speaks for this mysterious *Allgemeinheit?* The answer is to be found in a different part of the same monograph.

"There is never a shortage of men who because of their old age, spotless character, long experience and mental superiority, gain such an extent of moral influence that it is equal to a peculiar domination" (Gusinde 1937: 803).

These strong men are called *tiamuna* by the people, and they are active in the local groups (*Lokalgruppe*) that form the important units in the Yaghan social structure.

The picture in other cases of an alleged absence of authority is usually quite similar to this example. When we go deeper into our investigation, the *Allgemeinheit,* or absence of an authority, changes into more definite factors of social control. We find particular individuals initiating action in the group, resolving problems, and occupying more or less definite positions of importance. The difficulty lies in the problem of what the respective author actually means by the term "authority." The concept is usually not clarified and its meaning is taken for granted. Implicit in most of the statements of an absence of an authority is a definition that identifies the concept with a person of rather absolute power, whose acts, especially those involving the passing of decisions, are very formal. We may ask whether absoluteness and formality are the most important characteristics of an authority. The present writer has postulated that the essence of the concept does not rest with these descriptive characteristics peculiar to some cultures only. On the contrary, he believes that the fact that the decisions or advice of the authority are followed by the rest of the members of the group forms the only important criterion of the disputed term. The concept of an authority, therefore, is considered in this monograph not as a descriptive but as a functional one. Absoluteness and formality are only its specialized, nonuniversal attributes. An authority comprises one or more individuals who initiate actions in a functional group and whose decisions are followed by the majority of the group's members.

The postulate that an authority so defined is universal to all cultures is substantiated by the findings of psychologists in situations where the cultural factor emphasizing authority has been virtually eliminated. For example, Muzafer Sherif made experiments with the autokinetic effect (Sherif 1947: 77–89). An individual was brought into a dark room where no lights could penetrate. A tiny lighted dot appeared to him in the darkness. Although this dot was fixed and motionless, the person observing it was under the purely subjective impression that the light was moving, for there was nothing with which the observer could compare the point of light to be able to observe a possible motion. The same experiment was conducted with other observers. After this, the observers were permitted to tell each other their perceptions and discuss their experiences. Thereafter they were asked to look at the dot once again and were told that this was done so that they could correct their observations and be more accurate. An interesting result was reported. The individual perceptions in the second trial tended to cluster in a narrow range, which was called by Sherif the group norm. For the purpose of this thesis it is important that the individuals within this "group norm range," who changed their original statements of observations very slightly, or not at all, were functioning as persons with authority. The rest of the group were merely their followers. This experiment suggests that there are always individuals differing in intelligence, assertiveness, temperament, and aggression who influence others and who are looked to as leaders.

Kapauku society is one of those considered by Western observers as having no individuals of authority. However, even superficial observers had to notice a kind of reverence exhibited toward a man called *tonowi,* as well as the fact that some of the *tonowi*'s wishes were respected by the rest of the group. In order to make a concession to those observable facts, the Europeans called this individual *"primus inter pares,* the first among equals." We have discussed at length the attributes of this authority, his followers, as well as the different motivations for the compliance of the parties to a dispute with the *tonowi*'s verdicts. In the preceding discussion,[1] we have also shown his strange way of making decisions. In the description of our 176 cases of clashes of interests, we may notice that in 132 cases it was this authority—or the house owner and the husband in household and family cases—who passed weight-carrying decisions. In only three cases the advice and solutions were not respected. Thus we may conclude that the

---

[1] Not reprinted here.

Kapauku do have authorities who settle by decisions most of the disputes.

The objection of the Europeans to calling a rich man "the authority" is based upon disregard of the functional connotation of the concept. The attributes of the Western judge—the formality with which he adjudicates cases, the finality and absoluteness of his decisions, as well as the reverence and ceremony of the Western court—these purely descriptive criteria, are held as a measure for deciding the presence or absence of an authority. The title *primus inter pares*, assigned to the Kapauku leader by some Europeans, exemplifies the above statements. The insistence on the functional definition of authority and the following analysis of its different attributes results from comparative research.

Various cultures give to their authorities special attributes that sometimes differ fundamentally. In one culture, an aggressive individual with absolute power may be favored, while in another, the opposite may be true.

These different attributes allow the authorities to be classified as different types. For our purpose we may be interested in two attributes: formality and extent of power. The strength of these attributes will change from case to case, and so we shall get two mutually independent and qualitatively different ranges of types. The extreme positions in the first range will be occupied on one end by a totally informal authority (with a minimal amount of formality) and by a strictly formal authority (with a maximal amount of formality) on the other. In the second range pertaining to extent of power, there will be a gradation from an authority with narrowly limited power to one with the most absolute control. The extreme positions should be considered ideal instances, approximated by only a few concrete examples. The examples will differ from one another according to the degree of the criterion measured (the formality or extent of power).

To give some tentative definitions of our ideal extremes, we may say this: by formal authority is meant an individual (or individuals) with his (or their) role, rights, duties, and activities defined by custom and/or law. The public and ceremonial parts of the action tend to be emphasized more than in the opposite extreme of informal authority.

The informal authority, on the other hand, has no ceremonial importance and little public emphasis. In his case everything tends to depend on the personality of the individual, on his skill and personal achievements, and on his conformity with the ideal pattern of legal authority set up by the particular culture. His rights, duties, and procedures are not defined by law or custom.

A limited authority is acquired by a procedure which is controlled by the society. Approval by the majority of the members of the society is necessary, or nomination by another person with relatively greater authority must take place. An authority of this type has very little power. If he breaks the law, he is punished either by the members of the society or by a superior. His power thus is checked by another authority or by constitutional law.

An absolute authority is different in many respects. His power is not limited by someone else. The subordination of his followers is emphasized in personal contacts. He is not checked to a marked degree by the other members of the society or by any other institution. The tendency is to see in such an authority the end and not the means for achieving something.

By measuring the two variables discussed above, we should be able to place each authority in a definite position that indicates his qualities within the two ranges. An authority then will be defined by the following possible combinations of the two measured attributes and their negatives: formal and absolute, informal and absolute, formal and limited, or informal and limited. The distance from the limits of the ranges can be designated qualitatively or quantitatively.

The Kapauku concept of *tonowi*, by the lack of emphasis upon the ceremonial aspects in passing a decision, by the dependence upon personal skill and the achievements of the individual, and by the fact that the rights, duties, and procedures of adjudicating cases are not explicitly defined by law or custom, has to be classified as extremely informal. The amount of power that a specific Papuan authority possesses, of course, differs from individual to

individual. The average Kapauku authority is of the limited type
because the acquisition of the position is controlled by the members of the group and the duration of the role is determined by
the approval of the group's constituents. Custom and the rules
provide a check on the amount of power wielded by the leader
and prevent excessive arbitrariness. With respect to groups in a
descending order of inclusiveness, we may generalize and say that
a village leader would have more control over his followers than
a leader of a lineage would have over the constituents of his unit.
Thus Ekajewaijokaipouga, the leader of the Ijaaj-Pigome con-
federacy, would have the least power over Pigome people, more
over Ijaaj people of the Gepouja lineage, even more in his own
Jamaina sublineage, and most of all in the village of Aigii and his
own household. In summary, we may call all Kapauku authorities
informal with varying degrees of limitation in their power. Since
the word headman has been used in current ethnographies to con-
note an informal native authority as differentiated from the more
formalistic institution of chieftainship, the word headman has
been adopted by the present author in translating the native word
tonowi.

A Kapauku authority, however, does not limit himself to the
legal field. In every instance, the headman is a political authority
as well. Ekajewaijokaipouga, who has a reputation of being an
excellent shaman as well as a legal and political authority, has a
combination which lends him the greatest influence on his followers. Usually only in the most complex cultures such as our own
do we find a specialized legal authority.

To sum up our discussion of the attribute of authority, we may
say that the hypothesis of its universality, arrived at by cross-
cultural research, has been substantiated in a culture where its absence was claimed by several observers.

THE ATTRIBUTE OF INTENTION OF UNIVERSAL APPLICATION

While analyzing the data arrived at from cross-cultural research,
the writer conceived of the field of law as an ellipse surrounded

by a zone of transition which separated the field from the rest of the culture (see figure, page 34). Phenomena placed within the peripheral zone combined the overlapping criteria of the neighboring categories so that it was difficult to determine which ones dominated the field. Our attribute of authority, discussed in the previous section, constitutes the criterion which defines the lower boundaries of the ellipse and helps us to separate law from the neighboring field of custom. Repetitive behavior which does not form the subject of the authority's decision is simply custom. When we turn to the upper end of the ellipse, we find that our attribute of authority covering the whole field of law goes beyond it in this place and penetrates the adjacent field of political decisions, which is situated in the figure, above the field of law.

Since in the culture investigated both political decisions and legal judgments are made by the same authority, the Kapauku material shows a need for an additional criterion which would be effective in separating the legal and the political fields. This need is met by the attribute of legal decisions called by the writer the intention of universal application. This attribute, found to be present in all legal decisions, if applicable as a criterion of law, demands that the authority in making a decision intends it to be applied to all similar or "identical" situations in the future.

In the decisions of Kapauku authorities, this intention is usually made explicit either by mentioning the pertinent rule or by using the obligatory-repetitive tense aspect while referring to the guilt and the punishment. When the decision is claimed to be made according to a rule, this incorporated rule constitutes the ideal. In the phrase, *"kou dani te tija,* one does not act like that," the verbal suffix *-ja* expresses not only the moral obligation "ought," but it also stands for the customary, repetitive action which may be translated as "used to." Thus this phrase, used in all the decisions which the writer heard, confirms the statement with respect to the ideal component of law which we have discussed while dealing with the form of law. Not only does the decision solve a specific case, but it also formulates an ideal—a solution intended to be utilized in all similar situations in the future.

The ideal component binds all other members of the group who did not participate in the decided case. The authority himself turns to his previous decisions for consistency. In a way, they also bind him. Lawyers speak in such a case about the binding force of precedent which is legal justice.

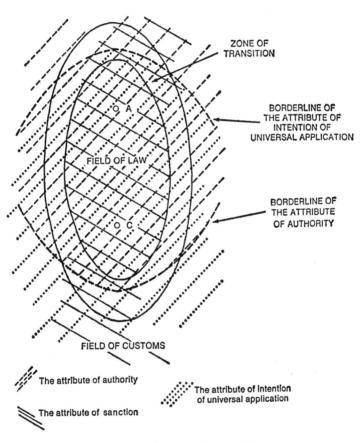

FIELD OF POLITICAL DECISIONS

ZONE OF
TRANSITION

BORDERLINE OF
THE ATTRIBUTE OF
INTENTION OF
UNIVERSAL APPLICATION

FIELD OF LAW

BORDERLINE OF
THE ATTRIBUTE
OF AUTHORITY

FIELD OF CUSTOMS

The attribute of authority

The attribute of intention
of universal application

The attribute of sanction

Diagram of the Attributes of Law.

According to what has been said above, the following cases represent legal injustice on the part of the authority who failed to be consistent with respect to his past decisions because his own, or his protégé's, interests were at stake.

In all the above cases the authority used his power to obtain personal advantages. Ijaaj Awiitigaaj of Botukebo certainly failed to emphasize an ideal when by sheer force of his following he repelled his creditors' requests for payment. However, he failed to apply discriminatory "unjust" decisions in some cases where his own interests were not involved. Because of the absence of the attribute of intention of universal application, the decisions cannot be considered legal according to this theory. Kapauku informants agree, calling the decisions "unjust."

The reader, however, should be cautioned against an assumption that inconsistency with the precedent alone excludes a decision from the legal sphere. A radical inconsistency, being perpetuated and having the intention of universal application, does constitute law. It is the absence of this intention rather than of the inconsistency which excludes a decision passed by an authority from the legal field.

THE ATTRIBUTE OF OBLIGATIO

The third attribute arrived at analytically is *obligatio*. It corresponds to that part of the decision of an authority which determines the rights of one party and the duties of the other. Both parties, it has been contended, must be represented by living persons. A decision which does not fulfill this requirement is not considered legal. The *obligatio,* it will be noticed, is different from the popular concept of obligation which only includes duty. Our concept is a statement about a social relation and has two directions: one going from the privileged party to the obligated one, which is called the right; and the other from the obligated party toward the privileged one, which is called the duty. . . .

A statement by the authority which gives one party a right, while not stating the duty of the other one, is not law even though both the attributes of authority and of the intention of universal application are present. The statement becomes law only when a duty on the part of someone is implied or included in the decision. . . .

Another important characteristic should be noted while dealing with this attribute. The *obligatio* that forms part of the decision is necessarily a new phenomenon created by the authority. It should not be mistaken for the obligation incurred previous to the decision, an infringement of which brought about the suit and legal decision. This is because the person with authority, no matter how objective and just he may be, is in most cases unable to find out all the facts about the pre-existing obligation and its violation. What counts in a legal decision is not what objectively existed but what is stated in the decision to have existed, since this leads to the solution of the problem being adjudicated by the authority. The question of how far the actual facts differ from those included in the *obligatio,* and of whether the decision is therefore proper, belongs to the factual part of the problem of justice, which is not our concern here.

The *obligatio* is a relation between two parties who are both represented by living individuals. Hence, all obligations toward the dead and toward the supernatural are excluded from the realm of law unless the interests of the dead or of the supernatural are represented by living people. It is an opinion of the present writer, who differs with Llewellyn and Hoebel (1941: 286) on this point, that a religious taboo "with no officials to enforce it" is not law, but a strictly religious phenomenon. If we were to include such taboos (where the privileged party is not represented by living people) in the legal field, this field would cease to exist because any kind of custom could creep in and break down its boundaries.

THE ATTRIBUTE OF SANCTION

The last but not the least important of the legal attributes is sanction. This criterion has played a paramount role in different legal theories; sometimes law has been almost equated with it. The writer does not attempt to underestimate its importance. Nevertheless, he would question the use of this attribute as an exclusive criterion and its superordination above the rest of the legal factors, the coexistence of which we have found as forming the essence of law. We have to realize that although many of the political decisions are provided with sanctions, they are not laws, for there is a lack of repetitive aspect, or, in other words, an absence of the attribute of intention of universal application.

As to the legal sanction itself, it has been usually conceived of as having a physical nature. In his early work, Hoebel has defined a social norm as legal ". . . if its neglect or infraction is met by the application, in threat or in fact, of absolute coercive force by a social unit possessing the socially recognized privilege of so acting" (Hoebel 1940: 47). Hoebel means absolute coercive force when he writes ". . . the exercise of physical force to control or prevent action is the absolute form of compulsion . . . the characteristic feature of law, as distinct from mere force, is the recognized privilege of a person or social group to apply the absolute form of coercion to a transgressor when conduct deemed improper may occur" (Hoebel 1940: 47).

In his later work Hoebel (1954: 28) gives the following substantially similar, definition: "A social norm is legal if its neglect or infraction is regularly met, in threat or in fact, by the application of physical force by an individual or group possessing the socially recognized privilege of so acting."

If we were to accept this definition of sanction, many of our Kapauku cases would not be "legal" and law would not be a universal phenomenon, for cultures exist where physical sanction is practically lacking. We may ask if the form of sanction is so important as to make the existence of law dependent upon it. Is not the effect (social control, conformity) of a sanction more important than its form? In this case, as in defining the concept of authority, the writer prefers a functional approach. He suggests that effective social control is the important qualification of a legal sanction. Some psychological sanctions, although of nonphysical nature, perform as strong a control as do physical sanctions. Ostracism, ridicule, avoidance, or a denial of favors—sanctions that are sometimes very subtle and informal—nevertheless may become more drastic than the corporal punishment to which we tend to attach over-importance even in our own culture.

The Kapauku, for example, consider being shamed by a public reprimand, which sometimes lasts for several days, much worse than anything except capital punishment.

In our sample of 176 cases, there are twenty-four which have reprimands as the sanction. Because all the other attributes of law are present, they belong in our legal field.

From cross-cultural research and the above discussion, it follows that a legal sanction does not need to be corporal punishment or a deprivation of property. The form of a sanction is relative to the culture and to the subgroup in which it is used; it may be physical or psychological. We can define a legal sanction as either the negative behavior of withdrawing some rewards or favors that otherwise (if the law had not been violated) would have been granted, or the positive behavior of inflicting some painful experience, be it physical or psychological.

In the following outline, the writer presents the various sanctions used by the Kapauku with the number of cases in which they were applied. The reader is reminded of the simultaneous occurrence of different sanctions in one case, as well as of the fact that forty-four have been disqualified as legal cases on the basis of the absence of some of our attributes of law.

Corporal sanctions

a. AN EXECUTION   Capital punishment is administered either by a close relative of the culprit's sib, such as a brother, son, father, or paternal parallel cousin, or by the plaintiff or his close relative. A bamboo-tipped arrow is usually the instrument used for the execution.

Reasons for execution   Murder, sorcery, violation of taboo, incest, ungenerousness (in the case from the Paniai region), and instigation of war.

b. BEATING WITH A STICK   Sticks of various lengths and thickness are utilized. Most blows are applied on the head and shoulders.

Reasons for beating   Beating is used for all possible delicts, ranging from murder to treason or a refusal to pay a debt.

c. SLAPPING   The Kapauku slap a person over the ears with the palms of both hands simultaneously. Slapping is used mostly on children and wives for minor delicts.

d. BANISHMENT   Banishment is always voluntary. It is an alternative to submitting oneself to punishment.

Economic sanctions

a. BLOOD MONEY   For killing a man, blood money is paid as compensation in order to avoid a war or capital punishment. The customary payment amounts to 120 Km. Blood money was used in cases of murder and manslaughter.

b. INDEMNITY   By offering an adequate indemnity, the defendant can avoid application of most of the other types of sanctions. Incest, most probably, would be the only exception from this generalization. The amount of indemnity varies according to the damage done to the other party. It seldom varies with the status of the plaintiff. A rich defendant, however, may be charged a higher indemnity than an objective estimate of the damage would suggest.

c. PAYMENT OF SUMS PROMISED IN CONTRACT   In this category are included cases in which the monetary stipulations made to one contractee have not been paid and where the verdict asks for such a payment.

Reasons for the disputes   The above disputes started because of the failure to pay rent, to pay a debt, to pay for goods, wages, or a bride price.

d. RESTITUTION   Here belong all the sanctions that pertain to the restitution of a commodity or money acquired by the defendant in a contract or through a delict.

Reasons for the disputes   Nonagreement about boundaries or a disagreement about the return of a payment or commodity.

e. DESTRUCTION OF PROPERTY   This sanction is used only after the refusal of the defendant to pay what he owes or in a case when he has escaped corporal punishment. It is usually the plaintiff who destroys the property.

Reasons for the disputes   Adultery, theft, insubordination.

f. CONFISCATION OF ALL PROPERTY   This type of punishment is used in cases of treason when a man allies himself with the enemy and participates in a war against his own village. The Kapauku assume a fictional death for such a person, and his property is inherited according to the rules governing those who die intestate.

g. ASKING THE RETURN OF LOANS   To ask a defendant for the return of a loan serves as a very effective punishment in cases of insubordination to the authority.

h. ORDERING THE CESSATION OF OFFENDING BEHAVIOR   This sanction is used against defendants who interfere with the rights of another party to the dispute. Such interference is always of the kind which has not yet caused damage, as for example, to dispute someone's rights or to make a claim which would preclude a right of another person.

Psychological sanctions

a. REPRIMAND   This is the favorite sanction of the Kapauku. It consists of intermittent public scolding, shouting of reproaches, and the dancing of the mad dance in front of the squatting defendant. The Kapauku consider this punishment the most effective of all.

b. WARNING   Individuals who commit a minor crime but who otherwise have good relations with the authority are subject to this type of sanction. The warning is informal and it is given to the defendant in private.

c. DIVORCE   Divorce is used as a sanction against a spouse who has violated his or her marital duties.

d. PASSIVE RESISTANCE   The followers of an unjust or immoral authority can punish him by ignoring his wishes and by refusing to support the authority in his personal problems.

Supernatural sanctions

a. PUNISHMENT FOR THE VIOLATION OF A TABOO   The violation of a general taboo is believed to be punished automatically "because Ugatame, the creator, determined so." Violations of taboos imposed upon individuals by the shamans are believed to be punished by the live spirits. Disease or death are the usual effects of such violations.

b. SORCERY   Killing by the use of black magic is a rare sanction in the Kamu Valley. Only in cases where all other means of punishment became impractical did the authority resort to sorcery.

Self-redress

An action of the plaintiff by which he regains his property or punishes the offender without authorization by the legal authority is called self-redress. Such an action, if later approved by the authority, becomes legal.

THE DIFFERING REALMS OF THE LAW

Paul Bohannan

A NTHROPOLOGY, including legal anthropology, is faced with a problem that may be unique in social science: In order to present the results of our field research without seriously warping the ideas, we must undertake a second job of research, on the homologous institutions of our own society, and in the scientific disciplines that have investigated those institutions. This paper is an exercise in the anthropological investigation of jurisprudence. It investigates three things: (1) definitions that jurisprudence has used, and the anthropological usefulness of such definitions, (2) the "double institutionalization" of norms and customs that comprises all legal systems, and (3) some of the problems of the association between legal institutions and certain types of political organization.

LEGAL LANGUAGE

It is likely that more scholarship has gone into defining and explaining the concept of "law" than any other concept still in central use in the social sciences. Efforts to delimit the subject matter of law—like efforts to define it—usually fall into one of several traps that are more easily seen than avoided. The most naïve, on the one hand, beg the question and use "law" in what they believe to be its common-sense, dictionary, definition—apparently without looking into a dictionary to discover that the

Reprinted from *American Anthropologist* Special Publication, *The Ethnography of Law,* edited by Laura Nader, Volume 67, No. 6, Part 2, pp. 33–42. Reprinted by permission of the editor of *American Anthropologist*.

word "law" has six entries in Webster's second edition (1953), of which the first alone has thirteen separate meanings, followed by five columns of the word used in combinations. The most sophisticated scholars, on the other hand, have been driven to realize that, in relation to a noetic unity like law, which is not represented by anything except man's ideas about it, definition can mean no more than a set of mnemonics to remind the reader what has been talked about.

Three modern studies, two in jurisprudence and one in anthropology, all show a common trend.

Hart (1954) concludes that there are three "basic issues": (1) How is law related to order backed by threats? (2) What is the relation between legal obligation and moral obligation? (3) What are rules, and to what extent is law an affair of rules? Stone (1965) sets out seven sets of "attributes usually found associated with the phenomena commonly designated as law": Law is (1) a complex whole, (2) which always includes norms regulating human behavior, (3) that are social norms; (4) the complex whole is "orderly" and (5) the order is characteristically a coercive order (6) that is institutionalized (7) with a degree of effectiveness sufficient to maintain itself. Pospisil (1958) examines several attributes of the law—the attribute of authority, that of intention of universal application, that of *obligatio* (the right-obligation cluster), and that of sanction. In his view, the "legal" comprises a field in which custom, political decision, and the various attributes overlap, though each may be found extended outside that overlapping field, and there is no firm line, but rather a "zone of transition," between that which is unquestionably legal and that which is not.

It was Hermann Kantorowicz (1958) who pointed out that there are many subjects, including some of a nonlegal nature, that employ a concept of law. He proceeded to a more questionable point: that it was up to "general jurisprudence" to provide a background to make these differing concepts sensible. Kantorowicz' method for supplying such a jurisprudential background is very like Pospisil's in anthropology—examination of some characteristics of law that are vital to one or more of the more specific concepts. Law, he tells us, is characterized by having a body of rules that prescribe external conduct (it makes little immediate difference to the law how one feels about it—the law deals in deeds). These rules must be stated in such a way that the courts, or other adjudging bodies, can deal with them. Each of the rules contains a moralizing or "ought" element—and Kantorowicz fully recognizes that this "ought" element is culturally determined and may change from society to society and from era to era. Normative rules of this sort must, obviously, also be distinguished from factual uniformities by which men, sometimes with and sometimes without the help of courts and lawyers, govern their daily round of activity. Law is one of the devices by means of which men can reconcile their actual activities and behavior with the ideal principles that they have come to accept in a way that is not too painful or revolting to their sensibilities, and a way that allows ordered (which is to say predictable) social life to continue.

DOUBLE INSTITUTIONALIZATION

Law must be distinguished from traditions and fashions and more specifically, it must be differentiated from norm and from custom. A norm is a rule, more or less overt, which expresses "ought" aspects of relationships between human beings. Custom is a body of such norms—including regular deviations and compromises with norms—that is actually followed in practice much of the time.

All social institutions are marked by "customs" and these "customs" exhibit most of the stigmata cited by any definition of law. But there is one salient difference. Whereas custom continues to inhere in, and only in, these institutions which it governs (and which in turn govern it), law is specifically recreated, by agents of society, in a narrower and recognizable context— that is, in the context of the institutions that are legal in character and, to some degree at least, discrete from all others.

Just as custom includes norms, but is both greater and more precise than norms, so law includes custom, but is both greater and more precise. Law has the additional characteristic that it must be what Kantorowicz calls "justiciable," by which he means that the rules must be capable of reinterpretation, and actually must be reinterpreted, by one of the legal institutions of society so that the conflicts within nonlegal institutions can be adjusted by an "authority" outside themselves.

It is widely recognized that many peoples of the world can state more or less precise "rules" which are, in fact, the norms in accordance with which they think they ought to judge their conduct. In all societies there are allowable lapses from such rules, and in most there are more or less precise rules (sometimes legal ones) for breaking rules.

In order to make the distinction between law and other rules, it has been necessary to introduce furtively the word "institution." I use the word in Malinowski's sense (Malinowski 1945; Bohannan 1963).

A legal institution is one by means of which the people of a society settle disputes that arise between one another and counteract any gross and flagrant abuses of the rules (as we have considered them above) of at least some of the other institutions of society. Every ongoing society has legal institutions in this sense, as well as a wide variety of nonlegal institutions.

In carrying out the task of settling difficulties in the nonlegal institutions, legal institutions face three kinds of tasks: (1) There must be specific ways in which difficulties can be disengaged from the institutions in which they arose and which they now threaten and then be engaged within the processes of the legal institution. (2) There must be ways in which the trouble can now be handled within the framework of the legal institution, and (3) There must be ways in which the new solutions which thus emerge can be re-engaged within the processes of the nonlegal institutions from which they emerged. It is seldom that any framework save a political one can supply these requirements.

There are, thus, at least two aspects of legal institutions that are not shared with other institutions of society. Legal institutions—and often they alone—must have some regularized way to interfere in the malfunctioning (and, perhaps, the functioning as well) of the nonlegal institutions in order to disengage the trouble-case. There must, secondly, be two kinds of rules in the legal institutions—those that govern the activities of the legal institution itself (called "adjectival law" by Austin, and "procedure" by most modern lawyers), and those that are substitutes or modifications or restatements of the rules of the nonlegal institution that has been invaded (called "substantive law").

Listed above are only the minimal aspects that are all shared by all known legal institutions. There may be other aspects, as for example the commonly recognized fact that legal institutions on both the procedural and the substantive sides can be in the fullest sense innovatory.

Seen in this light, a fairly simple distinction can be made between law and custom. Customs are norms or rules (more or less strict, and with greater or less support of moral, ethical, or even physical coercion) about the ways in which people must behave if social institutions are to perform their tasks and society is to endure. All institutions (including legal institutions) develop customs. Some customs, in some societies, are *re*institutionalized at another level: they are restated for the more precise purposes of legal institutions. When this happens, therefore, law may be regarded as a custom that has been restated in order to make it amenable to the activities of the legal institutions. In this sense, it is one of the most characteristic attributes of legal institutions that some of these "laws" are about the legal institutions themselves, although most are about the other institutions of society —the familial, economic, political, ritual, or whatever.

One of the reddest herrings ever dragged into the working of orderly jurisprudence was Malinowski's little book called *Crime and Custom in Savage Society*. It is unfortunately almost the only anthropological book that appears on the standard reading list used in many law schools, "The Dean's List," and it has had an undue and all but disastrous influence on the rapprochement be-

tween anthropology and jurisprudence. Malinowski's idea was a
good one; he claimed that law is "a body of binding obligations
regarded as right by one party and acknowledged as the duty by
the other, kept in force by the specific mechanism of reciprocity
and publicity inherent in the structure of . . . society." His error
was in equating what he had defined with the law. It is not law
that is "kept in force by . . . reciprocity and publicity." It is custom, as we have defined it here. Law is, rather, "a body of binding
obligations regarded as right by one party and acknowledged as
the duty by the other" *which has been reinstitutionalized within
the legal institution so that society can continue to function in
an orderly manner on the basis of rules so maintained.* In short,
reciprocity is the basis of custom; but the law rests on the basis
of this double institutionalization. Central in it is that some of the
customs of some of the institutions of society are restated in such
a way that they can be "applied" by an institution designed (or,
at very least, utilized) specifically for that purpose.

One of the best ways to perceive the doubly institutionalized
norms, or "laws," is to break up the law into smaller components,
capable of attaching to persons (either human individuals or corporate groups) and so to work in terms of "rights" and their
reciprocal duties or "obligations." In terms of rights and duties,
the relationships between law and custom, law and morals, law
and anything else, can be seen in a new light. Whether in the
realm of kinship or contract, citizenship or property rights, the relationships between people can be reduced to a series of prescrip-
tions with the obligations and the correlative rights that emanate
from these presumptions. In fact, if it is not carried too far and
unduly formalized, thinking in terms of rights and obligations of
persons (or role players) is a convenient and fruitful way of investigating much of the custom of many institutions (Hohfeld
1923; Hoebel 1954). Legal rights are only those rights that attach
to norms that have been doubly institutionalized; they provide a
means for seeing the legal institutions from the standpoint of the
persons engaged in them.

The phenomenon of double institutionalization of norms and

therefore of legal rights has been recognized for a long time, but analysis of it has been only partially successful. Kantorowicz, for example, has had to create the concept of "justiciability" of the law. It would be better to say that legal rights have their material origins (either overtly or covertly) in the customs of nonlegal institutions but must be *overtly restated* for the specific purpose of enabling the legal institutions to perform their task.

A legal right (and, with it, a law) is the restatement, for the purpose of maintaining peaceful and just operation of the institutions of society, of some, but never all, of the recognized claims of the persons within those institutions; the restatement must be made in such a way that these claims can be more or less assured by the total community or its representatives. Only so can the moral, religious, political, and economic implications of law be fully explored.

Law is never a mere reflection of custom, however. Rather, law is always out of phase with society, specifically because of the duality of the statement and restatement of rights. Indeed, the more highly developed the legal institutions, the greater the lack of phase, which not only results from the constant reorientation of the primary institutions, but also is magnified by the very dynamic of the legal institutions themselves (Stone 1964: Chapter 1, Section 1).

Thus, it is the very nature of law, and its capacity to "do something about" the primary social institutions, that creates the lack of phase. Moreover, even if one could assume perfect legal institutionalization, change within the primary institutions would soon jar the system out of phase again. What is less obvious is that if there were ever to be perfect phase between law and society, then society could never repair itself, grow and change, flourish or wane. It is the fertile dilemma of law that it must always be out of step with society, but that people must always (because they work better with fewer contradictions, if for no other reason) attempt to reduce the lack of phase. Custom must either grow to fit the law or it must actively reject it; law must either grow to fit the custom, or it must ignore or suppress it. It is in these very interstices that social growth and social decay take place.

Social catastrophe and social indignation are sources of much law and resultant changes in custom. With technical and moral change, new situations appear that must be "legalized." This truth has particular and somewhat different applications to developed and to less highly developed legal systems. On the one hand, in developed municipal systems of law in which means for institutionalizing behavior on a legal level are already traditionally concentrated in political decision-making groups such as legislatures, nonlegal social institutions sometimes take a very long time to catch up with the law. On the other hand, in less developed legal systems, it may be that little or no popular demand is made on the legal institutions, and therefore little real contact exists or can be made to exist between them and the primary institutions (Stone 1965: Chapter 2, Section 17). Law can, as we have seen in another context, become one of the major innovators of society, the more effective the greater a people's dependence on it.

BEYOND THE AUSTINIAN SOVEREIGN

To summarize the position so far, it is the essence of "law" to present a double institutionalization of norms. A secondary criterion was added: a unicentric political unit (no matter how pluralistic) is the device most commonly utilized to carry out the secondary, or legal, institutionalization (a "sovereign"). Such a theory—although it may be charged with being simplistic—is, it would seem, consonant with the state type of organization. However, the theory of double institutionalization seems inadequate thus far to explain three related situations: the situations of (1) law in a stateless society, (2) law in a colonial society, and (3) international law.

So far we have two assumptions. First, we have assumed a power or a state, whether it be seen as an Austinian sovereign, or as the greater entity that assumes the court whose actions are to be predicted with greater or lesser accuracy. Second, we have assumed that there is also only one legal culture in such a situation—no matter, for the moment, how many contradictions are to be found in it. A legal culture, for the present purposes, is that which is subscribed to (whether they know anything about it or

	Unicentric Power	Bicentric (or Multicentric) Power
One culture	Municipal systems of "law"	Law in stateless societies
Two (or more) cultures	Colonial law	International law

The Legal Realm.

not, and whether they act within it or "agree" with it or not) by the people of a society. The secondary institutionalization forms a more or less consistent cultural unit.

With these ideas in mind, it is possible to question both assumptions and hence to build a four-square diagram in order to extend our views for examining the realm of the legal (see figure). Municipal systems, of the sort studied by most jurists, deal with a single legal culture within a unicentric power system. Subcultures in such a society may create vast problems of law's being out of phase with the customs and mores of parts of the society, but it is a problem of phase.

Colonial law

Colonial law is marked by a unicentric power system, with greater or lesser problems of conjoining the colonial government with the local government, and more and less overt theories (such as the British "indirect rule") of accomplishing the conjunction. All are marked, however, by two (or more) legal cultures. Sometimes this situation is recognized, as it was in preindependence Kenya with its two hierarchies of courts, one for "European" law and the other for African law joined only at the top in the Supreme Court. The mark of a colonial situation might be said to be a systematic misunderstanding between the two cultures within the single power system, with constant revolutionary proclivities resulting from what is, at best, a "working misunderstanding."

In colonial law, the problem of disengaging a problem case from the milieu in which it arises is often complicated by the existence of directly opposed ideas about the motives and goals to be achieved in resorting to court action. Once disengaged, the culture of the court officials may be completely different from that of the principals and witnesses in the cases, so that the outcome at best may seem arbitrary. Once "settled" in this more or less arbitrary way, the re-engagement in the institutions of society may be very imperfcct, because of lack of consensus about what was decided or lack of agreement about the binding qualities and the justice of it.

We are only now far enough removed from colonies—now that they are obsolete—to begin a thorough examination of the effect that colonial powers had, via such a system, on the legal systems of the countries in which they were found.

Law in stateless societies

The mark of the stateless society is the absence of a unicentric power system. All situations of dispute that occur between people not within the same domestic unit *ipso facto* occur between two more or less equal power units. The prime example of a bicentric system is, of course, the lineage system based on the principle of segmental opposition, but there is no reason that this type of solution need be limited to such situations. There is, however, only a single culture: the principals and witnesses in a case may be at vast odds about who did what and to whom, and hence where justice lies. But they understand one another's activities and plots —perhaps they understand them only too well.

In such a situation, all trouble cases are settled by some form of compromise, more or less in accordance with a set of overt "rules." Instead of "decisions" there are "compromises." In a unicentric system, it is possible to have judicial decision and a recognized mechanism of enforcement which presents problems merely of efficiency, not of substance. In a bicentric situation, nobody can be in a position to make decisions—it is organized so that there cannot be. The "judges" must make compromises, and their compromises must be enforced from two power centers, which often—to a citizen of a "state"—looks like no enforcement at all. Instead of implementing decisions, the parties are made to accept the principles and provisions of a compromise.

It is my feeling—but I cannot claim it is any more than that—that the compromise, bicentric solution of problems leads to very much less precise restatements of norms as law than does the decision-based unicentric solution. Bodies of rules in stateless societies seem to be less precise, scarcely made into anything resembling a *corpus juris* although, of course, the anthropologist or the intellectually inclined informant can create a system—even a system of precedents—from the regularities that result from compromise between units in terms of their common cultural recognition of their common institutions.

In some societies the compromiser may be quite firmly institutionalized. Among the Nuer (Evans-Pritchard 1940), for example, the leopard-skin chief is a firmly institutionalized compromiser who may or may not be resorted to in any specific instance. If he is, his task is to create a compromise to which both parties will concur, saving the face of all by his religious position and "sanctions."

Most specifically, perhaps, the court—a body of men representative of the political power—cannot have any part in a bicentric system, unless there is some mode of organizing multiple judges. The more common methods of procedures are moots, contests, oracles, and self-help. In short, the bicentric, unicultural system may not have a very great potential for organized, neat systems of "law."

INTERNATIONAL LAW

This section is set forth with great circumspection, because I know very little about international law. Yet it is obvious, even to a rank amateur, that there has been a long dispute in jurisprudence about whether international law is *really* "law" (Williams 1945–46).

The difficulty arises among scholars who derive their model too narrowly from that law which is associated with a unicentric power system. It is undoubtedly true that the most "developed" legal systems occur within organizations such as states that have a single power system—indeed, the growth of states has been co-incident with the growth of such legal systems. For all that such a power system may be pluralistic, it nevertheless is not legally divisible into warring and treating factions. "Law" is seen as one of the supreme activities of such an institution. The elements of coercion and prediction that have been emphasized in the definitions of law have lent credence to the point. These qualities have carried over and indeed obscured discussions of international law.

The situation in international law is, however, made more complex in that two or more unicentric power systems are bound together by means other than a more inclusive unicentric power system. In each of them, custom is "legalized." In international law, then, the process of "reinstitutionalization" must take place yet again—but with the qualitative difference that this time it must be done within the limitations of a multicentric power system. The difficulties in this secondary reinstitutionalization of international law are compounded because there are likely to be cultural differences in the two or more primary legal systems.

The "law" must, in short, be reinstitutionalized not out of a single related set of institutions, but rather out of two separate sets of interrelated institutions, including the interrelationship of the two unicentric power systems. Many cultures can exist within a unicentric system—the United States provides a vivid example; moreover, what might in other aspects be neatly regarded as a single culture may be representative of two or more states. However, it is usually reasonable to assume that the two separate but interrelated sets of institutions on which international law must draw in the process of legalization, exhibit somewhat different cultures. Therefore legalization must take place in terms of two cultures that are often vastly foreign to one another.

Obviously, the legal institutions of a bicentric and bicultural system exhibit different types of organization, different goals—different customs all round—from those of unicentric systems. More specifically, they must have different ways of disengaging the trouble situation from its matrix. Probably those ways must be more subtle precisely because the power distribution stems from two centers, and a preliminary legalization has likely been made in each. We do not as yet have adequate legal institutions for bicentric systems, nor do we have agreed ways for legalizing international law that is sufficiently subtle and consonant with multiple cultural evaluations (Jones 1962). The problem will not be solved merely by the creation of a single "sovereign," as was supposed only a few years ago.

It is a characteristic of unicentric legal systems that they are empowered to reach and enforce decisions. It is, just so, characteristic of bicentric systems that they must reach legal compromises that are sufficiently compatible with both cultures as to be acceptable and ultimately enforceable from the two power centers. Western judges have lost and are just regaining some of their rights to compromise within the framework of the adversary procedure. Other societies such as some of those in Africa, are only beginning to adopt a "decision" procedure in place of or in addition to a compromise procedure.

In short, it would appear that in international law—or at least in the old-fashioned view of it—there is a *treble* institutionalization: once at the level of custom, once at the level of the legal institutions of states, and again at the level of the bicentric, bicultural "international" accord.

THE DIFFERING REALMS OF JURAL ETHNOGRAPHY

It is a truism to say that if the law is to be discovered in differing realms, that legal ethnography must also be found there. But the question comes up: What should we and our students be doing?

Without in any sense wanting to close any avenues, it seems possible to list several important tasks:

(1) First of all, we must study the relationship between the social institution and the legal institution in which some of its norms are (doubly or trebly) reinstitutionalized. We must know the relationships between families and family law or between received behavior and criminal law.

(2) We must get a full range of the types of institution that fulfill legal functions, and the social situations under which each is either tried or has proved successful.

(3) We must discover which customs are reinstitutionalized into law in different social, cultural, and political situations, and in accordance with what postulates. We must examine the institutions that precede and follow from such reinstitutionalization.

(4) We must seek out situations of cross-cultural conflict resolution and examine them against a set of legal qualities. (Anthropologists have been lax here.)

In short, jural ethnography, like the law itself, has no bounds. It is, on the one hand, as broad as life itself; on the other, as narrow as the recognizable reinstitutionalization in given situations of power structure and cultural field. There are three grave dangers: We may, like Barton, report all our ethnography as if it were law. We may, like Gluckman's first book, cut our insights short by defining the "legal" too rigidly before we start to write. Or we may, like my own *Justice and Judgment,* stop a chapter too soon so that neither does the ethnography fit easily into the mainstream of jurisprudence nor are methods made overt that allow ready comparison among legal systems, of all the sorts discussed here.

Part II | THE ETHNOGRAPHY OF LAW:
THE JUDICIAL PROCESS

THE JUDICIAL PROCESS
AMONG THE BAROTSE

Max Gluckman

THE LOZI ARE the ruling people of Barotseland. According to
Lozi legends, some time after God *Nyambe* first created Man,
one of His sons by His own daughter founded a kingdom in the
Upper Zambezi Valley. The Lozi believe that with this king there
came into existence Lozi Law (*mulao waMalozi*) as a whole body
of rules defining rights and duties and of procedures for seeking
justice from the king. The Lozi recite many instances of later kings
amending laws, of the institution of new customs and laws, and
of the adoption of customs and laws from other tribes. Nevertheless they consider that their Law as an embracing body of rights
(*liswanelo*) and justice (*tukelo* or *niti* = truth) has existed from
time immemorial. They have partially absorbed into it all the requirements and social changes which have flowed from British
overlordship.

European historical records, as well as Lozi legends, enable us
to affirm with certainty that this Lozi kingdom was well established by the middle of the eighteenth century. It had extended
dominion over many surrounding tribes, to whom collectively I
shall refer as the *Barotse*, since they are thus marked on general

Extracts from Max Gluckman, *The Judicial Process among the Barotse of
Northern Rhodesia,* published on behalf of the Rhodes-Livingstone Institute
by Manchester University Press. The original pages are 1–3, 7, 9, 10, 15,
21–24, 32–35, 37–42, 44–51, 322–23, 357–66. Reprinted by permission of
the author, the Rhodes-Livingstone Institute, and the Manchester University
Press. [This selection follows closely, but does not duplicate precisely, that in
Glendon Schubert (ed.), *Judicial Behavior, a Reader in Theory and Research,* Chicago, Rand-McNally, 1964.]

maps. This will enable me to keep references to the conglomerate
nation distinct from references to the dominant *Lozi* tribe, with
whom this study principally deals, though subjects of all tribes under the Lozi king are, in native parlance, *Lozi*. The Barotse nation has had for at least two centuries a governmental political
organization including a hierarchy of courts which had power to
enforce their decisions.

Since the establishment of the British Protectorate by treaty
with the British South Africa Company in 1900, the organization
of this hierarchy of courts has been altered, and their powers and
jurisdiction, especially in dealing with crimes and delicts, have
been radically curtailed.

In brief, Barotse courts have lost their power to try:

(*a*) Cases 'in which a person is charged with an offence in consequence of which death is alleged to have occurred and which
is punishable under any law with death or imprisonment for life';

(*b*) 'Cases relating to witchcraft', except with special permission;

(*c*) 'any case in which a non-native is a witness' [or, as stated
above, a litigant] (Section 11 of No. 26 of 1936).

Secondly, the courts have lost the power to inflict certain punishments and remedies, including the death penalty, throttling,
and unlimited flogging; and they have acquired the power to imprison, an unknown practice in the past (Sections 14 and 16 of
No. 26 of 1936).

Finally, appeals now lie from the highest Barotse court to the
High Court of Northern Rhodesia in civil matters, and to the
Provincial Commissioner of Barotse Province in criminal matters,
from whom there is further appeal to the High Court (Section 33
of No. 26 of 1936). In addition, under Section 22, reports of all
criminal cases must be submitted to Government officers, and
under Section 25 a District Officer, subject to the directions of the
Provincial Commissioner, may sit as adviser in a native court.
Obviously, many offences, and all cases in which non-natives are
involved as parties or witnesses, come directly under British
courts.

The old political and juridical organization into which these villages were tied can only be described if we begin at the capitals. Before 1890, there were two capitals only, both situated in the Plain. The king (*Mbumu-wa-Litunga* = great-one-of-the-earth) ruled the main capital, north of the middle of the Plain; another ruler (*Litunga-la-Mboela* = earth- [chief] -of-the-south), held a capital which has never been more than thirty miles farther south. Since the Lozi reconquered their homeland from a band of Sotho invaders, the Kololo, who subjugated it from 1838 to 1864, the southern ruler has been a princess (referred to henceforth as the princess chief). The southern ruler has always been subordinate to the king, though she has a capital which duplicates his faithfully. These capitals in the period with which we are concerned have been built at Lialui in the north, moving at flood to Limulunga, and in the south at Nalolo, from where the court moves a short distance at flood. All villages throughout the Barotse kingdom were attached to one of these two capitals. In the 1890s the Lozi began to establish subordinate capitals in their outer provinces to cope with invasions of other Bantu and with the incoming Whites. . . .

Every capital has at its heart a central cleared space (called *Namoo* at the two main capitals) on one side of which is the palace, and on the other the council-house. The ruler resides in the palace; the full council meets in the council-house to deliberate or try cases. Since the council is not only a court, I use the native term *kuta* throughout, save in general analytic passages. The court-houses, particularly the one at Lialui, are imposing buildings. In the center at the back is a dais on which the king or ruling member of the royal family sits if he (or she) is present. Usually the ruler does not attend the hearings of cases, though the kuta's judgment is referred to him for confirmation. Even if the ruler chooses to sit in the kuta while a case is being tried, it proceeds as if he were not there. He takes no part in the hearing, and the facts and judgments in the case are referred to him as if he had not heard them.

All Lozi kutas are divided into three sets of councillors, each of which may be called a 'mat', as the Lozi name them, since the councillors by virtue of their titled offices are entitled to sit on mats. The positions of the titles on each mat are fixed, and if a titleholder is discharged, is promoted, or dies, his successor (who is appointed by the ruler-in-kuta) takes his position on the mat. . . .

The most powerful group of councillors are those who sit on mats to the right of the king. Their senior member, the *ngambela,* is head of the kuta: he is so powerful that he is described, in relation to the king, as 'another kind of king'. He cannot be a prince who has a right to succeed to the kingship. I shall call these councillors-of-the-right *indunas,* the general Southern African word for 'councillor' (in Lozi *nduna,* pl. *manduna*), since it has passed into English from Zulu, and we need to standardize a term for African political authorities with varied duties. The Lozi use this term to distinguish councillors-of-the-right from the other 'mats', but there are two words to distinguish two groups among these indunas. The senior indunas are called *makwambuyu; malume* are the group of junior indunas who sit in a row behind them. On mats to the left of the royal dais sit councillors called *likombwa,* which in Barotseland has been translated as 'stewards'. This is an appropriate word, because while they are powerful councillors in national affairs, they are also more specifically responsible for the royal household. The stewards are also divided into seniors and *malume* juniors. At right angles to the stewards, or at the front of the kuta, is the royal mat for princes and for the consorts (*boishee,* sing. *ishee*) of princesses, who exercise power for their wives. Opposite the indunas' mat sit clerks, police, and royal bandsmen, leaving a space in the middle for suppliants and litigants.

The litigants, supported by their witnesses and kinsmen, sit before the judges against the posts which hold up the roof. The plaintiff, without interruption, states his case with full and seemingly irrelevant detail. The defendant replies similarly. Their witnesses, who have heard their statements, then speak. There are no lawyers to represent the parties. The kuta, assisted by anyone present, proceeds to cross-examine and to pit the parties and witnesses against one another. When all the evidence has been heard, the lowest induna on the right gives the first judgment. He is then followed by councillors on the three mats (indunas, princes, and stewards) in ascending order of seniority across from one mat to the other, until the senior councillor-of-the-right gives the final judgment. This is then referred to the ruler of the capital, who confirms, rejects, or alters it, or refers it back to the kuta for further investigation and discussion. It is this final judgment by the last induna to speak which, subject to the ruler's approval, is binding.

Most Lozi relationships are multiplex, enduring through the lives of individuals and even generations. Each of these relationships is part of an intricate network of similar relationships. Inevitably, therefore, many of the disputes which are investigated by Lozi kutas arise not in ephemeral relationships involving single interests, but in relationships which embrace many interests, which depend on similar related relationships, and which may endure into the future. This, at least, is usually the desire of the parties and the hope and desire of the judges and unbiased onlookers. The Lozi disapprove of any irremediable breaking of relationships. For them it is a supreme value that villages should remain united, kinsfolk and families and kinship groups should not separate, lord and underling should remain associated. Throughout a court hearing of this kind the judges try to prevent the breaking of relationships, and to make it possible for the parties to live together amicably in the future. Obviously this does not apply in every case, but it is true of a large number, and it is present in some degree in almost all cases. Therefore the court tends to be conciliating; it strives to effect a compromise acceptable to, and accepted by, all the parties. This is the main task of the judges. . . . This task of the judges is related to the nature of the social relationships out of which spring the disputes that come before them. In order to fulfil their task the judges constantly have to broaden the field of their enquiries, and consider the total history of relations between the litigants, not only the narrow legal issue raised by one of them. Since the kuta is an administrative body, as well as a law-court, it may take varied action to achieve its aim, or convert a 'civil suit' into a 'criminal hearing' in the public interest. The result is that in cases of this sort the court's conception of 'relevance' is very wide, for many facts affect the settlement of the dispute. This applies particularly to cases between blood-kin and between fellow-villagers. The relationship of husband and wife is more ephemeral, and in disputes between them the court concentrates more on the immediately relevant facts. When a contract between strangers, or an injury by a man on a stranger, is involved, the court narrows its range of relevance yet further.

Lozi, like all Africans, appear to be very litigious. Almost every Lozi of middle age can recount dispute after dispute in which he has been involved: most of these have been debated in family and village 'courts' but many have also gone to political courts. Many Lozi are ever ready to rush to court where they dispute with great bitterness and determination. In cases where they clearly cannot win, they will proceed from court to court. Their bitterness must be understood from the way in which a dispute provoking a lawsuit precipitates ill-feeling about many trifling incidents in the past both between the parties and among their kin, incidents which may go back over many years. Men may sue knowing they will lose, but that they thus bring to the kuta a kinsman who has slighted them and who will be rebuked. Or a man will commit an offence to induce another to sue him, with the same end in view.

The kuta should not achieve a reconciliation without blaming those who have done wrong. The litigants in coming to court have appealed for a public hearing of their grievances, and these are examined against the norms of behaviour expected of people. The judges therefore upbraid all the parties where they have departed from these norms: judgments are sermons on filial, parental, and brotherly love. This is not inappropriate since the kuta is the central administrative chapter for national religious affairs. People involved indirectly, as well as the litigants themselves, are admonished on how to behave.

When we assemble the norms which are stated in this exemplary way, we shall see that they form that figure which is so prominent in all legal systems—the reasonable man. This figure is also used by the judges as the basis of their cross-examination to arrive at the truth: therefore I pause in my argument to consider the problem of evidence (the significance of direct, circumstantial, and hearsay evidence; the use of oath and ordeal, etc.), before investigating the nature of the reasonable man in Lozi society. Here we shall find that he is highly specified, in accordance with the specific social positions which the parties occupy. Following up this point, we shall find that many disputes, apparently over gardens or chattels, are in fact suits by the plaintiff to have the kuta state that the defendant has not behaved reasonably in accordance with the norms of their relationship.

It will have already emerged from this summary account, that in assessing whether behaviour is reasonable the judges lay blame on those who have erred. Implicit in the reasonable man is the upright man, and moral issues in these relationships are barely differentiated from legal issues. This is so even though the Lozi distinguish 'legal' rules which the kuta has power to enforce or protect, from 'moral' rules it has not power to enforce or protect. But the judges are reluctant to support the person who is right in law, but wrong in justice, and may seek to achieve justice by indirect, and perhaps administrative, action.

In the course of this account of Lozi trials we shall also cover a number of other problems. I indicate a few here. First, since almost all a man's relationships exist in his positions in the political and kinship systems, a litigant in many cases arising from these multiplex relationships comes to court not as a right-and-duty bearing *persona,* but in terms of his total social personality. That is, in most disputes a person is not involved merely as buyer, seller, lessor, lessee, landowner, the injured party and the wrongdoer—briefly, the plaintiff and the defendant, the complainant and the accused—but he is involved as an individual in specific relationships with a whole set of other people. In administering the law the judges consider these total relationships, not only the relations between right-and-duty bearing units. But concepts of these units exist as nuclei for the substantive law.

I conclude this section of the analysis by surveying the relation of the judicial process to 'law' as a whole among the Lozi, and find that it is in essence similar to that process in Western law. The judges have to apply certain normative rules to a particular set of circumstances in dispute. These rules, known somewhat vaguely as 'the law', are contained in customary usages; in statutes; in institutions common to all tribes of the region and in some institutions which they believe are common to all humanity and derive from God; in general equity and justice; in judicial precedent; and in the regular processes of the natural world (in our sense). Customary usage—ritual and secular—is one of the sources of Lozi law, as it has been in all systems; and the Lozi have the same other sources as those other systems.

Theoretically, this total body of law is known and certain and the judges are supposed only to pronounce it, abide by it, and apply it. However, since the law has only recently and barely begun to be recorded, the judges do not make a systematic survey of all the sources and decide what rules are applicable. Generally they tend to form a moral and equitable judgment on the case and then state—and amend—the law to accord with this judgment. Often they cannot do this, and must abide by some well-known statutory law or customary rule. But especially in cases between kinsmen, they are generally able to satisfy their ethical view of the facts. This process emerges notably in the fact that judges refer less often to judicial precedents in previous disputes, than to precedents of people behaving morally in circumstances similar to those of the case they are trying.

This process of judicial reasoning begins with the pleadings of the parties and the judges' examination of the evidence, which at every point is evaluated against moral norms. Nevertheless, the process is controlled by logical reasoning, which proceeds from premises of fact and premises of law ('reasons' as the Lozi call them) to certain conclusions, and the Lozi have a developed vocabulary to evaluate the skill or clumsiness of judicial analysis. Judges also try to develop the law by reasoning by analogy and logical development to meet new situations. Thus they employ Cardozo's methods of philosophy, evolution, and tradition. They also employ his so-called 'method of sociology', by which they import equity, social welfare and public policy, into their applications of the law. They are able to do so because the main certainty of the law consists in certain general principles whose constituent concepts are 'flexible'—as law itself, right and duty, good evidence, negligence, reasonableness. The judges' task is to define these concepts for a particular set of circumstances, and in this process of specification they introduce into judgment through the flexible concepts all sorts of social values and prejudices, and indeed personal prejudices and values.

Finally, I conclude by making bold to submit that Western jurists, in maintaining or attacking the myth of law's certainty, have not fully explored the flexible 'uncertainty' of legal concepts; and have particularly failed to arrange these concepts in order either of flexibility or of moral implication. I suggest that this ordering is necessary if we are to understand the relation between law and ethics; for I see the judicial process as the attempt to specify legal concepts with ethical implications according to the structure of society, in application to the great variety of circumstance of life itself. In this process the judges are able to develop the law to cope with social changes.

My study of the judicial process in Loziland is based primarily on the analysis of cases tried in 1940–47. I have in parts referred to judgments and matters found in archival material or reported by informants from the past, and have sought for information from books by early visitors to Loziland. Strictly, my conclusions state that Lozi judges worked and thought thus in the 1940s. At that time Loziland had been under the British protectorate for forty years. The powers of Lozi courts to punish and modes of punishment had been curtailed by a British overlordship which is partially hostile to the Lozi authorities, and this overlordship had reduced the possibility of arbitrary action by king and kuta. But I believe that my observations not only yield a valid analysis of judicial practice in Lozi courts at present, but also that this analysis gives, with reservations for the past made clear in the text, a true view of their judicial *process* in that past. It may not do so for judicial *practice,* since this may have been influenced by political and economic factors in ways which we cannot now assess. But I observed Lozi kutas trying disputes and offences affecting land, cattle, and other property; social position, marriage, and succession; theft, assault, and slander; etc. From these trials, checked against earlier records and informants' texts, I have in this volume extracted the way in which judges approach their task, how they assess evidence, what sources they draw on for judicial decision, the logic of their arguments, and how they apply legal rules to the varied and changing circumstances of life. The modes of reasoning involved in this complex process are so deeply imbedded in Lozi institutions and thought, that I consider my whole analysis emphasizes their indigenous existence. There is no evidence that in these respects the Lozi have been influenced by the work of British courts, whose procedures are alien and often incomprehensible to them. Hence I assert that my study of the Lozi judicial process, which is akin to our own judicial process, faithfully depicts modes of reasoning which are probably found wherever men apply norms to varied disputes. I consider that more specific aspects of this study record processes which are likely to be found in other African states, and indeed in the arbitral processes of societies without governmental institutions. Since the study has by implication wider reference than to the Lozi alone, I argue here that some of its conclusions require that certain current ideas about 'primitive law' be abandoned and others be reformulated.

THE TASK OF THE JUDGES

The way in which the judges try to reconcile the disputing parties, or in which they convert a 'civil suit' into a 'criminal hearing'

in the public interest, is best illustrated, without further introduction, by records of cases. The main part of my analysis is based
on detailed anthropological inquiries over a period of thirty
months between 1940 and 1947, and especially on cases I heard
being settled in various kutas, in which I sat for several months.
I do not mean here records of the bare bones of judgments: it
will soon be apparent that these do not by any means reflect
either the judicial process or the substantive law. The record of
a case involves the pleas of the parties, the evidence of witnesses, and cross-examination, as well as the judges' decisions.
It is of course impossible for me to reproduce any verbatim record
of a whole case. The cases proceeded at high speed in Lozi, which
I understood very well but not perfectly. I took down notes in a
longhand mixture of Lozi and English. During the hearings I got
lost over some details. It was particularly difficult for me to follow
the references by parties and witnesses to others by various kinship terms. Where I got confused I asked the head of the kuta,
next to whom I was invariably seated, to clear things up for me.
Secondly, while the kuta is trying a case some councillors may
also at the same time be transacting administrative business,
and in trying to follow this I missed some passages in cases. Nevertheless, I am certain that the records I present are fair.

CASE 1: THE CASE OF THE BIASED FATHER

This was a land dispute between Kwangwa[1] kinsmen and fellow-
villagers, heard at the Saa-Katengo Kuta of Lialui on 27th August, 1942, on appeal from subdistrict induna SIKWA.

> A, B and C sued their 'father' (i.e., father's elder brother), Y,
> who is the headman of their natal village, for certain gardens on the
> margin of a small plain. Their own father, K, died when they were
> infants and Y raised them. The law in this case seems clear: 'if you
> leave the village, you lose your gardens in it.'
> Nephew A opened the case: 'We are disputing these gardens. The
> trouble began when our "brother" Z committed adultery with the
> wife of C. C caught him and injured Z till others intervened. B was
> away working in White country. We failed to settle the matter at

---

[1] A tribe related to the Lozi and living in the woodland near the Plain.

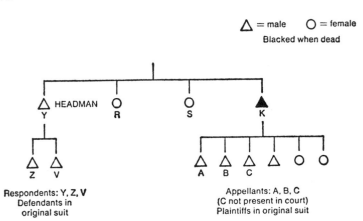

home, and went to the subdistrict induna SIKWA. C's wife paid the kuta's fine of a beast, and Z was to pay C two beasts but did not do so' [until 1946 when the damages and fine were increased, an adulterer paid his cuckold two beasts or £2 damages, and the adulteress paid the kuta a fine of one beast or £1]. 'Z insulted C. When C complained to our "father" Y, Y drove him out of the village. He built a short distance away. I remonstrated with Y that C was aggrieved and was not causing the trouble. Y came to me in the night and told me to get out of the village. I said goodbye to my female fathers [paternal aunts, R and S], but not to Y' [elicited under cross-examination by the court]. 'B returned from White country, and that evening left the village to join us. Then I found that Z was cultivating our old gardens, and eating our sweet-potatoes and mangoes. These were manured gardens. I protested to our "father" Y who said it was done without his agreement—he would put it right. He did nothing, so I saw that he was supporting his own son, Z, against the children of his younger brother. We complained to the induna SIKWA who said we could not live together, we must separate [because they would kill each other—see below]. The induna said we had lost our land. I cannot see how a person without a fault can lose his land, and his mangoes and other crops, so we have appealed.'

The son Z was called on to speak for the defence: 'Before I committed adultery with C's wife, A had cuckolded the son of the sister of our father Y. I admit I committed adultery. I admit I took their gardens, but they were not driven away, they fled in the night. Would I, their brother, drive them away—I who raised them and made them big? I did not insult C, C insulted me.' He then proceeded to complain of a long series of actions of his 'brothers', alleging that they took back poles and thatching-grass which they had cut and which his father Y had used in his hut, that they stinted Y fish they caught and goods they brought from White country, etc. He did this in order to show their hardness of heart. 'After they left, they told me that they had put medicine [magical substances] against thieves on the mangoes, so the children should not enter. Can you do this, get your child bitten by a snake?' [i.e. the magic makes a snake bite a thief, and his child is their child]. 'As for their crops, their wives pulled these up. How can a man who has moved, work gardens that he has left? There is the law of the Whitemen, about cleaning the village of weeds: will they be clearing in the village, or my wives? Is it fair for them to have gardens there, and live elsewhere? My hens and children and calves will enter their gardens. If they live in the village it balances out, for theirs will enter my gardens. But it is not the same if they live elsewhere.'

B told more or less the same tale as A, and added: 'When I got back from White country I tried to get Y, our "father", to call together the people to settle the quarrel. Y said it was no longer possible. I saw that Y was deciding with partiality (*sobozi*), supporting his own child. So I moved out after A and C.' He turned to A and corrected him: 'We were not driven out, because our father did not burn our huts.'

The kuta called on headman Y, the father. He began with a diatribe on how wicked and irresponsible the modern youth are. He described how K [his younger brother and father of A, B and C] died when K's children were small and they grew up on each side of him. 'I raised them. If I had been childless, they would have cared for me. Would I drive away the children of my brother, all of whom are on my foot? But the children of today are bad. When they stab fish at the battues, they give me none; they killed an ox, and my wife bought meat with cassava; they brought me nothing from White country. I sent my sister, their female father [paternal aunt], to remonstrate with A after he left the village. B said someone hated him and had planted medicines to burn up his crops. I said the sun had burnt B's crops; let him dig up the medicines. B replied that the person who had done it, had dug up the medicines when the crops were scorched. I took some poles of A's to make a partition in my hut, and A came and pulled them up, and took the grass from the roof. I did not drive them away—they went at night without reason or farewell. I gave the four sons of K eight cattle with which to marry.' Questioned by the kuta, A and B admit this.

These are the main statements of the litigants. Y's sisters R and S and his wife and son V gave evidence. I briefly indicate the points on which the kuta cross-examined them.

Steward AWAMI asked Y: 'Is it true that B asked you to call the people together to discuss the quarrel?'—Y denied it, and B reaffirmed that he had. The same councillor asked about A's taking away the poles; A said the partition had not yet been made. The poles had been taken and leant against Y's hut. A argued: 'It was after I was driven out—I did not see why if I were driven out, Y should have my poles.' Y asserted that he had made the partition, and the two sides divided on this, each side's witnesses supporting its leader.

Steward ALULEYA questioned A and B about whether they gave Y food generally, and clothes when they returned from White country with their earnings and purchases. They recited a long list, which Y and Z denied.

Induna INYUNDWANA asked A: 'What were the words which drove you out of the village?'—A: 'He told us to get out.'

INYUNDWANA: 'What did you do?'—A: 'We went to the sub-district induna SIKWA, who said we must move out or there would be fights.'

INYUNDWANA turned to question Y, but Induna KALONGA, (sitting as head of the kuta) intervened: 'You have not finished, INYUND-WANA. A, when you went to SIKWA, why did you not ask SIKWA to call you together with your father Y so that the kuta could decide between you?'—A: 'When SIKWA told us to move, we moved.'

Z denied this, so KALONGA said: 'We need witnesses.'

The king's Nkoya [another tribe] bandleader, sitting in the kuta, had already volunteered to give evidence and he now came forward.

Bandleader MWIBA: 'I know this family well because I live close to them, and Z abducted my daughter from another man to whom she was married. . . . The family lived together amicably until Z took C's wife. I was there with the late INDALA [leader of the king's Lozi and Simaa bands], getting the royal Nkoya drum. I heard that Y had driven out K's sons. I went to Y and rebuked him, saying, "It is very bad, you must not drive away your children. You must not back your own son, but must settle quarrels." [Here he began to judge, in effect.] 'Children of one womb do not go to court, but do as B suggested to Y—they meet and settle the quarrel. Y has driven away his family by supporting one person. A man's elder brother is his chief: but the trouble came from Z, as it should not, for he as the elder brother is the chief. Y has spoilt the village and will be left alone. You councillors know the land; it is the land drained by King Lewanika at Simululwa plain that they live on. I told A, B, and C to come to me and take there the land of their fathers whose village had died out.' The councillors pitted Y against the bandleader; Y again denied that he had driven out his 'children.'

The councillors questioned A and B at some length about their respective gifts to Y, and those of their absent brother C, and about the poles and grass and the allegation by Z that they stinted Y fish. They pressed Y on what he would do if his own son quarrelled with his sons by his younger brother; he maintained that he would support the one who was in the right.

Then Steward AWAMI asked Y: 'Do you want your sons back?'—Y: 'Yes, I do, emphatically.'

AWAMI asked A and B: 'Do you want to return?'—B: 'Yes, it is to our father; if the gardens . . .'

Several councillors interrupted: 'Leave the gardens, that is easy. Do you want to go home?'—A: 'We still pay tax in Y's book . . .' [the list of members of the village in the District tax-register].

The councillors interrupted: 'The tax register is easy. If the kuta decides, we can fix the book.'—A: 'We want to return. I don't know if our younger brother, C, driven away at night, and cursed by Y if he returns, will do so' [A had alleged that Y struck the ground in the lower court saying: 'May I split inside if C returns'].

Steward AWAMI: 'This is the final kuta. Speak your hearts. We know nothing of your brother who is not here.'—A: 'How can we refuse to return home, to our father?'

Z (questioned): 'I want my brothers to return home.'

(The councillors muttered to each other, condemning the sub-district induna SIKWA for not bringing A and Y together.)

AWAMI to Y, the headman: 'Then do you agree that Z as well as A is in the wrong?'—Y: 'Yes, Z and A are bad, but not B.'

After going again into details about the poles, etc., the kuta entered into judgment:

Induna MBASIWANA: 'You children return home. As for the gardens, no-one lives elsewhere and cultivates in the home. It is good that you return, and if you refuse to return home, you cannot return to your gardens.'

Two junior stewards gave the same brief judgment. The second added: 'If C were here, I'd see that he agreed. He was afraid of Z so he left home. Return home, A and B, and bring C with you. If you do not return, you cannot cultivate the gardens. They clean the village and you cultivate only!—no, it cannot be done! As for this story about medicines to kill the maize, you, B, brought a quarrel. Return home.' (B attempted to speak and was silenced: 'Be silent, your lord has judged.')

Induna IMUTUKO: 'I say you A have seduced the others. It is an astonishing affair—one leaves the village, and the others follow! If you get out, you get out—you cannot still cultivate the gardens. You, Z, you have heard your father. When A and the others return home they get the gardens. If you still quarrel, we'll try another path.'

A prince consort: 'I rebuke Y. You acted badly, Y, but I think it good that your children return home. They are the children of your younger brother. And if there is a quarrel again, and it is your own son's fault, you must right it. You, A and B, you must return and tell your brother C to return. Live well with your father, and get your soil, and live well with your elder brother Z. If there is another quarrel we must try another path.'

Induna SAYWA: 'Y, listen carefully to what the Malozi [reference to a chief or the kuta] say. You must finish quarrels among your children. If your own son starts quarrels with the others, do not support him. You must strengthen your children. Perhaps one of them will care for you—they and their sisters. Finish the quarrels and pray together [to your common ancestral spirits]. You, Z, you have heard this. Your father wants A and B. You and they must listen to him and end your quarrels. You, A and B, you return home and go to your soil. This is right. Leave the quarrels.'

Induna INYUNDWANA: 'A, if you return to the village you get your gardens. The people at home have dogs and children and cattle; it is not fair that you live elsewhere and have gardens there. Take the gardens even if Z has cultivated there.' (All the parties clapped.[2]) 'If you leave the village you do not have the gardens. You, A, have behaved badly. As for you, Y, on the bandleader's evidence you sent your children away. This is very bad. However, if they don't return, the gardens are yours.'

Induna KALONGA (sitting as 'finisher', *mufelelezi*, on the right): 'Y, I have nothing to say to you beyond what the Malozi said. I am shocked at your children taking the poles and grass. You are their only father, they have not two or three. I feel pain, I am sad at a child who does not respect his father. They can cut trees for themselves and go to White country. A child is like a man who is cured by a person.

'What I do not like about you children are the words reported by induna SIKWA[3]—that you said you cannot still live with your father. The affair that settled the matter for SIKWA was your saying that your crops, burnt by the sun, were burnt by sorcery [i.e. when they made charges of sorcery, SIKWA felt relations were too embittered for them to live together amicably]. You deceived this kuta saying you want to return, swearing by medicines [i.e. you have medicines to protect you from the consequences of false oaths here]. I do not believe you want to care for your father. I think tomorrow induna SIKWA will bring this affair of yesterday. We will wait and see. I do not prevent your going home because your father has asked for you. If the affair comes again, you will not be judged as today, but you

---

[2] Clapping, *kukandelela*, is the Lozi method of greeting. In any formal discussion a man claps to acknowledge any favourable reference to him, and in a lawsuit the parties and witnesses do this, especially when they agree with one of the judges' statements. The judges similarly acknowledge references to themselves by their fellows.

[3] I have not given all the evidence. The hearing spread over two days and R and S, sisters of Y and K, and Y's wife also gave evidence. KALONGA had stated the kuta needed SIKWA's evidence on what happened before him. He arrived at Lialui on the evening of the first day's hearing on other business, and gave evidence.

will be fined. You trouble your father, taking the grass and poles from him. No child can do this. You, A, this elder brother Z with whom you quarrel, you do not let the quarrel die. It is you who is spoiling the village of your father [i.e. as the eldest of K's sons, A is trying to lead them into a rebellion which will make him independent head of their group]. When your brother B came back from White country, instead of going with him to your father, you seduced him to leave home. Live well with your elder brother Z, so that you may both strengthen your father. So I do not agree that you return home, but your father and elder brother have asked for you. If you make trouble, and the case comes here again, we will fine you.

'Y, strengthen your children, hold them well. If you do not, we will hear from SIKWA. If there is trouble, it will not be you, but their changing.'

This was the final judgment, and all councillors, litigants, and people in kuta clapped it.

SOLAMI, head of this kuta, and other councillors returned from working at the palace fences. After consulting SOLAMI, KALONGA said that SOLAMI entered into the judgment of the kuta. 'If you have told the truth that you want to live with your father, who asks for you, all right; if your father finds that you were deceiving us, and returns to the kuta, the kuta will see what it will do. You, children, hear this —we do not want to hear again of your taking goods from your father. You will all give the royal salute [with which the successful litigant acknowledges that he has received justice].' KALONGA asked the kuta who should get back his deposited court fees, or should all, since all had won? [Both sides deposit fees, and the loser's is forfeit.]

ALULEYA: 'Their father won, so he gets his money again.'

Y, Z and V went to give the royal salute. A and B remained sitting in the kuta, and were ordered by the kuta to join Y in saluting the king and kuta.

This case involved more than the question, who had the right to cultivate the disputed gardens? On that point the law is quite clear and was stated early in cross-examination by several judges: 'If you leave the village you lose your rights in its land.' This was how the clerk recorded the case in his records. Sub-district induna SIKWA, who had heard the case, first gave evidence on a chance visit to the capital next day. He had not initially considered this issue but had ruled that the nephews must dwell apart lest they and their cousin fight each other, and therefore they lost the gardens. The quarrel simmered, and it was only when Z began to cultivate the gardens that his cousins brought the case to the capital. By building new huts nearby the nephews did not commit themselves to leaving the village: it is significant that they did not accept the royal bandleader's suggestions that they return to other ancestral lands near his village at another plain. Unfortunately, they hurried away from Lialui before I could interview them, but it seems possible that they were waiting for overtures of reconciliation from the 'father'. During this interim period their wives took fruit from the land, and Z's allegation that they protected the crops with medicine shows that he did not regard their departure as final.

However, when Z began to cultivate the gardens and his father did not forbid him to do so, a legal issue was raised on which his cousins went to court in the capital. They sued not for the land alone, but to be established as in the right in the whole quarrel. . . .

Stated in the most general terms, each party was concerned to show as far as possible that throughout he behaved lovingly, justly, and generously to the others, as a father should to all his 'sons', 'sons' to their 'father', and 'brothers' to each other; and that his opponents had been niggardly and quarrelsome. The measure of these valued emotional attitudes is the rendering of material gifts and of help to each other. The headman and his son heatedly denounced the others for stinting him; they as heatedly asserted their generosity. Though in relationships between kin there is no formal system of equal exchanges, people in practice balance what is done to them against what they do. When a major quarrel occurs their sense of being stinted or not recompensed, together with feelings of envy and dislike, comes to the surface. A, B, and C, those who were forced into patent loss by the quarrel, were the ones who showed this in charges of sorcery. The case therefore became a general venting of grievances, into which the judges patiently inquired, ruling out nothing as irrelevant. That is, to achieve their purpose of reconciliation, the judges' concept of relevance had to be very wide. Indeed when it became apparent to the Lialui judges that the parties could be reconciled they complained of sub-district induna SIKWA's failure to bring the parties together to thrash out the matter. SIKWA was in a weaker position than the Lialui judges, not only because he had less power but also because he was related to the parties. He had sought to avoid open charges of sorcery or bloodshed by ruling that it was not safe for A, B, and C to continue to live in the village—they should found an independent village, and this entailed losing their gardens.

The Lialui kuta was deeply concerned to avoid this break-up of the village and the breach of relationship between Y and his nephews. It is the duty of the councillors, who are administrators and legislators as well as judges, to try to maintain public order and national strength; this includes the unity of existing villages and the maintenance of kinship ties. The kuta therefore inquired into all the quarrels and all the feelings of the parties. . . .

In the end all the councillors gave the same judgment: A, B, and C should return to the village where Y and Z were to receive them, and they were to regain their gardens by Y's favour. This was made clear in Y's final interpolation when KALONGA, who disapproved of the young men, ruled that Z was entitled to the gardens by SIKWA's judgment [i.e., that on this point it was *res judicata*]. If they refused to return to the village, they lost their gardens.

Large parts of the judgments read like sermons, for they all lecture on the theme 'your station and its duties'. The standards publicly stated for the parties are the norms involved in their social positions and relationships: people have rights in land by virtue of birth and membership of a village; members of a village must be loving and forbearing, accepting mischances in a spirit of give-and-take, since the children and stock of fellow-villagers spoil gardens equally; the headman must be impartial in settling disputes among his followers; children must love and help their parents, and brothers one another. These are statements of Lozi law and morals, in which the ultimate values here are that 'children' should love one another to strengthen their 'father' and their village that 'the country may be well built'. The essence of the judicial process is to state these norms to the world and to assess against them the behaviour of the parties in a specific series of situations. The aim of the judicial process is that when the parties have had their rightdoings and wrongdoings indicated to them, they will be reconciled and live together harmoniously in the future. Nine years later I heard by letter that these disputants were living in amity.

Litigants and witnesses work with the same legal and moral rules as do the judges. Thus all the parties accepted that the break-up of the village was bad: the nephews felt that they had to justify their departure by alleging that they were 'driven out' or compelled to leave by the headman's bias against them, while the headman and his son asserted that they left without cause. This son, Z, conscious that he had done wrong in seducing his cousin's wife, tried to defend his wrongdoing by accusing the cousin's brother of the same fault. Similarly A, aware that he should not have taken the poles from his uncle, claimed he did so only after he and his brothers had been wronged. And so on. It is not clear in this case what exactly the truth about all these matters was, but we can note that if the parties lied, or were mistaken, they cast their story in such a form that they appeared to have acted rightly and to have been wronged. This point is of fundamental importance, because it means that the judges, working with these same norms, can cross-examine the parties and can give judgments for and against them in comprehensible and acceptable terms, even if the parties continue to deny that they have done wrong.

. . . because the full family dispute was only brought to a head in the suit over the gardens, the court's standard of relevant evidence is very wide. In fact no evidence about the gardens or who worked them was questioned: all the cross-examination was on other matters. Throughout the court was concerned with all the moral issues involved in the family dispute. Therefore it considered all the circumstances involved over several years. These circumstances were presented from the beginning in the pleas of the parties which were not confined to the claim over the gardens. Other circumstances, some bearing on the character of the litigants, were presented in the evidence, full of hearsay as well as of judgment, given by Bandleader MWIBA, as they might have been by any of the judges. There is no refinement of pleadings in Lozi procedure to whittle a suit down to certain narrow legal claims so as to present the judges with a mere skeleton of the facts relevant to those claims. The judges are immediately made aware of the moral perspective of the suit, and they themselves can take judicial notice of anything that falls in their own knowledge which they consider relevant.

I tried and failed to relate a series of judgments by particular judges to their personal histories, characters, circumstances, and social positions. I found that I had not sufficiently detailed information about their personal histories, characters, and circumstances; and I also lacked an appropriate variety of cases. A survey of the opinions of judges in cases I did record showed no particular consistency: it was difficult however to subject this material to quantitative analysis. I was left with certain general impressions. One judge who has had much trouble with his own children tended to be severe on youths who had come into conflict with their elders, and to place disproportionate blame on them as against other judges. Another junior judge who is notorious for his unusual jealousy of his wife—an attitude attributed by the Lozi to the wife's magic—tended to convict of adultery more often than his fellows.

Lozi judges are drawn widely from the tribe as a whole and are related by kinship throughout the Barotse nation. This applies to princes as well as commoners. The judges include young and old, Christians and pagans, educated and illiterate, rich and poor. I do not believe that anyone could tell from particular judgments whether judges were Christian or pagan, educated or illiterate. The pagan SOLAMI tended most often to bring God into his exhortations. The judges do not deal with the important conflicts between Whites and Blacks. In cases over land, which are economically the most important cases they try, princes, title-holders, and headmen did not unwarrantably support superior landholders against their inferiors. This is manifest in 'The Case of the Headman's Fishdams', as it is, in another context, in 'The Case of the Violent Councillor'. Indeed, my impression is that the royal family, which ultimately owns the land through the king, is as ready to enforce the rights of ordinary people in land as are commoner councillors. All judges seem to vary in their judgments according to their ability, rather than their personal or group prejudices and self-interest. The Lozi themselves—and indeed all Barotse—ascribe differences in judicial decision to differences in individual knowledge, wisdom, and courage, and not to differences in social status or acquirement.

The main presumptions which influence Lozi judges are, aside from a few personal prejudices, general social presumptions. This accords with the persisting comparative homogeneity of their society.

These social presumptions are drawn from the existing system of relations in the society, with a certain nostalgia for the good old days. The rising intelligentsia castigate the kuta for being conservative. But this charge has to be evaluated in political terms. The members of this intelligentsia are themselves anxious to obtain power in the kuta, and complaints about judgments are a handy weapon. I have very rarely heard one of them differ from the appointed judges in his judgment on a specific dispute.

CONCLUSION

We may glance summarily at the main points which have emerged from this analysis of the Lozi judicial process. On the whole, it is true to say that the Lozi judicial process corresponds with, more than it differs from, the judicial process in Western society. Lozi judges draw on the same sources of law as Western judges —the regularities of the environment, of the animal kingdom, of human beings; and customs, legislation, precedent, equity, the laws of nature and of nations, public policy, morality. They assess evidence in the same way. They manipulate the different types of legal rule which can be applied to a particular situation, and the ambiguity of the concepts which make up the legal rules, in a similar attempt to achieve justice according to their lights. Nevertheless their work is affected at every point by the general level of technology, and the economic and social structure, of Lozi society. The dominant factors which produce important differences are the comparatively egalitarian and undifferentiated nature of social relations, the absence of pleadings and counsel and complex procedure, and the unwritten state of the law.

Analyses of African adjudication have stressed that the judges try to effect reconciliation of the parties—'to restore the social equilibrium'. In Loziland this process applies where the parties are kinsmen or lord and underling, in a permanent multiplex relationship which the judges are trying to preserve. Then—though the judges will only inquire into a breach of a legal right—the concept of relevance is wide and the judges broaden their examination to investigate everything that the parties and other related persons may have done. They are not restricted by a doctrine of judicial ignorance or concepts of irrelevant, incompetent, etc., evidence. This tendency is less marked in cases between spouses, since the marital relationship is easily broken, and it is barely present in cases between strangers involved in delictual or contractual relationship. But it may reassert itself at any moment where the judges consider that a public or other interest is involved: they will inquire into this issue, and give judgment on it. What we would call a criminal or administrative trial may thus emerge from a civil suit. Lozi judges are also administrators and legislators, and, as they are accustomed to reason in these capacities, they may take administrative decisions; for though they have several rôles, they distinguish these clearly.

Even when the judges are striving to reconcile disputants who are kinsmen, they will not do so at the cost of glossing over wrongdoing. Those who have erred are always reprimanded. It is a basic axiom of Lozi law that wrongdoers should be scolded and punished: hence if it is impossible or inappropriate to secure this end by making them pay recompense to those they have harmed, the judges inflict a fine or other punishment. Again, a criminal trial may emerge from a civil suit. This is the reasoning at the basis of legislation which levies damages on an adulterer in favour of the cuckolded husband, and a fine on the erring wife. The requirements of good morals and public policy prevent her paying her husband: she can only pay the state. This may well be one spring of differentiated criminal law.

The standards of right behaviour against which the behaviour of the parties is assessed to see if they have acted rightly or wrongly, are those of 'the reasonable and customary man'. This exists as a distinct concept in the Lozi language, though it is not always explicitly stated by the judges. There is both a generally reasonable man, acting sensibly and conforming to custom, and a particular reasonable and customary incumbent of any social position—father, son, husband, wife, son-in-law, lord, underling. The chief standards of good behaviour and the customary usages of these various social positions are widely known to all Lozi. It is expected that everyone should conform to these standards and usages. Hence wherever it emerges in evidence that a person has departed from them, his actions and motives become suspect, and the judges attack him in cross-examination, demanding that he explain his deviation. This deviation may convict him. Therefore the standard of the reasonable man may be said to provide the main check on evidence and to be the main weapon in judicial cross-examination. The judges thus use custom as a yardstick for controlling the variety of social life. Custom has a social certainty akin to the physical, ecological, and physiological certainties of diurnal and seasonal time, vegetation growth, gestation, etc., which are also checks on evidence.

Custom can operate in this manner because it is widespread and generally known, and because every relationship tends to have its distinctive usages. These usages and customs are known to and accepted by litigants and witnesses as well as judges. Even when a person lies in court, he tries to cast his story so that he appears to have conformed to custom, and to standards of upright behaviour. This enables judges to cross-examine on the story by the standards of reasonable and customary behaviour and to expose lies. Further it enables them to give judgments which are intelligible to the litigants even if these reject the judicial conclusions. It is only rarely that litigants are operating with quite different values, though situations of this kind are probably increasing in number. In effect, in this process the judges hold that a person intends the reasonable or natural consequences of his actions. In practice, in the judicial process the argument is transposed, to say that a person has those motives which can be reasonably deduced from his witnessed actions. The courts therefore punish for wrongful actions, but judgments lay stress on the motives associated with those actions. 'The reasonable man' therefore imports psychology into the judicial process, and it is an ethical psychology.

Judges work not only with standards of reasonable behaviour for upright incumbents of particular social positions, but also with standards of behaviour which are reasonably interpreted as those of particular kinds of wrongdoers. There are social stereotypes of how thieves, adulterers, and other malefactors act. If the witnessed actions of a defendant assemble into one of these stereotypes, he is found guilty, though the judges prefer direct evidence to convict. It is a pertinent, and on my part not properly investigated, problem to ask whether these stereotypes in fact influence the behaviour of wrongdoers.

In this summary of how Lozi judges assess evidence, as in the text, I have started by emphasizing the importance of the reasonable man, because this point is often overlooked. It entails recognition of the fact that any departure from normal behaviour, reported by a litigant himself or by other witness, contributes to judicial conviction. Its importance is heightened for Lozi judges because, to establish guilt or innocence, they have not the support of detectives or of a technology of expertise on fingerprinting, handwriting, blood-tests, etc. But departures from custom must be established by good evidence, and Lozi judges distinguish various kinds of evidence as good and bad. No decision should be given before both sides are heard (this is due process of law), and all available evidence should be ascertained. There are direct and circumstantial evidence, direct and hearsay evidence, corroborative, impartial, and cogent evidence. All these kinds of evidence, and the evidence of reasonable and customary behaviour, are tested by judicial cross-examination. The Lozi quite explicitly affirm that it is by cross-examination that they arrive at the truth. Only in sorcery cases, and some charges of theft, were oracles used in the past.

Lozi judges expect cross-examination to establish the truth of an accusation or a plaintiff's suit. They will dismiss a case if the evidence is not conclusive enough. They do not convict on a past bad record. Since the judges, and not counsel for the parties, cross-examine, it may appear as if they consider a person guilty until he proves he is innocent, but this is a fallacious appearance. A person is innocent until he is proved guilty. The apparent assumption of guilt flows from the fact that it is only possible to cross-examine if the cross-examiner frames his questions as if he believes the examinee is lying—hence, guilty. Where judges conduct the cross-examination, this makes an onlooker assume they believe in the guilt of defendant or accused. Again, Lozi judges are well-aware of the implications of their technique; and I stress that there is no assumption of guilt in Lozi law.

The standard of reasonable and customary behaviour has importance as a technique for arriving at the truth. In addition, it often forms the crux of a law-suit. A wife sues for divorce on the grounds that her husband has not been a reasonable and customary husband to her; or a headman claims that he is justified in expelling a man from gardens because the man has not been a reasonable villager; or a lord claims the right to dismiss an underling from position and lands because of unreasonable behaviour. In all these situations, the standards of 'reasonable' and 'customary' vary with the social positions involved. They also vary with outside circumstances and with the changing conditions of life in Loziland. 'Reasonable' and 'customary', like other legal concepts, are highly flexible, and they become permeated with changing social presumptions, values, and conditions of life, and can absorb a variety of actual situations. Their flexibility has enabled Lozi judges to adjust rules of law to cope with Christianity, schools, work for money in Loziland and at distant towns, and so forth.

The Lozi have a developed vocabulary to define different kinds (legal, moral, decent, natural) of rules, rights, duties, wrongs, injuries, taboos. As in other languages, some of these words have many referents and several definitions, and others are elastic to cover a series of events or things. This leads to some confusion, but they have a clear idea that there are certain approved rules which their courts will enforce, while other approved rules they can only recommend as worthy of decent observance. They recognize that hard cases may make good law. This gives them a distinctive body of legal rules, as against other rules which are only morally binding. But where strict adherence to the letter of the law leads to an unjust decision, the judges strive to interpret the law so as to avoid this unpalatable conclusion. In all cases they apply 'general equity' in their reasoning, and they seek for a 'particular equity' to achieve justice in special hard cases. In doing so they may 'create' new law, albeit within the established body of law which Lozi believe derives from antiquity and which binds king and judges. They achieve these particular equities chiefly in two ways. First, they may specify—give temporary definition to —a particular legal concept to meet special circumstances. Secondly, a variety of different *kinds* of legal rules apply in varying ways to some situations, and the judges have considerable latitude in the way they apply these rules. They may achieve justice in one relationship, by enforcing a sanction in another. Here their power as administrators, acting as supreme controllers of land and village settlement and in other ways, is important.

Equity—justice—morality: these are therefore sources on which the judges draw in adjudicating on disputes. Formally, they recognize these sources under several terms, of which we may here note chiefly 'the laws of God' and 'the laws of humankind'. Their principles are axiomatic and patent to all reasonable men. These constitute at least an embryonic *jus naturale*. This *jus naturale* is applied by the Lozi in deciding which of the laws of their subject tribes they will protect. Here they also recognize 'the laws of nations' (*jus gentium*), being those rules and institutions which are common to all African tribes of the region, and many of which are also accepted by Whites. Since the economy of the region, insofar as it is controlled by Lozi courts, is largely based on status and not on contract, their *jus gentium* covers chiefly the law of persons and constitutional law: marriage, succession, citizenship, overlordship, etc.

It emerges from this analysis that certain problems, such as the distinction between law and custom or the relation of law and religion, which have concerned students of 'primitive law', are resolved if we see that 'law' in the sense of judicial decision—*legal rulings*—has the same material sources everywhere. When Lozi judges have to give a decision on a dispute, they draw, both during trial and in adjudication, on custom, legislation, judicial precedent, equity, the laws of nature and of nations, and good morals and public policy. They do so in a very complicated process, but it is a process which is controlled by publicly known logic. The whole process is conditioned by the absence of writing, which prevents the development of a forensic science. Its chief effect is that the judges are able to come to a moral decision on the dispute and then select those statutes, precedents, etc., for attention which support this decision. However, they cannot go against certain well-known statutes or 'common law' rules. Statutes overrule customary law. Custom must pertain to a group, be well-known and reasonable: the last proviso enables some customs to become obsolete while new ones are recognized. This latter process of development is assisted by the absence of historical records: new usages and standards can be graced with antiquity, and old standards and usages which are in conflict with new values are forgotten. Morality and equity control the weighing of laws, besides being a particular source of judicial rulings. Precedents are not surveyed, since they are barely recorded, and are quoted haphazardly. Indeed, the judges less often cite a precedent in the form of a previous judicial decision, than they cite moral exemplifications of rightdoing from their own actions or experience with others. The course of Lozi life, where it runs smoothly and without dispute—customary life—thus is a prime source of judicial decision, under the guise of precedent.

In drawing on these sources of law, and applying them to the facts of a particular dispute, the Lozi act by a logic which is akin to our own. It was necessary to make this point in view of frequent statements that African courts operate by oracles, or fetishes, and to cite in support their syntactical devices and conjunctions which enable them to build up coherent, reasoned arguments. Indeed, they have a vocabulary to describe 'arguments', and the 'reasons' and 'presumptions', 'probabilities' and 'indications', which go into them. Moreover, they have a developed vocabulary to evaluate the skill of good judges, and the stupidity or cowardice or corruption of bad judges. 'The unjust judge' is an accepted figure to explain away bad judgments.

Judicial logic operates in three stages, recognized as such by the Lozi: the hearing of and cross-examination on evidence, the taking of a decision on evidence, and the exposition of the law in support of the decision. Each stage has its own techniques, but the stages are not always kept apart. This is particularly so among the Lozi since the judges carry out examination and cross-examination. They may begin to arrive at a decision, and even to state the law for the case under trial, while hearing evidence. However, they have words to distinguish each stage and think little of judges who come to decision before all the evidence has been heard.

This is how judicial logic works in all cases. Some cases may fall in 'gaps in the law', and then different kinds of logic are employed by the judges. I have cited examples to show that here Lozi judges have been effective in aiding their people to cope with changes in social life due to British overlordship and all it entails. They have developed the law by employing all the methods isolated by Cardozo for Anglo-American adjudication: the method of philosophy by the rule of analogy; the method of evolution along the lines of historical development; and the method of tradition along the line of the customs of the community. Finally, they use Cardozo's method of sociology, which works along the lines of justice, social welfare, good morals, and public policy.

Consideration of this last method led to an attempt to resolve the paradox of the 'uncertainty' of legal concepts and the 'certainty' of law. I defined legal concepts as being *general* and *unspecific* in that they rarely referred to a particular person, thing, occurrence, or action; *flexible* in that they are *elastic,* capable of being stretched to cover various circumstances, and/or in that they are *multiple* in having several referents or definitions; *permeable* in that they can be pervaded by mores, values, and social and individual presumptions; and *absorbent* in that they can absorb the raw facts of evidence into their categories. In trial, the judges have to *specify*—give extrinsic referents to—these categories. In this process of specification the judges are able to operate the method of sociology, since general morality can control the adaptation of the flexible concepts to new circumstances. The judges manipulate the flexibility of the concepts—what is often denigrated as their 'ambiguity'—as they do the multiplicity of laws, to achieve justice.

This judicial manipulation is aided by the fact that, as I suggest, the concepts can be arranged in a number of hierarchies. In one hierarchy, that of the laws of persons and property, 'law' itself occurs at the top, rooted in government, in regularity of the natural and social order, based on the laws of God, nature, and nations, on customs, statutes, precedents. Law in this sense exists in a structure of social positions. This is law as *corpus juris,* a set of rules accepted by all normal members of the society as defining right and reasonable ways in which persons ought to behave in relation to each other and things. It includes right and reasonable ways of seeking protection for one's rights—adjectival as well as substantive law. The *corpus juris* consists of rights and duties as against wrongs and injuries. Rights and duties rest in ownership over things and persons. Wrongs and injuries give rise to responsibility which creates a liability giving rise to other rights and duties. Wrongs and injuries are assessed by guilt and innocence as judged on particular actions—particular rightdoings and wrongdoings. The standards of 'reasonableness and customariness' pervade the hierarchy as a whole. It is characteristic of this hierarchy, that the higher level concepts are the most general in meaning and their ambiguity consists chiefly in that they are *multiple*. Lower level concepts are chiefly *elastic*, measuring guilt or innocence, care or negligence, along a scale between two poles. A similar hierarchy is suggested for the law of contracts; and a distinctive one for the law of trial and evidence. In the latter, concepts are both elastic and multiple, which increases their flexibility.

I examined a series of apparently conflicting decisions on land cases to show that what the judges do in practice is to decide that one party has done *right* and the other done *wrong* in particular actions. From these decisions, they jump to decide that the party who has done *right* has *the right* to the land: in Lozi, as in English, the same word is used for these quite different meanings of 'right'. This is a typical example, which must suffice in this summary, to illustrate how the judges manipulate the flexibility of the concepts, in their hierarchical value, to achieve justice. My conclusion is that the way as a *corpus juris* remains certain, through some uncertainty of judicial decision, because of the flexible uncertainty of legal concepts. This is particularly marked among the Lozi since their *corpus juris,* what I call law in general, consists of general statements linking social positions —in custom, in statute, and in morality. Since they lack writing, these statements are not circumscribed by refining precedents or constricting terminology.

I do not suggest that these concepts, many of which are shared with other systems of law, exist *in vacuo*. I argue that they carry the historic, political, and economic load of their social milieu: they are permeated with a specific set of social presumptions, interests, values, etc.

Empirically it is clear that the Lozi believe there exists 'the law'—a *corpus juris* which binds king and court. It is well known to judges and litigants and they reason with it. It operates in social life unmarred by dispute. 'Law' in this sense is certain. Empirically also 'law' consists of a series of decisions by judges not all of which are certain in that they can be predicted in advance. This apparent contradiction can be resolved by examining the nature of Lozi legal concepts in all their flexibility, and seeing how judges manipulate them. But the Lozi share most of these concepts with Western law. I was therefore emboldened to apply my analysis, in all humility, to some recent studies of the Western judicial process and to suggest that it offered some solution to a number of controversies in jurisprudence. Western jurists on the whole have treated the 'ambiguity' of legal concepts as a weakness, without examining in general how the judges operate the ambiguities. I think this statement is justified, despite praise of particular flexibilities. I suggest that we must accept that words like law, right, property, have several meanings, and examine how these varied meanings function in the judicial process, in legal practice, and in social life. If we do this we avoid the sterile disputes which have raged over the many offered definitions of law, of criminal and civil law, and so on. For against every definition another can be offered, or an instance cited of what is by commonsense 'law' or 'crime' but is not covered by the proffered definition. More particularly, we dispose of the dispute between what I may call the orthodox jurists who consider 'law' to be on the whole certain, and the American sceptical jurists who argue that it is not. The case is made clear by Judge Jerome Frank's attack on the 'myth of certainty of law'. He examines litigation and probable litigation, calls them 'law', and concludes that they are uncertain: which they are. But he concedes that there are rules of law, which are more or less certain, and which control judges—and, one might add, control social life. If he talked about 'litigation and adjudication' instead of about 'law', there would be at least only factual discussion, and not sterile terminological disputation about his analysis. I go further, and suggest that a theory based on an analysis of actual judicial logic, and the nature of concepts of law, can resolve the paradox of certainty in the *corpus juris* and uncertainty in adjudication or legal rulings.

JUSTICE IN MOSCOW:
TEN DAYS' NORMAL FARE

George Feifer

*In capitalist society the court was primarily an apparatus of oppres-
sion, an apparatus of bourgeois exploitation. Therefore, it was beyond any question an obligation of the proletarian revolution not to
reform court institutions . . . but to destroy them completely, to
sweep away the old court and its apparatus to the foundations. The
October Revolution fulfilled this task, and fulfilled it successfully. In
place of the old court, it began to create the new people's courts . . .*
                                                    VLADIMIR I. LENIN

Truth is straight, but judges are crooked.
Fear not the law but the judge.

                                        OLD RUSSIAN PROVERBS

I BEGAN an unhurried, unguided tour of the People's Courts,
bottom rung in the Soviet judicial hierarchy. To the great
mass of Russian people, the Law means the People's Courts, for
almost all civil and criminal cases are heard here first. Here,
where the printed words on the page—the articles of the code,
the rules of socialist behavior—are translated into terms of human conduct, where the living law is germinated.

There are seventeen People's Courts in Moscow, one to each
city district: Kalininskii, Leninskii, Oktyabrskii, Kirovskii, Dzerzhinskii, Moskvoretskii, Krasnopresnenskii, Pervomaiskii. . . .
The courthouses are scattered about town in buildings of every
sort. Most of them, however, are worn and dry, mournful and

bare. They reminded me of the ancient, soulless city hall in the town where I grew up: no comfort anywhere to mitigate the civic gloom.

Each court has eight to twelve judges—"People's Judges"—and a "chairman" in charge. The judges have a courtroom more or less permanently assigned to them and, adjacent, a tiny, sparsely furnished office which serves as chambers, lunchroom, deliberating room and, for some intimate personal cases, courtroom. Somewhere in the building is a larger office for the court as a whole, dealing in the inevitable exasperations of petty bureaucracy. Somewhere sits a duty lawyer on watch, offering on-the-spot consultations for a trifling fee.

Here, in these plainest of settings, the coating of mystery, enigma and mumbo jumbo surrounding the law dissolves, leaving the commonplace.

The corridors of all the People's Courts offer similar joyless scenes. A crowd, made up of quiet couples waiting their turns, bunches outside the room in which suits for divorce are being heard. Police lead defendants, heads bowed and hands clasped always behind their backs, to and from their trials. Inquisitive time-wasters open doors, peek in, search for a good case. Witnesses pass around cigarettes and the morning's *Pravda*. Relatives—mostly older, black-clothed, wrinkled relatives—wait out the writing of verdicts. Lawyers between cases prepare their next speech, or answer queries of prospective clients. A queue forms haphazardly to see the judge, who is giving consultations about alimony, the necessary papers, the procedure for appeal, the insults of a neighbor or a foreman.

Opening a door along one hallway, I would come upon a typical scene. The first impression of a court in session was of drabness and routine; had I been seeking sensation, I would have left soon. I stayed a long time, however, even after my understanding of trial procedure was clear, for here was exposure to Soviet working-class life that a foreigner can get nowhere else. Here was detailed scrutiny of life in a country where such material is not much publicized.

Behind a door picked at random, the case on trial was likely to be minor, one I had seen many times before. For there is no summary procedure in Soviet criminal law, and the simplest cases are tried under the same general rules of procedure as the most serious and complex. The People's Judge—who is more often than not a woman—would be questioning the defendant or a witness in tones that reached the back of the room as a drone. The lay assessors would simply be in attendance, like bodyguards for the judge. The court secretary, often a fresh young girl just out of school, would be jotting down essential facts at a desk alongside the judge's bench. A small, dark group of spectators smelling of pomade, strong tobacco and uncleaned wool—mostly the family and friends of the parties involved—would be listening glumly, whispering their comments and sometimes shouting them to the bench. The door would creak as stray spectators or extra policemen would wander in or out.

Probably there would be no procurator, for he, the Moscow equivalent of an American district attorney, is overworked and cannot afford to assign his men and women to minor trials. (Or, as a procurator explained to me, he does not want to—for the law requires that when a procurator prosecutes, the accused *must* be represented by counsel, and "dragging a lawyer in makes unnecessary difficulty for everyone; it is better to keep him out, to keep a simple case simple.") More often there would be a defense counsel, for defendants *may* be represented whether or not the procurator attends, and Muscovites seem to value representation, even when the facts are obvious.

Sometimes the accused would be in the dock, watched by a surprising number of policemen. His head is shaved (in accordance with Russian prison rules), and in all respects he is a marked man, silly- or sad-looking. Among certain middle-aged Russian men a shaved head is still a mark of fashion, but for prisoners it is humiliating, a badge of guilt which keeps the head hung low. Sometimes, if he has not been taken into custody but has appeared at the trial still a free man, the defendant may sit in the first row of public benches and testify from his place.

In the first weeks, I was surprised by the informality, the lack of legal phraseology, of practiced, self-conscious precision, of esoteric procedural niceties and devotion to form. Much has changed since the early years of Soviet rule, when judges drew upon their "revolutionary consciousness" as the new law. But something of that amateur spirit has remained. A Soviet trial is informal by any standards; there is nothing a layman cannot understand. The rules of the game (or compulsions of the ritual) are not treasured like intricate, ancient plumage. What the people in court have to say is more important than how they must say it. In the trials that I observed, when an interested observer had some relevant information to give, he gave it, even if it would have been inadmissible as evidence in a foreign court and even if he was not, at the moment, in the witness stand.

As time went on, I sensed a lack of excitement and suspense—though not a lack of drama and emotion. There was a matter-of-factness, an everydayness, a quiet sadness, a weariness. All issues seemed to move, very slowly, to their fated ends, and the sameness of the cases and the repetitiousness of the "story" compounded the feeling of *déjà vu*. Heard once, the events sounded like a crime, but like fiction; heard ten times at each trial, through a hundred trials, they became heavy with some sort of personal meaning—inevitable, inexorable, confessional.

I was reminded in these courts of what I had read and seen of peasant Russia—of strength, simplicity and endurance; of human tragedy, official severity, and personal compassion. For the People's Courts are enclaves of old Moscow, tucked away among the modern, optimistic façade of the new capital.

People's Court, Dzerzhinskii District. The courthouse is the second and third floors of a narrow old office building on Srentenka, a busy central shopping street. Its façade is nineteenth-century Russian classical, the pasty-yellow plaster surface of most of downtown Moscow. The interior is dark and in need of paint. Just inside the entrance is a red banner with an inscription lettered in white: "THE TINIEST ILLEGALITY, THE

TINIEST VIOLATION OF THE SOVIET LEGAL ORDER IS A CHINK
WHICH IS IMMEDIATELY USED BY THE ENEMIES OF THE TOILERS.
—V. I. LENIN." A tinted portrait of Lenin hangs in every room.

Open a door along one of the corridors . . . I am selecting
from ten days' normal fare.

Article 144: Theft[1]

The accused is a muscular young man, born in Moscow but, like
so many, reeking of peasant ancestry. He has admitted stealing
a *papakha* (a tall fur hat popular in winter), which had been
lying on the seat next to his, late one evening in the metro. Next
to it, dozing, had been a hatless man, obviously the owner. This
man, the complainant, works for the K.G.B. [secret police].

"What do you do there, if it is not a secret?" the judge asks.
"Do not tell us anything you shouldn't."

"I am a driver. I don't know *anything* secret."

The accused has been convicted of crimes twice before, for
hooliganism and for theft of a watch.

"Now this is the third time, Solovyev. What's it all about?

---

[1] The articles are those of the Criminal Code of the Russian Soviet Feder-
ated Socialist Republic—Russia. Soviet criminal and civil law fall under the
jurisdiction of the constituent Republics, and each of the fifteen—Russia,
Ukraine, Georgia, Estonia, Moldavia, Armenia, Kazakhstan, Uzbekistan, et
cetera—legislate their own codes.

These fifteen codes vary only slightly, however, because they all conform
to general principles established by the central, All-Union government. The
federal principles, called "Fundamentals," settle all major problems of criminal theory and outline the law in considerable detail; the Republics are left
to fill in the gaps and adjust for local peculiarities. This is the way balance
between local and national interests is sought.

The current Fundamentals were enacted by the Supreme Soviet of the
Union in 1958; the Russian code by the Supreme Soviet of the Russian Republic in 1960.

As it affects the courts, Soviet federalism is far less confusing than American. The court structure resembles a simple pyramid, local arrangements
moving up to national. There cannot be any conflict between national and
state law in a given territory, nor any conflict of jurisdiction. Organization-
ally, it is a simple, logical system.

What are you doing with your life? Do you want to be a common criminal? That's where you're headed, you know."

No answer.

"What is your explanation, if you please?"

No answer.

"I don't understand. You know there is nothing romantic about this—you know jail. Do you like it there?"

An answer is formed but not spoken.

"Now look, you are a trained worker, you were taught a trade valuable to Soviet society, you have a decent income; your mother and father are both on pension. *How do you explain this thing?* Were things difficult for you? I would like to understand what made you steal again. I cannot. *Why?*"

"I did it, I told you that, I admit I took it. I already told you everything." The youth half whines, half defies.

"I'm trying to find out *why*."

"I . . . didn't know it was his hat."

"Why didn't you ask? Why just take it?"

"I don't know. I didn't know who to ask. I thought . . ."

"In February, a man walking around with a bare head, and on the seat next to him an unattached hat. Nonsense! Do you think anyone is going to believe that?"

"It's not so strange. There are lots of people without hats. *I* don't always wear one."

"Maybe you'll think this over a minute and tell the court what really happened. Don't think I'm talking you into anything. But if you have made mistakes in life you yourself must be the first to recognize them; then things will go better for you."

Solovyev winces. "I didn't intend to steal it."

"But it's still theft. When you take someone else's things without asking, that is theft. Do you understand that?"

"I understand . . . but I wasn't trying to steal."

"What *were* you trying to do? For heaven's sake, isn't it the normal thing to ask before you walk off with a hat that belongs to someone else? What did you have in mind?"

"I don't know. I really don't know what I had in mind. I just did it."

"Come on, tell us now. What were your motives? We want to hear what you were thinking in that metro."

"I wasn't thinking anything. I just picked up the *papakha* when I came to my station and . . ."

"You *stole* the *papakha*. Look, Solovyev, I want to hear one thing from you. When you take a hat from a seat without asking, do you understand that that is a *crime,* that you are stealing?"

"Yes, I do understand."

A second lesson remains to be taught. It turns out that the young man, a lathe operator, had not been working for some ten weeks before the incident. He had quit his job, drifted around, gone to movies, met his buddies in the park, done odd jobs, drunk in the afternoons and evenings, and lived principally on doles from his parents. Hearing this confirmed by the offender, the judge berates him.

"How could you permit yourself to go for weeks without work? Why did you quit? Why didn't you get a new job? Where is your honor as a Soviet citizen? How could you, a healthy young man with strong hands and an honest profession, refuse to work, disregard your civic duty for the sake of loafing? Aren't you ashamed of yourself? Do you understand how wastefully and decadently you spent your time? Do you understand that there is a direct correlation between not working—the idle hours, the drinking, the loss of self-respect—and the crime? What right have you to expect the support of society without your support of it?"

Solovyev seems indifferent. He replies in words of one syllable.

"And how do you regard your actions now? What can you say about the way you behaved?"

"Not very good."

"That's all? 'Not very good'?"

"Terrible."

In appointing punishment, the court takes into consideration the defendant's disrespect for his obligations as a citizen as evidenced by his unwillingness to work. The sentence is one year in a labor colony, normal regime.

Article 211: Reckless Driving by a Professional Driver

The defendant, thirty-two, clean-cut, Driver Third Class, bounced the factory's *pik-ap* ("pickup truck") over a curb one icy February evening, slightly injuring two schoolgirls who had been playing in the snow. He had been rushing home from work "terribly upset" by a telephone call informing him that his brother, a tuberculosis victim, had been taken to the hospital after a relapse. He had dashed to the store for some things for his brother, forgetting his license in another jacket, had gulped a few swallows of vodka for his nerves, and then had skidded on the ice in the truck.

His own lawyer, counsel for the defense, grills him determinedly. Had he behaved well? No, very badly. Not *badly,* the lawyer says, but *criminally;* does he understand that he committed a serious crime, not only in hitting the girls, but in sitting behind the wheel with vodka in him? Does he know that every Soviet life is sacred? Will he do it again, will he drink and drive? Will he promise he will never, never do it again? Does he understand that that kind of irresponsibility cannot be tolerated in Soviet society?

The driver, voice unsteady and hands stiff at his sides, is too upset to play a part; he manages only a look of sincere shame and a simple apology: "I behaved very badly." While the court is out, his relatives pounce on him for his weak performance and for not emphasizing that he helps support his mother and invalid brother. "I couldn't say more; I am guilty, I hurt those poor girls. The court must decide what to do with me."

It decides mercifully: corrective labor[2] and loss of driving rights for a year, but no imprisonment.

---

[2] Corrective labor is performed by the penalized person in his regular place of employment, at his regular job. A part of his salary—from 5 to 20 percent —is deducted. Otherwise he is a free man, living a normal life.

Article 154, Paragraph III: Petty Speculation

At the famous outdoor market-fair in Luzhniki, alongside Lenin Stadium, a young man, the picture of innocence, had sold his place near the head of a queue for Polish raincoats to a Georgian —the latter had been 465th in line—for three rubles. When he had successfully made his sale, the accused realized another ruble profit by selling to his victim two pairs of men's socks for six rubles instead of the five he had just paid. He had a history of such speculation: a camera bought and sold, jazz records, a rug; and once he peddled a trip to Leningrad that his brigade had been awarded for outstanding production.

The Georgian glowers menacingly, seemingly galled for having been taken in. His excuse is that he had wasted the entire previous afternoon standing vainly in line for a sweater; the supply had given out before his turn came up. The judge gives him a lecture, and to the speculator a look of disgust and a year's corrective labor.

Article 96: Petty Theft of State Property

Dozens of packs of Dukat cigarettes, totaling twenty rubles in value, had been filched from a tobacco factory in several installments. The accused is twenty-eight; like many Russian workers, he looks ten years older. He had been caught stealing before, had been warned, and had been reprimanded by the factory's Comradely Court. Now he can offer the judge no excuse other than vodka. He agrees that his wages had been sufficient for a comfortable life and that nothing had forced him to steal.

When the court retires, the man's wife turns on him. "Oh God, Andrei, why did you pretend we are not lacking for anything? You *know* that we hardly manage each month, with the children and everything. You were never able to speak up for yourself, you! Why didn't you say that your father and brother are sick and that you have helped them all these years? Oh, God. Or that our girl is weak and constantly needs milk? Besides, you earn sixty rubles, not seventy. The children ask already, 'What are we going to do without papa?' We will go hungry, that's what we'll do. Oh, God, Andrei."

The children are with them in the courtroom, two well-formed blond cherubs, too young to understand. They have a grand time, playing peek-a-boo behind their parents' motionless forms, giggling quietly, forming their newly learned words, and crawling up on the bench from time to time to embrace *mamachka* and *papachka*.

Then mother and father embrace, before he is led away to begin a two-year term in a labor colony.

Article 145, Paragraph II: Robbery

"I was on my way home at midnight," recounts the victim, a plump woman in her thirties, "when he grabbed me, took my watch, and searched my bag. I told him I had nothing besides the watch. When he unbuttoned my coat, I screamed—hard. Lord knows what he had in mind. I'm a married woman."

The attacker, an unskilled laborer, does not know himself what he had in mind. He was drunk. Now he admits his guilt "fully and completely," is eager to explain how it happened, and keeps repeating, "That's correct, that's correct," to all the charges. "Yes, it was a stupid, criminal action."

He looks up plaintively. "Comrade Judges, what can I say?"

"That is your affair."

"I have nothing to say."

This was his third robbery in three years. The court, "considering that the earlier sentences had no educative effect," orders deprivation of freedom for four years.

Article 211: Reckless Driving by a Professional Driver

A woman was slightly injured by a truck and spent three days in a hospital. The driver had been drinking.

The judge informs her that she is entitled to make a claim against the driver.

"Do you mean money? Oh no, I don't want any money."

"Are you sure?" the Judge asks. "Nothing?"

"Well, perhaps enough to replace my stockings and skirt which were ruined. But money has nothing to do with it; my claim is only that such an untrustworthy man should not be allowed to drive in our socialist society."

Article 206: Hooliganism

The code defines hooliganism as "intentional actions grossly violating social order and expressing obvious disrespect to society." Rowdyism, in other words; being drunk and disorderly and disturbing the peace.

Predictably, it is the most frequent single charge; twenty-eight cases fall under this article during the ten-day period—more than one third of the total calendar. The defendants are mostly men, mostly seedy, mostly repeaters—and mostly drunk. After drinking followed scenes, slaps, street fighting, or swearing—foul language in public is also hooliganism.

"Hooliganism" is an indispensable word in Moscow. A mother tells her young son to stop "hooliganizing"; a procurator says it can be grounds for capital punishment.

The criminal code provides a wide range of punishments: social censure, fine up to fifty rubles, corrective labor up to year, detention up to five years (when the defendant has been convicted before of hooliganism or has resisted the police or has behaved really outrageously). The twenty-eight cases here fell in between: from six months' corrective labor to two years' detention in a labor colony.

Articles 91, 144, 145 and 146: Armed Robbery with Intent to Seize State Property; Theft; Robbery; and Armed Robbery

Ten thin seventeen-year-old boys, their faces already hardened by vodka and factory work, sit on two benches in the dock, watched by nine policemen in boots, belts, and pistols, five facing the boys, a foot away.

The youths formed a neighborhood gang, which grew spontaneously, and spontaneously went wild, beating up and robbing people (with a 1903 German pistol that did not work), to keep themselves in vodka, or just for the fun of it. There were nine incidents in a three-week period. The victims were boys they disliked, random boys, a taxi driver, a policeman, salesgirls, and watchmen.

The judge is old enough to be their mother and acts as if she is. With tender concern, she asks each boy to have respect for the court, and then: *"Why?* What made you do it? What were your thoughts? Tell the court how you feel about it now. It is your future we are concerned with. Do you realize what you have done with your young life?"

Two boys got ten years; the others, eight, six, and five.

Suddenly, in an ordinary case of hooliganism, a drunken voice and meaningless whistling disrupt the orderly routine of the judge. "Yea Castro, Onward with Castro! Hurrah for Lenin! Give it to him like Lenin." It is a disheveled, red-nosed spectator, sprawled out on the rear bench, announcing his political creed. Some old women near him try to hush him up, but the soused man, who had been dozing, bellows on. "Let him have it like Castro and Lenin." He whistles and smirks.

The judge looks up calmly, stops the trial, and quietly orders a recess while the secretary fetches a policeman from the corridor. The big man is led away by the ear, protesting to Lenin's portrait. No one is surprised or outraged; it has happened here many times before.

Article 147: Swindling

A young Gypsy couple are charged with fortunetelling and short-changing drunks. Their entire tribe, it seems—about fifty persons, of three generations—have come to the trial to encourage the accused. During the deliberation they wait in the corridor—on one side, men; on the other, women, each with at least one infant, some of them nursing openly while squatting on the floor. There is no mingling of the sexes.

The Gypsies are dark and colorful, wretched and filthy. They are openly resentful, sneering at "this court, this law." When

Russians pass by for a look, the women swear foully and make obscene gestures with their hands and bodies. "What are you looking at, you dirty Jew," one screams at an astonished blond onlooker.

"I'm not a Jew," he assures me. "I'm one hundred percent Russian."

I cannot push my way past the tribe into the courtroom to hear the sentence.

Article 206: Hooliganism

The accused is not present; he is not permitted to leave the mental hospital where he is confined. He is charged with systematically creating disturbances in his apartment house, swearing vilely, distributing foul letters, frightening children, shutting off the electricity, chasing women with knives—for no apparent reason. His neighbors[3] confirm it, each standing about two minutes in the witness stand. Various remedies have been tried in vain.

The procurator says that psychiatrists have found him mentally unbalanced, and he urges that the accused be absolved from criminal responsibility. The defense counsel agrees, referring to war wounds and a medical history. The court is out eight minutes: it finds the accused guilty, but applies "enforced medical treatment" in the hospital, instead of criminal punishment. For how long? I ask. Until the doctors say he is well.

This is the shortest case, thirty-five minutes in all. Obviously, procurator and judge had settled everything beforehand on the strength of the psychiatric report.

Article 196, Paragraphs II and III: Forgery and Counterfeiting of Documents, Stamps, Seals and Forms

A year and a half earlier, a thirty-two-year-old bus driver in

---

[3] Throughout this account, "neighbor" usually refers to someone sharing the same multifamily apartment with the person involved. He is, literally, a next-door neighbor, since the rooms in most of Moscow's pre-World War II apartments are split up into separate family units and the kitchens and bathrooms are shared.

Odessa stole two tires from a parked car. He was discovered, and while his case was under investigation—he was not taken into custody—he fled to Moscow, moving in with an old army buddy and his wife, trusted friends. "I don't know what happened to me. I never had anything to do with the police before and I was frightened, frightened to my depths. And ashamed."

He sold his suit and raincoat and—"What does a man do in such a situation?"—wandered the streets and drank. Soon he was broke. He could not apply for work because his documents remained in the hands of the Odessa police. He feared that his friend would become suspicious of his unexplained idleness and his depression. He prepared to return to Odessa.

One day, at his wit's end, he spilled his sad story to a man with whom he happened to be sharing a bottle of vodka at a café. The man told him to relax, that everything could be fixed —for a fee, of course—and that he would never have to go to jail.

Two weeks of intense work followed, under the direction of the mysterious man. Passport, labor book, draft card and registration in a Moscow reserve unit, health card, permission to reside in Moscow, driver's license (second class), certificates—all the documents necessary to make a Muscovite—were forged by the two men. "I can't do it, I just can't," said the bus driver at first. *"Nichevo,"* said the older man. "You'll train a bit and you'll learn." He learned so well that it became his hobby, and on his own he forged twenty-six supplementary documents, whose quality flabbergasted investigators when he was finally discovered.

Armed with new papers, he started a new life. Aleksandr Akimovich Bobrenko became Aleksandr Akimovich Bobrenkov. "I wanted to work, to begin again, to pay for my crime and then forget it." His friend found work for him, driving a truck on a construction project, and a bunk in the dormitory at the site. Soon he moved again—in with a woman in her twenties and her seven-year-old son. He worked well, accumulating letters of recommendation and awards. His circle of friends grew. He became an outstanding Soviet toiler. He took his new family to visit his old mother in Odessa. He was appointed brigade leader of a section of the new circular superhighway around Moscow. Only good was said of him.

How he was found out is not revealed at the trial. Nor how much he paid the counterfeiter who started him on his way, nor what happened to the counterfeiter, nor where blank documents were obtained . . . "We are not interested in such details," the judge explained afterward in his chambers. "They're not important. Maybe he was lying—lying about the whole story of how he got the documents. Everyone in trouble meets some 'man in a café.'"

Bobrenko-Bobrenkov is deeply penitent, confessing in great streams of self-accusation and apology: "I stole and I lied and I falsified. I don't know whether I shall ever be able to redeem myself." Some of his Moscow friends who have come to the trial weep; and his army buddy and the buddy's common-law wife testify that they did not believe the investigator when the accusation was made, so honorable had his conduct been. "Comrade Judges!"—counsel for the defense begins his plea—"a little over a year ago, there was a fine Soviet worker . . . what made him stray? Fear and shame over a minor crime which, considering his heretofore exemplary life, would have been punished lightly . . . This proves that he is not a hardened criminal; on the contrary . . ."

The sentence, incorporating the year meted out for the two tires in Odessa, is four years in a labor colony, strict regime.

Article 89: Plunder of State Property by Means of Theft

A civil suit for eighty-five rubles—the value of a defective refrigerator which had been trucked out of a local factory by two enterprising workers between shifts and sold to a fence—is attached (as it may be in Soviet law) to this otherwise ordinary criminal prosecution. The lawyer presenting the factory's claim is a diffident young woman, who stumbles and falters as if it is her first case. (It is one of the rare times that I have seen a participant, other than defendants, self-conscious and inarticulate in court.) Although both men sit as defendants in the dock, the eighty-five-ruble claim is brought against only one. This puzzles the judge.

"You consider only Yegorov guilty?" he asks the lawyer gently.

"No . . . I . . . suppose not."

"You consider that *both* defendants are guilty as described in the indictment?"

"Yes . . . I think so."

"Then the court does not understand your reasoning. Why is your claim directed only against Yegorov?"

The embarrassed girl tries to think. The second defendant, having confessed voluntarily soon after the theft to factory administration and police, was still at his job; most likely she excluded him because he seemed *less* guilty than criminal-looking Yegorov, who denied all knowledge of the refrigerator and was taken into custody awaiting trial.

"I don't understand. If you consider both men guilty, you should bring your claim against both."

"Oh . . . well . . . all right . . . I'll make it both. In equal amounts?"

Articles 112 and 130: Intentional Light Bodily Injury, and Insult

These two charges, plus petty slander, are the only "private" crimes in the code: they must be initiated by the offended party (rather than the procuracy) and may be dropped by mutual consent if the parties are reconciled before the court retires for deliberation. The judge, moreover, is obliged to seek reconciliation; and this one—in his black shirt and yellow knit tie looks as if he belonged on the opposite side of the bench in a third-rate gangster film—does his best. "This is a shameful thing—Soviet adults behaving like children; it ought never have come to court. Now, we can dismiss the charges and forget everything if you will settle amicably and promise to stop this childishness. Otherwise you are going to have criminal records, and that would be sad—especially for the Communists among you."

The defendants are four respectable-looking, suited Ukrainian *gentilhommes,* all well-educated professional men, and all members of the same family. Three of them are co-occupants of one apartment—seven adults and four children in three small rooms and a kitchen—and the fourth is a frequent visitor. For months the apartment has been a circus of snarlings, fracases and sieges, with everyone worn to a fine edge in the close quarters. "Positively childish," says the judge, "a family of your background slapping and swearing at each other like guttersnipes!"

After the sermon, the accuser-defendants agree to reconcile. The judge has them sign a pledge: "In the future we obligate ourselves not to insult and hit each other, and to observe all the rules of socialist communal living. If anyone violates this pledge we ask that he be given maximum punishment. We request that the present case be dismissed."

The judge dismisses it. "But may I come back again if they keep annoying me?" whines the youngest man. "You may come back tomorrow if you must," the judge retorts. The oldest man says soulfully, "This is embarrassing, I am deeply ashamed. You will never see us again. Thank you, Comrade Judge."

But as they reach the door on their way out, the old antagonisms suddenly ignite. Insults, pushing, swearing—". . . purposely making noise when my baby is sleeping . . ."; ". . . if you ever throw a teakettle at me again . . ."; ". . . bully and boor . . ."; ". . . calling my wife a cunt . . ." The judge stuffs the pledge into the record book, hurries from the dais into his chambers, and shuts the door before they can come back.

Articles 92, 170 and 172: Theft of State Property by Misusing an Official Position; Misuse of an Official Position and Criminal Carelessness

The case is in its third week; seven bulging tomes of records lie on the judge's desk; four expert witnesses sit alongside the procurator; mountains of testimony have been taken down (will the court take time to review any of it when making its decision?), and much remains to be given. Two stories of an apartment house under construction in the suburbs collapsed, and during the investigation a plethora of financial, organizational, and technical

irregularities by the construction firm came to light. The administrators of the firm, a few key foremen, and officials in the trust
to which the unit was subordinate had been getting rich in a
platitudinous variety of ways—skimping on materials and selling
them elsewhere, taking kickbacks from workers, beefing up costs,
hiring relatives, neglecting finishing touches . . .

"*Vryad li* [Not a chance that] the case would have come to
court had the building not collapsed," the procurator admits
downheartedly in the corridor during a recess.

*Articles 96 and 206: Petty Larceny of State Property and
Hooliganism*

The defendant is a frizzy-haired, thin-lipped, hard little woman,
an ex-convict, guarded by a policeman and a policewoman.
When, as her rights as accused are read to her, she is asked
whether she has any petitions, she requests counsel. "Gimme a
lawyer."

The judge is annoyed—"Why didn't you ask for one earlier?"

"Because I didn't think it was important."

This is an open-and-shut case, and bringing in a lawyer is
going to waste time. Nevertheless, he grants the petition. The
appointment of a lawyer will be at the expense of the court in
this instance, since she is penniless, and the law requires that
every defendant who requests representation must have it.

Article 206: Hooliganism

The judge is disturbed: there is something amiss in the record.
The defendant insists that he has been in jail only once before
and seems to be telling the truth; the judge seems to believe
him. But the dossier lists two previous convictions.

"Look, I've admitted everything here. Why should I lie about
this? You can believe your papers if you want, but I know that
I was sentenced *once*. I told that to the investigator, but he wrote
down the other conviction anyway—said it wouldn't make any
difference."

The judge rummages in the record, puzzled and unhappy; this

is the kind of uncertainty—a slip-up in the *dokumentatsiya*—that most disconcerts them.

Articles 147 and 198: Swindling and Violation of Passport Regulations

The defendant, a skinny, dark, itinerant Azerbaijanian born in Baku, grins uncontrollably. (Is it the pleasure of confession, or the embarrassment of being caught, that forces that grin on so many defendants' faces? It is the grin of young boys found at mischief and not entirely ashamed. Defendants realize, of course, that they ought to look contrite; but the confessional grin operates on its own.)

He has admitted guilt on both charges. The swindling was attempted in a local *rinok* (an open market where collective farmers are permitted to sell produce from their private plots). With a fellow Azerbaijanian he worked a variation of an old confidence game, known in both the East and West as the "pocketbook drop," on a dashing Uzbek soldier on leave in Moscow. Promising to split the contents of a wallet they supposedly found, the two accomplices enticed the victim to part with his own fortune of sixty-three rubles. (The mustached soldier, a Lermontov character, carried his money in a clip under his tunic, next to his golden skin.) A plainclothes policeman became suspicious when he saw the transfer of money. The soldier had to be restrained when he realized he had been duped.

The second charge is illegal residence in Moscow: the accused has no *propiska* (a residence permit, issued by the police). This permission, which is stamped in the citizen's (internal) passport, is required in the major Soviet cities—Moscow, Leningrad, Kiev—and in the coastal strip along the Black Sea and in other popular areas. A Soviet citizen cannot simply take up residence in these areas as he could, for instance, in Irkutsk. For a newcomer, permission to stay usually depends upon his having a job which would entitle him to a *propiska;* but for most jobs—to complete the vicious cycle—possession of the *propiska* is a prerequisite. The purpose is to deter migration to already overcrowded cities.

Thus, the Azerbaijanian, having no steady job, has no legal right to live in Moscow; he has been warned four times during the past two years about his being there.

The judge is a ponderous man who plays with his words and his fingers. "Young man, you have got to get a job, you have got to find yourself an honest place in our socialist society. And you cannot do it in Moscow. Do you understand that you are living at the expense of society? Young man, you are a piece of fungus. You have done nothing with your life but practice the bourgeois creed of getting something for nothing. Why didn't you go back to your homeland and work, like a Soviet man?"

Grinning, the skinny defendant asks for mercy. He knows that he must be punished, of course; he understands that he did wrong—but could the court please make it as light as possible? You see, he has a sick mother in Baku, he has asthma, and he has a burning desire to reform. . . .

But the sentence is four years in a labor colony, strict regime. The Azerbaijanian is stunned; the grin becomes a mouth agape, then a grimace of hatred.

"Defendant, is the sentence of this court clear to you?"

"Yes, your great humanity is very clear. Thank you"—and under his breath, but loud enough for the fat judge to hear—"you bastard."

Four youths stole three rolls of tar paper from their factory: three years each. A drunk sneaked a mirror from a grammar school on Election Day: two years. A sober man took the windshield wipers and mirror from a parked car: one year. An obviously imbecilic old lush insisted on annoying strangers at a metro station: one year. A waitress had been pouring each glass of wine a few drops short and taking home a bottle a fortnight for herself: two years. A man rolled a drunk for his greasy jacket and scruffy shoes: one year. The punishments are astonishingly severe.

Much is written in Soviet legal literature about the need to re-educate and reform, rather than simply to punish, criminals.

Lenin's pronouncement that it is the inevitability of punishment, rather than its severity, that is crucial to the elimination of crime, is everywhere quoted. And the penal policy seems to conform to this enlightened spirit. In labor colonies, at least under normal regime, the lot of prisoners is said to approach the level of ordinary backwoods life. Men live in barracks, work at jobs that are not humiliating, receive wages, and are visited overnight by their wives. It is a far cry from the rot of jail, which in Russia is reserved only for the most dangerous criminals.

Yet, in the courtroom, the doctrine of rehabilitation seems to evaporate. Judges are simply impatient with the wrongdoer and quick to hand him a stiff sentence. "We are building Communism," they seem to say (and often they do say it), "and if you are not willing to help after we have given you every opportunity to do so, then you are not worth our effort and we are not willing to help you."

In these ordinary trials the cardinal concern is much broader than the facts and the juridical significance of a single crime, or even a single criminal. A greater task faces the court—no less a task than the remaking of a society. Remaking society means work, toil, labor, in its most direct sense, on farm and in factory. The task of the court is to put every man behind his machine.

But these defendants, like defendants everywhere, are mostly society's outcasts, those who do the least to improve it. Rarely are they the capable, respectable, steady citizens who keep the wheels turning. Usually the wrongdoer has an indifferent history of employment at an unskilled trade. "No established place of work" is mentioned often in indictments and sentences. And much is made of this; for these undesirables, the law is harsh.

The trials run aground on universal human frailties: a judge misses the crucial point in a defendant's testimony because she is fuming at her secretary for opening the window. A witness remembers, after he sits down, that he has forgotten to mention the most important fact. A court is so annoyed with a lawyer's nasal interruptions that it deafens itself to his client's appeal. And trials run aground, too, on the limitations of the trial form

itself; no code, indictment or summation is exact enough to re-
capture the subtleties of even the simplest case. A trial is an
attempt to reproduce episodes and circumstances from life. But
where to stop and where to start? How deep to probe? What to
simplify and what to leave out? A woman defendant wants to
talk about her family troubles, her husband's drinking; a mother
thinks she can explain why her son went wrong; a witness strug-
gles to remember who insulted whom first, who bought the vodka,
why blows were reached. . . . But the court has neither time nor
means for exactitude of that kind. It is a cardinal principle of
Soviet legal theory that the sentence in every criminal case should
reflect *materialnaya istina*—"material," or "objective," or "absolute truth." But it is a regular condition of Soviet trial practice
that judges are satisfied with much less in dealing with the oral
testimony. Even to the untrained ear many facts go undisclosed,
and seemingly essential questions go unasked.

These are the People's Courts. After some months in them
one feels the absurdity of the notion that "there is no law in
Russia"—even though the law is harsh in these ordinary cases
and the judges seem to place a subordinate importance on ascertaining the facts. And in time, the drab little chambers seem not
inappropriate as courtrooms; whether because of the bareness
or in spite of it, they preserve that dignity and solemnity that
means a court. People, not furniture or ornaments, dominate
those rooms; simple people, unintimidated by pomp and polish,
tell their stories and make their excuses in a setting natural for
them, and they seem stronger for it.

One feels, too, a sense of social (if not professional) equality
in these courts, a real absence of class distinction that is more
than a propagandist's invention. Equality between those on the
bench and those below it: the judge is not "your honor," and
there is no obsequiousness to his person as to someone of higher
social stuff. He is, if not always a comrade, then at least a *prostoi
Sovietskii chelovyek*—an "ordinary Soviet fellow"—made of the

same stuff and stock as his prisoners. No one is embarrassed, awed, or frightened by him.

And equality, too, between the defendants. Every statistic confirms that in American courts it's "the rich what gets the mercy and the poor what gets the blame." But it is no longer the same the whole world over. In the People's Courts, money talks softly, when at all. It can buy a better lawyer, and it has been known to bribe a weak investigator; but this is less common than the Soviet tendency to set an example by punishing the more affluent wrongdoers more severely.

In the People's Courts it is poor work in the factory, rather than a poor purse, that puts a defendant at a disadvantage.

AN ANALYSIS OF ZAPOTEC LAW CASES

Laura Nader

Aᴼᴼᴼᴼ FTER A DESCRIPTION of the background, this paper will present a descriptive analysis of a set of law cases collected in a Zapotec town involving decisions of the court, of town citizens and the court, and of family members and the court. The analysis of the case materials will explore specific aspects of Zapotec social life such as the kinds of people who use the courts, the range of grievances which they take there, the dyads which appear in opposition, the age of delinquency, and the relationship between type of conflict and outcome. Such law cases, in documentating interpersonal relations, enrich the understanding of data acquired by observation and interview techniques.

THE SETTING

Ralu'a, the bilingual Zapotec town with which this paper deals, is situated in the temperate region which lies between the higher mountains of the Mixe country and the Sierra de Juarez ranges, some 70 miles north of Oaxaca City, Mexico.[1] This region, referred to as the Rincón (Nader 1964a), is bordered by areas occupied by other Zapotec speakers, by Chinantec, and by Mixe.

Originally published in *Ethnology*, Vol. III, No. 4, pp. 404–19, 1964. Reprinted by permission of the author and of the editor of *Ethnology*.
[1] The material upon which the present study is based was collected intermittently between May 1957, and February 1958, in the Mexican town for which Ralu'a is a pseudonym. Research in this community was supported by grants from the Mexican Government and Radcliffe College (1957–58) and from Harvard University (the Milton Fund) and Radcliffe College (1959–60).

Until recently the Rincón has been isolated and hemmed in by impassable mountains, which prevented easy communication with the Valley of Oaxaca. The first motor vehicle entered the town in October 1959.

The town center of Ralu'a, located at an elevation of 5500 feet, possesses a population of 2000 people. A densely packed, compact settlement, its houses follow the lay of the hilly inclines. The inhabitants of the surrounding villages look upon it, in part respectfully and in part contemptuously, as the most "open" town in the area and the one most liable to rapid change, a "commercial center" in an agricultural region.

The land produces a livelihood for the inhabitants in the form of the staples—maize, beans, and sugar cane. Coffee, a cash crop, has been introduced only recently. The villages of the Rincón region share a basic unity in language and subsistence economy and, to a considerable extent, in formal social organization. There are, however, many subtle differences in crop distribution, in division of labor, in political and religious organization, and in the kinds of law cases taken to the courts of each town.

THE COURT SETTING

The *municipio* or town hall of Ralu'a is a spacious, rectangular building with two rooms and two small jails. The size and elegance of this edifice, and in part the history of law in Ralu'a, may be attributed to the use that this town has made of the traditional animosity which prevails between the inhabitants of Ralu'a and those of the neighboring village of Tsaquat. The prime reason for this resentment is land. Tsaquat has more land than any community in the Rincón but refuses to sell any of its holdings to outsiders. Ralu'a is land poor and has almost exhausted its possibilities for land accretion. Trespassing for firewood on the land of Tsaquat threatens the inhabitants of the latter and frequently gives rise to quarrels. The Ralu'ans get their revenge on Mondays, when the people of Tsaquat, as visitors to the Ralu'an market, consistently get drunk and are then thrown into jail and fined. The Ralu'ans ease their consciences by saying: "If we didn't jail these drunken Tsaquats, they would fall into the barrancas on the way home." The anthropologist cannot but note, however, that by these fines, in pesos and hard labor, Ralu'a has built its elegant town hall.

Within this building three officials constitute the town court of justice: the *presidente,* the *alcalde,* and the *sindico.* These three men, nominated by draft and elected by the town citizens (all adult males either married or over the age of twenty-one), are recruited for their experience and skills. They are men deemed capable of *erj.goonz,* "making the balance." All three are accountable for their behavior directly to the district court in Villa Alta and to the town citizens in Ralu'a.

The *presidente* and the *sindico,* who share one room, have administrative and judicial duties. The duties of the *alcalde* are only judicial, and he and his aides share a room apart. Although the state code of Oaxaca formally defines the duties of these officials, town citizens have their own folk definition of the functions of each. The *presidente* deals with light problems and with disputes that are easily resolved, e.g., conflicts between man and wife, between creditor and debtor, between drunken individuals. The *presidente* also handles cases of rebellious behavior such as the refusal to comply with the obligations of a citizen. Cases of family conflict, debt, and drunken assault and battery which remain unresolved by the *presidente* are passed to the *alcalde.* If the *alcalde* cannot settle them, they are usually referred to the district court in Villa Alta. The kinds of conflicts handled by the *presidente* and the *alcalde* overlap; it is the seriousness rather than the class of the complaint that determines whether it is passed on to the *alcalde.* Either the *presidente* may decide that the case is too serious for him to handle, or the litigants may ask for referral if the verdict reached by the *presidente* is not to their liking. The *sindico,* in contrast, is primarily responsible for processing specific kinds of complaints, those classed as crimes. It is the duty of the *sindico* to investigate all cases of crime, such as murder and theft, and to render impartial judgment in the settlement of property disputes. If he is unable to resolve property disputes and theft cases, he is supposed to refer them to the *alcalde*. All murder cases, however, go directly to Villa Alta.

All three officials have the right to prosecute, judge, and enforce the verdict with the aid of the *policia*. The police officials, twelve in number with two additional lieutenants and one chief of police, are recruited by the outgoing police force who have given one year's service to the town. The nominations by the outgoing police officials are then passed on at a general town meeting. Their explicit function is to police the town by a vigilant twenty-four-hour watch in order to maintain peace, to bring disturbers of the peace to "justice," and to interfere and break up all fights and noisy public quarrels. With the aid of these police officials the court may readily seek redress in a situation where a party has not complained. On market day, for example, if the police notice the least bit of argument and pushing anywhere, they (under orders from the *presidente* or *sindico*) bring offenders to court (trial), sometimes by way of the jail. Neither party to an argument need have complained.

While this is the division of labor as described by the court officials themselves, and as understood by the citizens of the town, it is not, in fact, strictly adhered to. The administrative and personal family responsibilities of a *presidente* may make it impossible for him at times to be present to deal with grievances, and in such situations the *sindico* may substitute for him. Or both the *presidente* and the *alcalde* may be averse to making a decision, and in such circumstances the plaintiff must, unless the *alcalde* refers the case to the district court, either withdraw his case or seek aid external to the village court system.

THE COURT CASES

How people resolve conflicting interests and how they remedy strife situations is a problem with which all societies have to deal, and usually they find not one but many ways to handle grievances. This is true in Ralu'a. A husband may be furious that his wife has taken and spent some of the money which he has hidden in the wall of his house. After much arguing he may resolve the conflict either by making her replace the money, or by beating her, or by both—the most frequent modes of resolving family problems between husbands and their wives.

Other ways of handling such conflicts are expressed in the following case involving Mariano's married son. Very soon after the marriage the daughter-in-law complained to her father-in-law that her husband was always drunk, never worked, and was always arguing with her. The father warned his son to behave better. Soon the daughter-in-law complained again, and this time the father whipped his son. The behavior of the son changed very little, and some time later the daughter-in-law, in despair, carried her complaint to the village Catholic priest. The conflict gained momentum, and one night the son arrived home in a drunken state and beat his wife. To no avail the wife had tried the various remedies available to her. What was left for her to do? She took her husband to the town court. Thus people will try one remedy after another until they reach a resolution. These remedies usually begin outside the court, and only when they fail is the case taken to the court. There is a strong suggestion that the more remedies a person has outside the court, the less likely he will be to take his grievance to court.

In Ralu'a there are three different kinds of remedy agents which may be referred to when a grievance reaches a boiling point: the court, the family, and the supernaturals. An understanding of all three agencies is necessary for a complete analysis of social control and for a sophisticated contextual analysis of the court system itself. The following discussion, however, will be limited to an analysis of only one agency—the town court. The unit of analysis will be the law case, of which the following literal translation of a recorded case occurring in Ralu'a in 1957 is an example:

> June 1, at nine o'clock in the morning, José Hernandez and María Chávez appeared before the president. Both are citizens of this town by birth. A complaint is brought against José by María because of the irregularities with which José administers his home: (a) eco-

nomically José has his wife restricted; (b) he frequently arrives home late and in a drunken state, pesters his wife, and frightens his young children; (c) he has illicit relations with other women. The Municipal Authority is asked to intervene energetically in order to correct his arbitrary behavior.

The defendant, in answer to the first complaint, said that the money that he gives to his family is exactly what he makes as a day laborer and that for him to give his wife more than he makes is not possible. As for the second complaint, he confessed that it is true that upon certain occasions when he meets a companion he has felt obliged to take a few alcoholic drinks but that he never arrives home in a dishonorable condition. Finally he asserted that he does not have illicit relations with anyone except his own wife, unless this may be called illicit.

After investigating the case, and after long discussion, it was proved that in actuality he does spend a certain amount of money on vices, that when he is drunk he has been known to threaten his wife according to information given by the neighbors, and thirdly that he does have illicit relations with various women. The defendant was ordered to pay a 50-peso fine to the court. He promised in the future he would support his home in better fashion, and it was stated by the president that should he ever be caught with some other women he would be punished, as would his lover or lovers.

During one month in 1957 sixty such law cases were consecutively recorded in the courtroom of the *presidente*'s office. This sample is small if one considers the total number of cases which annually enter the *presidente*'s office and admittedly restricts the use which can be made of the information found therein. However, the generalizations made on the basis of this small sample served me as significant predictors of various aspects of social life, and the cases contain sufficient information on procedure to be useful in predicting judicial decision-making.

In the analysis of these cases eight categories were selected from a larger number for consideration: the sex of the contestants, their status in relation to one another (kin or nonkin), their age, whether they reside together or separately, the jurisdiction used, the number of individuals involved in the courtroom as plaintiff and defendant, the class of complaint, and the verdict and the sanctions awarded. The analysis illustrates the insights about Zapotec life which may be learned from a study of law cases.

DECISIONS OF THE COURT

The process by which judicial decisions are formed in a court is a complex one involving biases of one sort or another in any culture. Judicial decisions may be based on strictly legal data, as when a Ralu'an citizen unmistakably violates a clear-cut rule such as "Citizens must not give forth with the Mexican grito after the sky is dark." Or they may be based on adventitious factors, such as the inebriated state of the judge, or on personal factors, such as mutual dislike between judge and one or both of the litigants. Such decisions may also be based on more general or social rules of the community, such as the unwritten rule in Ralu'a which states that the judge should naturally favor his own when deciding cases involving a town citizen and a litigant from another town. Finally, decisions may be based on a concept of justice. Among the Zapotec, this implies a decision calculated to "make the balance"—i.e., to insure the termination of a grievance —between the involved litigants.

An analysis of these 60 cases only begins to suggest features important to decision-making. It would be unreasonable to expect that a thorough understanding of the judicial process could be gleaned from an analysis of such recorded cases. To understand law, one must view it in its social context and not as something which can be described by the analysis of a sample, however large, of cases alone. The findings recorded below deal with two limited aspects of the decisions made in the sample cases: the verdict and the sanctions imposed.

The verdicts available from the total sample present a rather puzzling statistic. Of 40 cases, the plaintiffs, i.e., the initiators of the proceedings, win 32 cases, lose 3, and tie with the defendant in 5. This means that the person who is being complained against loses 32 cases, wins 3, and ties with the plaintiff in 5. In no case, moreover, is a plaintiff who loses his case required to pay costs or damages; he is never penalized for resorting to the authorities.

We might well ask why the plaintiff prevails so often. In United States courts (with juvenile and small-claims courts as possible exceptions) formal procedure allows the judges to consider only the evidence presented by the two parties. No evidence may enter into a decision unless it is presented and judged admissible at the trial. Gossip, personal history, and hearsay evidence, for example, are excluded. In Ralu'a this is not so. The defendant is fully aware that the men who are rendering judicial decisions know him well. They are aware if he has been "playing around," if he is addicted to drink, if he has assaulted his wife, or if he is in general a problem citizen. They have a fair prehearing knowledge of his personal history and may use it as evidence in his favor or to his disadvantage. Realizing that the men who judge his case know his full history, the defendant pleads guilty in nine out of ten cases.

Finally, the majority of the cases taken to the *presidente* involve gross or visible transgressions. If the case is not fairly clear-cut, the plaintiff does not wish to risk an adverse decision and would rather try to settle the case out of court. Litigants consider the court a resolver of blatant violations. The gray cases tend to be settled outside of the *presidente*'s court unless they are serious enough to be passed on to the *alcalde*'s court or even the district court. (Really serious violations, such as murder, are immediately reported by the *sindico* to the district court and then investigated in accordance with orders from that court.) Ralu'ans in general, particularly women, do not want to jeopardize their social status by telling a judge in public about their squabbles if they think they might be judged adversely. In the three cases lost by the plaintiff the women guessed wrongly. It is interesting to note that these cases all involved ambiguity of marital status. Case analysis suggests that if a defendant who has lost his case in the *presidente*'s office appeals his case to the office of the *alcalde,* his chances of winning are enhanced by this appeal.

What sanctions follow the rendering of a verdict of guilty? In Ralu'a, legal sanctions take the form either of fines paid in pesos, of fines paid by labor on public works, of public reprimand, or of all three, in addition to jail sentences.

Data on sanctions may be ordered in several different ways, depending on the purpose of inquiry. If, for example, the sanctions are ranked from the least to the most severe, we have for one thing an index of the seriousness of the cases. At the bottom of such a ranking, involving the payment of between 10 and 40 pesos, we find such offenses as street fighting, drunkenness, disturbing the peace, nuisance to the court, failure to complete municipal obligations, and flirting of females. Grievances requiring payment of from 40 to 100 pesos include abandonment, abduction, assault and battery, attempted murder, slander, boundary trespass, and flirting when initiated by a man. Such ranking, besides its usefulness as an index of seriousness, gives us information about the range of possible sanctions for a similar set of offenses. An illustration is the case of the two flirts. A single woman complained to the court that a Sr. X had appeared beneath her window the previous night and made the equivalent of American "wolf calls." The defendant pleaded that he had done this only because this woman had flirted with him the previous week and had even invited him to collect firewood with her. The court fined her 30 pesos for flirting and the defendant 60 pesos for flirting when, as a married man, he should have been at home with his wife. The distinctive feature here, according to the judge, was marital status. The discrimination in fines was made primarily because the woman was single and the man was married, and only secondarily because she was a woman and he a man.

A classification of cases according to their common features reveals that the sanctions may be different in a number of cases involving the same complaints. Examination of the distinctive features in such cases helps us to understand the difference in the sanctions. For example, we may consider three family cases (see Table 1) which share the following features: all the plaintiffs are women; all the defendants are men; and the complaints are

drunkenness and assault. The question is on what basis are the
sanctions decided.

TABLE 1

Features of three family cases

Case No.	Plaintiff	Defendant	Drunken- ness	Assault	Battery	Sanction
1	wife	husband	x	x	–	50 pesos
6	wife	husband	x	x	x	75 pesos
14	mother	son	x	x	x	90 pesos

In Case 1 the defendant threatened the plaintiff but did not
actually strike her. The sanction was 25 pesos less than in Case 6,
where the defendant both threatened and struck his wife. In
Case 14, where the defendant likewise both threatened and struck
a woman, the woman was his mother. To the Ralu'ans this is an
important difference, and they consequently fined the defendant
15 pesos more than in Case 6, where the victim was his wife
rather than his mother.

In many cases, however, the "logic" in the difference in sanctions is not obvious, and the explanation may lie in facts that
may not be reported. These might include such factors as the
state of inebriation of the defendant (which would reduce his
punishment in a case of assault and battery), or the place of
residence of the two litigants, or the relationship between the
litigants and the judge.

If the sanctions are ordered in terms of sex (see Table 2), the
cases show that men are penalized either by money fines, or by
public work, or by jail sentences, whereas women are sanctioned
most frequently in pesos, only rarely by jail sentences, and never
by the performance of public work.

In the sample, thirty men and twelve women were involved as
defendants. For the most part, the complaints against women
are less serious than those against men. Of the six women sanctioned, five paid less than 30 pesos, the one exception being a

slander case in which the woman was ordered to pay 80 pesos. Among the men, on the other hand, eleven had to pay fines of more than 30 pesos. In summary, men's offenses are more serious than those of women; and this is reflected in the fact that they pay heavier fines. To be considered, also, is the fact that men have larger incomes than women and are thus able to pay higher money sanctions. A more detailed account would have to consider the relative incomes of men and women.

TABLE 2

Complaints contrasted by sex of defendant

| | Sex of defendant | |
| | M | F |
Complaints	(*Number of complaints*)	
Unpaid debt	4	2
Residence stability		1
Disturbing the peace	4	
Slander		4
Rape	1	
Assault	6	
Battery	4	1
Boundaries	3	1
Tax evasion	1	
Unfair business practices	1	
Failure to fulfill municipal obligations	4	
Disorderly conduct	7	
Curfew	1	
Lack of support	3	
Drunkenness	5	
Abandonment of home duties	2	
Adultery	2	
Paternity	1	
School problems	1	
Abandonment	1	2
Abduction	1	
Attempted murder	2	
Interference		3
Contamination of public utilities		1

The most serious cases occur between men or between men and women. If a case is serious enough to merit a fine of more

than 100 pesos or long-term imprisonment, it is sent to the
alcalde (judge) in the town and is then frequently passed on to
the district court.

TOWN CITIZENS AND THE COURT

Kinship, locale, common work interests, and shared obligations
and values link the citizens of Ralu'a in a myriad of social groups.
The town is divided into four sections—north, east, south, and
west—primarily for such purposes as census taking. Citizens do
not usually refer to their section as a means of local identifica-
tion, but rather to the Zapotec name of some natural land feature
close to their home. In many parts of Mexico the word *barrio*
is used to refer to such local sections, but this is not true in
Ralu'a and the Rincón in general, where the *barrio* functions
rather as a co-operative bank or a savings-and-loan association.
Ideally, any adult male is free to join any *barrio* he pleases, and
he may change *barrios* or not join a *barrio*. In fact, however, a
son usually joins the *barrio* of his father, and a wife belongs to
that of her husband. Instead of being localized, the *barrios* are,
as one informant expressed it, *revueltos,* i.e., scattered, criss-
crossing the town, tying together people from various families,
occupations, and sections. The four *barrios* are represented in
the town government. There are no large localized descent
groups in Ralu'a.

Men hold all the positions in the local government. These number about thirty and confer important kinds of prestige upon their
holders. Men also participate in musical groups, such as the orchestra and the band. Membership in these organizations re-
flects differences in social status. The band is made up of farmers
of the conservative element in town; the orchestra consists of "pro-
gressive" farmers, who are predominantly coffee producers and
merchants. The musicians perform on religious occasions, at
funerals and weddings, and in the entertainment of visiting engi-
neers. Men likewise hold church positions, which in some way

parallel the town government organization, and special associations of men serve to maintain and protect the wells near their homes. Men, and women as well, form more informal groups which come together for purposes of mutual aid (*gozona*); friends and kinsmen help one another in the building and repair of houses, in field work, and in carrying out wedding and funeral obligations.

Ralu'an women have fewer formal groupings than men. They participate in neither civil nor religious organizations except as helpers at fiestas. They are not required to take part in communal village labor projects. They may, however, belong to women's church associations, which carry out certain religious duties such as daily prayer and the decoration of the church with flowers. These associations are neighborhood groups and do not reflect *barrio* membership.

Perhaps the most important and most frequent social contacts among women are a result of the daily round. When the men go out to their fields, the town is left mainly to the women and children, the merchants, and the old people who can no longer work. The duties and activities of a woman bring her into contact with other women at the mills, the wells, and the church. At night, after their relatively solitary day in the fields, the men tend to spend their time talking with other men on the plaza or drinking in the *cantinas*. Sundays and market days break the monotony of life, especially for the men, who may spend these days either working around the house or out drinking mescal with their male friends.

None of these formal social groups are reflected in court cases as groups (as, for example, lineages might in a Moslem Arab village). Individual members of all social groups, whether formal or informal, however, utilize the courts, and the cases reveal valuable information about the behavior of citizens as citizens. They answer, for example, such questions as what people use the court, when in their life cycle they do so, and in what roles, for what complaints, and against whom.

Excluding cases which involve citizens from other towns and those initiated by the court, we learn, for example, that men and women use the courts to an approximately equal degree. In 22 of our cases the plaintiff is a female, and in 17 a male. The men, however, seek judicial remedies mainly in conflicts with nonkin. Of 17 cases initiated by men, 15 were with nonkin and two with affinal kin. On the other hand, of the 22 cases initiated by women, 14 were with kin and only eight with nonkin. From a cross-cultural view the number of women who contest cases in the court is extraordinarily high. Upon investigation of these 22 female plaintiffs it was found that more than two thirds lacked a male relative (father, father-in-law, husband) who might have defended them.

The complaints which the town brings against its citizens for drunkenness, disturbing the peace, unpaid debt, and insubordination have an outcome which is advantageous to the town. It sanctions such citizens by using them as labor on public works projects. With the increase in public works during the past few years resulting from various technical assistance projects, this is seen as one way to supplement communal labor, and appropriate advantage is taken of any citizen who steps even slightly out of line. Similarly, when the town treasury needs supplementing, what ordinarily might be acceptable as customary behavior conveniently becomes prosecutable. This technique of making or enforcing laws primarily for economic reasons is, of course, not unfamiliar in our own society.

It should also be noted that certain classes of people avoid using the courts. For example, the families of the *principales,* the leading government advisers, rarely utilize the town court. Their respect and authority relations are perhaps so well defined that they are able to handle family problems within the family, with the oldest member, usually a *principal,* acting as arbitrator, mediator, or judge. For any member of such a respected or respectable family to be found in court would be considered a shame, and any wise member of such a family hesitates before involving the name of his family in a public hearing.

The following tendencies were observed from the incomplete information on age in our sample. People seem to get into most trouble with the town officials and their fellow citizens between the ages of 30 and 50. (These are the years when most adults lose their parents.) Nine of the defendants were between the ages of 20 and 30, seventeen between 30 and 40, seventeen between 40 and 50, and six between 50 and 65. Among the plaintiffs, the age distribution is more widely spread: five were between the ages of 20 and 30, eleven between 30 and 40, ten between 40 and 50, and nine between 50 and 65. Young couples seem to begin having serious marital troubles between the ages of 23 and 33, usually after they have had several children, while older citizens (between 40 and 65) are primarily involved in grievances concerned with property and contracts.

One of the interesting observations noted when the content of the cases was tabulated was the co-occurrence of complaints. For example, cases of assault and battery are nearly always found in conjunction with instances of drunkenness. The one exception in the sample is a case of two sober women fighting on the street. We also found that adultery rarely stands by itself as a cause for complaint; it is usually associated with assault, or battery, or lack of support, or drunkenness, or a combination of these complaints. In other words, as long as the husband brings home the corn, as long as he does not verbally or physically insult his wife, she does not complain to the courts of his adultery. Such complaint complexes are as relevant to an understanding of how the plaintiff or defendant presents and pleads his case as they are to description of the judicial decision-making process.

Sexual differentiation in complaints (see Table 2) is equally revealing. It has previously been noted that women and men use the court about equally, that men do so mainly for the resolution of marriage problems, and that many more men are accused than women. We may now ask what kinds of complaints are made against female defendants and how these contrast with complaints against men. As is revealed in Table 2, the variety as well as the number of charges against men is greater. However, other features should also be taken into account. For example, several women, but no men, are accused of slander and interference, and several men are accused of assault and battery but only one woman. In short, where men use assault and battery as an expression of hostility, women use gossip.

The overlap of complaints between men and women is an indication of the range of rights and duties which men and women share and have serious conflicts about. In Ralu'a the common range includes only a few cases: one battery charge, one boundary complaint, two unpaid debts, and two abandonment charges.

THE FAMILY AND THE COURT

The Ralu'an household, the largest number of related individuals who reside and eat together, varies in size and composition. At different stages in his life cycle, an individual's household may be composed of one, two, or three generations. When households contain members other than those of the nuclear family, these relatives most frequently include spouses of newly married children, grandchildren, or relatives of the grandparental generation.

In 1957, fifth and sixth grade children ranging in age from eleven to fourteen years filled out a census form. These children represented 45 households, numbering 228 individuals. Of these households 29 consisted of nuclear families. Six households had other relatives living with them: grandparents, mother's sister, father's brother's wife, or nephews. In ten families either the father or mother was missing; in eight of these it was the father who was absent.

Ideally, residence is patrilocal; at marriage a young man brings his wife home to reside with his parents. Although patrilocality is said to be preferred, in actual practice there is a great deal of variation in residence patterns. Under many circumstances, usually having to do with the availability of space, a couple will find it advantageous to live with or near the wife's family. The nuclear family, however, maintains a separate, independent economy, even if residing with the parents of either spouse. That the nuclear family is something apart is often symbolized by one kitchen in which separate cooking space has been allocated for each nuclear family.

Inheritance is bilateral and lineal. Parents ideally divide their property equally among their children or their grandchildren. Individuals rarely inherit lands from their siblings, from their parents' siblings, or from affines. Where land is scarce, parents may choose to give their lands to their son, their house to their daughter. The latter arrangement provides insurance, in a culture where marriages are brittle, against the event that a girl's marriage does not work out successfully.

The Rincón Zapotec's concept of property, which is based on individual ownership, modifies the traditional pattern of inheritance. Although a pair of siblings may inherit property jointly, such joint ownership is usually temporary. One sibling may buy out the other, or both may sell the property and divide the payment equally—procedures which avoid the inevitable conflict that joint ownership implies. That individual ownership prevails does not mean, however, that the use of property is individual. On the contrary, individual ownership is accompanied by joint use of property by the nuclear family. Control and disposition of the sale of property may also be under joint control of a married couple, but, in the last analysis, it is the individual owner of a piece of property who decides to sell or lend it.

Consanguineal and affinal ties are supplemented by ritual kinship relations, the *compadrazgo* system. This refers to the relation established between godparent and godchild and—equally important—that established between godparents and a child's parents. Godparents are usually not related to the family of the godchild, as they are in some Mexican towns. The *compadrazgo* in Ralu'a thus operates to extend solidarity and reciprocity beyond the limits of the family. Ritual kinsmen are those people to whom a child may go for advice or for aid in resolving problems or who may come to give advice and aid unsolicited.

The family never participates as a group in a case at law. Most family cases deal with dyads within the family. I will briefly describe four of these dyadic relations—those between father and child, between mother and child, between siblings, and between husband and wife.

A quotation from my field notes describes the father-child relationship rather succinctly:

> They were discussing a case at dinner of a son who had to go to jail in Villa Alta because he hit his father. I said, "For that they sent him to jail?" The father said, "Of course," and sounded surprised at my question. I probed further: "But many men beat their wives, and they never go to jail." He answered, "Wives are one thing, fathers another." Then I asked what if a father was in the wrong. The son in the family said, "Fathers are never in the wrong for beating their sons. They always do it for their own good." I asked if a father under their law could ever be proved guilty for doing wrong to a son, no matter what the son's age. The answer: "A father cannot do wrong with his children."

The father is the principal authority figure and the disciplinarian in the family. He does not have to suffer back talk. He cannot only threaten the child with present physical punishment or future disinheritance, but he also knows that the court of law will probably support whatever he may do.

The mother-child relationship is primarily one of affection, rather than of fear or strong respect. While a woman may let either her husband or his parents punish her child, she avoids doing so herself. She rarely says, "I will spank you." Rather she threatens: "Your father will beat you"; "The witches will get you"; "X will inject you"; etc. The child runs to her for present support and protection, and in return she sees her children as future security should her husband die or separate from her.

Relationships between siblings differ considerably with sex, age, and order of birth. In general, younger siblings show respect toward elder ones. However, siblings talk freely about each other in public, and often derogatorily, especially if they have married and separated from their family of orientation. Sibling rivalry over the mother's affection and in regard to questions of inheritance is common, but a brother often helps a sister when she is involved in serious marital problems. Ideally, siblings should be treated equally by their parents. Nevertheless, a mother is said to be closer to her daughters than to her sons and to a youngest son than to older ones.

The relationship between husband and wife presents a variety of difficulties. For the most part, marriages are arranged by the parents, who consider the preferences of a son but often ignore those of a daughter. Men usually marry between the ages of eighteen and twenty; women, between fourteen and eighteen. If the young bride likes the chosen groom, all may go well. If not, she faces a dilemma. If she disobeys her father and chooses to marry someone else, she must bear the consequences alone. Obedience to her father, on the other hand, means future security in case her marriage fails. The changes involved in marriage are often a shock for the bride. She and her husband are likely to spend the first months sleeping in the same room with his mother and father. She must accustom herself not only to such intimacy but also to living in a new part of town, to washing at a different well, to patronizing a different mill. The first years of marriage are indeed difficult.

With this brief summary in mind, we can consider the cases in our sample which deal with family grievances. Of the sixteen family cases brought to the *presidente*'s office during one month, eleven were settled by the *presidente,* and only four were referred to the *alcalde*'s office. Both offices, as indicated earlier, have the authority to enforce the law and the duty to act as counselors of domestic relations. The cases handled by the *alcalde*'s office were referred there because the *presidente* decided the case was too involved for him to settle in a short review or else were appealed with his consent because the litigants were not satisfied with his proposals.

If we consider the classes of kin relations involved, we find twelve cases of wife versus husband, one of son-in-law versus mother-in-law, one of a widowed mother versus her son, one of daughters versus their mother, and one of sister versus sister. Conspicuously missing are child versus father and child-in-law versus father-in-law; their absence is understandable since paternal authority is strong and unquestioned. There are no cases involving related males; should they occur they would be considered serious enough to be heard by the *alcalde* or even by the district court.

Thirteen cases in the sample deal with affinal kin conflict and only three with consanguineal. We might deduce from this that affinal ties are weak, and indeed this agrees with the observations of daily life. For a mother to take her son to court would be unusual unless she were a widow. Her husband, the father of the son, would be able to control the situation because his authority is considered binding. Of the thirteen cases involving affinal kin, wives are the plaintiffs in eleven; the others are single cases each of husband versus wife and son-in-law versus mother-in-law. Wives clearly make use of the courts to defend their domestic rights—in strong contrast to many Mexican villages where women rarely, if ever, take their husbands to court (Nader and Metzger 1963).

In two of the three cases which involved consanguineal relatives the parties maintained separate residences. In the third case, a mother was asking her son to leave her home. In general, therefore, affinal cases involve coresidents; consanguineal cases, relatives who live apart.

Decisions concerning married couples hinge upon the court's determination of whether the marriage is legal. In Ralu'a the priest and some avowedly strong Catholics define legal marriage as marriage in the Catholic church, whereas the town government defines it in terms of the civil ceremony. In the minds of a great number of the inhabitants, however, neither ceremony alone constitutes a legal marriage. For them, marriage involves a long series of rituals which begin with the first formal negotiations which the family of the boy initiate with the girl's family and end with the presentation of a gift to the girl's family in the presence of kinsmen and friends. Only after they are completed is the marriage considered legal in the cultural context. Only then do the couple begin to live together, though they may have been married by civil and/or religious authorities weeks or even months before. Marriage ceremonies thus assume three different forms: the religious, the civil, and that of customary exchange between families. All three forms, either separately or in combination, are recognized by the town courts, and the rights of a wife or husband are protected accordingly.

These ceremonies relate primarily to a girl's first marriage. Second marriages are usually common-law unions. In the past, a woman who had lived with a man long enough to bear him a child would have been protected by the courts. If her common-law husband left her and his children, he could have been taken to court to answer to the complaint of abandonment. Now the system is changing. The concept of marriage recognized by the court no longer includes common-law unions. This change has created marriage instability, many fatherless families, and a large number of confused women who may not understand why their rights are not being protected. The *municipio* makes no attempt to reconcile a couple in such a predicament; the woman is simply told that she is not legally married and thus has no rights binding on her man.

There are some exceptions to this. The Ralu'a court interprets differently the cases which arise in the small neighboring settlements for which it acts as appellate court before the case goes to Villa Alta. In these settlements, called *agencias,* whose inhabitants are considered backward by Ralu'ans, the custom of second marriages, the informal joining together of a couple, is recognized by the people, and the Ralu'a court, in what seems a contradiction, protects the common-law wives.

SUMMARY

This has been a brief analysis of the manifest content of law cases adjudicated during one month in a small Zapotec town. I have not attempted to describe or explain exhaustively Zapotec legal procedure (see Nader 1964b) or Zapotec law in its relation to the rest of the social organization (see Nader and Metzger

1963). Rather, my analysis of law cases as part of the legal order in Ralu'a has specifically called attention to the range and kinds of grievances handled by the office of *presidente,* the classes of people who bring these grievances, and the conditions that seem to be associated with special types of conflict such as the presence of drunkenness in assault and/or battery cases.

Further, the analysis has revealed patterned outcomes for specific classes of complaints. For example, slander is punished more severely than citizen insubordination and, in some cases, more severely than assault and battery. The analysis of different classes of participants, such as plaintiffs and defendants, reveals certain tendencies. We can predict, for example, that if a woman takes a man to court, he is likely to be her husband. The reverse is not true; indeed, if a man takes a woman to court, she is likely not to be his wife. The implication is that patterns obtained in the analyses of law cases allow us to predict other aspects of social organization much as the analysis of kinship systems has been shown to be predictive in the areas of economic and political behavior. The fact that women regularly take their husbands to court tells us something about the status of women; it also shows that the authority of a male household head is often overruled by the elected town officials.

Some patterns of interpersonal relationship were discovered in the analysis, for it is often difficult to elicit satisfactory descriptions of the less formalized roles and statuses in a society. Some indication as to the degree of conformity to particular patterns is obtainable by the comparison of ideal patterns of behavior, e.g., between husband and wife, with legal cases, such as those involving husbands and wives. The analysis of law cases is thus capable of enriching our knowledge of social organization.

SOME NOTES ON LAW
AND CHANGE IN NORTH INDIA

Bernard S. Cohn

I THE LITTLE KINGDOM

A S THE ANTHROPOLOGIST has turned from the study of primitive, isolated, preliterate societies to that of social units
which are parts of great civilizations, a new range of problems
calls for description and analysis. The following paper is a description of the dispute settlement process in a local region in
North India and the effects that the establishment of British rule
had on indigenous dispute settlement procedures.[1]

The complexity of the situation in an Indian village as regards
law and the process of settling disputes can be only briefly cata-
logued in this paper. To start, let me briefly summarize the social
system of a particular region in India. Senapur is a large, multi-
caste village in Jaunpur District of Eastern Uttar Pradesh, and my
remarks, unless otherwise specified, relate to Senapur and the
immediately surrounding locality, which is called Dobhi Taluka

Reprinted from *Economic Development and Cultural Change*, Vol. VIII, No.
1, October 1959, by permission of editor, author, and The University of Chicago Press.

[1] The field work on which this paper was based was carried out in 1952–53,
when the author was a fellow of the Social Science Research Council and
Fulbright scholar. The Social Science Research Council's Summer Seminar
on Law and Social Relations, 1956, provided the stimulus for a preliminary
analysis of the data on legal change.

I would like to express my thanks to Shri Rudra Datt Singh, Shri shri
Nath Singh, Professor Morris Opler, and Professor McKim Marriott for comments on the paper or assistance during the field work; and my appreciation
of the suggestions made by the late Robert Redfield.

or Tuppah. Dobhi Taluka is an area of forty square miles with roughly one hundred villages. All the villages were "owned" at one time by one lineage of Rajputs, locally termed "Thakurs." Thakurs are descendants of an agnatic ancestor who conquered the area in the seventeenth century. One of the underlying assumptions in this paper is that a local area of this kind, which I will style the "little kingdom," was the basic jural unit of upper India in the eighteenth and nineteenth centuries.

The political organization of upper India in the latter part of the eighteenth century has to be viewed at two levels. At the top level were the successor states of the Mughal Empire, most of them established by conquerors. Beneath this level were lineages which, as corporate groups, acted as the local rulers. A lineage, usually Rajput but occasionally Brahman, Bhumihar, Ahir, Jat, or Gujar, controlled anything from a few villages up to several hundred. The British recognized a lineage or the headman of a lineage as the landlord of a village or a group of villages and made the lineage or headman responsible for the regular payment of land revenue and maintenance of law and order. In Mughal times, in addition to payment of land revenue, the lineage was also responsible for the provision of troops. These lineages governed the little kingdoms. In Mughal times, there was little interference in the little kingdom on the part of the ruling state as long as the ruling lineage did not try to abrogate its tax or military obligation and as long as internecine warfare among the Rajput lineages did not break out into major battles.

One of the lineage functions in the little kingdom was the settlement of disputes. Disputes regarding caste matters, such as marriage, rules of commensality, and caste occupational regulations, were settled by the caste *pancayats* (councils) of the local region. As far as I could determine in the field of 1952–53, the jurisdiction of the various caste *pancayats* fell entirely within the boundary of the little kingdom. Caste matters that could not be settled by the caste *pancayat* could be, and often were, referred to the dominant caste, the Thakurs (Rajput landlords), whose lineage controlled the little kingdom. This referral of caste disputes to the Thakurs was usual in questions of poverty right, inheritance, intercaste disputes, or disputes which threatened the peace of the village or the region.

The Thakurs' power to settle disputes arising in other castes resident in the little kingdom was based on their position as land-lords, the fact that all castes were tied to them through social, economic, ceremonial, and traditional ties, and the fact that the Thakurs were the *Rajas* (kings) for the inhabitants. The Thakurs defined themselves and were defined by those below as the "Lords." The Thakur attitude was summed up by one elderly Thakur, who said, "We took this land with the sword, these other people are our dependents."

During the eighteenth and nineteenth centuries, in a little kingdom, the dominant caste controlled all castes beneath it. The outside government did not ordinarily interfere with this relation-ship. Disputes among members of the dominant caste within the little kingdom, at least in Eastern Uttar Pradesh, could ultimately be settled by a formally constituted council. Membership in this council was based on a regional division into twelve lineage seg-ments, the basis of the judicial and governing body and land-holding. The principal basis of dispute settlement in this council was probably arbitration and the balancing of power so well analyzed by students of African political organizations. The sys-tem of arbitration and power balance was reinforced by the expectation, in pre-British times, that internal strife in the domi-nant caste would be used by surrounding groups to destroy the suzerainty of the lineage over its little kingdom.

Thakurs also derived important status in their role as settlers of disputes and judges, from their claims to be kings in a tradi-tional social order. In Hindu political and legal doctrine, part of the function of the king was the maintenance of the social order, which entailed prevention of what the law books term "the con-fusion of castes." Every caste had its prescribed duties to per-form, as well as the obligation of marrying within the caste. The king wielded the *danda* (literally, a stick) to enforce the rules of the caste system. The Brahman was the advisor of the king and the interpreter of law, and he could prescribe punishment in form of a ritual expiation, but it was the king's duty to see that the punishment was carried out. Theoretically, the castes were self-governed in terms of setting and enforcing their own standards of behavior, but the king could always be resorted to by appeal from caste rulings. This aspect of the function of the king was preserved even into the twentieth century in those parts of the Indian subcontinent ruled by the Indian princes.

The Thakurs in a particular village, backed ultimately by the local council of twelve, ruled and adjudicated for themselves, and for the dependent castes in matters which the dependent castes could not settle themselves. The separate subcastes below the Thakurs lived, worked, and were the dependents (*praja*) of the Thakurs. These separate and independent subcastes usually settled intracaste disputes. I will describe a typical procedure of settlement of disputes in one subcaste, the Chamars.

II THE CHAMARS

In 1952 there were over 600 Chamars, scattered in six hamlets, living in the village of Senapur. The basic social and economic unit of the Chamars is the household (*ghar*), which is usually a nuclear family; the households in turn are united into lineages (*khandan*), normally traced through the male line. We may view the Chamars' social organization somewhat as the cross-section of an onion, the center ring being the household, the next the *khandan,* the next ring the hamlet, the next the six hamlets of Senapur, the next ring the network of villages into which Chamars marry and from which they take brides—a circle of four to ten miles, and finally the named subcaste, Jaisvara, whose members spread over many of the districts of Eastern and Central Uttar Pradesh.

A The household

Many disputes arise in the household, primarily concerned with land, other property, marriage, and divorce. Theoretically, the eldest capable male is the head of the household, who, as part of his role, is responsible for maintaining the peace of the household. Often disputes arise in the household which are adjudicated at different levels in the Chamar organization and at times are adjudicated by persons outside the Chamar social organization.

B   The khandan (*lineage*)

Disputes that arise within the household are usually taken first to the leader of the *khandan*. Since the *khandan* is localized in one part of the hamlet and since there is little that does not take place within earshot of the other households, the *khandan* leader is aware of the dispute from its inception. Minor quarrels can usually be settled by allowing the participants to vent their anger and then suggesting a simple compromise.

Many disputes arise among members of different households of the same *khandan*. Disputes are frequent over use of land in front of houses, the hamlet well, property still held in common after partition, insults, suspicion of petty thefts, and the use of witchcraft. If a dispute cannot be settled easily by the *khandan* leader, the leader or one or both of the participants may ask the hamlet at large to hold a meeting (*pancayat*) to hear and settle the dispute. Hamlet meetings to settle disputes may be formal or informal. An informal meeting will include leaders of all the *khandans* in the Chamar hamlet, heads of the households who are available, and any interested persons in the hamlet. The meeting will assemble in a traditional spot, usually the open space near one of the hamlet wells. Everyone who attends will have considerable knowledge of the dispute in question and know and be affected by the chain of relations and disputes which lie behind it. The meeting is opened by the hamlet leader; he asks the party calling the meeting to explain the reason for doing so. Then each side states its case in a declamatory fashion, with no attempt at cross-examination or rebuttal except to dismiss the whole story of the other side. The other people attending the meeting comment on the facts, either to support or deny the statements made, and may also comment upon human nature, the stresses of life, the evil of Thakurs, the disputatious nature of women, or general morality. There is no apparent systematic method of determining the facts of the situation. Probably all the listeners are aware of the facts. When questions of fact do arise, they usually pertain to actions which took place out of the hamlet or village. Throughout the meetings the *khandan* leaders or the hamlet leader take members of the contending parties aside to talk with them and urge them to compromise. If the dispute concerns an insult or a simple land or marriage question, it might be settled by the informal hamlet meeting or a series of hamlet meetings. If the dispute is complicated or if it entails direct infringement of caste regulations which could result in the outcasting of one or more of the participants in the dispute, the participants in the informal meeting ask for a formal meeting of the hamlet with the addition of outside leaders from the other Chamar hamlets, possibly some other low caste leader noted for his ability as a mediator, the Thakurs of the disputing Chamars. And if the case entails witchcraft, some noted divines and exorcists are summoned.

The procedure of the formal hamlet meeting is very similar to the informal one with the exception that the outside leaders are called upon for advisory opinions. As they are not as directly involved, they often ask direct questions of fact.

When divines and exorcists are present, they appeal to their spirits through rituals to get information about the witchcraft charges. If Thakurs are present, they usually take the lead in questioning and suggest formal solutions. As far as I could determine, there was little question of what the "law" was in disputes. Everyone knew what was appropriate behavior in marriage and inheritance. Many Chamars could make general statements as to what were rules of behavior, and then back up their statements with cases and decisions of meetings (*pancayats*). There was no recourse to a knowledge of sacred texts, law books, or current civil or criminal law. The law which the Chamars know is customary law, often at variance with aspects of traditional Hindu law.

C   Hamlet councils

Disputes arising among members of different *khandans* in the hamlet are treated in much the same fashion as disputes within the *khandan,* with the exception that there will almost certainly be outside Chamar judges. In matters that come up for consideration before the hamlet council the question of outcasting is present from the beginning of the dispute, since disputes at this level most often entail caste regulations, such as nonfulfillment of the social and ceremonial obligation to invite a hamlet mate to a feast, irregularity in marriage, or disobeying a caste rule regarding occupational activities. Theoretically these questions could arise at the *khandan* level, but it is very rare that one *khandan* mate will charge a member of his own *khandan* with such a serious matter, and if he did, the charge would be discussed at least before the whole hamlet.

Let us look at the situation in which a hamlet mate has not invited another hamlet mate to a feast and ceremony which is given at one of the life-cycle ceremonies. The general rule is that, when a household is celebrating a life-cycle rite, all adult males from the *khandan* and at least one adult male, usually the head, from every other household in the hamlet is invited. An invitation requires attendance. If a feast is being held and one household is not invited, its members call for a hamlet meeting and ask for an explanation for the breach. If the explanation is not satisfactory, they demand that the offending household be outcaste.

When a Chamar family is outcaste, no other Chamar will allow its members to share the *hukka* (waterpipe)—symbol of caste solidarity. In extreme cases people will not allow an outcasted family to draw water from the hamlet well; they will not even give the outcasted family fire from their hearths; and ultimately, outcasting entails the inability to marry off children, since Chamar will not take daughters from or give daughters to an outcaste household.

Outcasting among the Chamars is not a permanent condition. The most severe outcasting that I know of is twelve years, the penalty for incest. Usually a family is fined a certain amount of cash and charged to give one or two feasts. If the family promises to pay the fine and give the feasts within the stipulated period, its members will not be outcasted to the fullest extent (i.e., not being able to use the hamlet well or get fire). Usually they will not be invited to feasts or allowed to use the *hukka* until they fulfill the requirements of the fine, but ordinary social intercourse continues.

D   Village and intervillage

In Senapur a full meeting of the leaders and representatives of all the Chamar hamlets is rare. There is little likelihood for personal disputes to arise among the Chamars across hamlet lines, since they do not share land and property and, since, except in work situations, they do not interact much. There are meetings, which could be termed all-village meetings, to consider general rules of behavior; for example, thirty or more years ago the Chamars decided to stop taking cow dung out to manure their Thakurs' fields, since they felt this was too degrading. It is difficult to reconstruct how this was decided, but some informants said there was a general meeting on the question.

Intervillage meetings among the Chamars are not uncommon; the main impetus is to settle disputes about marriage and divorce. Typically, the conjugal problem is a wife running off and her refusal to return to her husband's village, or a husband's refusal to support a wife. In cases of this sort, the aggrieved party will call upon his *khandan,* hamlet, or village leaders to have a meeting with his counterpart in the other village. A meeting will be held, usually in the village of the accusing party or in some neutral spot. Leaders from both groups of Chamars will assemble, plus some neutral Chamar leaders or other law caste leaders to hear the case. It is my impression that proceedings in these intervillage meetings are much more formal, with an attempt to present the evidence systematically. When a decision is reached entailing a penalty, enforcement is the responsibility of the leaders of the hamlet or village in which the penalized party dwells. The general sanction enforcing the ruling of the intervillage Chamar meeting is the threat to cut off marriage relations by the aggrieved group, and then to get other Chamar hamlets and villages with which they have relations to do the same, thereby in effect outcasting the whole village group of Chamars.

III   THE DISPUTE SETTLEMENT PROCESS AMONG THE CHAMARS

This description very much oversystematizes and simplifies the actual processes of intracaste disputes among the Chamars. The distinctions between the types of meetings (*pancayats*) are not explicitly made by the Chamars, and as can be seen from my description, one type of meeting can easily flow into another type. In general, the processes of settlement are similar in all types of meetings and might be summarized as follows:

A   Leaders and audience

The general rule is that the leaders of the units of the persons involved will act in some sense as mediators, since by social definition the position of each leader depends on his ability to function not only as a leader of one unit but to lead in the next larger unit and take a wider role and more active part in it; hence, he would endanger his role of leader in the wider circle if he were to push the claims of his immediate followers too much. In essence, I judge it is the role of the leader to bridge the gaps between the rings of the social "onion," by balancing between advocacy of the rights of his immediate followers and the demands of the wider social group. All interested parties, whether they be leaders or directly concerned with the dispute, are free to attend meetings, to comment, and to take part in the proceedings. The people attending form the "public opinion," and part of the leader's function is to sense, as well as direct, "public opinion" as it develops at the meeting.

B   Talk and time

Essentially, a dispute among the Chamars seems to get settled through talking it out. The act of talking seems to relieve some of the aggression built up in the dispute. No one is cut off, and a person can raise any issue or problem he wants. On several occasions I attended meetings in which what appeared to be completely irrelevant issues were discussed for hours. The Chamars do not expect to settle the dispute in any specified number of meetings. A meeting will last three or four hours and then be adjourned for a week; meanwhile, mediators will talk to the parties in the dispute. The meeting will be reconvened, and there will be more talk. Eventually a "compromise" will be suggested, and even though it may be more favorable to one party, as long as it can be defined as a compromise in a rhetorical sense, both parties seem to be satisfied.

C   The relevant dispute

Very often a meeting will be held ostensibly to hear one dispute, and people will then discuss and adjudicate another dispute which lies behind the antagonism and comes to the surface as a side issue. They feel no necessity of "sticking to the point." The Chamars do not lead a segmented life in which behavior or situations can be compartmentalized easily, and they see no point in trying to decide matters only on the basis of an immediate situation.

D   The personal characteristics of the disputants

The Chamars in their daily lives have clear ideas about the relative worth of their fellow Chamars. When it comes to settling a dispute, the Chamar sees no reason why he should not include his knowledge of the disputants in his evaluation of the dispute. Some men's promises are worth more than others, some are known to be quarrelsome, some are relatively rich, well-connected, or dependents of important Thakurs. Some come from honorable Chamar families, some are educated, some have traveled, some are loose morally, some are stupid, some lazy—all these personal characteristics are known, enter into the adjudicative process, and need not be made explicit.

Thus far we have described only two aspects of disputes and dispute settlement in a North Indian village: the traditional organization and position of the Thakurs in the little kingdom of the late eighteenth century; and the process of intracaste dispute settlement among the Chamars. The description dealt with the horizontal organization of the society and disputes arising in segments of this horizontal organization, but did not treat vertical organizations of the village and disputes which arise in this organization nor with the far-reaching social, economic, political, and legal changes which have affected the wider society of North India, the little kingdom, and the village.

IV   INTERCASTE DISPUTES

Central to the settlement of intercaste disputes within the village is the role of the Thakurs. When the British established their rule in the lands of the Raja of Benaras at the end of the eighteenth century, they tried to maintain the *status quo* of the dominant caste relating to other castes and to the land, by recognizing the dominant caste as *zemindar* (landlord). In Dobhi Taluka, these were the Thakurs.

Castes other than the Thakurs in Dobhi Taluka were tenants and/or servants of the Thakurs. In pre-British times the servants (Chamars, Kahars, Barais, and other low castes) were little better than slaves. James Thomason, a British civil servant in the early nineteenth century in upper India, described the relationship in the following terms:

> They the Urzal neither have nor assert in general any rights, other than the will of the Zemindar. They take what land he gives them, and pay the utmost that they can, either in money or in kind. Besides their direct contribution to his rental, they render him many personal services. If Kuhars, they carry his Palankeen, merely receiving in return food to support them during the time. Other classes bring him wood, tend his cattle, or perform numerous other similar

services for very inadequate remuneration. Under former Governments this power was no doubt recognized, and permitted. They were the predial slaves, who were beaten without mercy for misconduct, and were liable to be pursued, and brought back if they attempted to escape. Their state is now much improved. The power is now conventional. (Thomason *n.d.:* 115)

The Thakur, given his position as *zemindar* and his caste status, settled disputes which the caste meetings could not. At present the Thakurs are most often involved as mediators in disputes among low castes which involve questions of land and property, but sometimes they are involved in disputes which threaten the peace of the village, or which involve a particular Thakur's dependents and cause him to feel that the dispute is disrupting the dependent's work for the Thakur.

Usually, in a dispute in which a Thakur is taking a role, the disputants are called to his house, and he hears both sides. He may ask a low-caste leader to attend and give advice on a particular point of "law," as customary law varies from caste to caste. The Thakur has considerable power as landlord to enforce his decision. Until fairly recently Thakurs beat low-caste men, with little fear of the consequences. One respected Chamar leader described a situation in which he was beaten by his Thakur:

> I was plowing in my field when he came. My Thakur started to beat me with a *lathi* (a large bamboo club). I kept right on plowing. I told my Thakur that I did not strike him back because he was my Thakur, otherwise I would not stand to be beaten.
>
> My grandfather was *chaudhri* leader of the subcaste, my father was *chaudhri*, and I am *chaudhri*, so for three generations our word has carried weight, and I have never been insulted except by my Thakur. I was capable of taking revenge, but I thought BBS was my Thakur and therefore equal to my mother and father and he should not be insulted.

The Thakur could bring to bear the ultimate economic sanction of preventing dependent castes from cultivating the land, as theoretically, and until recently, actually, all dependent castes were tenants of the Thakurs.

In summary, one can say that the Thakurs had the economic, social, and political power to settle any dispute arising among the

castes below them. The question of a dispute between a Thakur
and a low-caste man rarely arose, because, as Thomason pointed
out, the relationship was that of master and servant. A dispute
could arise, but the only real recourse the servant had was to
withdraw his services by fleeing and to seek the protection of
some other dominant caste. There apparently was social pressure
on a Thakur to treat his servants and tenants with a certain
amount of *noblesse oblige*. This social pressure was exercised by
other Thakurs, who had a well-developed idea of the treatment
of their dependents. Before the twentieth century, the Thakurs
saw to it that their dependents were fed, clothed, and housed,
and the tenant knew that his Thakur would protect him in most
crises.

V SETTLEMENT OF DISPUTES AMONG THAKURS

Disputes among the Thakurs of the village were frequent, bitter,
and often violent, both in the nineteenth and twentieth centuries.
Older informants recounted incidents when Thakurs along with
their dependents would fight other Thakurs, often involving
bloodshed. These fights would often be over questions of land,
but more frequently would arise over insults. Some Thakur families appear to have had traditional feuding relations, sometimes
stretching over four or five generations. There were always several
Thakur families in the village who were recognized as more
powerful and important than others, and when a dispute arose,
the disputants would try to enlist the aid of these powerful families (Opler 1956). It is important to note that a tremendous
amount of time, energy, and money went into these Thakur disputes, but as divisive as they were, they were limited to the little
kingdom. The Thakur council of twelve mentioned earlier provided a court of final adjudication for disputes. The process of
settlement of disputes among the Thakurs was one of balancing
of antagonisms and mediation and compromise, and the process
described for the settling of intracaste disputes among the
Chamars is probably similar to the process of settlement of dis-

putes among the Thakurs. The most important fact is that disputes ultimately were settled on a local basis within the little kingdom. The prestige and power system was largely bounded by the little kingdom. The Thakurs and other castes within it could always unite in the face of outside threats. The little kingdom was, however, far from self-sufficient; extensive networks involving marriage, ritual activity, economic activity, and military activity extended to the outside and related the little kingdom to wider networks, but questions of law and judicial procedure were concerns which affected only the little kingdom.

VI THE CHANGING POLITICAL, LEGAL, ECONOMIC, AND SOCIAL SITUATION

Thus far I have been writing as if the village and little kingdom were unchanging, isolated units, unaffected by outside events in North India society. Obviously this was not the case. I seriously doubt if the village of Senapur was at any time stable, since in the pre-British period warfare and famine must have had considerable effect on the social structure of the village and little kingdom. The description I have given is an abstraction and to some extent a caricature; however, since the establishment of British rule in the late eighteenth century, a number of developments have markedly changed the relationships within the village. The initial effect of the establishment of British rule was a stabilization of the society by guaranteeing the position of the Thakur as *zemindar* and by eliminating internal warfare. The British strengthened the position of the dominant caste by the extension of the cash-crop economy. In the nineteenth century the new sources of income were used by the Thakurs to strengthen their traditional way of life and their traditional position vis-à-vis low castes.

Opler and Singh (1948: 1952a: 1952b) have outlined the forces that have affected Senapur from the beginning of the twentieth century to the present. The period has seen a large rise in population with the concomitant rise in pressure on land, coupled with a rise in agricultural prices that have made land a very valuable commodity. During this period, Senapur, through the building of railroads and the spread of Western-style manufactured goods, has increasingly been drawn into an all-India market and ultimately a world market. Higher standards of education and the rise of urban occupations in commerce, industry, and administration have increased opportunities for employment outside the village and have exposed the villager to a wide range of urban contacts. The establishment of British and, later, Indian administrations has greatly weakened, if not destroyed, the importance of the little kingdom as a political-judicial unit. Land reform has altered the relationships among Thakurs and their dependents, and the nationalist struggle, democratic elections, and movements for social and economic uplift of the low castes have destroyed the moral base of the relationships of super-ordination-subordination among the Thakurs and their low-caste dependents. Even this brief listing of some of the variables at work indicate the far-reaching changes taking place in Senapur and the little kingdom.

VII LEGAL CHANGES

In 1795, after twenty years of indirect rule, the full legal and administrative structure of the East India Company was extended to Benaras. The company's goal was the full and regular collection of the land revenue, and as a step toward this goal, courts were established, the judges of whom were British employees of the company. The principal disputes in these new courts were questions of ownership of land and rates of revenue and rent.

In the area of personal law (marriage, divorce, inheritance, and adoption), the district courts administered Hindu law for Hindus and Muslim law for Muslims. The courts administered criminal codes, written in the middle of the nineteenth century, which were a mixture of British and Muslim criminal law, and acts and laws passed by the various provincial legislatures and governors. This latter group includes the very important top of land law.

When the British established their courts in India, they were cognizant of substantive law, but did not think that the procedural law and the courts, as they found them in the late eighteenth century, were adequate. In fact, some of the early British administrators thought there was no court system other than that which the Mughals had imposed in North India. They ignored local indigenous adjudication procedures and modeled the process of adjudication in the courts on that of the British law courts of the period.

Almost from the establishment of British courts in India, it was apparent to the British that there were serious faults in these courts. It took years for disputes to be resolved, and there were too many appeals from lower courts. Use of forged documents and perjury in the courts became endemic (Spear 1951). It was evident that courts did not settle disputes, but were used either as a form of gambling on the part of legal speculators who were landlords or merchants and who turned to the courts to wrest property from the "rightful" owners, or as a threat in a dispute. There is apparently no quicker way of driving an opponent into bankruptcy than to embroil him in a lawsuit. Most people would go to any length to avoid going to court. It is likely that most of the cases that went into courts were fabrications to cover the real disputes (Carstairs 1912; Moon 1945; Walsh 1912). The British were constantly concerned with reforming the courts. This concern entailed, in Uttar Pradesh, the shifting of the language of the court from Persian to Hindu, Urdu, and English, imposing severe penalties for bringing false cases, reform of the police, and establishment of local *pancayats* (village courts). But the flood of cases continues, and, at least based on my experience in 1952–53 and on a brief revisit in 1958, there is no apparent abatement in this cycle of false cases and what an historian, Percival Spear, has termed the Indian peasants' "slot machine" attitude toward the courts.

It is my thesis that the present attitude of the Indian peasant was an inevitable consequence of the British decision to establish courts in India patterned on British procedural law. The way a people settles disputes is part of its social structure and value system. In attempting to introduce British procedural law into their Indian courts, the British confronted the Indians with a situation in which there was a direct clash of the values of the two societies; and the Indians in response thought only of manipulating the new situation and did not use the courts to settle disputes but only to further them.

The British thought that, by providing an honest judge and establishing firm rules of evidence and court procedure, the judge could determine the facts in the case and, with his knowledge of the law, hand down a just decision. But from the brief description of the process of adjudication of intra- and intercaste disputes which I have given above, several value conflicts are apparent.

A   Equality in the eyes of the law

Basic to British law is the idea of the equality of the individual before the law. North Indian society operates on the reverse value hypothesis: men are not born equal, and they have widely differing inherent worth. This theme or value is basic to the whole social structure and is expressed most clearly in the caste system. When Indians go into a court, they are supposed by definition to lose their outside statuses. It is not Thakurs and Chamars who are having a dispute, but a defendant and a complainant. The adversary system has developed to equalize the persons in court. To an Indian peasant this is an impossible situation to understand. The Chamar knows he is not equal to the Thakur. He may want to be equal, but he knows he is not. The Thakur cannot be convinced in any way that the Chamar is his equal, but the court acts as if the parties to the dispute were equal.

B   Status and contract

As in the nineteenth century when Sir Henry Maine wrote about India, the Indian peasant society is one still largely dominated by values surrounding the concept of status. The landlord-tenant tie is not just a contractual relationship, as it is treated in law, but rather it is a hereditary relationship having important social and ceremonial concomitants which cannot be treated as contractual relationships. Two Thakurs disputing over a piece of land are not only buyer and seller with a contractual tie, but in classificatory kinship terms are brothers or uncle and nephew. In Max Gluckman's terms, the Indian village is a multiplex society in which people are tied by a network of relationships, and some of these ties cannot be summarily cut by a decision of a court. People must continue to live and work together in the multiplex society. So decisions of the courts based on ideas of contract do not fit the value system and social structure of the Indian village.

C   *The importance of the decision*

Central to British law is the necessity of a decision, if a case comes to court. It appears that the indigenous adjudication procedure of India is geared to postponing a clear-cut decision as long as possible. The goal is to have the parties to the dispute compromise their differences in some way. If a compromise is not possible, the minimal requirement is to maintain at least the fiction of a compromise, especially in an intracaste dispute. This fiction is not possible in the court, where the situation is defined in terms of winning or losing.

D   *Settling the case and only the case*

The British legal system, as it has been adopted in India, rests on the idea that the courts will adjudicate the dispute that is presented to it. Very often, even in the caste meetings, the case which is ostensibly the crux of the dispute is only a minor expression of a long-standing antagonistic relationship between two families or groups. Often when I discussed a case with a villager, he would start out by discussing events and disputes of twenty years ago. A specific case does not stand alone, but is usually part of a string of disputes. The caste meeting can and does deal with the string of disputes, and over a period of time will try to mediate the basis of the dispute. The British court, given the nature of the adjudication process, can deal only with the specific case presented by the contending parties.

I have detailed the areas of change and conflict which brought about the situation in which law is used not for settling disputes but for furthering them, and where the courts are looked upon as a place for harassment or a place in which to gain revenge.

The Rajputs, their way of life, values, and power were dominant in the little kingdom. Everyone else was subservient to them within the little kingdom, and although the dominant Rajputs were in a position of subordination to the Mughal Government or, later, to the Raja of Benaras, these superordinate political powers did not in any way challenge the Rajputs' control in their own little kingdom. The Rajput landlords settled all disputes arising among the castes below them that were not of an intracaste nature, and through the functioning of their own Council were able to settle disputes among themselves.

British legislation regarding land revenue was the first assault, albeit unintentional, on the solidarity of the Rajputs, by making engagement for revenue with individual members of the lineage and recognizing individual interests in the land of the little kingdom, rather than assessing the *taluka* as a unit and considering the land to be held by the entire lineage—both practices in effect before British rule. As a result of the British policies, the Rajput saw that his economic position was not as tightly bound with that of the other members of the community as it had been. Although separate engagements were part of the land-revenue settlements of 1789 and 1839–1942, they do not seem to have impinged strongly on the little kingdom until the settlement of 1880–82, when in conjunction with a rapidly expanding role network and increasing urban experience, the Rajputs began to look outward for prestige and power.

Before the end of the nineteenth century, the little kingdom was an almost closed prestige system; prestige depended on the amount of land one inherited from his ancestors, the status of his family in relation to the founding ancestors, and the number of low-caste followers that he could muster. When the Rajputs began to turn to government employment, education, and business outside the little kingdom, a new source of wealth and prestige was introduced. A Thakur could now convert the money he had made as a police officer in the British administration to buying land, building a large house, marrying his daughter into a more prestigeful clan; and in a generation's time, a family could move from a lowly position into one of great importance in the village and the local area. Election to a position on the district board enabled a Thakur to use his knowledge of the government and his acquaintanceship with government officials to better his position and to help his followers in the village. Education, in addition to opening up new opportunities which could be converted to higher status within the community, also resulted in a growing familiarity with law and the courts.

In addition to new sources of prestige and power which were in opposition to the principles on which the old prestige system was built, the expanded role network made the Thakur more aware of the possibilities of manipulation in the courts and what could be done through influence and the use of questionable practices.

The Rajputs have always had a highly developed sense of their own importance, honor, and position. Their traditional occupation was warfare and they have a highly developed martial ethic. With the coming of the British, outside warfare stopped; the basis of the solidarity of the group was cut away; they no longer had to cooperate from fear of outside invasion or subjugation; and with the changes in land tenure it became advantageous for individuals to break their ties with the group. This change led to increased feuding, competition for position, and attempts to ruin fellow Thakurs. In this new scramble for prestige, the courts provided an excellent battleground in which to carry out a fight against both their caste fellows and the lower castes. A wealthy Thakur who went to court looked forward to not just one quick case, but to a series of cases, appeals, adjournments, and counter appeals, through which a poorer competitor could be ruined. Since British procedure and justice appeared capricious to the Indians, someone with a bad case was as prone to go to court as someone with a good case. The standard was not the justice of his case, but his ability to outlast his opponents. It became a mark of pride among the Thakurs to outwit an opponent through the use of the courts and law, and the prestige of a family was tied to its success as a litigant and its ability to ruin its competitors in court.

PROCEDURE AMONG THE IFUGAO

R. F. Barton

THE FAMILY IN RELATION TO PROCEDURE

THE MUTUAL DUTY of kinsfolk and relatives, each individual to every other of the same family, regardless of sex, is to aid, advise, assist, and support in all controversies and altercations with members of other groups or families. The degree of obligation of the various members of a family group to assist and back any particular individual of that group is in direct proportion: *first,* to the kinship or the relationship by marriage; *second,* to the loyalty the individual in question has himself manifested toward the family group, that is, the extent to which he discharges his obligations to that group.

The family is without any political organization whatever. It is a little democracy in which each member is measured for what he is worth, and has a voice accordingly in the family policy. It is a different body for every married individual of the whole Ifugao tribe.[1] There are a great many relationships that complicate matters. An Ifugao's family is his nation. The family is an executive

Originally published in *Ifugao Law* by R. F. Barton, University of California Publications in American Archaeology and Ethnology, Vol. 15, No. 1, pp. 1–186, February 15, 1919. The extracted portion is from pp. 92–109. Reprinted by permission of University of California Press.

[1] Thus A and B, two brothers, are members of the same family until they marry. After marriage A's family consists of his blood kin and of his relatives by marriage, and the same holds of B's family. Thus after marriage only half the individuals of the families of the two brothers are identical. The families of two cousins are identical as to one-half the component individuals before their marriage and as to one-fourth of the component individuals after their marriage.

and a judicial body. Its councils are informal, but its decisions are none the less effective. The following rules and principles apply to the family and to individuals in the matter of procedure.

Brothers of the blood can never be arrayed against each other. They may fall out and quarrel, but they can never proceed against each other. This is for the reason that their family is identical (before marriage at least), and a family cannot proceed against itself.

Cousins and brothers of the half-blood ought never to be arrayed against each other in legal procedure. In case they should be so arrayed, the mutual kin try to arrange peace. Only in the event of serious injuries may a cousin with good grace and with the approval of public opinion collect a fine from another cousin, and even then he should not demand as much as from a non-related person. In the case of minor injuries he should forego punishing his kindred. The following is an example:

> A steals some rice from his cousin B. Theft and thief become known. A takes no steps against the thief; but A's wife cannot overlook it—and the injury was an injury to her as much as to A. Her kin take the matter up. They collect half the usual indemnity for their kinswoman. A foregoes his half of the indemnity.

In cases of minor injury, procedure against more distant kin is frowned on, but sometimes occurs.

It is the duty of mutual, equally related relatives and kin to try to arrange peace between opposing kin or relatives.

In the event of procedure on the part of one kinsman against another, those who are related to both take sides with him to whom they are more closely related. Besides blood relationship, there is marriage relationship oftentimes to make it a very complex and difficult problem for a man to decide to which opponent his obligation binds him. This is most frequently the case among the remoter kin. A man who finds himself in such a position, and who knows that on whichever side he may array himself he will be severely criticized by the other, becomes a strong advocate of compromise and peaceful settlement.

In case a kinsman to whom one owes loyalty in an altercation is in the wrong and has a poor case, one may secretly advise him to compromise; one must never openly advise such a measure. One may secretly refuse him assistance and backing—one must never oppose him.

One owes no obligation in the matter of procedure to another merely because he is a covillager or inhabitant of the same district.

The obligation to aid and assist kinsmen beyond the third or fourth degree is problematic, and a question into which elements of personal interest enter to a great extent. One of the greatest sources of the power of the principal *kadangyang* lies in their ability to command the aid of their remote kin on account of their prestige and wealth and ability to dispense aid and favor.

There is also a class, small in number, corresponding somewhat to the "clients" of the chiefs of the ancient Gauls. This body is composed of servants who have grown up in the service and household of a master, and who have been well treated, and in times of need sustained and furnished with the things needful to Ifugao welfare; another division consists of those who habitually borrow or habitually rent from one who stands in the nature of an overlord to them. This class is most numerous in districts where most of the lands are in the hands of a few men. The duty of the clients to their lord and of their lord to them seems to be about the same as those duties have always been in a feudal society; that is to say, the duty of rendering mutual aid and assistance.

The first step in any legal procedure is to consult with one's kin and relatives. In initiating steps to assess a fine or collect an indemnity, the next step is the selection of a *monkalun*.

The monkalun or go-between

The office of the *monkalun* is the most important one to be found in Ifugao society. The *monkalun* is a whole court, completely equipped, in embryo. He is judge, prosecuting and defending counsel, and the court record.[2] His duty and his interest are for a

---

[2] The word *monkalun* comes from the root *kalun,* meaning *advise.* The Ifu-

peaceful settlement. He receives a fee, called *lukba* or *liwa.* To the end of peaceful settlement he exhausts every art of Ifugao diplomacy. He wheedles, coaxes, flatters, threatens, drives, scolds, insinuates. He beats down the demands of the plaintiffs or prosecution, and bolsters up the proposals of the defendants until a point be reached at which the two parties may compromise. If the culprit or accused be not disposed to listen to reason and runs away or "shows fight" when approached, the *monkalun* waits till the former ascends into his house, follows him, and, *war-knife in hand,* sits in front of him and compels him to listen.

The *monkalun* should not be closely related to either party in a controversy. He may be a distant relative of either one of them. The *monkalun* has no authority. All that he can do is to act as a peacemaking go-between. His only power is in his art of persuasion, his tact and his skillful playing on human emotions and motives. Were he closely related to the plaintiff, he would have no influence with the defendant, and *mutatis mutandis,* the opposite would be true.

Ultimately in any state the last appeal is to a death-dealing weapon. For example, in our own society a man owes a debt which he does not pay. Action is brought to sell his property to pay the debt. If he resists, he is in danger of death at the hands of an agent of the law. Much more is he in danger if he resists punishment for crime. The same is true in the Ifugao society. The lance is back of every demand of importance, and sometimes it seems hungry.

An Ifugao's pride as well as his self-interest—one might almost say his self-preservation—demands that he shall collect debts that are owed him, and that he shall punish injuries or crimes against himself. Did he not do so he would become the prey of his fellows. No one would respect him. Let there be but one debt owed him which he makes no effort to collect; let there be but one insult

---

gao word has the double sense, too, of our word *advise,* as used in the following sentences, "I have the honor to advise you of your appointment" and "I advise you not to do that."

offered him that goes unpunished, and in the drunken babbling attendant on every feast or social occasion, he will hear himself accused of cowardice and called a woman.

On the other hand, self-interest and self-respect demand that the accused shall not accept punishment too tamely or with undue haste, and that he shall not pay an exorbitant fine. If he can manage to beat the demands of the complainant down below those usually met in like cases, he even gains in prestige. But the *monkalun* never lets him forget that the lance has been scoured and sharpened for him, and that he walks and lives in daily danger of it.

The accuser is usually not overanxious to kill the accused. Should he do so, the probabilities are that the kin of the accused would avenge the death, in which case he, the slayer, would be also slain. The kin of each party are anxious for a peaceable settlement, if such can be honorably brought about. They have feuds a-plenty on their hands already. Neighbors and covillagers do not want to see their neighborhood torn by internal dissension and thus weakened as to the conduct of warfare against enemies. All these forces make for a peaceful settlement.

It is the part of the accused to dally with danger for a time, however, and at last to accede to the best terms he can get, if they be within reason.

Testimony

Litigants do not confront each other. From the time at which a controversy is formally entered into, the principals and their kin are on a basis of theoretical—perhaps I ought to say religious—enmity. A great number of taboos keep them apart. Diplomatic relations between the two parties have been broken off and all business pertaining to the case is transacted through the third party, the *monkalun*. He hears the testimony that each side brings forward to support its contention. Through him each controversant is confronted with the testimony of the other. It is greatly to the interest of the *monkalun* to arrange a peaceful settlement, not only because he usually receives a somewhat larger fee in

such case, but because the peaceful settlement of cases in which
he is mediator builds up a reputation for him, so that he is frequently called and so can earn many fees. To the end of arranging
this peaceful settlement, the *monkalun* reports to each party to
the controversy the strong points of the testimony in favor of the
other party, and oftentimes neglects the weaknesses.

There are no oaths or formalities in the giving of testimony.

Ordeals

In criminal cases in which the accused persistently denies his guilt,
and sometimes in case of disputes over property the ownership
of which is doubtful, and in cases of disputes over the division line
between fields, ordeals or trials are resorted to. The challenge to
an ordeal may come from either the accuser or the accused. Refusal to accept a challenge means a loss of the case, and the challenger proceeds as if he had won the case.

If the accused comes unscathed from the ordeal, he has the
right to collect from his accuser the fine for false accusation.

If two people mutually accuse each other, *panuyu,* they are
both tried by ordeal. If both be scathed, they are mutually responsible for the indemnity to the injured person. If only one be
scathed, he is responsible for the indemnity to the injured person
and for a payment of the fine for false accusation to the one
whom he accused.[3]

THE HOT WATER ORDEAL   A pot, a foot or more in depth, is filled

---

[3] When a crime such as theft has been committed, and it cannot be determined from any evidence at hand who was the culprit, the injured person
frequently resorts to the *hapud.* One form of this ceremony consists in placing an egg or areca nut on the edge of a knife or the bevel of a spear and
repeating the prayers necessary to make the egg or areca nut balance and
stand on end at the mention of the guilty person. Another form consists in
spanning an *agba* stick. At the mention of the guilty person the stick grows
longer, as revealed by its length in relation to the span of the priest. These
sticks are kept for generations. Many of them are over a hundred years old.
These ceremonies are not of virtue as evidence and are entirely without the
pale of Ifugao procedure. They are of value only to the injured person in
assisting him to determine who has committed the crime.

with water and heated to a furious boiling. A pebble is dropped
into it. The accused must reach his hand into the water without
undue haste, extract the pebble, and then replace it. Undue haste
is interpreted as a confession of guilt. This ordeal is used in certain
sections of Ifugao, while in others the hot bolo test is used. It is
interesting to note that neither of them is efficacious in determining accusations of adultery. This is for the reason that the gods of
animal fertility and growth do not permit an accused to receive
an injury for that act which is so eminently useful in their particular sphere of activity. Thus, Ifugao religion looks with the greatest disfavor upon things which tend to restrict population, just as
our law frowns upon statutes in restriction of marriage.

THE HOT BOLO ORDEAL In this, if two persons mutually accuse
each other, their hands are placed side by side. The *monkalun*
lowers a hot knife on their hands. The knife burns the guilty person much more seriously than the guiltless one. If only one person
be put to the test, it is said that the knife bends away from the
hands of an innocent person. The *monkalun,* with all his might,
it is said, cannot put the knife down on the hand: the gods of war
and justice will not permit it. But if the person be guilty, the knife
grips the hand in its eagerness. If the accused show fear and try
to withdraw, the kin of the accuser may catch him and burn him
well. I know a man whose fingers were burned off in this way, the
thumb adhering to and coalescing with the palm.

THE ALAO OR DUEL Eggs, *runo* stalks, or spears are used in trials,
the accused facing each other and, at the word of the *monkalun,*
hurling their missiles. The duel is not without its dangers. Even
though eggs or *runos* be used, the one struck is likely to return a
stone; and from throwing stones to throwing spears is an easy
step. The two parties of kin are likely to take a hand. How much
more likely are they to take a hand and avenge their kinsman if
spears be the missiles and he be wounded!

The duel is used in cases of adultery, sorcery, and in some disputes over ricefields, everywhere in Ifugao. In adultery cases, only
eggs are used in the duel.

TRIAL BY BULTONG OR WRESTLING This ordeal is used throughout

Ifugao, preëminently to settle cases of disputed ricefield boundaries.

The Ifugao clearly recognizes that the processes of nature—landslides, the erosion of rainfall in wet weather, and caking and crumbling in dry weather—tend to wear away a terrace not maintained by a stone wall. A terrace maintained by a stone wall is a rarity in the Kiangan district. Should the boundary not be well marked, a dispute is nearly sure to result sooner or later. These disputes are usually settled by wrestling matches. The wrestling matches are usually friendly. The Ifugao believes that the ancestral spirits of the controversants know which party is in the right, that they know just where the true boundary is, and that they see to it that he who is right shall win, provided always that they be invoked with the proper sacrifices; and that they "hold up" even the weaker of the wrestlers, and cause him to win, provided his cause be just. Notwithstanding this belief, the people are sufficiently practical to demand that the wrestlers be approximately evenly matched. The owners of the adjacent fields may themselves wrestle, or they may choose champions to represent them. Between kinsmen these matches are presumably friendly; and only sacrifices of dried meat are offered the ancestral spirits. But between those not related, there is often a great deal of unfriendly feeling. In this latter case numerous chickens and two or three pigs are sacrificed, and ceremonies like those against enemies are performed.

On the appointed day the two parties meet at the disputed boundary and occupy opposite ends of the disputed land. A party of mutual kin follows along and occupies a position midway between the adversaries. With each party is one of the family priests. Taking betels and dried meat (presuming the contest to be a friendly one) from a headbasket, the priest prays very much as follows: "Come, Grandfather Eagle, Grandfather Red Ant, Grandfather Strong Wind, Grandfather Pangalina; come, Grandmother Cicada, Grandmother Made Happy, Grandmother Ortagon; come, Grandfather Gold, etc. [throughout a list of perhaps a hundred ancestors]. Here are betels and meat; they are trying to take our field away from us. And was it here, Grandmother Grasshopper, that the boundary of the field was? No, you know that it was a double arm's length to the right. Hold us up, you ancestors, in order that *we* may be the wearers of gold neck ornaments; in order that *we* may be the ones who give expensive feasts. Exhort [here the priest names over the gods of war and justice] to hold us up. Was it here, Grandfather Brave, that the boundary was when you bought the field? Do not let them take our land away from us, for we are to be pitied. We are sorely tried!"

After the prayers of the priests, each champion is led by one of his kinsmen to the place where the first wrestling is to occur. This leading is very ceremoniously done, and suggests the heralding of the champions in feudal days. The dike of the upper terrace has been cleaned off at intervals of fifteen to twenty-five feet in order that the owner of the upper field may have no advantage. The champions frequently work themselves down half-thigh deep in ricefield mud, water, and slime. Catching fair and even holds, they begin to wrestle, encouraged each by the shouts and cries of his kinsmen and by the calling of the old men and old women on the spirits of the ancestors. Each wrestler tries to push his opponent into the territory that that opponent is defending and to down him there. If A throws B in B's field, ten feet from the line on which they wrestle, A wins ten feet of the ricefield at that point. Finally, there is a fall that more than likely capsizes one or both of them in the black mud. One point in the boundary is determined. Frequently the lower terrace is eight or ten feet lower than the upper one, but there are no injuries for the reason that the mud is at least two feet deep and is a soft place in which to fall.

At every fifteen or twenty feet along the disputed boundary there is another wrestling match. Sometimes the champions are changed. The new boundary runs through every point at which there has been a fall.

THE UMPIRE AND THE DECISION   The *monkalun* is the umpire in trials by ordeal. He interprets undue haste or a faulty performance as a confession of guilt. On the day following the trial by fire or hot water he goes to the house of the accused and examines the hand and forearm. If he finds white inflamed blisters, he pronounces him guilty. In the case of a duel, he pronounces the one struck by the missile guilty. The Ifugaos believe that the gods of war and justice turn missiles aside from the innocent in these duels. For the umpire to be manifestly unfair, would be for him seriously to imperil his own life.

As a matter of fact, a person whose skin is rough, dry, and horny has a great advantage in these ordeals. Since sword climbing and the walking on hot stones and live coals have occurred in other parts of the world, it would seem that a question might be raised whether *state of mind,* or other factors as yet unexplained, may not enter these affairs.

Execution of justice

RETALIATION   In the case of lives lost in feuds, sorcery, murders, and head-hunting, capital punishment inevitably follows, provided the kin of the slain be sufficiently daring to execute it.

Capital punishment is the rule, and is almost invariably inflicted in cases of the refusal to pay proper fines, for which demand has been made in correct form, and after a reasonable length of time has been given in which to raise the sum demanded, in punishment of adultery, manslaughter, the putting of another in the position of an accomplice in case of murder or death in feud, or for wounds, provided the culprit be not a kinsman or person closely related by marriage. Rarely would there be much trifling in the infliction of this penalty. Seizure of something of sufficient value to cover the fine assessed might sometimes be made, except in the cases of adultery and manslaughter. To practice seizure in the case of adultery—except when a kinsman were the offender —would have the aspect of anxiety to profit by the pollution of the wife's body and might give rise to suspicion of conspiracy on the part of husband and wife to bring about the crime in order to profit financially. In the same way, a self-respecting family would disdain to accept payment for the life of a kinsman except as a matter of forbearance and mercy to the taker thereof.

The crime of arson undoubtedly justifies the death penalty; but it is so rare a crime that it is impossible to say what is the usual Ifugao practice in punishing it.

The nonpayment of a debt when there is the ability to pay it, and after many and repeated demands have been made in the proper manner for it, justifies the infliction of the death penalty.

Capital punishment is administered by the injured person and his kin. In all cases it is fraught with the greatest danger to the inflicters. Usually it is inflicted from ambush, although it may be a sudden slaying in the heat of passion. The culprit is never notified that he has been sentenced to death. The withdrawal of a go-between from a serious case is, however, a pretty good warning. It has about the same significance as the withdrawal of an embassy in an international complication.

The infliction of a death penalty has been the starting point of many an interminable feud between families. For this reason the injured person exhausts every effort to effect a punishment in some other way if any other punishment be consistent with his dignity and respectability.

SEIZURE OF CHATTELS   If a kinsman of remoter kinship than that existing between brothers commits a crime punishable by death, except sorcery or murder, and obstinately refuses to pay the fine assessed, seizure of his property or part of it is made.

Seizures are made from unrelated persons to cover fines due in punishment of theft, malicious killing of animals, arson, and the minor crimes, also to secure payment of a debt.

The following is a list of the things usually seized: gongs, rice-wine jars, carabaos, gold beads, ricefields, children, wives.

A seizure may be made by fraud or deceit, or it may be made in the absence of the owner of his household, or it may be made by superior force. Considering only the manner of the seizure, there is but one law to be followed: the seizure must be made in such a manner as to leave no doubt as to the identity of him who seizes. Thus if B persistently refuses to pay a fine owed to A, A may go to B's house when there is nobody at home and may run away with a gong. If he leaves his bolo, his scabbard, his blanket, or some other personal effect in the house as a sort of a visiting card, his seizure is legal. Or A may go to B's house and, pretending friendship, borrow the gong, representing that he wants to play it at a feast and, having secured possession of it, refuse to return it till the fine be paid. Or suppose that an agent of B's is bringing a carabao up from Nueva Vizcaya, and that the agent has to travel through A's village. A and his friends stop the agent and take the carabao away from him, telling him to inform B that the carabao will be delivered to him when the fine is paid.

There is a second kind of seizure, a seizure of the property of some relative or kinsman of the culprit. The property of a wealthy kinsman may be seized to cover a fine due from a poor kinsman who has no property. This kind of seizure is more likely to lead to a lance throwing than a seizure from the culprit himself. The danger of such an ending increases with the remoteness of the kinship between the culprit and the person from whom the seizure is made.

A third kind of seizure is practiced against neighbors of delinquents who live in another district. Suppose a man, B, in one of the districts to the west of Kiangan to have gone to Nueva Vizcaya (east of Kiangan) and there to have purchased a carabao. He owes no debts, nor have any fines been levied against him. He returns through Kiangan, however, and his carabao is seized by A, a Kianganite. B is informed that C, a resident of the same district as he, stole a pig a year or two ago from A. The evidence against C is placed before him in the minutest details. He is given thirty pesos as *patang* (interest in advance) and told to collect from C the payment proper to the case, and in addition the thirty pesos advanced as *patang*. When he makes these collections, and delivers them to A, he gets back his carabao. If C is innocent of the crime charged, he may kill A for this, or he may do so even if guilty. More likely he kidnaps A's wife or child and sells them for a ransom sufficiently great to repay B, and leave a substantial surplus for himself. A may or may not retaliate with the lance.

In quarrels between *kadangyang* (for their dignity is very dear to them) and between persons of different districts or contrary parties, it is more frequently than not the case that the thing seized is not returned. Powerful individuals in a district are rather glad to have a seizure made of their property, since they can nearly always manage to come out winner in the finish. Thus in the case above, B, if a powerful individual, probably collects two or even three carabaos or their equivalent value from C, and besides he receives thirty pesos *patang.* It would seem that the obligation rests on every Ifugao—notwithstanding there is no political government—so to conduct himself as not to involve his neighbors in trouble with individuals of inimical or semi-inimical districts; and that should he so involve them, he is liable to whatever punishment circumstance metes out to him.

In the case of altercations between individuals of different districts, seizure of animals was generally practiced by persons of those districts through which the road led to the region from which the animals were imported. Of all districts, Kiangan was most advantageously situated in respect to this matter; since, for the greater part of Ifugao-land, the road to Nueva Vizcaya (whence most of the animals imported into Ifugao came) led through it.

SEIZURE OF RICEFIELDS   The seizure of ricefields is practicable only in case the fields are near the village of him who seizes them. For if located in a distant district, the working of the field would be extremely hazardous, and its protection and continuous holding impossible.

Fields may properly be seized for collection of debt or for refusal to pay fines or indemnities. Portions of fields are seized sometimes in disputes as to ownership or boundaries.

Disputes over ownership and boundary come to a head during spading time. One party begins to spade for the next year's crop the land claimed by the other. The other party sticks up *runos,* tied "ethics lock" fashion (*alpud*), along the line which he claims to be the true boundary. The first party then pulls up these *runos,* and sticks down others along the line claimed by it as the true boundary. The issue is joined. The defendant has made his "rejoinder." A *monkalun* is now selected by the plaintiff party, and tries to arrange—and in case of disputed boundaries nearly always does arrange—a means of peaceful settlement, either by compromise or through trial by wrestling. Sometimes the ownership of a field itself is in question. Usually the question is one of inheritance; although there are a number of other causes that may give rise to dispute.[4] Ownership is usually peaceably settled by means of a wrestling match.

We come now to those cases in which a field is seized for debt as payment of a fine or indemnity. The plaintiff or prosecutor seizes the field at spading time by planting *runo* stalks, *alpud,* in it. The defendant probably pulls up these stalks and throws them away.[5] An attempt may be made by mutual friends and relatives to secure a peaceful settlement of the trouble. A ricefield is a thing so dear to the Ifugao, and so necessary and useful to him, that such attempts are extremely likely, however, to come to naught.

If the matter be not arranged otherwise, the seizer of the field sends a body of men to spade it, holding in reserve an armed force of kinsmen and relatives to protect and maintain the spaders if they be attacked. The other party emerges with an armed force to drive the spaders away. The two parties meet. If one be greatly superior in strength, the other usually retires and surrenders the field. If they be fairly evenly matched, a battle is likely to ensue. If the first wound be a slight one, the party receiving it is likely to withdraw; but if it be serious, or if one of their number be killed, they fight to avenge him. Sometimes four or five men are killed in one of these frays.

But in the meantime, and often before actual fighting begins, a

---

[4] The very day that I wrote this, the ownership of a field was settled by a wrestling match. An Ifugao some time before pawned a field to a Christianized Ifugao. This worthy had the temerity to sell the field. Although the pawner would have surely been sustained in his right had he appealed to the lieutenant-governor, nevertheless, he was so confident, being in the right, that he would not lose, that he consented to settle the ownership by a wrestling match. He won. The Christianized Ifugao may possibly now have more faith in the tenet of his former religion that the ancestral spirits uphold him who is in the right.

[5] He may gratuitously add an insult by implanting a few of them in a pile of fecal matter.

body of mutual relatives, friends, and neighbors emerges and tries to make peace and secure an amicable settlement.

ENFORCED HOSPITALITY   Sometimes a creditor and a numerous and powerful following of kinsmen descend upon a debtor's house as unwelcome guests, consume his stores of food, and force his hospitality until appeased by the payment of the debt.

This form of collection can only be used in the case of debts, for in all other controversies, taboos forbid the eating of the adversary's food, drinking his water, chewing his betels, etc. Even in the case of debt, if a go-between has been sent to the debtor, this means may not be used. It can only be used in a case where "diplomatic relations" have not been ruptured.

KIDNAPPING OR SEIZURE OF PERSONS   Interior districts had no opportunity to seize animals from those districts nearer than they to the region whence animals were imported. Of necessity, then, they kidnapped and sold or held for ransom women and children from those districts. The following instances actually occurred in times past. They are excellent and veritable illustrations of this phase of Ifugao administration of justice:

Bahni of Tupplak spoke scornfully of Bumidang of Palao. Some time subsequently he sent a man to buy carabaos in Nueva Vizcaya. The man bought two, and returned on the homeward journey, travelling through Palao. Bumidang took one of the carabaos away from him there, and with his kin, killed it and ate it. Bahni with his kin shortly afterward went to the house of Dulauwan of Bangauwan, a neighboring village, and stole away with Dulauwan's carabao. Dulauwan followed after them, hotfoot, and was given as *patang* three pigs, and told to collect his carabao from Bumidang. Dulauwan gathered together a great host of kinsmen and neighbors, descended on Bumidang's house, and camped there demanding three carabaos. To show that they meant to get them, they helped themselves to rice needed for their daily food from Bumidang's granary. Bumidang was unable to get together a sufficient force to frighten away his guests, and accordingly he paid the three carabaos.

Ginnid of Umbul presented a demand to Guade for the payment of a long-outstanding debt. Guade denied that the debt was owed. Ginnid seized Guade's field. Each party led a force of kinsmen to the field. There they fought with spears and shields. The first man wounded was Tului of Pindungan, a kinsman of Guade. He received a slight wound. Guade's party then withdrew. Guade paid the debt and got his field back.

Gumangan of Ambabag when a youth, sent an advocate to ask for the hand of the daughter of M of Umbul. He was accepted. But he changed his mind about the girl, and went to Baininan, where he engaged himself to a girl of that village without assuaging the mental agony of his jilted fiancée by paying the *hudhud* indemnity. M seized a carabao belonging to Gumangan. Gumangan gathered together his kin and went to Umbul—only a quarter of a mile distant—to prevent the slaughter of his animal. But M's party was so much more powerful that Gumangan's kin ran away. M's party then killed and ate the carabao.

Gumangan married in Baininan, and bearing in mind his former humiliation, decided to do something that would restore his prestige and at the same time assure him a sufficiently large body of followers to make him strong to demand and to resist demands. He consequently gave a great *uyauwe* feast at which the unheard of number of six carabaos was slaughtered, to say nothing of innumerable pigs. And later, he gave the *hagabi* feast—an even more expensive operation.

Dumalilon of Tupplak borrowed a carabao of Gumangan. Five years elapsed, yet he made no move to repay the debt, notwithstanding repeated demands of Gumangan. Gumangan seized Dumalilon's field, which had already been spaded, and threw his seedbed away. Both men led armed parties to the field, but this time Gumangan was careful to have a sufficient number of backers on hand. Dumalilon's party took to flight.

In Burnai, a fight occurred over the seizure of a ricefield that resulted in the killing of four men.

Kodamon of Pindungan and Katiling of Ambabag[6] had a dispute over the boundary of a field. There were *paghok* to mark the boundary, but Kodamon contended that all memory of the planting of the *paghok* was absent, and that they were, consequently, without significance in the matter of dispute. They wrestled, and Kodamon lost a little ground, but Katiling tried to take more than was due him according to the verdict of the wrestling matches. Katiling sent men to spade the disputed territory, and led an armed force out to support them. Kodamon led an armed force to the field. At the same time and at a safe distance, the mutual kin of the two parties and a goodly number of neighbors gathered. Kodamon was armed with a Remington rifle whose trigger was broken; Dulinayan, a kins-

---

[6] The villages of Pindungan and Ambabag are less than a mile distant from each other.

man of Katiling, with a revolver for which he had no ammunition. The other members of each force however were substantially, if less spectacularly, armed with spears which they well knew how to use. Women rushed in between the two parties, and catching the warriors by the waist tried to lead them away. One can well believe that the air was riven by curses, threats, accusations, upbraidings, imprecations, invocations. The male neutral kin shouted from their safe distance that if Kodamon killed Katiling, they would kill Kodamon (as a vengeance for the death of their kinsman) while if Katiling killed Kodamon, they would avenge their kinsman's death by killing Katiling. "What kind of a way is this for covillagers to settle a dispute," they shouted. "Go back home and beget some children, and marry them to each other, giving them the two fields, and then it will make no difference where the division line is!" There was an exchange of spears in which Buaya, a kinsman of Kodamon's, was wounded slightly. The matter was then left in abeyance with the understanding that as soon as possible, the two families be united by a marriage, and the two fields given the married couple.

It happened, however, that on account of the sexes of the unmarried children of the families, a union between them was impossible. Accordingly, Kodamon gave his field to his son Dulnuan, and Katiling traded his field to Pingkihan, his brother. Both of these young men had pregnant wives. Pingkihan's wife gave birth first, the child being a girl. Shortly afterward, Dulnuan's wife gave birth. I met Dulnuan, and not knowing of the event, and noticing that he seemed downcast, asked him why he was so sad. "My wife has given birth to a *girl* baby," he said. The quarrel over the boundary is as yet unsettled.

Kuyapi of Nagakaran, before the Spanish occupation, sent a slave child to Guminigin of Baay, to be sold in Baliwan (Nueva Vizcaya), stipulating that the child must bring at least five carabaos. Guminigin sold the child for seven carabaos, delivering five to Kuyapi, and kept two.

The Spaniards came. They were exceedingly partial to the people of Kiangan district in which the village of Baay is located. They paid little or no attention to complaints of people of other districts against people of Kiangan district. Many debts owed by Kiangan people were unpaid, for the Kianganites took advantage of the protection given them by the Spaniards. And yet the Nagakaranites and Kianganites were very closely united by marriage and by blood. Indeed Kuyapi and Guminigin were second or third cousins.

Owing to the difficulty the Nagakaran people had in collecting debts owed them by the Kianganites, they conceived for the latter and for the Spaniards a most violent hatred, and began to make reprisals. The Spaniards punished these reprisals by making an expe-

dition to Nagakaran in which they came off second best.[7] They sent
another and stronger expedition, which killed a number of people
and which burned all the houses in the district. To this day the
Nagakaran people have not been able to rebuild their houses—the
large trees having long since been cut from nearby forests—and live
in wretched shacks built on the ground. They blame the Kiangan
people, saying that the latter invited the Spaniards into Ifugao.

Kuyapi claimed that the terms on which he sent the slave to
Guminigin were that Guminigin was to receive only one carabao for
having effected a sale, and that all the rest were to be delivered to
him, and that there was consequently a carabao still due him. It
seems likely that the claim was false, and that it was advanced merely
as an excuse for making a reprisal.

Pagadut, the son of Guminigin, to whom demand was presented
for the payment of the carabao claimed to be yet due, refused to
pay this debt. The Nagakaran people made an expedition into
Kiangan district (about two miles distant) and captured Ormaya,
the daughter of Pagadut, a very comely girl of sixteen or seventeen.
In order to make her walk, and in order that she should not continually offer resistance, they took her skirt off so that she would
have to cover her shame with her hands and would also hurry to
arrive at the journey's end.[8] But the Baay people managed to cut
off Lubbut the son of Kuyapi, and imprison him. They took him
to a granary in Baay, intending to keep him as a hostage for the
return of Ormaya. But word was carried to the ears of the Spanish
commandante of this capture. He had Lubbut brought before him.
He struck Lubbut, tied although he was, twice in the face, and
would have continued, had not Alangwauwi the husband of
Ormaya seized and held his arm and beseeched him not to use
Lubbut harshly. The *commandante* promised not to take his life.
But a soldier called attention to the fact that a gun had been captured with Lubbut, which gun, it was claimed, was that of a Spanish
corporal whom the Nagakaran people had killed. Alangwauwi and
his companions started back to their homes in Baay. But on the
road, they saw, across the valley, Lubbut with his back turned to a
firing squad, saw a puff of white smoke, and saw Lubbut fall into
a ricefield. Alangwauwi says he burst into tears, for he realized that
this meant serious trouble for him and his relatives, and placed
Ormaya's life in the greatest peril.

When the Nagakaranites heard of Lubbut's death, they at first

---

[7] The Nagakaran people claim that only five out of forty of the first expedition returned.

[8] This was the usual method of treating kidnapped persons. It is interesting to
note an almost parallel practice on the part of the Allies in the present war
[World War I]. When prisoners are taken, the buttons are cut off their clothing, in order to keep their hands engaged during the march to the rear.

blamed the people of Baay for it. Inasmuch as it is against the ethics of people of the Kiangan-Nagakaran-Maggok area to kill women, or at least to kill any but Silipan women, they considered walling Ormaya up in a sepulchre and leaving her to die for want of food and drink. The women relatives of Lubbut wanted very much to kill Ormaya, and pointed out that while it would not be permissible for the men to kill her, there would be no disgrace in their doing so. But Kuyapi would have none of it. He himself guarded his prisoner two or three nights to see that her life was not taken.

Soon a *monkalun* was sent to ascertain the true details of Lubbut's death. His report exonerated the Baay people. The Nagakaran people held Ormaya's ransom considerably higher, however, because of that death. They received five carabaos, twenty pigs, two gold beads, and a great number of spears and bolos, and death blankets. It was five months before the Baay people could raise the amount of this ransom. During this time, Ormaya was well treated—for was she not a kinswoman?—but she was carefully guarded.

The paowa or truce

The word *paowa* means literally prohibition. As most commonly used, it denotes a period of truce imposed by the *monkalun* in cases that cannot be peaceably arranged. It is a period that gives both sides to a controversy a chance to cool off. It avoids that rash and ill-considered action that would be likely to follow the breaking off of diplomatic relations between the two parties.

I say the *paowa* serves these purposes. However, it is imposed by the *monkalun* in order to allow him to withdraw with dignity from the case, and without loss of reputation. A lance throwing or a seizure made while he is acting as *monkalun* or occurring soon after he has severed his connection with the case is an insult to him. People say to him: *Dinalan-da tolban-mo,* "they went over your head." Such an occurrence is exceedingly hurtful to his reputation. People will not employ him as *monkalun* for the reason that his cases do not end in peaceable settlements. He thus loses many fat fees.

Assuming that the Ifugao's culture would some day, if left alone, develop courts somewhat after the fashion of the courts of civilized nations, have we not here the embryo of "contempt of court"?

The period usually set by the *monkalun,* as truce, is fourteen days. During this time, should one of the parties to the controversy commit any act hostile to the other, the *monkalun* must avenge or punish it. At the conclusion of this period of truce, the two parties may fight out the dispute to suit themselves, kidnapping, seizing property, or hurling lances, without injuring the dignity of the *monkalun;* or the aggressive party may employ another *monkalun. . . .*

Termination of controversies: peacemaking

The word *hidit* has three senses: It refers to a class of deities, the offspring of one of the principal deities of war; it refers to sacrifices to these deities; it refers to peacemaking. Deities, sacrifice, and peace may seem widely distinct, but a glance into the Ifugao's religion will show the connection.

The *hidit* (deities) desire peace: but the peace must be made in the proper manner, and accompanied by sacrifice to themselves. The *hidit* have established the taboo that those who are involved in a controversy or enmity must not chew betels with an adversary, nor be in the same house or gathering or feast with him, nor drink with him, nor receive gifts or hospitality from him. The penalty for breaking this taboo is the affliction by the *hidit* with diseases of the lungs, throat, voice; the condition known as "big belly," *leukemia,* short wind, swelling of the feet, dropsy, etc. This may be said to be the punishment for making peace without ceremonies. But sometimes the *hidit* punish the prolongation of a feud, enmity, or controversy, by afflicting one or both of the parties as set forth above. Those who are involved in long enmities sacrifice continually to the *hidit* in order to offstand such affliction.

The *hidit* or peacemaking ceremony is performed in the following cases:

(*a*) At the termination of the funeral of a married person. It is performed between the kin of the dead spouse and between those of the living spouse.

(*b*) Between adversaries in case of adultery, rape of married woman, sorcery, murder, manslaughter, malicious killing of animals, false accusation, disputes over ricefields, theft (sometimes), or other serious controversy, *provided* the controversy terminate peaceably.

(c) At the peaceful termination of all ordeals and trials.

(d) Between the kin of a dead spouse and the widow or widower on occasion of remarriage of the latter.

(e) Between parties to a controversy ending in payment of the *tokom* fine.

(f) At the termination of a feud, between the families involved in the feud. A feud was rarely—my belief is that it was never—terminated except by a marriage or on request of one of the members of the family afflicted by the *hidit* deities. In the latter case, peace might or might not be purchased. At any rate, the family suing for peace furnished the animals for sacrifice.

In most parts—I believe all—of Ifugao, peace was never made between *districts* or *villages*. Peace was always made between *families;* but peace between the principal families of two villages or districts was sometimes *in effect* a peace between the districts or villages involved—I say *sometimes* because such a peace was uncertain and undependable.

When peace was made between families of different districts, or between families of the same district in cases of serious controversy, two men were chosen, one by each party to the peace, and with appropriate prayers and ceremonies, were given good spears. It was understood always that these spears were for the purpose of killing the first one of either party who reopened the feud, war, or controversy. After this ceremony, other spears were broken and tied together as a symbol of the breaking and tying up of all enmity; as a symbol, too, that spears were no longer needed.

LAW-WAYS OF THE COMANCHE INDIANS

E. Adamson Hoebel

THE COMANCHES in the nineteenth century roved the entire
southern plains as hunters following the buffalo and as warriors whose raiding parties reached down through the pueblo
country deep into Mexico. But the place the Comanche called
his was the territory extending from the Wichita Mountains across
the plains and streams to the Red River in Texas. There was no
strictly defined tribal territory, however; some Comanche camps
could be found scattered among the Kiowa villages on the north
side of the Wichitas.

The languages of the Comanche and northern Shoshone are
mutually intelligible, the differences being found in slight phonetic
shifts, not in grammatical morphology.

Shoshone and Comanche legends retain the tradition of the
separation.

The culture of the Comanche tribe in the third quarter of the
nineteenth century—the period from which the materials of this
study derive—was a growth developing from the Shoshonean base
under the impact of new influences met with on the Plains and in
the Southwest.

First among these influences were war and the horse. Aggression from the northeast and the lure of trade and loot in the southwest drew the Comanches to the Spanish frontier, where they be-

Extracted from E. Adamson Hoebel, *The Political Organization and Law-
Ways of the Comanche Indians*. Memoirs of The American Anthropological
Association, No. 54, 1940. The extracted material is from pp. 9–12, 17, 21–
24, 35, 45–48, 50–55, 59–65, 96–97, 99–100. Reprinted by permission of the
author and of The American Anthropological Association.

came one of the earliest tribes to acquire horses. By adjusting itself to a horse and buffalo economy, Comanche society attained a mobility and plenitude unknown to the northern Shoshones. Fortified with these resources and ultimately with guns, stiffened by the aid and example of their Kiowa associates with whom they ended their enmity in 1790 (Mooney 1898: 162–65), the Comanches succeeded in adopting the war patterns of the Plains with complete success. The war ideal permeated male behavior and markedly colored their legal system. Out of this matrix the Comanche brought new and significant legal forms.

TRIBAL ORGANIZATION

There was no political unit which could be termed the Comanche tribe. The tribe was no more than a congerie of bands held together as a peace group by the bonds of a common tongue and culture. There appears to have been no machinery for institutionalized political action on a tribal scale. It is the present belief of the Comanches that Echo Of The Wolf's Howl convened the first tribal council of the Comanches in order to debate the problem of peace with the United States at the time of the proposal of the Medicine Lodge Treaty in 1876.

The population of the Comanche tribe was distributed among a number of autonomous bands, each loosely organized and each centering its activities in a vaguely defined territory within the Comanche country (Mooney 1898: 235; 1928: 13).

The Comanche band, or local group, ranged in size from a single family camping alone, through the small camp of related individuals who formed a composite extended family, up to the large band of several hundred persons.

Clan organization was absent. The kinship principle was weak even within the extended family band (Hoebel 1939: 440–57). Marriage was commonly intraband when a person was a member of a larger group, but there was no fixed rule of residence. Since marriage seems to have been to a great extent within the band, a couple lived customarily in the same group as both their parents.

Comanche residence was semi-patrilocal. Children, as a result, usually belonged to the band of the father. But, except for habituation, there was nothing to prevent change of residence to another band at any time, mere whim being sufficient cause.

The crude economic picture of the Comanches in the last century is one of a tribe with a simple culture adapted to high mobility, which, in a setting of buffalo plenty and prosperity of booty derived from enterprising raiding and trading in the Spanish territories, freed the Comanches from problems of economic want. Much of the Comanche male's energy was directed toward individual aggrandizement in war and coup-counting and the maintenance of prestige within the tribe. The law picture is largely a reflection of this.

WAR AND WAR LEADERSHIP

Comanche war notions conformed to the general Plains pattern of raiding and coup-counting (Grinnell 1910: 296–310). The raid might be made by a party of any size, from a single warrior up. The coup was an individual exploit, made in any contact with the enemy, *after* it had been socially recognized both as achieved in fact and as worthy of distinction.

The life of the Comanche male centered around warfare and raiding. The main objectives were the taking of horses, the counting of coup, and the killing of enemies. It required more bravery to hit an adversary with a spear or a war club than to pierce him with a bow-driven arrow or a gun-driven bullet. Thus striking an enemy gave ground for an honored coup, while long-distance killing did not.

The stealing of tethered horses from within a hostile camp ranked as a very high honor, but it was not nearly so valued as striking a fallen enemy who lay near his own lines, or drawing blood from an enemy in hand-to-hand combat.

The Comanche honored two coups struck on the same victim by different persons. This arrangement was an efficient way of providing sufficient coups to meet the cultural demands of the so-

ciety—an inflation of the currency of war prestige. The first man
to reach the body of a fallen enemy struck it with his weapon and
uttered the cry, *"ahɛ́"* ("I claim it"), gaining thereby equal honor
with the man who had done the killing. But if a bow or gun had
been used to bring down the enemy, this second coup-counter received greater honor for his deed than did the slayer himself.

The prosecution of warfare was very much a matter of individual discretion. Any Comanche was theoretically eligible to lead a
war party. Were the individual not, however, a man of proved reputation or the possessor of potent medicine, his raid would remain
strictly personal and private.

There were two primary motivations for organizing a war party.
The first was an entirely personal matter, depending simply upon
desire for action, honors, or horses. Merely to feel the urge was to
be at liberty to muster such men as would volunteer to go. On the
other hand, a war party instigator might bind himself to avenge
the death of a fellow tribesman by enemy hands.

The invariable conviction of the Comanche is that a man never
failed to do what the leader asked. It was always said that a
brave leader never asked of his men what he himself would not
readily do. Each knew this. Each knew, too, that to disobey might
bring disaster on the party. Each did what he was told. Not a single instance of the use of force or other punishment as sanctions
in the hands of the war leader could be uncovered.

Some Comanche raiding parties were gone for an entire year
or more. Disaffection could and did set in in such a period of
time. The solution of such difficulties was simple. The party split.
The disgruntled fighter and those who sided with him withdrew to
go their own way. This, be it noted, is also the procedure followed
when a man and his friends did not like the way in which things
were being run in the band in times of peace. A man followed
only the leader in whom he had confidence; he obeyed that leader
to the utmost; when he lost confidence, he withdrew from that
leader's sphere of influence.

The waging of war was a matter of individual initiative, but
the making of peace was a prerogative only in the hands of the

war chiefs. A war leader on a raid could make peace in behalf of his own raiding party on his own authority. Such a peace, however, had no binding effect upon other members of the band and not at all upon the tribe. Band peace was made only upon unanimous consent of the warrior class.

IS THERE A COMANCHE LAW? *An Anthropological Hypothesis*

The practical absence of a recognized authority makes the machinery relied upon by the Comanches just that much more significant for the student of jurisprudence and social control. Here we are confronted with legal patterns which are more than mere custom, with norms as to which there is no binding force of hypertrophied reciprocal obligations as in Melanesia, norms which exist without the sustaining force of courts, or police, or other expression of state sovereignty. Since sibs were lacking and associations nearly so, there were no permanent organizations which functioned as equivalents of what we know as government.

No prevailing concept of the nature of law as given in current definitions will fit the facts as we find them in Comanche society. The ideology of orthodox political science and jurisprudence, expressed in terms of "commands of the sovereign," "rules of the state," "an obligation imposed by the lawmaker" have no meaning here. In Comanche society reciprocity is not developed to an exaggerated degree, so that Malinowski's approach (1926) is even less applicable here than it might be elsewhere.

Without courts and without strongly developed obligations of reciprocity to serve as criteria of law, what then is there in Comanche practice that can be identified with what can reasonably be considered "law"? *A social norm is legal if its neglect or infraction is met by the application, in threat or in fact, of the absolute coercive force by a social unit possessing the socially recognized privilege of so acting.*

The term "social unit" means, of course, any individual, subgroup, or the society in its entirety. The subgroup may be a group of kinsmen, or friends, or any association within the society. "Socially recognized privilege" means that the action taken is generally looked upon as justifiable and acceptable by the majority of persons in the society concerned. Acceptance by the majority is by no means a clear-cut picture in many situations. Law is a thing of growth and conflict. The substance of an old rule may be under challenge. The formulation of a new rule may be meeting with stiff resistance. A point of friction may have existed in a society for generations without an effective legal solution having been attained. Feud is a case in point. A murder done may be punished by death at the hands of the murdered man's kin in accordance with prevailing custom. But the privilege of a revenge killing is not recognized (again in accordance with custom) by the kin of the murderer. They strike back, and the siphoning of blood is on.

"In threat, or in fact"; this, because compensatory and restitutive damages, as well as punitive fines (confiscation of property) are ofttimes substituted for coercive force. But the defaulter in damages and fines finds that force has been merely veiled.

The Comanche materials which are to follow serve to demonstrate (as one example) that in primitive society the application of law is not limited to the "political state," whatever that may be, nor even to government. When this fact is realized it will also be seen that "law" in our own society is somewhat more than has ordinarily been allowed. "Primitive law" is the henchman of Legal Realism (Pound 1930: 697–711; Llewellyn 1930: 431–61).

Procedure in adultery and wife-absconding

A Comanche male who had suffered a legal wrong was under social obligation to take action against the offender. For a man not to do so was not looked upon as an act of social grace; indeed, such behavior was a social disgrace. A man so acting was stamped not as magnanimous, but as lily-livered. Adultery and taking another's wife were direct attacks upon the prestige of the wife's husband. Both acts were unmistakable challenges which could not be ignored by the man who would maintain enough face to make life livable.

Naturally, the aggrieved party was not always inclined to act, nor was the reason always cowardice. If the wrong were not made public, it is obvious that public opinion could not drive a man to institute prosecution. Ridicule was the weapon used by society to cause a man to proceed after the cause for action had become public.

This is clearly brought out in the account of an adulterous youth as told by That's It.

Case 4. Adultery: Husband Slays Boy's Pony; Also That of Boy's Grandfather
Informant: That's It

An old man had a handsome grandson. Being very proud of the boy, the old man liked to boast of him in public.

One day the boy sat in a tipi playing the stick game. There were many people present. The grandfather came in and squatted beside the boy as he was playing. The old man looked around and saw a good-looking woman there. He nudged his grandson in the ribs.

With a sly look he whispered, "That looks like the woman you had last night."

The boy looked up and told his grandpa to go away. Then the old man was hurt and said he said nothing wrong. He said it looked like her; no harm in that, is there? Then he was quiet for a few minutes.

But the old man just couldn't keep still. He kept repeating his observation, how that good-looking woman looked like the one the boy had had the other night. He wouldn't shut up.

The woman's husband was also there. Pretty soon he spoke up, saying, "Yes, that's the fellow."

The old man left the tipi.

Pretty soon the game broke up, and all the people went home. The woman's husband just got on his pony and rode over and shot the red mare which was the old man's favorite horse. Then he went and killed the boy's pony. He had been letting the matter ride until that old grandpa talked about it in public.

The boy was real sad and he said, "Grandpa, you sure done wrong. Look what you got us into."

The old man couldn't say anything. He just went off and wept.

Since there were no courts or assizes to be waited upon, action could be instituted at any time. Each case was met by the parties concerned as it arose, and the location was limited only by the necessity of carrying the action to wherever the offender could be found. At home, this was usually at the doorway of his tipi. If the offender was with a raiding party, the aggrieved could await the return of the absconder, or could pursue him. In prosecution, the aggrieved (a) accosted the defendant himself, stating the offense and the extent of damages which would satisfy him. This he might do if he were brave enough. Or, (b) he sent others to prosecute for him, signifying that he considered the matter not worthy of his personal attention, and at the same time minimizing the chance of violent outbreak. An extreme instance of this method of procedure was to send the unfaithful wife herself on the onerous task of demanding damages from her lover.[1]

If the aggrieved deemed it wise to form a party to act in the prosecution of the case, he (c) took his group and sat aloofly astride his horse while his confreres laid the charge and negotiated. But he sometimes got impatient with the progress of the action

---

[1] *Case 5. Adultery: Husband collects damages through wife*
Informant: Visits Her Relatives

A woman used to go regularly to a hill to get power. Claiming to be a medicine woman, she induced her parents to build her a special tipi in which she could go to rest when she had returned from her pilgrimage for power. This went on for some time, when her husband began to suspect that her movements were not in the interest of medicine, as she claimed. He followed her one day and found her horse down by the creek. Turning back, he went by the tipi of a young man and heard his wife's voice inside. Looking in stealthily, he saw the pair lying together.

Feeling very wrathful, the husband went home and asked his mother-in-law to take down his wife's special tipi. She refused. He then told his sister to do it, and she could not refuse him, so she removed it.

When the woman came home and went to rest in her tipi, she found it gone. She went to her husband to ask where her tipi was. He invited her to come into his tipi and sit beside him. When she had done so, he pulled out his knife and cut her hair off close to the scalp, then cut her skirt short. In this bedraggled state he drove her through the camp with his whip. When they came by her lover's tipi the husband bade his wife call to him to come and see her. She called, but her lover did not appear.

Her husband then sent her to collect damages from him. He demanded six horses, a saddle, bridle, and war costume. When she appeared before the young man in her sad state he was sorry for her and said, "You look so pitiful; you may have anything you want that I have!"

His mother loaded his horse with all his portable belongings, and the wife led it publicly through the camp to her husband. This satisfied him, so he kept her as a wife.

and interceded himself. This led to violence. At every step, strong individual reactions threatened the proceedings.[2] It was not unusual, however, for the aggrieved to (d) send his group to carry out the whole procedure, refraining from appearing upon the scene himself. The situation is not the same as in (b) above.

Another alternative relied upon by men without war honors, lacking in self-confidence, and who were unable to muster a party for themselves, was (e) to entreat a war chief to act for the plaintiff in the matter. The ţékniwʌp undertook to see the matter to its close, whatever the consequences, once he agreed to open proceedings on behalf of the aggrieved. An aberrant form of the same type which completely reversed the principle involved was (f) the sending of an old woman to "prosecute" in a situation where the aggrieved feared the defendant, hoping through presenting his cause pitiably to touch the compassion of the offender and so gain larger damages than he himself would dare demand.[3]

The crux of the procedure was bargaining. There was no question of evidence—except in sorcery. In the damage-seeking cases

---

[2] *Case 6. Adultery, Homicide: Procedure breaks down*
Informant: Post Oak Jim

While one of the bands was out on the warpath, a man learned that his wife had committed adultery. He decided to let the matter ride until they were back in safer territory. When again out of danger the aggrieved husband went with two friends to the culprit to ask for damages.

Negotiations were proceeding amiably when the husband became impatient with the procedure and shouted, "That's no way to talk. Why don't you beat him up or kill him!"

This made his adversary so angry that he stabbed the husband dead. At that the two friends of the slain man killed the offender.

[3] *Case 7. Wife-Absconding: Husband sends old woman to collect*
Informant: Rhoda Bluefoot

A woman deserted her husband by joining a raiding party led by a noted warrior, who took her as wife. On their return to the main camp her husband did nothing to get her back because he was afraid of the warrior and his three brothers. So he sent an old woman to plead for her. Since the warrior wished to keep her, he sent back a gift of horses and goods to the husband in place of the woman.

This gift the husband had to accept, and he dropped proceedings.

Later the warrior was killed in a battle, and one of his younger brothers inherited the woman as wife.

the evidence was obtained before action was brought. In wife-absconding cases the presence of the woman with the absconder was *prima facie* evidence which need go no further. In all our cases but one the bargaining was begun with guilt accepted by both parties. In cases of adultery, beyond *in flagrante delicto,* evidence came from witnesses or by confession of the wife. However it may be, except for cases of sorcery, there was no technique for obtaining evidence from the defendant. Nor was the defendant usually confronted with witnesses. The aggrieved had to ascertain to his own satisfaction who the guilty party might be. After this had been done the defendant could then be confronted.

And what if guilt was denied? Usually it was not. When the defendant refused to own up, the procedure apparently came to an impasse. The aggrieved might be angry enough to take illegal steps (violence), or he might possibly kill some of the accused's horses to satisfy his desire for damages. The latter course would be likely to lead to retaliation, however, for the defendant, in denying guilt, denied cause for damages and such peremptory taking of damages was to him illegal. The reaction of the defendant if the first recourse were taken by his accuser is problematical; it would depend pretty much on his temperament and guilt in fact. Denial of guilt by an accused (except in sorcery) was so uncommon that there are not cases enough to draw sound conclusions.

Cases were opened with formal politeness and smooth words; the man who had come to prosecute addressed the one he was about to accuse as "brother" (Hoebel 1939: 448–49). While the defendant listened, he was told why the accuser had come as prosecutor and informed what must be given in damages to satisfy his visitor. Inasmuch as the defendant usually knew what had called forth the visit, the prosecutor was not invited into the tipi to take the seat of the guest of honor opposite the door. Ordinarily the defendant was sitting beside the door of his tipi as the prosecuting party arrived, and the negotiations took place before the tipi.

The aggrieved usually stated his demand for damages specifically, but the damages rendered were those which the defendant agreed to give and the aggrieved was willing to accept. "Willingness," with either or both, could of course be anything but willing. There was no judge to determine what should be paid in composition for the wrong, nor was there any specific customary code regulating payments in accordance with degree of wrong. Consequently, only by agreement could the case be settled. Without the aid of an arbitrator, the sole way to agreement was bargain.

The factors which operated in the process of settlement were manifold and delicate, each factor having many shades and facets. Who can say what the forces shaping the attitudes which determine the actions of any individual in any special circumstance may be? It is clear, however, that the will to push or resist was of greatest moment. Sometimes the defendant acquiesced only too willingly to the first demands made upon him. Sometimes the prosecutor placed a timid request for compensation, which he accepted with a sign of relief, glad that the thing was done. It is in this very will to push or to resist that the personal factor entered and resists reduction to written words. Nevertheless, personal courage and aggressiveness were the potent traits which counted in the Comanche male. Each party mentally weighed the other and decided accordingly, most of this being done before any action recounted in a story could occur. The one outstanding factor around which the settlement of a dispute turned was not the question of the right or wrong of the situation, but rather the relative bravery in warfare of the two parties involved. A reputation as a doughty slayer of enemies was a handy thing. The real point was that in Comanche law, as in all law, the ultimate power was resort to force. But the right to use—or threaten with—force was not reserved to the government. It was a privilege reserved to the interested parties in case the adjudicative process broke down. In other words, there existed a situation exactly comparable to that observed among nations which recognize certain practices of international law, but which reserve to themselves the sovereign right to resort to force if things don't suit them. Then, in the words of Post Oak Jim, "Lots of trouble, lots of people hurt."

It is very clear, however, that the Comanches tended to attribute moral rightness to the braver man. This is revealed, for instance, in the settlement of a land-rights squabble in the early days on the reservation:

Case 8. Land Dispute
Informant: Eagle Tail Feather

When land allotments were made by the government, two neighbors quarreled over a quarter section of land which both wanted. One of them succeeded in establishing his claim on the disputed land. The other protested the action and contested the claim. Feeling ran higher and higher over the matter until each was threatening to kill the other.

Quanah Parker, who was chief of the band at the time, was called upon to settle the dispute. He asked two warriors to testify as to the past war record of the disputants. Since one of the warriors was late in coming to report, Parker sent Eagle Tail Feather, then chief of the Indian police, to find him to hear what he had to say. Eagle Tail Feather took another warrior with him as witness. The first disputant also went in the party, thinking to gain an advantage by confronting the witness personally.

When the four men were assembled at the warrior-witness's house, this disputant spoke up, saying, "Which is better, I or this other fellow?"

"All right," said the warrior, "now that you've asked me, I'll speak out plain. That other one (the opponent in the case) is the better man. I was in a battle where I saw him get off his horse and help a dismounted comrade from the midst of the enemy. He is a brave man and did a great deed; you'd better look out or he'll whip you, or kill you."

These words silenced the claimant. He knew that he would lose the land unless he could speak up and tell of a braver deed which he had performed. This he could not do, so he remained speechless while the others waited for his words. When they were satisfied that his adversary was the braver man, Eagle Tail Feather and his aide returned to Quanah and told him what had ensued at the meeting.

Quanah decreed that the disputed quarter section should belong to the warrior who had made the rescue. The other released his claim to it without further word.[4]

---

[4] This is, of course, an atypical case, involving as it does, land rights which are not a part of the aboriginal culture. However, it *does* show the carryover of old attitudes to new procedures.

Intermediaries and the champion-at-law

Women who were deserting their husbands rather consistently chose brave men as partners in absconding. Or, if the absconder was doubtful as to his own fighting ability, he placed himself and his runaway woman under the temporary protection of a war party leader. It is also said that a would-be absconder sometimes induced a war party leader to steal the desired woman, then to release her for the lover after the settlement had been made. Consequently, the husband was more frequently than not the weaker party in the bargain situation. He was impelled to take action by the force of social opinion; yet he had small chance of succeeding.

It is true that his kin would avenge his death if he were killed in carrying out his social obligation to prosecute. Small comfort in that. What he sought was not death but an adjustment in accordance with his legal rights. Where the balance of prowess lies normally on the side of the wrongdoer in an individualistic system, the process of law will be checked. This is because the ultimate legal sanction is force, the very power in which the prosecutor may find himself shorthanded. If this prevails generally, then the foundation is sapped from under the structure of legal order. But if the power of the wronged party equals that of the transgressor, a different situation exists. A settlement can be effected through bargaining. Here the sociological principles of compromise are clearly operative: an avoidance of force to effect exchanges in terms of mutual concessions. John R. Commons (1901: 325) writes, "Arbitration is never accepted until each party to a dispute is equally afraid of the other, and when they have reached that point, they can adopt something better than arbitration, namely, negotiation."[5]

Unconsciously operating on this principle, a Comanche prosecuted by himself only if sure of his own courage in relation to that of the defendant. But Comanche society took an important step

---

[5] Commons' truth is an overstatement. Not "equally afraid," but "enough to make battle highly inconvenient," is more accurate.

forward in effecting an equalization of powers when the aggrieved was not strong enough to prosecute by himself. The aggrieved was allowed the privilege, apparently not customarily granted the defendant, of marshalling his kin and friends to aid him in seeking restitution. In many instances these partisans took over the complete responsibility of negotiations. In other cases, the aggrieved accompanied them on their mission, but refrained from entering the bargaining activities. In no single specific case did the defendant take recourse to similar reinforcements. It does not seem to have been his privilege. Consequently, the collectivization of the bravery of blood relatives and friends by the prosecutor may be viewed as a social mechanism whose function was to give added protection to the rights of the husband.[6]

This practice often allowed for such a show of force on the side of the aggrieved that the defendant could actually be cowed. Though this might seem unfair, there is more justice and stronger check to illegal action if it is the defendant and not the wronged party who is thus intimidated. Accordingly, this occasional overbalancing of forces on the prosecuting side does not so much defeat the aim of law as would the alternative condition, and is socially more defensible. Nevertheless, as we shall see, abuse by the plaintiff could lead to repercussions. Defendants, too, were within the protection of the law.

A number of conditions entered into the matter of group aid in such endeavors. The "rightness" of the aggrieved party's case was a strong operative factor when it came to gathering his group. To participate in such a group if petitioned was a kinship responsibility, though not an obligation. It was rather reciprocity, in this case, which made the responsibility a reality. Theoretically any man could refuse to help a relative, but it was the better part of wisdom to go along with him. Who knew but what the day might

---

[6] The only contradictory evidence to this is the statement by Post Oak Jim that once there was trouble over damages between a couple of groups fighting with rifles, "so I didn't get close enough to see much." The fact of rifles indicates that it is a late case.

come when each man in turn would need the help of the others? And there was material gain to be had by participation.

Brothers and friends who were called "brother" were those obligated to act for the aggrieved, if he called upon them. This obligation was fortified by a right to a share in the damages collected; the participants' right to a cut in the compensation took precedence over the aggrieved's. The ludicrous result was that sometimes a man's "lawyer" brothers got all, while he was left to contemplate the satisfaction of having seen the law through. This is a stated principle, but does not appear in our case material. To be accurate, however, these "brothers" had more than a lawyer's interest, and a closer responsibility than that of other relatives was theirs. Through the institution of levirate they had a partial claim on the aggrieved husband's wife. They too were wronged. This claim could in itself give rise directly to occasional legal action. Hence their share in the damages was more than pay for helping in the procedure. It was a share in composition for a wrong mutually suffered. But why did the "brothers'" rights to the goods take precedence over the husband's? A hazarded explanation would be that it served as an inducement to reinforce the obligation the brothers held.

Or is it possible that a broader force was in operation here? The practice may be associated with prestige compulsions. It was more grandiose wantonly to kill a horse than to take one. It was more noble to reward one's helpers than to grab the take for oneself. The principal was under social compulsion to be noble. Is it a parallel to the rule of the raiding party that the leader should be the last to share?

The Comanches showed a sense of justice at work and an awareness of the function of legal institutions in their society when they accorded the aggrieved party a customary massing of subsidiary force which was apparently denied to the aggressor. The dynamic quality of Comanche culture and the mark of creative genius is to be seen in the way in which this principle of equalization was refined and fitted to meet the needs of the person who had no group of "brothers" to back him in need. Comanche juridical

processes were more than a mere phase of the status struggle
among males. Men whose status was so low that on the personal
and kinship basis they were, in effect, without status were still
guaranteed protection under the Comanche law. This was done
by harnessing the status drive in the society to the needs of the
weak and aggrieved. There was the institution of *champion-at-
law*.[7]

The functioning champion-at-law is best revealed in action
through cases.

*Case 12. Wife-stealing: Red Crooked Nose vs. a young warrior
Informant: Visits Her Relatives*

The wife of Red Crooked Nose absconded with a young, good-
looking warrior. In the raiding party were four other men and another woman. For two years the pair remained away, and no one
in the main camp knew where they were living. But one day some
hunters found their camp and reported it to Red Crooked Nose. He
was determined to get his wife back, but he had few war deeds to
his credit. So he asked a brave, well-known warrior to go with him.
The warrior consented to go.

When they reached the absconder's camp, the woman saw them
coming and ran to her young husband, saying that she wanted to
stay with him. But when the young man saw Red Crooked Nose's
champion he said, "Against such a man I have no chance to keep
you."

So they met outside the tipi. Red Crooked Nose picked up a
quiver of arrows belonging to the young man, but his wife told him,
"Put them down. You can't do any better with them than their owner
can."

Food was offered the newcomers, and they stated their mission.
They said that they would accept no damages in place of the woman,
that Red Crooked Nose needed her to care for their young child. So
the young man ordered her horse brought, upon which was a good
saddle, a silver-braided bridle, and good blankets. He told the woman
to dress up. He told her, "Take everything nice that belongs to you.
This old man can't get things like these for you."

She gathered all her belongings, including fifteen horses. She was

---

[7] There is no special word in the Comanche lexicon for this personage. A
man acting as champion-at-law was simply referred to as tékniwʌp (war
leader). Only men who were war leaders were sought to act as champions.
Their legal activity on behalf of others was merely an incidental function
of their status as ranking braves in the tribe.

ready to start back with them, but she cried pitifully to have to leave her young lover. After they had started, she lagged behind sullenly.

They had gone. The young absconder broke camp. He mounted and rode on past them. As his horses ran by, Red Crooked Nose killed one of them and called upon his party to take the meat he had shot for them. Then the owner of the dead horse scorned him, "My feelings aren't hurt. *I* can get plenty of horses—like the grass, so many!" And he rode on.[8]

He knew that Red Crooked Nose would not have dared to kill his horse without the warrior as protector.

While stopping one night they heard that enemies were coming. The women were sent on. The men prepared for war. Before the battle started, the young man donned his best war paraphernalia. With his feathers flying he rode past the camp of Red Crooked Nose. He fought conspicuously and was killed.

The champion saw him go down.

He called to Red Crooked Nose, saying, "It was we who caused him to be killed. I know you are a coward, but you have to go and walk in front of the enemy to protect us while I carry off his body."

Thus they took the young man off the field, and put his body on a horse. When the woman saw his body brought back, she tore her dress apart, slashed her body all over with her knife, and cut her hair off short. She embraced his body and wanted to throw her jewelry away in mourning. But the people pulled her away, telling her to keep it in remembrance of him.

Red Crooked Nose and his champion rode up and mourned him. Then he was wrapped in blankets and buried. The camp broke up and continued on its way.

Though it is the activities of the intermediary which we must here examine, the fine devices of sarcasm and ridicule which make this history so rich in intrinsic sanctions deserve attention. The woman mocks her husband. The lover mocks. These are expressions of rage, or attempts to egg him into overreaching his position. The latter occurs. Again the lover mocks. But the combination of grief and shame works in him as his mockery seems to have worked in the husband. He seizes the occasion for a protest-

---

[8] No empty boast for the young man. And it cut two ways. In itself, this killing of a horse, over and above taking back the woman, is wholly proper. The overdoing lies in these points: the woman had brought double a heavy indemnity, the adjustment was over, and the strength of the husband was not equal to the deed he was performing. He was overreaching, and the young man's disdainful ignoring of his act showed him up in just that way.

sacrifice equivalent to suicide, save that it serves his tribe. The champion turns upon the championed. Red Crooked Nose's mourning is a penance. And one may be certain that his later repute suffered. The people told *her* to keep her jewelry in remembrance of a "wrongdoer," who, overpenalized, had made himself a hero.

The institutionalized champion we see as a purely social device. None of the ordinary inducements used to lead a person to assume a difficult obligation or responsibility were operative for him. Unlike kin or friends, he received no material compensation for his pains. This is borne out both by the word of the informants and by the evidence of the cases. Nor did the principle of reciprocity of services operate for him. Men chosen to act as champion were always warriors of great renown. They could look to themselves; they had no need to ask for return of favors. It was a sense of *noblesse oblige* and self-esteem which forced the champion into the legal lists on behalf of weaker persons to whom he had no personal ties. A war leader who refused to accept the request for aid in prosecution was to be deemed unworthy of his rank, for it was imputed that he feared the defendant. No war leader could admit fear. The institutional capitalization of these factors for the legal protection of the weak is an amazing piece of social engineering.

In action the champion was not an arbitrator. It was not his purpose to serve as a go-between. He went to demand damages. The bare fact is that he confronted the defendant as a "tough guy" who could take as well as give it. He was ready, if need be, to close the matter, not with damage settlements, but with physical combat.

It is in the champion that we can see most clearly the social policy of balancing the opposing forces so as to clear the way for a bargain settlement. This phase of the Comanche legal system is therefore to be viewed as a not so badly balanced mechanism, which operated without the organization of government. Making certain that action was taken when an offense was made publicly known, it made possible a sort of justice by assuring that the guilty and the wronged parties were placed on a bargaining level.

There were no officials in the picture. The peace chief could not act in damage suits, because he had no social authority to do so. As an old and gentle man he lacked the physical prowess to enter an affair in a personal capacity. The champions who participated in actions, because they were the bravest men, were also war chiefs. But the role of champion which they played was a function of their bravery, not of their rank as a chief.

Forced confessions: the third degree

There were various techniques available to the husband as a prosecutor. These were ritualistic and nonritualistic. The latter were simple and direct third-degree forms. A man took his wife to a lonely spot to build a fire. If the threat of what was coming did not force a confession from the lips of the wife, the husband then held her prone over the fire, lowering her closer and closer to the flames until she gave the information he wanted. Another method was to choke the woman until a confession was forthcoming. Whipping also served the end. One or the other of these methods was used in six out of the twenty-three adultery cases recorded in this study.

Not only was the confession of unfaithfulness forced in this way, but also the naming of the corespondent. On the basis of such confession, suit for damages could be begun.

The case of Bone and his wife is illustrative of how evidence given by a witness was reinforced by such confession.

Case 28. Adultery: Bone vs. Cómatsit
Informant: Visits Her Relatives (niece to Bone)

Bone and his younger brother were living together with Bone's wife. She was called Little. One day Little was out collecting sticks for the fire; it took her a long, long time, until Bone began to suspect things. He called on his little ten-year-old sister to go see what his wife was up to. The little girl went looking about. Finally she found the pile of wood near a tipi, so she went over and looked in. There she saw her grown-up sister-in-law lying in bed with a man.

"What are you doing there, auntie?" the little girl asked. "My brother wants you to come home right away. You'd better hurry up."

"Oh," Little tried to reassure her. "I just came in here for a smoke. You run along now."

The little sister did just that. She ran home as fast as she could to tell her brother she had seen his wife lying in bed in a certain tipi: how she had seen her there with Cómatsit (a Mexican name). Soon after, Little came home. "Now we are going hunting," announced Bone. "Come, brother, we are going after game. We shall not stop to eat. You are coming, too," he told his wife. Then they started out, but as soon as they were out of sight of the camp, Bone stopped the procession. He ripped the clothes from Little and violently threw her upon the ground. "Now tell me," he thundered, "what were you doing in that tipi?"

"Oh, my husband," Little wept, "I did nothing there. Your little sister has told you an untruth. She does not know what she says."

"We'll see," muttered Bone. So saying, he placed his hands firmly on her throat. "Now tell me," he commanded. Then he choked her and choked her and choked her.

At last she gasped, "Yes, I did it."

Then he let go of her. With his freed hands he drew his knife and deftly cut off half her nose. "Come, brother," he said. So the brother picked up their wife's clothes, and away they went, leaving poor Little lying on the ground where they had mutilated her. When they got back to the camp, Bone sent his little sister out again. "Go to our wife's grandmother and tell her to go get her." So the old grandmother went and found Little and took her home.

Next Bone and his brother went to Cómatsit to sue for damages because of the offense he had committed. They got most of that man's fine clothes and six horses from him besides.

The rough-and-ready third degree techniques fit well into the Comanche picture of warlike life. But beyond these forms there were other means at hand for the husband who chose to use them. These were ritualistic approaches to the supernatural which entered when called upon as a legal force. The supernatural was invoked through conditional curse and oath.

The use of the conditional curse for proof was very specialized, indeed confined seemingly to adultery and sorcery cases. It was known as "sun-killing" (ṭaβέβekʌt). In adultery procedure the husband took his wife to a lonely spot and, making smoke with his pipe, he addressed the charge to the sun and the earth and sometimes the moon. By these same powers the wife swore her innocence. These powers in their omnipotence knew the truth, and if the wife were guilty, they afflicted her with consumption. The usual fate of erring women who took the curse was, according to native dogma, that of Short Dress, wife of Kóhi. She denied her husband's charge, placing her hands flat upon the earth and calling upon the powers, while her husband smoked. She bade the sun, "May I die when the geese fly from the south to the north if I have done the thing he has charged me with."[9] She died the next spring.

In adultery, as in sorcery, the supernatural played the double role of judge and executor. The case was rested by the prosecutor and there was no more for him to do but await results.

More recent developments put another angle on the conditional curse. As Comanche women began to feel the emancipating effects of the impact of white contact, they refused to submit docilely to the curse. It was very unsettling to the men, but even so, That's It laughed as he thought of the startled discomfiture of the first husband to feel its effects. This man had accused his wife of adultery and did not believe her denial, so he prepared a smoke to the sun. And just as he was about to pronounce the fatal words, his wife broke in.

"You are going to make smoke. You want to kill me," she expostulated. "But you listen, I deny this thing. Now look out! I am going to smoke too. If you are putting the lie on me, the sun will get you instead." That put a different complexion on the situation; the husband was not begging for such a bargain. "So," as That's It put it, "he called off his sun-killing and gave his wife sugar words."

Later another husband called the deal and paid the price. A man named Brother-in-law, according to Holding Her Sunshade, tried his wife on false evidence. When he put her to the curse, she made her denial and ended by calling to the supernaturals, "If he cuts off my nose, grant that he shall not live long." Brother-in-law accepted the challenge. He did cut off her nose, and within a month he was dead.

---

[9] Some Comanches evaded repeating this oath to us for fear of its dangerous implications.

DISPUTING IN TANGU

K. O. L. Burridge

TANGU[1] LIVE in hilly terrain some fifteen miles inland from Bogia Bay on the north coast of New Guinea in the Madang District. Composing in all some two thousand people distributed through about thirty settlements of varying sizes, and grouped into four named neighborhoods, they are hunters, gatherers, and gardeners whose known history has been characterized in the last fifty years by upheaval and instability. An epidemic plague or, as Tangu view the event, a particularly violent and uncontrolled increase in sorcery, helped to set in motion, at the turn of the century, a series of local migrations combined with much internecine fighting which broke down the former large communities. The larger kin and local residential units—which were also jural groups and landholding units—fragmented into households and, extensive tracts of unsettled land then being available, segments of varying size and composition scattered and resettled themselves over a relatively wide area. Soon afterward the first Europeans came to the region. Over the next thirty years Tangu were gradually brought under control: peace was enforced, labor recruiting became ordered, a mission station was established, and native administrative representatives were appointed. However, the pop-

Originally published in *American Anthropologist,* Vol. 59, 1957, pp. 763–80. Reprinted by permission of the author and of the editor of *American Anthropologist.*
[1] The names of persons involved in the disputes are fictitious. The word *Tangu* refers to both place and people; the context makes clear which is meant. Field research was carried out in 1952 while a Scholar with The Australian National University.

ulation remained dispersed—indeed, additional settlements were
founded. When, after the Japanese war, Tangu were persuaded
to concentrate into larger aggregations, it was not long before
families began to return to their old homes in the bush. During
daylight the settlements are deserted. Families are out in the surrounding countryside in their hunting lodges, tending their gardens, or visiting friends or kinfolk. Only at dusk, on festive
occasions, or when some community task is afoot is any substantial proportion of a settlement present. Tangu say, "There is always trouble and quarreling in large villages or when we gather
together."

Within Tangu there are cultural diversities. Among individuals
there is disagreement on the significance and implications of many
situations, and where a consensus is found it often happens that
nothing is done by way of enforcement. Lacking a permanent
corporate jural group recruited from specified categories of genealogical kin, the strongest loyalties are to the household, the nuclear
family, at the expense of the community as a whole. Yet, inter-
marriage between members of different settlements, communities,
and neighborhoods is frequent, internal trading and exchange
relationships are numerous and regularly maintained, and while
participation in the political activity, *br'ngun'guni,* is theoretically
open to outsiders, examination shows it to be virtually confined
to those who call themselves Tangu. What primarily distinguishes
Tangu from their neighbors and makes them a distinct unity is
not a series of loyalties geared to levels of group organization,
but their adherence to a few interrelated notions and activities.

Everywhere in Tangu the basic and definitive social and economic unit is the household; and households are in significant
relationships with each other as they cooperate, exchange, or are
mngwotngwotiki—an agreement by free and mutual consent neither to exchange nor to cooperate. The work done by the members of a household goes into subsistence, exchanges with other
households, and feasting and dancing exchanges which take place
regularly during the harvesting months between two principal but
temporary cooperative groups to which the other households in

the community attach themselves. The cooperative relationship implies that the husbands of the households concerned are brothers or that the wives are sisters, while the exchange or oppositional relationship connotes households, severally or grouped, where the wife of one is the sister of the husband of the other. That is, the households of married siblings of the same sex are in actual or potential cooperative relationships, and the households of married siblings of different sexes are in actual or potential exchange relationships. However, the kin categories are in large measure putative. Though the kin idiom is always used, and though the core of a feasting exchange may consist of men and women in the requisite categories of genealogical kinship, there always remain households which find themselves equivocally placed in the particular feasting series and which are persuaded into joining one or another group of households by influential men—managers.

Managers create alliances—make for themselves brothers—by persuasive oratory, cunning, and making good their claims to productive ability. Normally, in each community, alliances are forged at the beginning of each horticultural cycle so that the participating households form two approximately equivalent groups in a mutual-exchange relationship. During such feasting exchanges, in the intervals between different phases of the dance, as food is placed before the exhausted dancers, men from either group of households make speeches. This is formal br'ngun'guni. The oratory is accompanied by staccato beats on the hand drum, thwacking the buttocks, and, if a man is really excited, wild leaps into the air. Men boast of their prowess in the gardens and bush, comment on the dancing, and throw out disparaging hints as to the productive abilities of others. Some take the opportunity to remind the assembly that it is time to harvest the yams, cut new garden sites, or that work in the ricefield is lagging behind. Others bring up their grievances whether they relate to hunting, fishing, gardening, administrative, mission, or kin matters, exchange obligations, or suspicions of sorcery. Visitors from other communities come to these feasts not only because they enjoy a party but because formal br'ngun'guni is the explicit occasion for submitting a cause or attempting to establish a claim. As the result of anger or an announcement or a complaint, however, br'ngun'guni may occur ad hoc, and though in the unexpectedness and heat of the moment many of the formal niceties may be omitted, the procedure, ends, and means are much the same. Managers are concerned with oratory, in the interplay of comment and discussion —in order to recruit allies, challenge other managers, and put to the test the abilities they believe themselves to have; individuals mediate, soften the hard lines of parry and thrust; the community in general works to restore equilibrium.

The political maneuvering and the domestic and kinship activities which lead to a feasting exchange and br'ngun'guni, or which result from a br'ngun'guni undertaken ad hoc, are dominated by a few firmly held and interrelated axioms. Amity exists within its own moral right, explicitly governs all Tangu relationships, and characterizes the ideal equilibrium. Mutual relationships tend to shift toward some kind of overt conformity with amity. At the same time, amity is no vague and emotional goodwill: it is expressed in and depends on equivalence, a notion of moral equality between persons which must be continually reaffirmed and reiterated lest someone become dominant. The focal assertion of equivalence occurs in food exchanges at every level of organization, whether the exchange is completed within the space of a day, weeks, or months. All such exchanges must be equivalent. If they are not, expectations are disappointed and trouble results. Yet no food exchange can be precisely equivalent; and because resources are limited households are forced to establish a scale of priorities, necessarily disappointing some to satisfy others. Since, in these circumstances, there is always room to find fault, exchanges that are regarded as equivalent reflect a true moral equivalence—and when this happens they speak of the households as being mngwotngwotiki: they have achieved equivalence, and neither exchange nor cooperate. An exchange that is not regarded as precisely equivalent, or remains not fully honored for long, indicates a lack of moral equivalence. One or the other party is thought to be attempting to demonstrate a dominance.

The one is suspected of trying to establish an overall dominance in virtue of what may be a simple physical competence, the other may be suspected of contempt, and either may be suspected of resorting to a technique to shroud the other in obloquy. The necessity for maintaining equivalence in this way, or for working toward a moral equivalence, results in a critical attitude which, together with disappointed expectations, may lead into expressions of anger and indignation.

Tangu have no noun to denote anger; it does not exist as an abstraction. Men are angry with one another, not merely angry; it is a transitive verb. Anger kept in the heart leads to sorcery and means sickness or death for someone. Anger made public, normally by a rapid onomatopoeic drumming on a slit-gong, may lead into a complaint and thence into br'ngun'guni. An angry man is a dangerous man, and the signal on the slit-gong is both a warning to keep clear and an invitation to a close friend or kinsman to inquire what the matter might be. Whatever may lie behind a particular show of anger, whether it is expressed as an unsettling device or whether it actually derives from some substantial antecedent cause, it is almost always explicitly related to a misdemeanor over food and its production. A theft is denying food or tools to another, a trespass implies the intent to seize flesh, fish, or fruits from another; either renders the wronged person less able to maintain equivalence with others through food exchanges. The breach of the norm finds concrete expression in relation to food, and restitution demands further activities in relation to food: anger indicates a breach of equivalence, and normally predicates a series of feasting exchanges in which br'ngun'guni will occur and through which public equivalence may be re-established.

Either formally, or by precipitating br'ngun'guni by an expression of anger when the opportunity allows, managers attempt to secure and define cooperative alliances. Since they may not dominate but have to maintain equivalence with all in the community, managers must control themselves and challenge men of roughly equivalent abilities and resources. To challenge a small man would be fruitless: if equivalence is adhered to, no evidence of productive ability emerges; if equivalence is breached, the offender becomes the target for mystical attack which—even if the manager himself is oblivious—results in the defection of allies. Ideally, the successful manager is one who, in spite of great productive ability, is able to maintain equivalence and can resist the temptation to dominate. One br'ngun'guni is the springboard for another. Each subtly confirms or refutes existing alliances and mutual interrelationships, the latter tending to shift so that amity can find expression in its most conventional forms. Formally, br'ngun'guni is a deliberative device which provides implicit authority for a series of activities; it is a mechanism for initiating, continuing, containing, or resolving disputes, and it is a vehicle for political management. Br'ngun'guni does not, and cannot, make any defined and explicit reallocations of claims to exercise rights.

The following summaries of four disputes are presented as illustrations of the principles outlined above.

1

One afternoon two teams of brothers were building houses for their sisters, Juatak, wife of Kwaling, and Nuongweram, Turai's wife and Kwaling's half-sister. Kwaling and Juatak were distributing food to the latter's brothers, and Nuongweram's brothers were working. The atmosphere was one of quiet and cheerful industry as men and women went about their tasks, smoked, talked, or chewed betel nut. Presently, Meakriz, the Luluai,[2] was approached by Igamas, his natural son, and Bunjerai, his adopted son. There was a short whispered conversation, and all three ran off into the bush.

The incident created a small stir. People thought a pig had been trapped, and expectations were aroused.

Sure enough, half an hour later the cries of a party returning with a pig were heard. There was a short pause and then, from a

---

[2] Title of native administrative representative. A Tultul aids a Luluai.

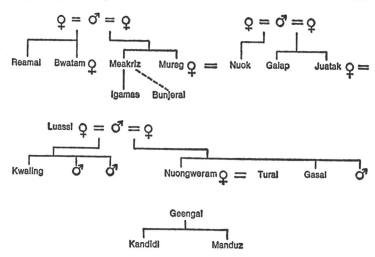

Genealogy of Participants in Case #1, Tangu.

group of homesteads separated from the main settlement, the beaten rhythm of a slit-gong announced the trapping of a pig and to whom it was going to be given.

Mureg, who is a sister to Meakriz and his half-brother Reamai, and who, since Meakriz is a widower, normally cooks for him and his sons, was disappointed. She said in a loud voice to her husband, Nuok, "What is this? Why does he not bring the pig down here, carve it under my porch and give it to me to distribute? Why is he giving it to Bwatam? I cook for him every day."

Nuok, friend[3] of Kwaling and brother to Juatak, stepped out onto the dancing space to support his wife. "Why was the pig going to Bwatam? Why not to Mureg who cooked for Meakriz daily? Gasai, Nuongweram's brother, had killed a pig the day before and had given it to Nuongweram to distribute to the brothers building her house. It was appropriate that Meakriz and Reamai should give their pig to their sister Mureg to divide between the brothers building Juatak's house. Were not Kwaling, Meakriz, and Reamai brothers?"

---

[3] *Kwav:* a relationship entailing mutual aid. (See Burridge 1957.)

Reamai, who had actually trapped the pig and who was annoyed that his choice should be questioned, came down from the upper portion of the village and confronted Nuok. "We will do what we like with our pig," he said. "We are giving it to our sister, Bwatam."

"Who cooks for Meakriz?" asked Nuok. "Bwatam?"

Reamai did not answer. He strode away angrily, asserting that the pig would be given to Bwatam. Nuok walked off in disgust.

Suddenly—perhaps Mureg had fired a parting shot—Reamai lost his temper. Turning on his heel he ran back to Mureg's house, forced his way in, and started to thrash her.

Mureg screamed. She was still screaming when Nuok, hurrying to the rescue, confronted Reamai emerging from his hut. Nuok stooped, picked up a clod of dried earth and flung it at Reamai. He missed.

Reamai sprang to the attack. Being smaller and frailer, Nuok fled. Reamai gave chase and grappled. Meakriz pounced on them both, trying to separate them. Reamai whooped, Nuok cried for help, and others rushed yelling to the scene.

Kwaling was among them, a heavy digging stick in his hands. Bounding into the melee with a whoop, he cracked Reamai across the head. Reamai staggered back, blood spurting from his temples and pouring down his chest. Nuok broke free. Gaiap, Juatak's full brother, supported Reamai and helped him out of harm's way. Kwaling retreated. Women scuttled around to the backs of their huts. The village was in uproar.

Br'ngun'guni commenced.

Why has brother struck brother? Both Kwaling and Reamai are managers. They are classificatory brothers who ought to be in an amicable cooperative relationship, but they have been quarreling since boyhood and they dislike each other intensely. Reamai is the younger of the two, boastful, hot tempered, and very proud of being the son of a famous father. He is an excellent gardener, hunter, and dancer. Nevertheless, he is jealous of Kwaling who is quiet, withdrawn, cool, well known and respected far beyond the boundaries of Tangu. As Luluai of the village, Meakriz is responsible for keeping order, apprehending wrongdoers, and reporting misdemeanors to the administration. Because he is a widower with children, his sister Mureg has given him shelter, and has cooked for him and generally looked after him. She can reasonably expect generosity in return. However, Meakriz cannot find a new wife and he had been thinking of having his sons adopted by either Mureg or Bwatam on a more or less permanent basis. This means putting his potential as a food producer at the disposal of either Bwatam or Mureg—a matter on which the two women had come to blows and which had resulted in Bwatam moving her house from the main part of the settlement to the outlying cluster of homesteads.

Even apart from the economic issue, the two women have little love for each other. Bwatam is an attractive creature well liked by the men of the community, and it is no secret that Meakriz expresses his affection for her by many small favors. Having eaten a meal cooked by Mureg, Meakriz is wont to stroll over to Bwatam's house and there enjoy his leisure with tobacco and betel nut. Mureg herself swings her hips to some effect and enjoys the reputation she has among men of being somebody else's mistress. Reamai, however, regards Mureg's reputation as a blot on his name; he has had words with her before, and he has beaten her. Quite recently he had embroiled himself over an alleged theft of areca nuts and, since the popular suspect stood to him as son, he had attempted to clinch matters by threatening to beat up anyone who continued to speak of his son as a thief.

Into this generally uneasy situation has come a stroke of good fortune—the capture of a pig. Meakriz and Reamai are burdened with a choice, and their decision has angered and disappointed Mureg. Nuok, her husband, has made a complaint, and the impending dispute is across the brother-sister link. Reamai was presented with a second choice, for he might have returned with dignity to his pig and carved it notwithstanding. Instead, angered, he chose to beat Mureg. In consequence Nuok was angry, the two men start fighting, and Meakriz, as Luluai, tries to separate them. Kwaling has the choice of helping Reamai who is his brother, or Nuok who is his friend, or, like Meakriz, he might have tried to make peace. He chose deliberately to strike Reamai. Gaiap, Juatak's full brother, has already taken the first step toward a return to amity. By ostensibly supporting Reamai and shielding him from Kwaling, and incidentally shielding Nuok from Reamai, he has shown that this need not be a matter involving all of Juatak's brothers. It is a personal issue.

Nevertheless, a number of expectations have been disappointed, several relationships have been thoroughly disturbed, equivalence has been breached, and there is no longer amity.

Shouting, leaping, whooping, beating their buttocks with the palms of their hands, Kwaling, Reamai, and Meakriz ran up and down the dancing space, sweating, furious, livid with anger; boasting, threatening, calling witness. Nuok made himself scarce. Kwaling had taken the quarrel out of his hands and made it his own.

The blood streaming down Reamai's body was prima-facie evidence of a breach of amity. Meakriz, running, leaping, and thwacking his buttocks, said it was a deliberate assault and that he would take Kwaling to court at Bogia on the morrow.

Reamai passionately endorsed the proposal. Dizzy, eyes glazed, rubbing his hands in the blood, he demanded the court.

Kwaling countered. Reamai had beaten his sister, he said, and was in the act of assaulting Nuok when the blow was delivered. Should a man not go to the aid of his friend? His father and Reamai's father had been very close to each other. They had lived together in amity and cooperation, and their sons should behave in the same way. Right. Go to court. Tell the white men how they behaved—how a man of the village had beaten his sister, beat the husband who came to the rescue, and had threatened to beat others.

Meakriz withdrew, sitting down in silence.

Reamai and he, continued Kwaling, had been brought up together in Kimaimwenk. They were brothers. Was it necessary to fight?

Still dazed by the blow, Reamai stuck doggedly to court, rebutting the appeal to amity by stressing the deeper issues between them. Kwaling disliked him and had hit him on purpose from spite. He, Reamai, had left Kimaimwenk and settled on his own, all because of Kwaling. From there he had gone elsewhere, and it was Kwaling who had stopped him from settling in the village now. Court was the only way to settle it.

Kwaling continued to conjure moral or "ought to be" relationships, and by so doing he was looking ahead and placing himself in the stream of public opinion. He had taken advantage of the opportunity to give Reamai a knock and had everything to gain by returning to amity as quickly as possible. Reamai, on the other hand, was handicapped. He had suffered and wanted redress, yet it was not a fruitful course to pursue. If he was in earnest in calling for the court, and succeeded, it could only further postpone the eventual return to amity. If he was bluffing, and threatening to go to court is a stock maneuvering weapon, he was also invoking nontraditional values and procedures—a tactic in strong contrast to Kwaling who was referring the quarrel only to what was traditional, and who had also pointed out that the court might be equally severe about Mureg's bruises. Meakriz's withdrawal was a tacit admission that going to court was not a practical solution. By revealing the real relationship between himself and Kwaling, Reamai was deepening the rift and flying in the face of public opinion by making it so much the harder to return to amity. Kwaling withdrew from br'ngun'guni from time to time to have a smoke, a maneuver which highlighted Reamai's temperament and made it quite plain who was upset. Then other things came up.

Each accused the other of cheating in food exchanges. Each boasted of his own ability in producing food and accused the other of trying to steal the limelight when they had cooperated. Reamai called Mangai, his wife's brother. Mangai, an old manager, pointed to the blood, remonstrated with Kwaling, pleaded

with Reamai not to make too much of it, and was emphatic that
the affair should not go to court. Womak, a close friend of
Kwaling, tried to pacify Reamai; what other way was there?
Kusai, mother's brother to Kwaling and father to Reamai, scolded
Kwaling, saying he ought to go into the deep bush and stay there
awhile. Then, turning on Reamai, he entreated him to be more
reasonable. Dimunk, called by Kwaling, remarked only that this
was an affair between brothers. The matter of the adoption of
Meakriz's sons was brought up, and the incident between Bwatam
and Mureg was discussed. Previous assaults by Reamai on Mureg
were remembered, and the recent theft of betel and its consequences were thrown in as a makeweight. The air was clearing.

As the examples show, those who interjected remarks—and
many did so whether they were asked or not—did not take sides.
Explicitly supporting neither party, or blaming both, the remarks
were designed to mollify anger, soothe hurt pride, and prepare
the ground for re-establishing equivalence and amity. The specific
issues which triggered the incident could not be considered as
isolated acts, for each formed part of a complex of disappoint-
ments and grievances. At the same time, the focal issue in the
br'ngun'guni is clearly the personal rivalry between Kwaling and
Reamai, which has become a political rivalry. The principal disputants interacted with each other and also with the community,
the former attempting to influence and to manage, the latter to
mediate—a process which may be described as "mutual steering"
to equivalence and amity. What is also evident is a "looking to
consequences." From the moment he grasped his digging stick,
Kwaling seems to have been looking several moves ahead, and
Meakriz's behavior reveals the same concern for what the future
might have in store. Juatak and Nuongweram had fled from the
scene as soon as the fracas started. As far as the trapped pig
was concerned, Nuok's complaint had ranged their brothers in
opposition, and the presence of the sisters might have provided
concrete mobilizing points. After it was all over Nuongweram
said, "We went away because we might have had to say something which would have made more trouble." Gaiap, it will be

remembered, had made the first move to limit the range of the dispute by ostensibly protecting Reamai from Nuok. Only Reamai seems to have been hopelessly entangled in himself.

The present explosion may be taken to have ended when Gaiap, with two coconuts, and Gasai, with a bunch of areca nuts, placed their offerings in the middle of the dancing space to be shared among both sets of brothers. And this attempt to demonstrate "no quarrel" as between the groups of brothers was echoed in the way the pig was eventually disposed of: it was shared between all those who turned up to work in the ricefield the next day. That is, it came from Meakriz, the administrative representative, to all those who engaged in an administrative task, irrespective of kin affiliation or cooperative alliance. But the disposal of the pig that had triggered the events only marked the end of a phase. Reamai and Kwaling were committed to feasting each other and finding public equivalence through hard work and recruiting help. In the feasting exchanges more br'ngun'guni will occur. Meakriz shifted his residence to a site almost a mile distant from the larger settlement, and Bwatam and her husband went with him. Bwatam will look after Igamas and Bunjerai and Meakriz will work with Bwatam's husband in alliance with Reamai, who was left with the opportunity for making good his claims to respect and managerial ability: he has something to win. Kwaling, whose position before the incident had been fairly secure, was shaken. First, he is past his peak in physical energy and competence, and no amount of cunning or high reputation will offset his smaller production. Tangu prefer to be allied to plenty of yams in the present than to yesterday's reputation. Second, he made Reamai look small. He was beginning to dominate, and "fence sitters" went over to Reamai. Those who have been with Kwaling had their first apprehensions about the future, and in the days that followed Kwaling himself began to brood and think about sorcery. On the other hand, Reamai brightened and became cock-a-whoop.

2

Perhaps the most fascinating aspect of the first dispute is the personality of Kwaling and what he represents. He was too good for his nearest rival, too cunning and too shrewd. He lost out because by being too good he was unable to maintain equivalence, and a fortnight later he exploded again.

Twambar, Kwaling's four-year-old son, was playing with Geengai's young sons, Kandidi and Manduz. They saw a piglet defecating and, as children will, decided to stone the animal for being thus ungracious. Kandidi struck hard and true, crushing the delicate skull. Death was almost instantaneous.

Geengai, the local jokester, cackled with mirth. "Oh, well hit, well hit!" he cried.

The owner of the pig, Luassi, Kwaling's aged mother, started to grieve, complain, and scold. Kwaling himself tucked his pipe into his armlet, leaped to his feet, and grasping a large hunk of firewood gave chase. Whooping loudly he hurled his log, hit Twambar in the back of the neck, and brought him down. Juatak hurried to the rescue and dragged the screaming child to a safe place. Br'ngun'guni commenced.

Whooping, yelling, leaping into the air, and thwacking his buttocks, Kwaling had everyone's attention. Children fled from the dancing space, women sought out their huts, and a few men who were stitching sago fronds into roofing strips continued their work with studied concentration.

Geengai made a few half-hearted runs and then retired to his hut. Kwaling wanted to know what Geengai was about. Did he want a fight? What then? Did he think he had a garden of worth? Did he want a feasting exchange? Ha!

Luassi intervened. This, she said, was a fuss about little. The pig was dead. Kandidi was only a child.

Gently but firmly, Kwaling hustled her off and returned to the dancing space. Meakriz, who was sitting nearby, rose to his feet, but he had barely opened his mouth when Kwaling let fly at him.

The Luluai sat down in silence. Luassi came forward again, imploring her son to desist. Kwaling only took her by the shoulders and led her, protesting, back to her hut.

Geengai, who is an easygoing man with no pretensions to managerial ability, had seemed transfixed. However, at last he gave voice. He pointed out that the piglet deserved stoning: it should not foul the village. Everyone stoned piglets that defecated in the village; who could tell it would be killed? Besides, Kwaling ought to take more care of his pigs. Kwaling's pig had been into his garden, rooting and eating his yams.

"Come out of your hut!" Kwaling cried, livid and bouncing with rage. "Come out into the open!"

Geengai refused. He has a big enough garden, but as the village jester he is wont to laugh at the things others take seriously. He is not interested in prestige and influence; his métier is gossip, turning the phrase, mimicry, making fun of the pompous. He likes his joke.

"Ha!" With a last flourish and thwack of the buttocks, Kwaling sat down to relight his pipe. The village fell silent.

Seconds later, Geengai emerged from his hut, axe in hand. Walking deliberately, he went around to the back of his hut—to his coconuts.

Immediately there was uproar. Geengai's wife's brothers rushed down and pushed Geengai away from his coconuts. They argued, they placed themselves between Geengai and his coconuts, hugging the trees; gently, they relieved him of his axe. No, he must not cut down his coconuts.

Geengai said little. With a gesture of resignation he turned and went into his hut. In a few moments he emerged, spear on his shoulder, and, with Manduz following, he walked disdainfully out of the village.

Though the incident arose from the irresponsible act of a small boy who had not reached years of discretion, the critical choices cleared the way for a speedy return to amity. Kwaling had an interest in the piglet and there is no doubt he was angry over its death, yet he is in no kind of competitive relationship with Geengai. He struck Twambar, his own son, not Kandidi who had done the deed, and by so doing avoided a major issue with Kandidi's mother's brothers. Nor was the act an accident; it was done, as Kwaling afterward explained, specifically to avoid further entanglements. He was looking to consequences. The br'ngun'guni had to happen. The pig was dead, killed in public, and Geengai had laughed. Something had to be done. Nothing could bring the pig back to life but, especially in view of what had happened with Reamai, there had to be a retort.

Geengai refused to accommodate Kwaling. In his way a philosopher, and a Christian, Geengai had spent the last two weeks bringing out the funny side of the Reamai affair, and he had even succeeded in making it look ridiculous—a joke hardly appreciated by Kwaling. Yet, though Geengai refused to meet Kwaling on a ground of his own choice, he is so far locked in traditional values that the reply he made referred to the ravages of Kwaling's pig in his garden; and his final act, an apparent attempt to sever his connection with the village by cutting his coconuts, shows that he felt keenly his inability or reluctance to maintain equivalence in the traditional way. In the eyes of his friends and relations he was failing quite miserably.

Nobody will ever know whether Geengai was bluffing or whether he really meant to cut his coconuts. He had more to lose than to gain by so doing, but points in his hand if someone would stop him: his wife's brothers could hardly have been more timely. Kwaling had dominated in br'ngun'guni, but this was because Geengai had refused to accept. If Geengai had wholly submitted, sympathy would have gone to Kwaling because Geengai's behavior would have been thought contemptuous and therefore a deliberate breach of equivalence. Further, no one in the community would have failed to impute to Geengai a deliberate and malicious intent to get his own back by sorcery—a flagrant intent to do evil which would have made him very unpopular and an outlaw. If Geengai had succeeded in cutting his coconuts, the community would have fallen to pieces. Kwaling's reaction to the death of the pig was expectable and, in the circumstances, natural; Geengai ought to have engaged in br'ngun'guni. Yet no one would have had sympathy either for Geengai or for Kwaling had the coconuts fallen: Geengai should not have done it, nor should Kwaling have driven him to it. The whole village would have had to rearrange itself and most would have gone off into the bush to found new settlements. On the other hand, the evidence of intent served to equalize. Kwaling and Geengai went off into the bush and kept out of each other's way and three weeks later relations between them seemed to be quite normal. Geengai was as cheerful as ever, and Kwaling had recovered his confidence. They had finished equivalent.

3

It was thought in neighborhood M that a man of neighborhood B, who was a renowned and skillful hunter and who had been giving a series of feasts, had been taking his game from bush habitually used by a man of M. Private representations had been made to the people of B, but still the game was elusive. The conclusion in M was that the trespasser was continuing his mischief.

One night, at the start of a regular community feasting and dancing exchange in M, Ndori, the Luluai, who was leading the dance, became dissatisfied with some of his team who were blowing whistles. He halted the dance and asked his brothers to stop blowing their whistles. They nodded compliance and the dance continued.

A few minutes later, quite firmly, the whistlers piped up again.

Again, Ndori stopped the dance. It was his favorite dance, and he didn't want any whistling. Was that understood? Yes, it was. The dancers resumed their places in the line and the dance recommenced.

But the whistlers wanted to whistle. Gradually the soft little "peeps" grew into a chorus of shrill, fully blown screams. Ndori was obviously under some strain; glowering, stamping too hard, and cracking his hand drum in temper, he said nothing. Nearly everyone was whistling.

Suddenly, Ndori straightened. Tearing off his headdress of cockatoo plumes, he flung it to the ground, stamped it to pieces, and strode off to his hut.

The dance stopped. Nobody spoke. Seconds later the rapid tattoo on a slit-gong and the clatter of the wand being flung into the body of the instrument informed all within earshot that Ndori was very angry indeed.

After a hasty consultation the dancers decided that the mission boss-boy should go to Ndori and try to persuade him to rejoin the dance. But when he returned a few minutes later, he could only report complete failure. Ndori had shut himself in his hut, was very angry, and would speak to no one. "Let us stop dancing," suggested the boss-boy. "If we go on it will make him angrier."

There was general opposition to this. Someone struck up on a hand drum and the dancers resumed.

An hour later the boss-boy again repaired to the Luluai. He returned with the news that Ndori had gone to the stream to wash himself of paint. Speaking in formal br'ngun'guni, he exhorted all those present to abandon the dance. They refused. The boss-boy started to lobby individuals, pointing out that Ndori could use his office of Luluai to stop dancing for the year. He went again to see Ndori and spoke twice in formal br'ngun'guni, but to no effect. Someone always struck up on a drum and the dance continued.

A little after midnight Kavak, Tultul of B, who was attending the dance, rose to speak in formal br'ngun'guni. He was sorry, he said, very sorry indeed to see Ndori so angry. Why was Ndori so angry? There was nothing to be angry about. Perhaps it was the matter of—but no! Allegations of trespass could be settled in amity, by talking. True, there had been a little wild talk, but it could never be seriously meant. True, the men of B were tired of being accused of trespassing and there were some loose and irresponsible people who had spoken of stopping the trade in cooking pots if the accusations went on in this way. But now? Now it was different. Ndori was angry, angry in a dance! Angry because he had seen a man of B—himself! Right! (Kavak thwacked his buttocks and leapt into the air.) They of B would let no cooking pots into M; they would smash them to make sure! Anger such as this over an unproven trespass!

Kavak did not get through his speech without interruption. It was pointed out that Ndori's anger had nothing to do with the trespass, nor was it a reply to the threat of an embargo on cooking pots. It had to do with the whistling.

"Whistling?" cried Kavak, "Bah!"

Many muttered expletives under their breath. Others shouted, "You are a good fellow—come again next week!" Or, "Speak up —I cannot hear." Or, "We like you. Let us get on with the dance!" Or, "Oh true, oh true!"—a phrase always carrying explicit agreement but importing overtones of scepticism or frank or aggressive disagreement. One man sitting next to the writer very gently exploded with wrath.

Kavak whipped around. "Never mind!" cried the man, "You're a good chap. You carry on!"

But the position was serious. No one in M could make a clay cooking pot; they had to get them from B. The threat of the embargo was a fair weapon to use in reply to the allegations of trespass, but failure to establish Ndori's anger as resulting from the threat—followed up by carrying out the threat—was answering a pinprick with a bombshell. M was to be without pots, and unless B could establish anger in M, Kavak, as representative of B, had overreached himself.

The following night there was a dance in B, and to it went several men of M including Ndori. The Luluai had recovered his poise, but nevertheless the men of B studiously avoided him during the feast. Toward dawn, however, Wapai, Luluai of B, approached Ndori, offering betel and tobacco, and cautiously felt his way into a conversation. He joked, mentioning casually that there was no need for anger in this matter. He laughed with spirited gaiety. As tactfully, and quite as obstinately, Ndori refused to be drawn. In a few minutes Kavak joined them and contributed his quip. It was soon evident that he had abandoned his position of the previous night, and that his kinsmen in M had persuaded him that Ndori had been angry over the whistling and not over the threat to place an embargo on pots. Without taking sides, he became a mediator. He tried to show both Wapai—who, sincerely convinced or otherwise, would have liked the anger pinned to the trespass—and Ndori that it was an understandable mistake that Ndori's anger should have been connected with the trespass. Ndori said little.

Nor were they the only men talking. It had become recognized that although B was committed to stopping the trade in pots, the individuals concerned would like to recant without climbing down. If Ndori, or someone in M, would admit Ndori's anger to have been over the trespass all would have been clear sailing, but no one in M was willing to do this. Nevertheless, reconciliation had entered the decisive stage when it was agreed that B should come to dance in M. Throughout the interval between the feast in B and that to be held in M, there were meetings between private individuals. Kin links between the two neighborhoods facilitated the talks, but one factor stood out: how, in the circumstances, could one neighborhood reach equivalence with the other?

During the feast in M the men of B danced very well, but when food was placed before them there was no meat and the tubers were not so well cooked as they might have been. The men of B were highly indignant. One after the other they spoke in formal br'ngun'guni. Why was there no meat? What had they done? Were the men of M really this impossible? First there were allegations of trespass, then Ndori had been angry, and now there was no meat!

No one from M spoke a word. They gathered the empty food bowls in silence, and the dance petered to an end.

As soon as the dance was abandoned there was jubilation in both camps. "Now all the trouble is over," said a man of M. "We gave them no meat." A man of B said, "We shall have another feast. It is finished already but another feast will finish it properly." One insult had canceled the other.

With the parties roughly equivalent there only remained a few niceties of wit to show how close to one-up equivalence can be. Two days after the feast in M the slit-gongs of B announced the concluding feast together with dance *Surai*. When he heard the slit-gongs the Tultul of M, who was to lead the dancers, at once let it be known in B that he had a sore toe and would be unable to dance Surai. There was much indignation in B, since the Tultul's refusal was good for all of M. It was noted, however, that the refusal had not come by slit-gong but by messengers. Those with kinsfolk in M took up their spears, girded their betel bags, and set off for M.

Meanwhile, the Tultul sat on the platform of his hut, legs spread wide so that anyone who would might inspect his sore toe. "I do not like Surai," he confided in a whisper. "Besides, I do not have the proper regalia." It was also common knowledge in the neighborhood that the Tultul was an expert at *Dumari*.

As men from B began arriving in M to visit their kinsfolk, they passed by the Tultul. Some inspected the toe, clucking their sympathy, and went on their way. Others may have noted the Dumari plumes carelessly hung in the doorway. At any rate, a couple of hours later the slit-gongs rang out again from B. Surai was canceled, and Dumari was on.

Dumari in B was a great occasion. The man of M who had first alleged a trespass went, and the alleged trespasser provided most of the food. All the speeches in br'ngun'guni were conciliatory; the quarrel, the "talk," was dead. Both neighborhoods appeared to have clean sheets before them. The atmosphere was gay, the food excellent and prodigious, the dancing superb.

Then Ndori made a speech in formal br'gnun'guni, the last to be made. He praised the food, soberly approving its quality and quantity, and he remarked on the skill, industry, and generosity that had gone into the preparation of such a feast. There had been some trouble, he said, the beat of his hand drum beginning to quicken. There had been some talk, but now it was over. Ndori thwacked his buttocks for emphasis. He leaped into the air, bounding up and down the dancing space. Ha—what a feast! But let the men of B come to M! Let them come to show how they could dance! Let them come and see if they could eat all that M would provide!

A chorus of yells greeted this outburst. "Have you no shame? The talk is dead! There is no quarrel between us!"

Ndori sat down, gleeful and unchastened, and the hubbub died down.

With the dawn came the end of the dance. As men and women stole away to their huts or to their gardens to sleep, one or two remarked on the portent of Ndori's speech. Two months later men's ears were pricking as they reminded one another of what Ndori had said. For, though the two neighborhoods are separate entities, only fifteen minutes' walk lies between them, the kin links are many and strong, and both sides enjoy having reasons to entertain each other at feasts.

Ndori is a manager. He had failed to get his way with the whistling, but in his final speech in B he equalized personally and he also opened the door for another series of issues to be settled by interneighborhood feasting. His last speech is the peg on which future issues will be hung. Other managers, looking to consequences and susceptible to mediation, also tried to influence the course of events. The mission boss-boy, anxious because Ndori was angry and might stop dancing altogether, tried to have the first dance abandoned. Kavak used Ndori's anger to bring the bush dispute into the open, and to crystallize and justify what hitherto had only been rumored—an embargo on cooking pots. Later, knowing he had overreached himself, he was among the first to attempt to restore equivalence through mediation, particularly choosing Ndori who had become, as it were, the fulcrum of the dispute. Others, in other directions, were not slow to follow his example. Some managers in M felt that huge quantities of meat in the third dance, rather than no meat, was the proper response. Either would have neutralized the insult of placing an embargo on pots, but the scarcity of game forced them to select the cheaper way. Wapai, a manager, called for dance Surai. In B they were experts at Surai, well qualified to criticize others who attempted the dance. Knowing this, the Tultul of M, also a manager, maneuvered Wapai into canceling Surai and substituting Dumari, thereby serving a political as well as a personal interest. Finally, although Ndori's anger was over the whistling, it started the train of events, was used to make other issues explicit, and was directly responsible for reopening further possibilities between the two neighborhoods.

4

The following provides a brief glance at Tangu in their relations with outsiders, and illustrates the basic theme of Tangu disputes: whither equivalence?

A dog belonging to a man of A, where they speak an unintelligible variant of the Tangu language, fell into a pig trap dug by a Tangu of neighborhood R. The dog died.

Grieved and angry at the loss of his dog, the stranger repaired to the hunting lodge of the owner of the trap and demanded compensation of one pound (£1). Saying he would consider the matter, the owner of the trap returned to his settlement, spread the news, and started an informal discussion. A covillager, just returned from hunting, joined them. He said he had fallen in with some men from A and they had urged him to tell the others in R to forget about the demand for compensation. The men of A had no quarrel with the men of R.

One of those present said, "Pay the compensation and have done with it."

The latest arrival objected. "There is no quarrel. It is best to forget it."

"He was angry with me and demanded compensation," said the owner of the trap.

The argument continued.

Payment of one pound is a fair and recognized compensation for causing the death of a hunting dog, but who was responsible for the death? Surely the dog was trespassing? Surely the owner of the dog could not have been far behind and was also trespassing? The plain demand for compensation was a simple enough matter. It could be argued about and so mixed into other events that equivalence could be reached without actually making a payment. Withdrawing the demand after having made it makes the situation extremely complex. To pay or not to pay?

R could insist upon payment, but in so doing they would offend A where there are many notorious sorcerers much feared by Tangu. It is asking for trouble. Not to pay puts R at a decided disadvantage, for in any future contretemps men from A will say, "Remember how we let you off that compensation you owed us?" Even if the aggrieved party had not asked for compensation, the death of the dog would have become known and nobody in R could have imagined that the man was not angry about it. Failing the open expression of anger, the only reasonable construction would be that the owner of the dog was resorting to sorcery. So men of R would go to A and ask for the sorcery to cease. In A they would be suitably indignant, and counter accusations would be made. Other incidents would be remembered.

From the moment the man from A suffered his loss, some involvement of others was inevitable. Since it happened that the dog died in R, the affair could not but involve R in opposition to A. In the old days such an issue would have been resolved by armed demonstrations or warfare. Today, since warfare is forbidden and neither party can or will br'ngun'guni in the settlements of the other, the only way to settle issues between them is to steer clear, bicker intermittently, and resort to mystical attack.

The last dispute fairly describes the quality of relations between households, communities, and neighborhoods within

Tangu. Disputes are frequent.[4] Households are not organized into permanent jural corporate groups, and cooperators one year may be in an exchange relationship the next. All issues are basically matters for consideration by the independent household, and expectations between households are only definable in terms of those claims—which themselves are vulnerable to challenge—that are actually being made good. The claims of individuals are put to work for the household, and in a crucial conflict the household itself splits and a new one comes into being. When anger, which is evidence of a conflict of claims, can be related to food and its production, the equilibrium is maintained between households through br'ngun'guni and the necessity to establish equivalence in order to return to amity. When Tangu become involved with the administration and its officers, as Reamai threatened in the first dispute, normally an explicit decision is made. Since such a decision must in some way detract from the total personality of one or the other party, it is a breach of equivalence and cannot predicate amity. So, though Tangu often threaten to go to court they rarely go through with it; they know that to do so will further delay the return to amity. If an issue goes to the administration and a decision is made, failing physical enforcement on the ground by policemen, Tangu proceed much as they would have done otherwise. They have feasting exchanges and br'ngun'guni. The administrative decision becomes a factor on the level of Ndori's anger or the Tultul's toe: it is used to work for equivalence. By resorting to the administration a second time, a return to amity is still further delayed; for in order to return to amity it is necessary to establish equivalence, and the latter is as much dependent on the cooperation of the whole community as on the mutual respect of the individuals concerned.

Br'ngun'guni is an activity designed not to make explicit decisions. It allows personal relationships to work themselves out in relation to the community. Brothers, such as Kwaling and Rea-

---

[4] One year with Tangu produced some twenty major disputes and many more minor ones.

mai, should ideally be in a cooperative relationship. But it so happens that, first, they are the two best food producers in the community and, second, there is a personal antagonism between them. In a cooperative relationship the discord becomes vicious and cannot conform to amity. In an exchange relationship, on the other hand, personal animosity becomes larded with mutual respect, which in turn lays the basis for equivalence. It may even be that Kwaling and Reamai will end up mngwotngwotiki—precisely equivalent. Finally, since Kwaling and Reamai are the two best producers, with whom can they exchange and at the same time maintain equivalence and a reputation for productive ability if they cooperate? What is personally apparently desirable also emerges as a structural necessity. Only by shifting from the cooperative to the exchange relationship can they work toward a personal equivalence. Other households will join with them, help them toward their personal equivalence, and also work out their own equivalences.

The techniques of br'ngun'guni appear to be consistent with the ends. Management is the dynamic element which keeps interrelationships shifting toward conformity with amity even though, since amity depends on equivalence, it may have to be done through expressions of anger. Managers rise and fall, gain adherents and lose them. They are not what they are by virtue of their positions within a network of kinfolk, but because of their competences—productive ability, shrewdness, and convincing oratory. Each br'ngun'guni subtly redefines the expectations contained within personal and interhousehold relationships. Anger is evidence of unsatisfactory relationships, of inequivalence, and on anger's expression the community seems to be on the point of disrupting—but the contrary happens. Individuals collect as an aggregation, disputants and others interact, and expectations become redefined. In terms of the interrelationships of individuals and households, br'ngun'guni changes the community. Mediation, whether as an interruption in br'ngun'guni or in the form of private conversations, lobbying, or carefully prepared small talk, shades black into white and lays the foundation for re-establishing equivalence. Looking to consequences might, but does not, proceed from the idea of a precedent; it is a technique related to situations of choice, the inevitability of disappointed expectations, mutual participation and interdependencies, and the necessity to establish equivalence in order to have amity. The most common, generalized, and conventional technique is retiring to the bush so that an angry relationship is not sparked by personal contact into a series of incidents which may lead the persons concerned to a point of no return.

There is little doubt that as individuals managers are restrained by the fear of sorcery—mystical consequences. At the same time, so long as equivalence remains a firm value expressed in equivalent exchanges of foodstuffs, it is evident that no manager can possibly attain an outright dominance; sorcery acts in concert with, but independently of, the other factors involved. In the first dispute Meakriz, as Luluai, had to try to make peace. As Reamai's half-brother he came to his aid; as Luluai he demanded the court; and as Meakriz, the Luluai, a member of the community with a personal interest, he abandoned the idea. His behavior in the second dispute, where he might have made an ass of himself by trying to be Luluai, as well as the behavior of Kwaling, Reamai, Ndori, Kavak, Wapai, and the Tultul of M, shows a close coincidence of personal interest, political ends, and structural forms.

When anger cannot be related to food and its production, br'ngun'guni cannot occur. In the old days an offense such as incest would have been dealt with on the level of the jural group through the clubhouse organization, which included secret societies of sorcerers. Today, lacking both, there exists no machinery for dealing with such crimes apart from bringing in the administration, which Tangu do not like to do. One heinous incest on record, involving father and daughter, revealed that at the time when the act first became public knowledge there was general and hearty disapproval, but it was only diffuse. The union had persisted for over a year and had come to be accepted as a fait accompli—a claim made good and maintained in the face of an opinion which could not grow "teeth." Less serious incests gain disapproval and, in effect, "Oh well, that is how it is these days," if the parties adhere to their union. Complaints of adultery may be expressed through, or worked into, a br'ngun'guni but again, only on the level of the Tultul's toe. Adultery is a personal, nonpolitical issue; there are divorce, compensation in valuables, and sorcery. Equivalence can be found in more ways than one. In Tangu political power depends primarily on the production, exchange, and distribution of foodstuffs under equivalence, and these community issues br'ngun'guni deals with. It cannot cope with personal problems unless they are also politically relevant.

THE WAGER OF BATTLE

Henry Charles Lea

WHEN MAN IS emerging from barbarism, the struggle between the rising power of reason and the waning supremacy of brute force is full of instruction. When in the dark ages, we find the administration of justice so strangely interrupted by appeals to the sword or to chance, dignified under the forms of Christianized superstition, we should remember that even this is an improvement on the all-pervading first law of violence. When the strong man is brought, by whatever means, to yield to the weak, a great conquest is gained over human nature.

The curious mingling of procedure, in these untutored seekings after justice, is well illustrated in a form of process prescribed by the primitive Bavarian law. A man comes into court with six conjurators to claim an estate; the possessor defends his right with a single witness, who must be a landholder of the vicinage. The claimant then attacks the veracity of the witness— "Thou hast lied against me. Grant me the single combat, and let God make manifest whether thou hast sworn truth or falsehood"; and, according to the event of the duel is the decision as to the truthfulness of the witness and the ownership of the property.

In discussing the judicial combat, it is important to keep in view the wide distinction between the wager of battle as a judicial institution, and the custom of duelling which has obtained with more or less regularity among all races and at all ages. We have only to deal with the combat as a strictly judicial process, and

Extracted by Paul Bohannan from pp. 101–98 of Henry Charles Lea, *Superstition and Force: Essays on the Wager of Law—the Wager of Battle —the Ordeal—Torture*. Philadelphia: Lea Brothers and Co., 1892.

shall, therefore, leave untouched the vast harvest of curious anec-
dote afforded by the monomachial propensities of modern times.

The medieval panegyrists of the wager of battle sought to
strengthen its title to respect by affirming that it was as old as
the human race, and that Cain and Abel, unable to settle their
conflicting claims in any other mode, agreed to leave the decision
to the chances of the duel; while the combat between David and
Goliath was considered by the early schoolmen as an unanswer-
able proof of the favor with which God regarded such encounters.
Leaving such speculations aside, it is enough for us to know that
all the tribes which settled in Europe practiced the combat with
so general a unanimity that its origin must be sought at a period
anterior to their separation from the common stock, although it
has left no definite traces in the written records which have
reached us of the Asiatic Aryans.

While the laws of the Angles, the Saxons, and the Frisians bear
ample testimony to the general use of the wager of battle, it is
not a little singular that the duel appears to have been unknown
among the Anglo-Saxons. I can offer no explanation of the anomaly, and can only state the bare fact that the judicial combat is
not referred to in any of the Anglo-Saxon or Anglo-Danish codes.
There seems, indeed, to be no reason to doubt that its introduction into English jurisprudence dates only from the time of William the Conqueror.

The wager of battle thus formed part of the ancestral institutions of all the races who founded the nations of Europe. With
their conversion to Christianity the appeal was transferred from
the heathen deities to God, who was expected to intervene and
decide the battle in favor of the right. It was an appeal to the
highest court and popular confidence in the arbitrament of the
sword was rather strengthened than diminished. Enlightened
lawgivers not only shared, to a greater or less extent, in this
confidence, but were also disposed to regard the duel with favor
as the most practical remedy for the crime of false swearing which
was everywhere prevalent. Gundobald assumes that its introduction into the Burgundian code arose from this cause; Charle-

magne urged its use as greatly preferable to the shameless oaths
which were taken with so much facility; while Otho II, in 983,
ordered its employment in various forms of procedure for the
same reason. It can hardly be a source of surprise, in view of the
warlike manners of the times, and of the enormous evils for which
a palliative was sought, that there was felt to be advantage in
this mode of impressing upon principals and witnesses the awful
sanctity of the oath, thus entailing upon them the liability of
supporting their asseverations by undergoing the risks of a combat rendered doubly solemn by imposing religious ceremonies.

Various causes were at work to extend the application of the
judicial duel to all classes of cases. In the primitive codes of
the barbarians, there is no distinction made between civil and
criminal law. Bodily punishment being almost unknown, except
for slaves, and nearly all infractions of the law being visited
with fines, there was no necessity for such niceties, the matter
at stake in all cases being simply money or money's worth. Accordingly, we find the wager of battle used indiscriminately, both
as a defense against accusations of crime, and as a mode of
settling cases of disputed property, real and personal. Yet some
of the earlier codes refer to it but seldom. The Salic law, as we
have seen, hardly recognizes its existence; the Ripuarian code
alludes to it but four times, and that of the Alamanni but six
times. In others, like the Baioarian, it is appealed to on almost
every occasion, and among the Burgundians it superseded all
evidence and rendered superfluous any attempt to bring forward
witnesses. This variation is probably rather apparent than real,
and if in any of these bodies of laws there were originally substantial limitations on its use, in time they disappeared, for it
was not difficult to find expedients to justify the extension of a
custom which accorded so perfectly with the temper of the age.
How little reason was requisite to satisfy the belligerent aspira-
tions of justice is shown by a curious provision in the code of
one of the Frisian tribes, by which a man unable to disprove an
accusation of homicide was allowed to charge the crime on whom-

soever he might select, and then the question between them was decided by combat.

The elasticity, in fact, with which the duel lent itself to the advantage of the turbulent and unscrupulous had no little influence in extending its sphere of action. This feature in its history is well exemplified in a document containing the proceedings of an assembly of local magnates, held in the year 888, to decide a contention concerning the patronage of the church of Lessingon. After the testimony on one side had been given, the opposite party commenced in reply, when the leaders of the assembly, seizing their swords, vowed that they would affirm the truth of the first pleader's evidence with their blood before King Arnoul and his court—and the case was decided without more ado. The strong and the bold are apt to be the ruling spirits in all ages, and were emphatically so in those periods of scarcely curbed violence when the jurisprudence of the European commonwealths was slowly developing itself.

It is no wonder, therefore, that means were readily found for extending the jurisdiction of the wager of battle as widely as possible. One of the most fruitful of these expedients was the custom of challenging witnesses. The duel was a method of determining questions of perjury, and there was nothing to prevent a suitor, who saw his case going adversely, from accusing an inconvenient witness of false swearing and demanding the "campus" to prove it—a proceeding which adjourned the main case, and likewise decided its result. This summary process, of course, brought every action within the jurisdiction of force, and deprived the judges of all authority to control the abuse. That it obtained at a very early period is shown by a form of procedure occurring in the Bavarian law, already referred to, by which the claimant of an estate is directed to fight, not the defendant, but his witness; and in 819 a capitulary of Louis le Débonnaire gives a formal privilege to the accused on a criminal charge to select one of the witnesses against him with whom to decide the question in battle. It is easy, therefore, to understand the custom, prescribed in some of the codes, by which witnesses were required to come into court armed, and to have their weapons blessed on the altar before giving their testimony. If defeated they were fined, and were obliged to make good to the opposite party any damage which their testimony, had it been successful, would have caused him.

A still more bizarre extension of the practice, and one which was most ingeniously adapted to defeat the ends of justice, is found in a provision of the English law of the thirteenth century, allowing a man to challenge his own witnesses. Thus in many classes of crimes, such as theft, forgery, coining, etc., the accused could summon a "warrantor" from whom he professed to have received the articles which formed the basis of the accusation. The warrantor could scarcely give evidence in favor of the accused without assuming the responsibility himself. If he refused, the accused was at liberty to challenge him; if he gave the required evidence, he was liable to a challenge from the accuser. The warrantor was sometimes also employed as a champion, and served for hire, but this service was illegal and, when detected, involved the penalties of perjury. Another mode extensively used in France about the same time was to accuse the principal witness of some crime rendering him incapable of giving testimony, when he was obliged to dispose of the charge by fighting, either personally or by champion, in order to get his evidence admitted.

The result of this system was that, in causes subject to such appeals, no witness could be forced to testify, by the French law of the thirteenth century, unless his principal entered into bonds to see him harmless in case of challenge, to provide a champion, and to make good all damages in case of defeat; though it is difficult to understand how this could be satisfactorily arranged, since the penalties inflicted on a vanquished witness were severe, being, in civil causes, the loss of a hand and a fine at the pleasure of the suzerain, while in criminal actions *"il perderoit le cors avecques."* The only limit to this abuse was that witnesses were not liable to challenge in cases concerning matters of less value than five sous and one denier.

If the position of a witness was thus rendered unenviable, that of the judge was little better. As though the duel had not received sufficient extension by the facilities for its employment just described, another mode of appealing to the sword in all cases was invented by which it became competent for the defeated party in any suit to challenge the court itself, and thus obtain a forcible reversal of judgment. It must be borne in mind that this was not quite as absurd a practice as it may seem to us in modern times, for under the feudal system the dispensing of justice was one of the most highly prized attributes of sovereignty; and, except in England, where the royal judges were frequently ecclesiastics, the seignorial courts were presided over by warriors. In Germany, indeed, where the magistrates of the lower tribunals were elective, they were required to be active and vigorous of body. Towards the end of the twelfth century in England we find Glanville acknowledging his uncertainty as to whether or not the court could depute the settlement of such an appeal to a champion, and also as to what, in case of defeat, was the legal position of the court thus convicted of injustice. These doubts would seem to indicate that the custom was still of recent introduction in England, and not as yet practiced to an extent sufficient to afford a settled basis of precedents for its details. Elsewhere, however, it was firmly established.

Towards the latter half of the thirteenth century, we find in the *Conseil* of Pierre de Fontaines the custom in its fullest vigor and just on the eve of its decline. No restriction appears to be imposed as to the cases in which appeal by battle was permitted, except that it was not allowed to override the customary law. The suitor selected any one of three judges agreeing in the verdict; he could appeal at any stage of the proceedings when a point was decided against him; if unsuccessful, he was only liable in a pecuniary penalty to the judges for the wrong done them, and the judge, if vanquished, was exposed to no bodily punishment.

While the feudal system was supreme, this appeal to arms was the only mode of reversing a judgment, and an appeal in any other form was an innovation introduced by the extension of the royal jurisdiction under St. Louis, who labored so strenuously and so effectually to modify the barbarism of feudal institutions by subordinating them to the principles of the Roman jurisprudence.

Twenty years later, we find in Beaumanoir abundant evidence of the success of St. Louis in setting bounds to the abuses which he was endeavoring to remove. In capital cases, the appeal did not lie; while in civil actions, the suzerain before whom the appeal was made could refuse it when the justice of the verdict was self-evident. Some caution, moreover, was requisite in conducting such cases, for the disappointed pleader who did not manage matters rightly might find himself pledged to a combat, single-handed, with all his judges at once; and as the bench consisted of a collection of the neighboring gentry, the result might be the confirmation of the sentence in a manner more emphatic than agreeable.

The king's court, however, was an exception to the general rule. No appeals could be taken from its judgments, for there was no tribunal before which they could be carried. The judges of the royal court were therefore safe from the necessity of vindicating their decisions in the field, and they even carried this immunity with them and communicated it to those with whom they might be acting.

By the German law of the same period, the privilege of reversing a sentence by the sword existed, but accompanied with regulations which seem evidently designed to embarrass, by enormous trouble and expense, the gratification of the impulse which disappointed suitors would have to establish their claims in such manner. Thus, by the Suabian law, it could only be done in the presence of the sovereign himself, and not in that of the immediate feudal superior; while the Saxon code requires the extraordinary expedient of a pitched battle, with seven on each side, in the king's presence.

Thus carefully molded in conformity with the popular prejudices or convictions of every age and country, it may readily be imagined how large a part the judicial combat played in the affairs of daily life. It was so skilfully interwoven throughout the whole system of jurisprudence that no one could feel secure that he might not, at any moment, as plaintiff, defendant, or witness, be called upon to protect his estate or his life either by his own right hand or by the club of some professional and possibly treacherous bravo. This organized violence assumed for itself the sanction of a religion of love and peace, and human intelligence seemed too much blunted to recognize the contradiction.

There was, in fact, no question which might not be submitted to the arbitrament of the sword or club. If Charlemagne, in dividing his vast empire, forbade the employment of the wager of battle in settling the territorial questions which might arise between his heirs, the prohibition merely shows that it was habitually used in affairs of the highest moment, and the constant reference to it in his laws proves that it was in no way repugnant to his general sense of justice and propriety.

The next century affords ample evidence of the growing favor in which the judicial combat was held. About the year 930, Hugh, King of Provence and Italy, becoming jealous of his uterine brother, Lambert, Duke of Tuscany, asserted him to be a supposititious child, and ordered him in future to claim no relationship between them. Lambert contemptuously denied the aspersion on his birth, and offered to clear all doubts on the subject by the wager of battle. Hugh accordingly selected a warrior named Teudinus as his champion; Lambert was victor in the ensuing combat, and was universally received as the undoubted son of his mother. His triumph, however, was illegally brought to a sudden close, for Hugh soon after succeeded in making him prisoner and deprived him of eyesight. About the middle of the century, Otho the Great appears, throwing the enormous weight of his influence in its favor. As a magnanimous and warlike prince, the wager of battle appears to have possessed peculiar attraction for his chivalrous instincts, and he extended its application as far as lay in his power. Not only did he force his daughter Liutgarda, in defending herself from a villainous accusation, to forego the safer modes of purgation, and to submit herself to the perilous decision of a combat, but he also caused the abstract question of representation in the succession of estates to be settled in the same manner.

A duelist, in fact, seems to have been reckoned a necessary adjunct to diplomacy, for when, in 968, Liutprand was dispatched by Otho to Constantinople on a matrimonial mission, and during the negotiations for the hand of Theophania a discussion arose as to the circumstances which had led to Otho's conquest of Italy, the warlike prelate offered to prove his veracity by the sword of one of his attendants: a proposition which put a triumphant end to the argument. A more formal assertion of the diplomatic value of the duel was made when in 1177 the conflicting claims of the kings of Castile and Navarre were referred to Henry II of England for adjudication, and both embassies to the English court were supplied with champions as well as with lawyers, so as to be prepared in case the matter was submitted to the duel for decision.

It is not to be supposed, however, from these instances that the duel was an aristocratic institution, reserved for nobles and affairs of state. It was an integral part of the ordinary law, both civil and criminal, employed habitually for the decision of the most everyday affairs. Thus a chronicler happens to mention that in 1017 the Emperor St. Henry II coming to Merseburg hanged a number of robbers who had been convicted in single combat by champions, and then proceeding to Magdeburg he had all the thieves assembled and treated them in the same manner. So much was it a matter of course that, by the English law of the thirteenth century, a pleader was sometimes allowed to alter the record of his preliminary plea, by producing a man who would offer to prove with his body that the record was incorrect, the sole excuse for the absurdity being that it was only allowed in matters which could not injure the other side; and a malefactor turning king's evidence was obliged, before receiving his pardon, to pledge himself to convict all his accomplices, if required, by the duel.

[It was forbidden to] endeavor to influence God's judgment by the use of unlawful expedients. This was not confined to the laity. In 1355 there was an important suit between the Bishop of Salisbury and the Earl of Salisbury respecting the ownership of a castle, in which the combat was adjudged. When the champions entered the lists the customary examination of their arms and accoutrements was made, and the combat was adjourned in consequence, as it was said, of finding in the coat of the episcopal champion certain rolls containing prayers and charms. The case was finally compromised by the bishop paying fifteen hundred marks to the earl for the disputed property. That precautions against such devices were deemed necessary is shown by the oath required of all combatants, whether principals or champions, that they had on them no charms or conjurations to affect the result. A quaint formula for this is the oath of the champion in the case of Low *vs.* Paramore in 1571—"This hear you justices that I have this day neither eat, drunk, nor have upon me either bone, stone, ne glass or any enchantment, sorcery, or witchcraft wherethrough the power of the Word of God might be inleased or diminished and the devil's power increased, and that my appeal is true, so help me God and his saints and by this Book."

By the English law of the thirteenth century, a man accused of crime had, in doubtful cases only, the right of election between trial by jury and the wager of battle. When a violent presumption existed against him, he was obliged to submit to the verdict of a jury; but in cases of suspected poisoning, as satisfactory evidence was deemed unattainable, the accused had only the choice between confession and the combat. On the other hand, when the appellant demanded the duel, he was obliged to make out a probable case before it was granted. When battle had been gaged, however, no withdrawal was permitted, and any composition between the parties to avoid it was punishable by fine and imprisonment—a regulation, no doubt, intended to prevent pleaders from rashly undertaking it, and to obviate its abuse as a means of extortion. In accusations of treason, indeed, the royal consent alone could prevent the matter from being fought out. Any bodily injury on the part of the plaintiff, tending to render him less capable of defense or aggression, likewise deprived the defendant of the right to the wager of battle, and this led to such nice distinctions that the loss of molar teeth was adjudged not to amount to disqualification, while the absence of incisors was considered sufficient excuse, because they were held to be important weapons of offense. Notwithstanding these various restrictions, cases of treason were almost always determined by the judicial duel, according to both Glanville and Bracton. This was in direct opposition to the custom of Lombardy, where such cases were especially exempted from decision by the sword. These restrictions of the English law, such as they were, did not, however, extend to the Scottish Marches, where the trial by battle was the universal resource and no proof by witnesses was admitted.

There were three classes—women, ecclesiastics, and those suffering under physical incapacity—with whom personal appearance in the lists would appear to be impossible. When interested in cases involving the judicial duel they were therefore allowed the privilege of substituting a champion, who took their place and did battle for the justice of their cause. So careful were legislators to prevent any failure in the procedure prescribed by custom, that the North German law provided that the dead when prosecuted could appear in the lists by substitutes, and the Assises de Jerusalem ordered the suzerain to supply the expenses for forty days, when a suitor unable to fight was also too poor to pay for a champion to take his place; and when a murdered man left no relatives to prosecute the murderer, the suzerain was likewise obliged to furnish the champion in any trial that might arise. Equally directed to the same purpose was the German law which provided that when a crippled defendant refused or neglected to procure a substitute, the judge was to seize one half of his property with which to pay the services of a gladiator, who could claim nothing more. Guardians of women and minors, moreover, were bound to furnish battle in their behalf.

Women, however, did not always restrict themselves to fighting thus vicariously. The German laws refer to cases in which a woman might demand justice of a man personally in the lists, and not only are instances on record in which this was done, as in a case at Berne in 1228, in which the woman was the victor, but it was of sufficiently frequent occurrence to have an established mode of procedure, which is preserved to us in all its details by illuminated MSS. of the period. The chances between such unequal adversaries were adjusted by placing the man up to the navel in a pit three feet wide, tying his left hand behind his back, and arming him only with a club, while his fair opponent had the free use of her limbs and was furnished with a stone as large as the fist, or weighing from one to five pounds, fastened in a piece of stuff. A curious regulation provided the man with three clubs. If in delivering a blow he touched the earth with hand or arm he forfeited one of the clubs; if this happened thrice his last weapon was gone, he was adjudged defeated, and the woman could order his execution. On the other hand, the woman was similarly furnished with three weapons. If she struck the man while he was disarmed she forfeited one, and with the loss of the third she was at his mercy, and was liable to be buried alive. According to the customs of Freisingen, these combats were reserved for accusations of rape. If the man was vanquished, he was beheaded; if the woman, she only lost a hand, for the reason that the chances of the fight were against her. In Bohemia, also, women over the age of eighteen had the privilege of the duel; the man was put into a pit as deep as his waist; the woman was armed with sword and buckler, but was not allowed to approach nearer than a circle traced around the mouth of the pit.

There was one jurisdiction which held itself more carefully aloof from the prevailing influence of barbarism—that of the Admiralty Courts, which covered a large portion of practical mercantile law. This is a fact easily explicable, not only from the character of the parties and of the transactions for which those courts were erected, but from the direct descent of the maritime codes from the Roman law, less modified by transmission than any other portions of medieval jurisprudence. These codes, though compiled at a period when the wager of battle flourished in full luxuriance, have no reference to it whatever, and the Assises de Jerusalem expressly allude to the Admiralty Courts as not admitting the judicial duel in proof, while an English document of 12 Edward III attests the same principle. When, however, the case was one implying an accusation of theft or deception, as in denying the receipt of cargo, the matter entered into the province of criminal law, and the battle trial might be legitimately ordered.

There are some details which are of interest as illustrating both the theory and practice of the duel in its legal aspect. Thus the general principle on which the combat was conducted was the absolute assertion by each party of the justice of his cause, confirmed by a solemn oath on the Gospels, or on a relic of approved sanctity, before the conflict commenced. Defeat was thus not merely the loss of the suit, but was also a conviction of perjury, to be punished as such; and in criminal cases it was also a conviction of malicious prosecution on the part of a worsted appellant. That it was regarded as much more serious than the simple loss of a suit is shown by the provisions of the custom of Normandy, whereby a vanquished combatant was classed with perjurers, false witnesses, and other infamous persons, as incapable thenceforth of giving evidence in courts, or of serving on a jury. Accordingly, we find the vanquished party, whether plaintiff or defendant, subjected to penalties more or less severe, varying with time and place.

In the ancient laws of the Alamanni, when there was controversy as to the ownership of land, the contestants brought to the court of the district some earth and branches of trees from the disputed property. These were wrapped and sealed and placed in the lists, where the combatants touched the bundle with their swords and called upon God to grant victory to the right; the land passed to the victor, and the defeated party was fined twelve sous for having made an unjust claim.

The tendency, as civilization advanced, was to render the penalty more severe. Thus, in 819, Louis le Débonnaire decreed that, in cases where testimony was evenly balanced, one of the witnesses from each side should be chosen to fight it out, the defeated champion suffering the usual penalty of perjury—the loss of a hand; while the remaining witnesses on the losing side were allowed the privilege of redeeming their forfeited members at the regular legal rate. William the Conqueror imposed a fine of forty sous on the losing side impartially; this was increased to sixty sous by the compilation known as the laws of Henry I; and the same regulation is stated by Glanville, with the addition that the defeated person was forever disqualified as a witness or champion; but in practice the amount seems to have been indefinite.

It was not customary to order the combat to take place immediately, but to allow a certain interval for the parties to put their affairs in order and to undergo the necessary training. In Southern Germany this delay was for nobles from four to six weeks, and for others a fortnight, and during this period any assault by one on the other was a capital offense. They were required to give security for their due appearance at the appointed time, various fines and punishments being inflicted on defaulters. By the law of both Northern and Southern Germany, when default was made by the defendant he was held guilty of the crime charged upon him: and if he was allowed the privilege of redeeming hand or life either as defendant or appellant, he was declared infamous, and deprived of the protection of the law. In a case occurring in the twelfth century in Hainault, between a seigneur and a man whom he claimed as a serf, the latter demanded the duel, which was allowed, but on the appointed day he failed to appear by nine o'clock. His adversary had waited for him since daybreak, and claimed the verdict which was awarded him by the council of Hainault. At this moment the missing man presented himself, but was adjudged to be too late, and was delivered to his claimant as a serf. According to the custom of Flanders, indeed, the combatant who failed to appear suffered banishment, with confiscation of all his possessions. This extreme rigor, however, did not obtain universally. By the English law, the defaulter was declared infamous, and was also liable to a fine to the king, for which there was apparently no fixed amount. The Scandinavians punished him popularly by erecting a "nithstong" —a post inscribed with defamatory runes, and so flagrant was this insult considered that finally it was prohibited by law under pain of exile. Perhaps the most emphatic assertion, however, of the obligation to appear is the rule in the law of the Scottish Marches in 1249, that if the accused should die before the appointed day his body must be brought to the lists, "for no man can essoin himself by death."

The bail, of course, was liable for all legal penalties incurred by a defaulter, and occasionally, indeed, was made to share the fate of his principal, when the latter appeared and was defeated. In the law of Southern Germany, according to one text, the bail under these circumstances was liable to the loss of a hand, which, however, he could redeem, while another version makes him suffer the penalty incurred by his principal.

It may be briefly observed that when champions were employed on both sides, the law appears generally to have restricted them to the club and buckler, and to have prescribed perfect equality between the combatants. An ordinance of Philip Augustus, in 1215, directs that the club shall not exceed three feet in length. In England the club or baton was rendered more efficient with a "crook," usually of horn, but sometimes of iron, giving to the weapon the truly formidable aspect of a pickaxe or tomahawk. When the principals appeared personally, it would seem that in early times the appellant had the choice of weapons, which gave him an enormous advantage. When, however, the spirit of legislation became hostile to the wager of battle, this advantage was taken from the appellant. Frederic II appears to have been the first to promulgate this rational idea, and, in decreeing that in future the choice of arms shall rest with the defendant, he stigmatizes the previous custom as utterly iniquitous and unreasonable.

In the law of Northern Germany, care was taken that the

advantage of the sun was equally divided between the combatants; they fought on foot, with bare heads and feet, clad in tunics with sleeves reaching only to the elbow, simple gloves, and no defensive armor except a wooden target covered with hide, and bearing only an iron boss; each carried a drawn sword, but either might have as many more as he pleased in his belt. Even when nobles were concerned, who fought on horseback, it was the rule that they should have no defensive armor save a leather-covered wooden shield and a glove to cover the thumb; the weapons allowed were lance, sword, and dagger, and they fought bareheaded and clad in linen tunics. According to Upton, in the fifteenth century, the judges were bound to see that the arms were equal, but he admits that on many points there were no settled or definite rules. In Russia, each combatant followed his own pleasure; and a traveler in the sixteenth century relates that the Muscovites were in the habit of embarrassing themselves with defensive armor to an extent which rendered them almost helpless, so that in combats with Poles, Lithuanians, and Germans they were habitually worsted, until judicial duels between natives and foreigners were at length prohibited on this account.

As a general rule the combat ended at sunset or when the stars became visible, and in such case if it was a drawn battle the case was decided in favor of the defendant, because the prosecutor had not proved his charge. In Italy, however, the duel was fought to an end; if stopped by darkness the judge was instructed to note carefully the respective positions of the combatants and replace them exactly the next morning, so that neither might derive advantage from the adjournment.

The issue at stake being death or dishonor, with severe penalties hanging over the vanquished, whether principal or champion, no chivalric courtesy was to be expected in these combats. They were fought to the bitter end with persistent and brutal ferocity. A fairly illustrative example is furnished in an incident which followed the assassination of Charles the Good of Flanders in 1127. One of the accomplices, a knight named Guy, was challenged for complicity by another named Herman. Both were renowned warriors, but Herman was speedily unhorsed by his adversary, who with his lance frustrated all his attempts to remount. Then Herman disabled the horse of his opponent and the combat was renewed on foot with swords. Equally skillful in fence they continued the struggle till fatigue compelled them to drop sword and shield and they wrestled for the mastery. Guy threw his antagonist, fell on him and beat him in the face with his gauntlets till he seemed to be motionless, but Herman quietly slipped his hand below the other's coat of mail, grasped his testicles and with a mighty effort wrenched them away. Guy fell over and expired; he we adjudged guilty.

Restricted to cases of disability, the use of champions was a necessity to the battle ordeal; but at a very early period the practice received a remarkable extension, which was directly in conflict with the original principles of the judicial duel, in permitting able-bodied antagonists to put forward substitutes, whether connected with them or not by ties of blood, who fought the battle for their principals. With regard to this there appears to have been a considerable diversity of practice. The earliest Frisian laws not only grant unlimited permission for their employment, but even allow them to be hired for money. The laws of the Franks, of the Alamanni, and of the Saxons make no allusion to such a privilege, and apparently expect the principal to defend his rights himself, and yet an instance occurs in 590 where, in a duel fought by order of Gontran, the defendant was allowed to intrust his cause to his nephew, though, as he was accused of killing a stag in the king's forest, physical infirmity could hardly have been pleaded.

In England, until the first statute of Westminster, issued by Edward I, in 1275, the hired champion of the defendant, in a suit concerning real estate, was obliged to assume the position of a witness, by swearing that he had been personally present and had seen seizin given of the land, or that his father when dying had enjoined him by his filial duty to maintain the defendant's title as though he had been present. This legal fiction was common also to the Norman jurisprudence of the period, where in such cases the champion of the plaintiff was obliged to swear that he had heard and seen the matters alleged in support of the claim, while the opposing champion swore that they were false. In a similar spirit, an earlier code of Normandy prescribes that champions shall be taken to see the lands and buildings in dispute, before receiving the oath of battle, in the same manner as a jury of view. An English legal treatise of the period, indeed, assumes that the principals can put forward only witnesses as substitutes, and gives as a reason why combats in civil suits were always conducted by champions, that in such cases the principals could not act as witnesses for themselves. In a similar spirit, if on the field of battle one of the parties presented a champion who was not receivable as a witness and had not been accepted by the court, the case could be decided against him by default.

Looking on the profession of a champion in this light, as that of a witness swearing for hire, we can find a justification for the heavy penalties to which he was subjected in case of defeat—penalties of which the real purport presumably was to insure his fidelity to his principal. Thus, in Norman civil suits as to disputed landed possessions, the champion swearing to the truth of his principal's claim was, if defeated, visited with a heavy fine and was declared infamous, being thenceforth incapable of appearing in court either as plaintiff or as witness, while the penalty of the principal was merely the loss of the property in dispute; and a similar principle was recognized in the English law of the period. In criminal cases, from a very early period, while the principal perhaps escaped with fine or imprisonment, the hired ruffian was hanged, or at best lost a hand or foot, the immemorial punishment for perjury.

With such risks to be encountered, it is no wonder that the trade of the champion offered few attractions to honest men, who could keep body and soul together in any other way. In primitive times, the solidarity of the family no doubt caused the champion in most cases to be drawn from among the kindred; at a later period he might generally be procured from among the freedmen or clients of the principal. In the palmy days of chivalry, it was perhaps not uncommon for the generous knight to throw himself bodily into the lists in defense of persecuted and friendless innocence, as he was bound to do by the tenor of his oath of knighthood. Even as late as the fifteenth century, indeed, in a collection of Welsh laws, among the modes by which a stranger acquired the rights of kindred is enumerated the act of voluntarily undergoing the duel in the place of a principal unable or unwilling to appear for himself.

When the Roman law commenced to exercise its powerful influence in molding the feudal customs into a regular body of procedure, and admiring jurists lost no opportunity of making use of the newly discovered treasures of legal lore, whether applicable or not, it is easy to understand that the contempt and the civil disabilities lavished by the imperial jurisprudence on the gladiator of antiquity came to be transferred to the medieval champion; although the latter, by the theory of the law, stood forth to defend the innocent, while the former ignobly exposed his life for the gratification of an imbruted populace.

By the thirteenth century, the occupation of champion had thus become infamous. Its professors were classed with the vilest criminals, and with the unhappy females who exposed their charms for sale, as the champion did his skill and courage. They were held incapable of appearing as witnesses, and the extraordinary anomaly was exhibited of seeking to learn the truth in affairs of the highest moment by a solemn appeal to God, through the instrumentality of those who were already considered as convicts of the worst kind, or who, by the very act, were branded with infamy if successful in justifying innocence, and if defeated were mutilated or hanged. By the codes in force throughout Germany in the thirteenth and fourteenth centuries, they were not only, in common with bastards, actors, and jugglers, deprived of all legal privileges, such as succeeding to property, bearing witness, etc., but even their children were visited with the same disabilities.

The Italians took a more sensible and practical view of the matter. Accepting as a necessity the existence of champions as a class, they were disposed rather to elevate than to degrade the profession. The law required that they should not be criminals or infamous, and the fact that they fought for hire did not render them so. In the Veronese code of 1228, they appear as an established institution, consisting of individuals selected and appointed by the magistrates, who did not allow them to receive more than one hundred sous for the performance of their office.

In England, there were prolonged efforts to suppress their hiring. In 1150, Henry II strictly prohibited the wager of battle with hired champions in his Norman territories. A champion suspected of serving for money might be objected to by the opposite party, whence arose a secondary combat to determine his fitness for the primary one.

In France and the Frankish kingdoms of the East, there were limitations placed by law on the employment of champions in prosecutions for crime, while in civil actions there appear to have been, at least in France, no restrictions whatever. In appeal of judgment the appellant in criminal cases is bound to show satisfactory cause for employing a champion, while in civil affairs the right to do so requires no argument. This hiring of champions, moreover, was legally recognized as a necessity attendant upon the privilege of employing them. High rank, or a marked difference between the station of parties to an action, was also admitted as justifying the superior in putting forward a champion in his place.

There were two other classes of pleaders with whom the hiring of champions was a necessity, and who could not be bound by the limitations imposed on ordinary litigants. While the sexagenary, the infant, and the crippled might possibly find a representative among their kindred, and while the woman might appear by her husband or next of kin, the ecclesiastical foundations and chartered towns had no such resource. Thus, in a suit for taxes, in 1164, before the court of Verona, Bonuszeno of Soavo proved that the village of Soavo had exempted his father Petrobatalla from all local imposts for having served as champion in a duel between it and a neighboring community, and his claim to the reversion of the exemption was allowed.

As a rule, ecclesiastical communities were likewise under the necessity of employing champions to defend their rights. Sometimes, as we have seen, these were hired, and were of no better character than those of common pleaders. They seem to have been well paid, if we may judge from an agreement of 1258 between the Abbey of Glastonbury and Henry de Fernbureg, by which the latter bound himself to defend by battle the rights of the abbey to certain manors against the Bishop of Bath and Wells, for which he is to receive thirty sterling marks, of which ten are to be paid when battle is gaged, five when he is shaved for the combat, and on the day of the duel fifteen are to be placed in the hands of a third party to be paid over to him if he strikes a single blow. Sometimes, however, gentlemen did not disdain to serve God by fighting for the Church in special cases, as when, so late as the middle of the fourteenth century, the priory of Tynemouth had a suit with a troublesome neighbor, Gerard de Widdrington, over the manor of Hawkshaw, and Sir Thomas Colville, who had won great renown in the French wars, appeared in court as its champion and offered the combat. No one could be found hardy enough to accept his challenge, and the manor was adjudged to the priory. There was, moreover, another class of champions of the Church who occupied a distinguished position, and were bound to defend the interests of their clients in the field as well as in the court and in the lists; they also led the armed retainers of the church when summoned by the suzerain to national war. The office was honorable and lucrative, and was eagerly sought by gentlemen of station, who turned to account the opportunities of aggrandizement which it afforded; and many a noble family traced its prosperity to the increase of ancestral property thus obtained, directly or indirectly, by espousing the cause of fat abbeys and wealthy bishoprics, as when, in the ninth century, the Abbot of Figeac, near Cahors, bestowed on a neighboring lord sixty churches and five hundred *mansi* on condition of his fighting the battles of the abbey.

SONG DUELS AMONG THE ESKIMO

E. Adamson Hoebel

H OMICIDAL DISPUTE, though prevalent, is made less frequent in many Eskimo groups by recourse to regulated combat— wrestling, buffeting, and butting. Buffeting is found among the central tribes along the Arctic Circle from Hudson Bay to Bering Straits. Wrestling occurs in Siberia, Alaska, Baffinland, and Northwest Greenland (König 295). Head-butting as a feature of the song duel occurs in West and East Greenland. All three forms are a type of wager by battle without the element of divine judgment.

In buffeting, the opponents face each other, alternately delivering straight-armed blows on the side of the head, until one is felled and thereby vanquished. Butting accompanies the singing in the song duel in Greenland. The singer, if so inclined, butts his opponent with his forehead while delivering his excoriation. The opponent moves his head forward to meet the blow. He who is upset is derided by the onlookers and comes out badly in the singing. As juridical forms, boxing and butting are more regulated than feudistic homicide, since the contests are announced and occur on festive occasions, when they are looked upon as a sort of sporting performance before the assembled community. Stealth, cunning, and ambush are not part of such contests; the strongest wins by pitted strength. The object of the boxing and butting contests is not annihilation, but subjection. Nor is there

Extracted from E. Adamson Hoebel, *The Law of Primitive Man: A Study in Comparative Legal Dynamics.* Copyright 1954 by the President and Fellows of Harvard College. Reprinted by permission of Harvard University Press.

any more or less concern with basic justice than there was in the medieval wager of battle. Whatever the facts underlying the dispute, they are irrelevant to the outcome. The man who wins, wins social esteem. He who loses, suffers loss of social rank.

Boxing and butting are apparently available as means of settling all disputes except homicide.

Wrestling serves much the same function, though it may have a more deadly outcome in Baffinland and Labrador, where the loser may be slain by the victor. The wrestling duel is occasionally used as the means through which blood revenge may be carried out.

Deserving of fame are the *nith* songs of the eastern and western Eskimos. Elevating the duel to a higher plane, the weapons used are words—"little, sharp words, like the wooden splinters which I hack off with my ax" (Rasmussen 1922: 236).

Song duels are used to work off grudges and disputes of all orders, save murder. An East Greenlander, however, may seek his satisfaction for the murder of a relative through a song contest if he is physically too weak to gain his end, or if he is so skilled in singing as to feel certain of victory (Holm 1914: 87). Inasmuch as East Greenlanders get so engrossed in the mere artistry of the singing as to forget the cause of the grudge, this is understandable. Singing skill among these Eskimos equals or outranks gross physical prowess.

The singing style is highly conventionalized. The successful singer uses the traditional patterns of composition which he attempts to deliver with such finesse as to delight the audience to enthusiastic applause. He who is most heartily applauded is "winner." To win a song contest brings no restitution in its train. The sole advantage is in prestige.

Among the East Greenlanders song duels may be carried on for years, just for the fun of it. But elsewhere, grudge contests are usually finished in a single season. Traditional songs are used, but special compositions are created for each occasion to ridicule the opponent and capitalize his vulnerable foibles and frailties.

Some situations and their songs will illustrate the institution as it functions.

Ipa— took Igsia—'s third wife away from him. Igsia— challenged Ipa— to a song contest. Because he was not really competent, Ipa— had his former stepson, M—, sing for him. M— accused Igsia— of attempted murder. When Igsia—'s turn came to sing he replied with proper ridicule and satirical antics as follows:

"I cannot help my opponent not being able to sing or bring forth his voice." (He put a block of wood in his opponent's mouth and pretended to sew the mouth shut.)

"What shall we do with my opponent? He can neither sing anything, nor bring forth his voice. Since one cannot hear him, I had better stretch out his mouth and try to make it larger." (He stretched his opponent's mouth to the sides with his fingers, crammed it full of blubber, then gagged it with a stick.)

"My opponent has much to say against me. He says I wanted to do A— a hurt and would have slain him. When we came hither from the south, it was thou didst first challenge A— to a drum match." (He put a thong in his opponent's mouth and tied it up under the rafters.)

Etc., etc., etc. The song lasted one hour. Whenever Igsia— made mockery of his opponent with such tricks, M— showed his indifference by encouraging the audience to shout and laugh at him.

Other songs rely less on buffoonery, placing greater reliance on innuendo and deprecation. When K— and E— confronted each other they sang with dancing and mimicry in the following manner (E— had married the divorced wife of old man K—. Now that she was gone K— wanted her back. E— would not give her up, and a song duel occurred):

K—:

> Now shall I split off words—little,
>   sharp words
> Like the wooden splinters which I
>   hack off with my ax.
> A song from ancient times—a breath
>   of the ancestors

A song of longing–for my wife.
An impudent, black-skinned oaf has
    stolen her,
Has tried to belittle her.
A miserable wretch who loves
    human flesh–
A cannibal from famine days.

E–, in his defense, replied:

Insolence that takes the breath away
Such laughable arrogance and effrontery.
What a satirical song! Supposed to
    place blame on me.
You would drive fear into my heart!
I who care not about death.
Hi! You sing about my woman who
    was your wench.
You weren't so loving then–she was
    much alone.
You forgot to prize her in song, in
    stout, contest songs.
Now she is mine.
And never shall she visit singing,
    false lovers.
Betrayer of women in strange households.

K– and E– taunt each other in like manner as they sing out
their dispute:

K–:

Let me too follow the Umiak as kayak man!
To follow the boat with the singers
As if I could be afraid!
As if I were possessed of weak-kneed ways!
When I pursue the kayak paddler.
It is not to be wondered at
That he is pleased,
He who has nearly killed his cousin
He who has nearly harpooned his cousin
No wonder that he was so self-satisfied
That he felt such joy.

E– hurls back in rebuttal:

But I merely laugh at it
But I but make merry over it

That you K—, *are* a murderer
That you are jealous from the ground up.
Given to envy
Because you do not have more than three wives,
And you think them too few
So are you jealous.
You should marry them to some other men.
Then you could have what their husbands bring in.
K—, because you do not concern yourself
  with these things
Because your women eat you out of house and
  home
So you have taken to murdering your fellow men
                  (Rasmussen 1922: 235–36).

In West Greenland, the singer has the vocal backing of his household. In preparing for the contest he sings his songs until all his household knows them perfectly. When the actual contest is in full swing, his householders reinforce his words in chorus. In spite of the nastiness of the insults hurled, it is good form for neither party to show anger or passion. And it is expected that the participants will remain the best of friends thereafter. The West Greenlanders, in contrast to the men of the East Coast, use self-deprecation, "the self-irony which is so significant in the Eskimo character," though at the same time the opponent is lashed with weighty accusations and sneering references. Here, for example, is the song which a husband hurled at the man who had induced the singer's wife to so gash the covering of his kayak that it would open and drown him. Then she and the plotter could marry. The plot failed; the wife received a physical mauling, and the coconspirator received a verbal mauling:

Ah, how doubtful I feel about it!
How I feel about having to sing.
In my soul, which is not strong!
However could it occur to me to make a song
  of charge against him.
How stupid that now I really have to
  trouble on his account.
When we were up North there,
When we were up at Kialineq

It happened as usual that she made me
    angry,
That as usual I gave my wife a trouncing.
I was not angry without cause.
I was as usual displeased with her work,
Because my kayak cover was torn.
It had got an opening;
When I, a moment, went outside, they say,
You appear to have made a remark about me:
That I am always accustomed to behave so
    devilishly considerately:
That I on every occasion act so extraordinarily
    leniently.
How stupid I was then not to give him the
    same treatment,
That I did not also give him a stab with
    the knife.
What a pity that I acted so leniently
    towards you.
What a pity that I showed myself so
    considerate towards you,
You scoundrel, who so thoughtlessly
    received my anger (König 1927: 313).

Among the Polar Eskimos the song duel is also used, but without the head-butting and buffeting.

Among the Iglulik Eskimos, north of Hudson Bay, contest singing is also an important art. Among these people, anyone who would be considered an effective singer must have a "song cousin." This is an institution built upon the basis of "formal friendship," a comradeship bond which was widespread among the aborigines of the Western Hemisphere. Song cousins try to outdo each other in all things, exchanging costly gifts and their wives whenever they meet. Each delights to compete with the other in the beauty of his songs as such, or in the skillful composition and delivery of metrical abuse. When song cousins castigate each other, it is for fun, and is done in a lighthearted, humorous manner. When a man takes up a grudge song duel, however, the tenor of the songs is different. Though the cast of the songs is humorous for effect, insolence, derision, and the pictured ludicrousness of the opponents are the stuff they are made of. As in Greenland, the one who can win the audience, or silence his opponent, is victor, but in any event, winner and loser are expected to be reconciled, and they exchange presents as a token of settlement (Rasmussen 1929: 231–32).

Further inland, among the Caribou Eskimos, who are located at the very center of the whole Eskimo territory, the song duel is also found. From Rasmussen we have the composition of a man who is chastizing the deserted husband of a woman, who, mistreated by her spouse, ran away to join the singer. Its quality will by now be familiar to the reader.

> Something was whispered
> Of a man and wife
> Who could not agree
> And what was it all about?
> A wife who in rightful anger
> Tore her husband's furs across
> Took their canoe
> And rowed away with her son.
> Ay-ay, all who listen,
> What do you think of him?
> Is he to be envied,
> Who is great in his anger
> But faint in strength
> Blubbering helplessly
> Properly chastized?
> Though it was he who foolishly proud
> Started the quarrel with stupid words.

The occurrence of the song-duel complex all down the west coast of Alaska and even out into the Aleutian Islands (reported by the Russian missionary Weniamenow) (Weyer 1932: 227–28) shows how basic (and possibly, ancient) a form it is among the Eskimos.

The song duels are juridical instruments insofar as they do serve to settle disputes and restore normal relations between estranged members of the community. One of the contestants receives a "judgment" in his favor. There is, however, no attempt to mete justice according to rights and privileges defined by substantive law. It is sufficient that the litigants (contestants) feel relieved—the complaint laid to rest—a psychological satisfaction attained and balance restored. This is justice sufficient unto the needs of Eskimo society as the Eskimos conceive it. It is, so far as here achieved, an element in which "higher" cultures often fail.

Unlike wager of battle, however, there is no ordeal element in the song duel. Supernatural forces do not operate to enhance the prowess of the singer who has "right" on his side. Let it be remembered that "right" is immaterial to the singing or its outcome (though the singer who can pile up scurrilous accusations of more or less truth against his opponent has an advantage in fact). As the courtroom joust may become a sporting game between sparring attorneys-at-law, so the juridical song contest is above all things a contest in which pleasurable delight is richly served, so richly that the dispute-settlement function is nearly forgotten. And in the forgetting the original end is the better served.

DRUMMING THE SCANDAL
AMONG THE TIV

Paul Bohannan

*The following case took place in 1950, in the southern part
of Tiv Division, Benue Province, Northern Region, Nigeria.*

EARLY IN the spring of 1950, an argument occurred between
Torgindi of MbaYar and Mtswen of MbaGishi, both lineages
contained within MbaDuku. Mtswen was the secondary marriage
guardian of the wife of Torgindi's son, and had been guilty of
some rather highhanded tactics that caused the marriage to fall
through. Mtswen had then refused to act as intermediary to get
Torgindi's bridewealth refunded, and the two men exchanged
angry words. Torgindi went back to his compound and made up
a song in which he said what a skunk Mtswen was. That night,
when all was quiet, he drummed and sang the song as loud as
he could, for the whole countryside to hear—including Mtswen,
who lived a little over a quarter of a mile away.[1] The next night,
he again sang the song, and all the members of his own compound and some from other compounds of his lineage joined in
the chorus. The only thing for Mtswen to do was to make up a
song of his own against Torgindi. But knowing that he wasn't
much of a songmaker, he hired the best songmaker in Shangev
Ya to stay at his place and compose scurrilous songs about Torgindi and all his kinsmen and wives.

Soon Torgindi's inventiveness was also exhausted, and he too
hired a songmaker. By this time the two men were holding

Reprinted from Paul Bohannan, *Justice and Judgment among the Tiv*,
published for the International African Institute by the Oxford University
Press, London, 1957; pp. 142–44. Reprinted by permission of the International African Institute.
[1] Some Tiv can pitch their voices so as to be heard up to three miles away.

dances and song contests every night. They each brewed beer and made food in order to attract dancers to come to dance and sing the songs directed at the other.

There are some specific rules for these songs. Chenge told me that if an act attributed in such a song was possible of human performance, it should be true, or the slandered person could call a *jir*. However, if the act was not humanly possible anything could be said. In one of Mtswen's songs, he accused one of Torgindi's wives of stealing yams: this, by local consensus, was probably true because this particular wife was of the Udam tribe, and widely thought to be a thief. But if it was not true, Chenge insisted, Torgindi and the wife could call a *jir* against Mtswen and the songmaker. Another song, and one of the catchiest tunes which the contest produced, told how Torgindi changed himself into a pig at night and made it unsafe for every sow in the countryside. The Shangev songmaker (who later became a good friend and favorite guide) said that since even Torgindi couldn't actually do that, such a song couldn't be the basis for a *jir*. The songmaker said that he had thought of some much worse things to suggest that it was in Torgindi's nature to do, if it were only humanly possible, but that Mtswen had stopped him saying that all he wanted to do was to win the contest, not to "spoil Torgindi's heart permanently." They were, after all, neighbors.

The drumming contests continued every night for more than three weeks before the *mbatarev* took notice. Finally, Chenge decided that if the thing was allowed to continue it would almost surely end in a fight, for which he himself would be answerable to the District Officer. Therefore he sent word to both Mtswen and Torgindi that they and their people were to come to his compound the following afternoon, and both would sing and drum and he and the *mbatarev* would decide the case.

Both sides came fully prepared. Torgindi's group dragged a large *ilyu* drum for two and a half miles in order to accompany their songs and dances. Mtswen's songmaker and one of his sons hurried across to Udam and bought two small wooden figurines of the sort the Udam use in divination: a small male and a larger female. The male figurine they painted black; the larger female figurine they painted red. These two figurines represented Torgindi, a small and very dark man, and his tall, fat, light-colored wife. They were tied together at the top of a long pole in a somewhat compromising position, and were waved frantically in accompaniment to all the songs.

The *mbatarev* walked back and forth between the two performing groups. They noted this performer and that song. Then, about two hours later, they called for quiet and said that they would now hear the *jir*. As Torgindi began his story, the man carrying the two figurines put them up in the air and waved them—a roar of laughter followed. Chenge took them away from the offender and put them under his chair until the hearing was over.

The case, which was a simple marriage case, was very quickly settled, and both men—anxious to be rid of the vast expense they were incurring—concurred in the judgment. After the case was settled on its jural points, the *mbatarev* announced the winner of the song contest: Torgindi won the case, but Mtswen had the better songs. They then advised both songmakers to go home immediately and not return to MbaDuku for a couple of months until the feelings which had been aroused had died down.

The local chief and Mtswen's songmaker both told me that in the old days "drumming the scandal" was a favorite method of settling disputes, and almost always led to fighting. Whoever won the fight won the dispute.

THE ORDEAL AS A VEHICLE
FOR DIVINE INTERVENTION
IN MEDIEVAL EUROPE

William J. Tewksbury

THE ORDEAL is a primitive form of trial used to determine the guilt or innocence of the accused, the result being regarded as a divine or preterhuman judgment. The fundamental idea upon which the ordeal rests is that it is a device for regulating, under conditions of comparative fairness, the primitive law of force. The concept that victory would inure to the right—that divine intervention would prevail on behalf of the innocent—was a belief that was subsequently engrafted upon the concept of the ordeal. The earliest occurrences, which can be referred to as pseudo-ordeals, seem to turn on the idea of brute strength. Such was the wager of battle and other *"bilateral* ordeals" to which both sides had to submit. Only later do we see man, alleging his innocence and facing his Creator, on trial by himself.

To understand the ordeal and the use for which it was designed, one must recognize the tremendous impact that religion has on the daily lives of the people who rely on it. The usual conception of divine intervention to vindicate innocence and to punish guilt is illustrated through an occurrence which happened in 1626 in France. A master had two servants, one stupid, and the other cunning. The latter stole from the master and so framed the stupid servant that he could not justify himself. The doltish servant, allegedly guilty, was tied to a flagstaff and guarded by the accuser. In the night, the flagstaff broke, the upper part falling upon and killing the guilty cunning servant, leaving the innocent servant unhurt. Beliefs such as this lead to irregular judicial proceedings. One might refer to them as ordeals of chance. The innocence of a man often turned on pure luck.

I   ORDEALS BY FIRE AND HEAT

The ordeal of boiling water is important in medieval Europe and elsewhere because it combines the elements of fire and water. Water represents the deluge which was the judgment inflicted upon the wicked of old. Fire represented the fiery doom of the future —the day of judgment. This ordeal compelled the accused with his naked hand to find a small pebble within a caldron of boiling water. After the hand had been plunged into the seething caldron, it was carefully enveloped in a cloth, sealed with the signet of a judge, and three days later was unwrapped. It was at this subsequent unwrapping that the accused's guilt or innocence was announced, determined by the condition of the hand.

A related ordeal was that of the red-hot iron. Two forms of this ordeal were found in medieval Europe. The first, which can best be categorized as one of chance, is the ordeal of the red-hot ploughshares. Ploughshares are heated until they glow and are then placed at certain intervals. The accused walks blindfolded and barefooted through the prescribed course. If he escapes injury, he is acquitted. The second form of the ordeal is more widely discussed. The accused is compelled to carry a piece of hot iron for a given distance. The weight of the iron varies with the magnitude of the crime alleged. If the accused can carry the piece of iron without sustaining any burn, he is regarded as innocent.

II   ORDEALS BY WATER AND MEANS OTHER THAN
     A DIRECT APPEAL TO GOD

The basis of the ordeal of cold water was that water, being a pure element, will not receive into her bosom anyone stained with the crime of a false oath. Water was recognized as capable of ascertaining those things which had been injected with untruths.

The result seems, today, somewhat anomalous: the guilty floated and the innocent sank.

The success of this ordeal was less than perfect. Throughout the sources on this mode of ordeal were examples of malfunctions. Witches would sink like rocks, while leading members of the community, offering themselves to the rigors of the ordeal to test to their validity, would float, often not sinking at all, even with the efforts of the officiating executioner.

Some ordeals were designed for people with some type of infirmity, such as blindness, lameness, or old age. Such people had to endure less trying ordeals to determine their guilt or innocence. A person burdened by such an incapacity is placed in one scale of the balance with an equivalent weight to counterbalance him in the other scale. The accused then went before the administering official, who then addressed a customary adjuration to the ordeal of the balance. The accused ascended the balance again, and if he was lighter than before, he was acquitted. This association of lightness with innocence would seem to be contrary to the European belief that lightness is associated with the Devil, as the Devil was regarded as nothing but a spirit of air.

III   ORDEAL BY DIRECT APPEAL TO GOD

The ordeal of the cross is characterized by placing two parties, the accused and the accuser, in front of a cross with their arms uplifted. Divine service was performed, and victory was adjudged to the one who was able to maintain his arms in the upraised position for the longest period of time. If this procedure led to a stalemate, the accused was given a piece of bread or cheese over which prayers had been said. If the accused could swallow the consecrated morsel, he was acquitted. We must remember that at the time these ordeals were the vogue, the people had great faith in Christ. The criminal, conscious of his guilt, standing before God and pledging his salvation, was expected to "break" under the weight of his own conscience. The truth of the matter lies in the fact that bread or cheese is difficult to swallow when the saliva secretion in one's mouth is not functioning properly. The exorcisms which were said beforehand were subject only to the imagination of the presiding priest. The more ingenious and devising he was, the more constricted became the throat of the most hardened criminal (as well as God-fearing innocents), and, therefore, the more difficult became the function of swallowing.

It was only a slight modification of the above which resulted in the Eucharist as an ordeal. "He that eateth and drinketh unworthily eateth and drinketh damnation to himself" (I Corinthians XI). When the consecrated wafer was offered under appropriate adjuration, the guilty would not receive it; or if it were taken, immediate convulsions and speedy death would ensue.

The basis for all ordeals is that men are asking for divine help to relieve themselves of the responsibility of decision. The ordeal has as its greatest charactcristic the element of certainty. Such dependence on ordeals could be had whenever man waived his own judgment and undertook to test the inscrutable ways of his Creator—i.e., the laws of Nature are to be set aside whenever man chooses to tempt his God with the promise of right and the threat of injustice to be committed in His name. This passing the buck to God was particularly prevalent when there was no evidence as to the crime or where the crime was very difficult to prove judicially. The ordeal offered a ready and satisfactory solution to the doubts of a timid judge. Man believed that God would reverse the laws of Nature to accomplish a specified object.

The ordeal was thoroughly and completely a judicial process. It seems to have been used mostly to supplement deficient evidence and amounts to nothing more than an appeal to God.

A LIBERIAN ORDEAL

Esther Warner

It is the badness inside a man that burns him.

TRIAL BY SASSWOOD is an ordeal in which an accused person drinks an infusion made from the poisonous bark of the sasswood tree. If he is guilty, the poison will "catch" him, he will die. If he is not guilty, his stomach will acquit him. Vomiting establishes innocence. In common speech, *sasswood* has come to apply to any form of trial by ordeal, and there are many. Plucking a brass anklet from the bottom of a potful of (apparently) boiling palm oil is a popular variety in general use.

Several white persons have witnessed trials by ordeal in Liberia; a few have written about them. I have never discussed the matter with anyone who did not try to explain them away. "The oil was not really boiling," they say. Or, "The cutlass was not really red hot." (In hot-cutlass sasswood, a blade is heated in the fire and stroked across the bare backs of all the suspects. Only the guilty one is supposed to be burned.) If the trial has taken the form of drinking the red water, the brew of the sasswood bark, the usual comment, if the accused survives, is that the infusion was too weak to be fatal. If the victim dies, the explanation made is that he was a nuisance so the concoction was made purposely into fatal dosage. There is always from white people the suggestion that the trial was rigged. I grant that the possibilities for this are numerous and probably abused.

Ask the sceptics, "Do you believe that Hindu holy men can

Reprinted from Esther Warner, *Trial by Sasswood,* London: Gollancz, 1955, pp. 50–51; 241–47, with permission of Paul R. Reynolds Inc.

walk through live coals without feeling pain? Or that Indian dentists can pull teeth without the patient feeling discomfort?" "Some sort of hypnosis," they answer, as though giving it a recognizable name diminished the wonder of it. "Hypnosis must be the explanation of trials by ordeal."

Regardless of what one may choose to believe about these matters, there is one point on which everyone seems to agree: *the trials work for the Africans because they have implicit faith in them.* I have never heard of a tribesman questioning the verdict of sasswood.

An American doctor once established the potency of an infusion of sasswood bark. His sample came from a potful of the brew from which an accused old woman drank considerably more than a lethal dose. She evidenced her innocence and showed not the slightest ill effects. He observed that she gulped it down with complete confidence. It was his opinion that a smaller dose of the same strength, sipped haltingly and reluctantly by a victim who knew he was guilty, might have been retained and absorbed, resulting in death.

[Mrs. Warner witnessed a successful ordeal, carried out when Comma, one of her servants, returned to his tribal homeland among the Loma of Northwestern Liberia. Comma had been accused (unjustly, it turned out) of theft.]

Lega = Bola ♀   Keke is the "sassy-wood man,"
                                 as he is called in Liberian English
Comma

Cast of Characters.

I could look across the compound to Lega's house. Squatted in front of it, father and son were boiling up a midday snack. From that distance, they seemed of one age. Lega was as supple and had the same tardive grace about his movements as Comma. At intervals, I saw the white flash of their teeth as they spoke or smiled. One might think they had nothing more on their minds for the afternoon ahead than a comradely excursion into the jungle to set snares for game.

The sasswood-player (diviner) was an ancient from a nearby village, famous for his occult power. He was tardy for the trial, a cause of grave concern for the expectant throng.

Keke would allow no one to touch the wood for the fire. He built it up bigger and bigger, crouched so close to it that I thought his swishing robe would surely catch from the sparks. Although perspiration rolled into the crevices of his seamed face, he continued to shiver.

"The spirits are gathering inside him," Zabogi told me. "That is why he is so cold and full of shakes."

No one had thought to explain to me that the wood had to be "cleaned" by fire before it could be used in the trial. I saw that after a log was burned on the outside, Keke transferred the solid core of remains to a separate pile. From this fire-cleansed wood, he selected certain sticks for a third fire, which he placed on the ordeal spot. The crowd was not the least restless during this drawn-out proceeding; they sat hushed and tense.

Finally, he had everything just the way he wanted it, the fire properly placed and hot, a three-legged iron ring over it to support an enormous clay pot (not yet in place), the supply of rich red palm oil to be heated, the polished brass belled anklet which Comma was to pluck from the bottom of the pot, and a kettle full of leaves which he had bruised in a mortar until they were an arsenic-green paste. Besides these things, there was one other clay pot containing what appeared to be water.

Keke now placed the ordeal pot in the iron stand over the fire and poured the palm oil into it. I watched to see the shade of color of the oil. It has been said that the oil may be only a film on top of water in these trials and that the water would not be as damaging to living tissues as oil. As far as I could see, the oil was as rich a red-brown as palm oil ever is.

Keke made a long oration while the oil was heating.

"He is telling what an evil thing it is to steal," Zabogi explained to me. Zabogi and Bola and I were sitting as close to the fire as Keke would allow. "He is telling the people the names of different-different Lomas who stole."

From the length of the harangue, I thought he must be enumerating the tribe from the first man through "all his begats".

"Now, he is telling what was done to them," Zabogi said. "If any Loma does a bad thing, it is the man's own family who have to do the punishment. That punishes them for letting one of themselves go bad."

"The burns aren't punishment enough?"

"Oh, no," Zabogi said. "The burns are the smallest part of it."

Keke had the crowd completely under his spell. Some of the women began to sob.

"They remember now the terrible day they had to help punish someone in their own family," Zabogi said.

I hoped Zabogi would not feel it necessary to describe these punishments in detail. Before the trial I had told him over and over that he must translate *everything* that was said and done, so now it was too late to spare myself the grisly history Keke was repeating in order to admonish all the spectators to the upright life. Some of the offenders had been hacked to pieces with cutlasses, some of them had been laid in leaf-lined *kinjas* and covered on all sides with pounded hot-pepper pods, some had been tied in line of march of driver ants, some had been flogged with firebrands. "So it is done to those who break the law of the Lomas."

Slate-blue smoke was pouring off the heated oil by the time Keke finished his exhortations. Most of the crowd was moaning and swaying in a rhythm of misery. I was trembling and drenched with perspiration. Bola had her strong arm around me, whether to comfort me or to herself receive comfort, I don't know. Keke then sent Zabogi to fetch Comma. He came out of the house with Lega, both of them walking erect with long, brisk strides. Lega sat down beside Zabogi, Comma took his place behind the smoking pot.

Keke then talked to the pot, told it that if Comma had not stolen, it must not hurt him in the least, but that if he had spoiled the Loma name along with his own, it must bite him deep. Comma looked at his mother and me. Bola looked steadily back at him, steeling him with her own strength.

Keke next addressed Comma, telling him that he could refuse the trial, confess without the ordeal if he wished, and take the punishment the Old Ones would decide. Comma shook his head, indicated that the trial should go on. Lega nodded proud approval. Keke next took the paste of leaves and smeared it in a thick coating over Comma's right hand and arm, being careful to get it between all the fingers. Then he held up the three-knobbed brass ring and spoke at length about it. The paste of leaves was meanwhile drying into a crust over Comma's hand. It had turned a shade of sage-green where it was thinnest. There was less smoke coming off the oil now and it was less blue in color. After another coating of the paste was rubbed on Comma, the brass anklet was dropped into the pot. Quick as a flash, Comma dived his hand in after it and brought it up, dripping oil as red as blood. A great collective sigh swept like wind through the crowd, and then the roar of approval and triumph. They carried him off to the waterside on their shoulders. Keke was completely ignored now, and when they almost brushed his *baka* in the surge, he prated unattended. Bola crushed me to her and we wept unashamedly on each other's shoulders. After all the tense waiting, the imagined horror, it was over and done with in a moment and had come out all right!

I ask no one to believe one thing or another about trials by ordeal. All I can do is to tell what I saw, and leave it at that.

THE KPELLE MOOT

James L. Gibbs, Jr.

A FRICA AS a major culture area has been characterized by many writers as being marked by a high development of law and legal procedures. In the past few years research on African law has produced a series of highly competent monographs such as those on law among the Tiv (Bohannan 1957), the Barotse (Gluckman 1954), and the Nuer (Howell 1954). These and related shorter studies have focused primarily on formal processes for the settlement of disputes, such as those which take place in a courtroom, or those which are, in some other way, set apart from simpler measures of social control. However, many African societies have informal, quasi-legal, dispute-settlement procedures, supplemental to formal ones, which have not been as well studied, or—in most cases—adequately analyzed.

In this paper I present a description and analysis of one such institution for the informal settlement of disputes, as it is found among the Kpelle of Liberia; it is the moot, the *bɛrɛi mu meni saa* or 'house palaver'. Hearings in the Kpelle moot contrast with those in a court in that they differ in tone and effectiveness. The genius of the moot lies in the fact that it is based on a covert application of the principles of psychoanalytic theory which underlie psychotherapy.

The Kpelle are a Mande-speaking, patrilineal group of some 175,000 rice cultivators who live in Central Liberia and the adjoining regions of Guinea. This paper is based on data gathered in a field study which I carried out in 1957 and 1958 among the

Reprinted from *Africa*, Volume XXXIII, No. 1, January 1963, pp. 1–10, by permission of the author and of the editor of *Africa*.

Law and Warfare

Liberian Kpelle of Panta Chiefdom in northeast Central Province.

Strong corporate patrilineages are absent among the Kpelle. The most important kinship group is the virilocal polygynous family which sometimes becomes an extended family, almost always of the patrilineal variety. Several of these families form the core of a residential group, known as a village quarter, more technically, a clan-barrio (Murdock 1949: 74). This is headed by a quarter elder who is related to most of the household heads by real or putative patrilineal ties.

Kpelle political organization is centralized although there is no single king or paramount chief, but a series of chiefs of the same level of authority, each of whom is superordinate over district chiefs and town chiefs. Some political functions are also vested in the tribal fraternity, the Poro, which still functions vigorously. The form of political organization found in the area can thus best be termed the polycephalous associational state.

The structure of the Kpelle court system parallels that of the political organization. In Liberia the highest court of a tribal authority and the highest tribal court chartered by the Government is that of a paramount chief. A district chief's court is also an official court. Disputes may be settled in these official courts or in unofficial courts, such as those of town chiefs or quarter elders. In addition to this, grievances are settled informally in moots, and sometimes by associational groupings such as church councils or cooperative work groups.

In my field research I studied both the formal and informal methods of dispute settlement. The method used was to collect case material in as complete a form as possible. Accordingly, immediately after a hearing, my interpreter and I would prepare verbatim transcripts of each case that we heard. These transcripts were supplemented with accounts—obtained from respondents—of past cases or cases which I did not hear litigated. Transcripts from each type of hearing were analyzed phrase by phrase in terms of a frame of reference derived from jurisprudence and ethno-law. The results of the analysis indicate two things: first, that courtroom hearings and moots are quite different in their procedures and tone, and secondly, why they show this contrast.

Kpelle courtroom hearings are basically coercive and arbitrary in tone. In another paper (Gibbs 1962) I have shown that this is partly the result of the intrusion of the authoritarian values of the Poro into the courtroom. As a result, the court is limited in the manner in which it can handle some types of disputes. The court is particularly effective in settling cases such as assault, possession of illegal charms, or theft where the litigants are not linked in a relationship which must continue after the trial. However, most of the cases brought before a Kpelle court are cases involving disputed rights over women, including matrimonial matters which are usually cast in the form of suits for divorce. The court is particularly inept at settling these numerous matrimonial disputes because its harsh tone tends to drive spouses farther apart rather than to reconcile them. The moot, in contrast, is more effective in handling such cases. The following analysis indicates the reasons for this.

The Kpelle *bɛrɛi mu meni saa,* or 'house palaver', is an informal airing of a dispute which takes place before an assembled group which includes kinsmen of the litigants and neighbors from the quarter where the case is being heard. It is a completely *ad hoc* group, varying greatly in composition from case to case. The matter to be settled is usually a domestic problem: alleged mistreatment or neglect by a spouse, an attempt to collect money paid to a kinsman for a job which was not completed, or a quarrel among brothers over the inheritance of their father's wives.

In the procedural description which follows I shall use illustrative data from the Case of the Ousted Wife:

Wama Nya, the complainant, had one wife, Yua. His older brother died and he inherited the widow, Yokpo, who moved into his house. The two women were classificatory sisters. After Yokpo moved in, there was strife in the household. The husband accused her of staying out late at night, of harvesting rice without his knowledge, and of denying him food. He also accused Yokpo of having lovers and admitted having had a physical struggle with her, after which he took a basin of water and 'washed his hands of her.'

Yokpo countered by denying the allegations about having lovers, saying that she was accused falsely, although she had in the past confessed the name of one lover. She further complained that Wama Nya had assaulted her and, in the act, had committed the indignity of removing her headtie, and had expelled her from the house after the ritual hand-washing. Finally, she alleged that she had been thus cast out of the house at the instigation of the other wife who, she asserted, had great influence over their husband.

Kɔlɔ Waa, the Town Chief and quarter elder, and the brother of Yokpo, was the mediator of the moot, which decided that the husband was mainly at fault, although Yua and Yokpo's children were also in the wrong. Those at fault had to apologize to Yokpo and bring gifts of apology as well as local rum ['cane juice'] for the disputants and participants in the moot.

The moot is most often held on a Sunday—a day of rest for Christians and non-Christians alike—at the home of the complainant, the person who calls the moot. The mediator will have been selected by the complainant. He is a kinsman who also holds an office such as town chief or quarter elder, and therefore has some skill in dispute settlement. It is said that he is chosen to preside by virtue of his kin tie, rather than because of his office.

The proceedings begin with the pronouncing of blessings by one of the oldest men of the group. In the Case of the Ousted Wife, Gbenai Zua, the elder who pronounced the blessings, took a rice stirrer in his hand and, striding back and forth, said:

> This man has called us to fix the matter between him and his wife. May ɣala [the supreme, creator deity] change his heart and let his household be in a good condition. May ɣala bless the family and make them fruitful. May He bless them so they can have food this year. May He bless the children and the rest of the family so they may always be healthy. May He bless them to have good luck. When Wama Nya takes a gun and goes in the bush, may he kill big animals. May ɣala bless us to enjoy the meat. May He bless us to enjoy life and always have luck. May ɣala bless all those who come to discuss this matter.

The man who pronounces the blessings always carries a stick or a whisk (*kpung*), which he waves for effect as he paces up and down chanting his injunctions. Participation of spectators is demanded, for the blessings are chanted by the elder (*kpung namu* or '*kpung* owner') as a series of imperatives, some of which he repeats. Each phrase is responded to by the spectators who answer in unison with a formal response, either *e ka ti* (so be it), or a low, drawn-out *eeee*. The *kpung namu* delivers his blessings faster and faster, building up a rhythmic interaction pattern with the other participants. The effect is to unite those attending in common action before the hearing begins. The blessing focuses attention on the concern with maintaining harmony and the well-being of the group as a whole.

Everyone attending the moot wears their next-to-best clothes or, if it is not Sunday, everyday clothes. Elders, litigants, and spectators sit in mixed fashion, pressed closely upon each other, often overflowing on to a veranda. This is in contrast to the vertical spatial separation between litigants and adjudicators in the courtroom. The mediator, even though he is a chief, does not wear his robes. He and the oldest men will be given chairs as they would on any other occasion.

The complainant speaks first and may be interrupted by the mediator or anyone else present. After he has been thoroughly quizzed, the accused will answer and will also be questioned by those present. The two parties will question each other directly and question others in the room also. Both the testimony and the questioning are lively and uninhibited. Where there are witnesses to some of the actions described by the parties, they may also speak and be questioned. Although the proceedings are spirited, they remain orderly. The mediator may fine anyone who speaks out of turn by requiring them to bring some rum for the group to drink.

The mediator and the others present will point out the various faults committed by both the parties. After everyone has been heard, the mediator expresses the consensus of the group. For example, in the Case of the Ousted Wife, he said to Yua: 'The words you used towards your sister were not good, so come and beg her pardon.'

The person held to be mainly at fault will then formally apologize to the other person. This apology takes the form of the giving of token gifts to the wronged person by the guilty party. These may be an item of clothing, a few coins, clean hulled rice, or a combination of all three. It is also customary for the winning party in accepting the gifts of apology to give, in return, a smaller token such as a twenty-five-cent piece[1] to show his 'white heart' or good will. The losing party is also lightly 'fined'; he must present rum or beer to the mediator and the others who heard the case. This is consumed by all in attendance. The old man then pronounces blessings again and offers thanks for the restoration of harmony within the group, and asks that all continue to act with good grace and unity.

An initial analysis of the procedural steps of the moot isolates the descriptive attributes of the moot and shows that they contrast with those of the courtroom hearing. While the airing of grievances is incomplete in courtroom hearings, it is more complete in the moot. This fuller airing of the issues results, in many marital cases, in a more harmonious solution. Several specific features of the house palaver facilitate this wider airing of grievances. First, the hearing takes place soon after a breach has occurred, before the grievances have hardened. There is no delay until the complainant has time to go to the paramount chief's or district chief's headquarters to institute suit. Secondly, the hearing takes place in the familiar surroundings of a home. The robes, writs, messengers, and other symbols of power which subtly intimidate and inhibit the parties in the courtroom, by reminding them of the physical force which underlies the procedures, are absent. Thirdly, in the courtroom the conduct of the hearing is firmly in the hands of the judge, but in the moot the investigatory initiative rests much more with the parties themselves. Jurisprudence suggests that, in such a case, more of the grievances lodged between the parties are likely to be aired and adjusted. Finally, the range of relevance applied to matters which are brought out is extremely broad. Hardly anything mentioned

---

[1] American currency is the official currency of Liberia and is used throughout the country.

is held to be irrelevant. This too leads to a more thorough ventilation of the issues.

There is a second surface difference between court and moot. In a courtroom hearing, the solution is, by and large, one which is imposed by the adjudicator. In the moot the solution is more consensual. It is, therefore, more likely to be accepted by both parties and hence more durable. Several features of the moot contribute to the consensual solution: first, there is no unilateral ascription of blame, but an attribution of fault to both parties. Secondly, the mediator, unlike the chief in the courtroom, is not backed by political authority and the physical force which underlies it. He cannot jail parties, nor can he levy a heavy fine. Thirdly, the sanctions which are imposed are not so burdensome as to cause hardship to the losing party or to give him or her grounds for a new grudge against the other party. The gifts for the winning party and the potables for the spectators are not as expensive as the fines and the court costs in a paramount chief's court. Lastly, the ritualized apology of the moot symbolizes very concretely the consensual nature of the solution. The public offering and acceptance of the tokens of apology indicate that each party has no further grievances and that the settlement is satisfactory and mutually acceptable. The parties and spectators drink together to symbolize the restored solidarity of the group and the rehabilitation of the offending party.

This type of analysis describes the courtroom hearing and the moot, using a frame of reference derived from jurisprudence and ethno-law which is explicitly comparative and evaluative. Only by using this type of comparative approach can the researcher select features of the hearings which are not only unique to each of them, but theoretically significant in that their contribution to the social-control functions of the proceedings can be hypothesized. At the same time, it enables the researcher to pinpoint in procedures the cause for what he feels intuitively: that the two hearings contrast in tone, even though they are similar in some ways.

However, one can approach the transcripts of the trouble cases with a second analytical framework and emerge with a deeper understanding of the implications of the contrasting descriptive attributes of the court and the house palaver. Remember that the coercive tone of the courtroom hearing limits the court's effectiveness in dealing with matrimonial disputes, especially in effecting reconciliations. The moot, on the other hand, is particularly effective in bringing about reconciliations between spouses. This is because the moot is not only conciliatory, but *therapeutic*. Moot procedures are therapeutic in that, like psychotherapy, they re-educate the parties through a type of social learning brought about in a specially structured interpersonal setting.

Talcott Parsons (1951: 314–19) has written that therapy involves four elements: support, permissiveness, denial of reciprocity, and manipulation of rewards. Writers such as Frank (1955: 524–25), Klapman (1959), and Opler (1959: 296–98) have pointed out that the same elements characterize not only individual psychotherapy, but group psychotherapy as well. All four elements are writ large in the Kpelle moot.

The patient in therapy will not continue treatment very long if he does not feel support from the therapist or from the group. In the moot the parties are encouraged in the expression of their complaints and feelings because they sense group support. The very presence of one's kinsmen and neighbors demonstrates their concern. It indicates to the parties that they have a real problem and that the others are willing to help them to help themselves in solving it. In a parallel vein, Frank, speaking of group psychotherapy, notes that "Even anger may be supportive if it implies to a patient that others take him seriously enough to get angry at him, especially if the object of the anger feels it to be directed toward his neurotic behavior rather than himself as a person" (1955: 531). In the moot the feeling of support also grows out of the pronouncement of the blessings which stress the unity of the group and its harmonious goal, and it is also undoubtedly increased by the absence of the publicity and expressive symbols of political power which are found in the courtroom.

Permissiveness is the second element in therapy. It indicates to the patient that everyday restrictions on making antisocial statements or acting out antisocial impulses are lessened. Thus, in the Case of the Ousted Wife, Yua felt free enough to turn to her ousted co-wife (who had been married leviratically) and say:

> You don't respect me. You don't rely on me any more. When your husband was living, and I was with my husband, we slept on the farm. Did I ever refuse to send you what you asked me for when you sent a message? Didn't I always send you some of the meat my husband killed? Did I refuse to send you anything you wanted? When your husband died and we became co-wives, did I disrespect you? Why do you always make me ashamed? The things you have done to me make me sad.

Permissiveness in the therapeutic setting (and in the moot) results in catharsis, in a high degree of stimulation of feelings in the participants, and an equally high tendency to verbalize these feelings. Frank notes that "Neurotic responses must be expressed in the therapeutic situation if they are to be changed by it" (1955: 531). In the same way, if the solution to a dispute reached in a house palaver is to be stable, it is important that there should be nothing left to embitter and undermine the decision. In a familiar setting, with familiar people, the parties to the moot feel at ease and free to say *all* that is on their minds. Yokpo, judged to be the wronged party in the Case of the Ousted Wife, in accepting an apology, gave expression to this when she said:

> I agree to everything that my people said, and I accept the things they have given me—I don't have *anything else* about them on my mind. (*My italics.*)

As we shall note below, this thorough airing of complaints also facilitates the gaining of insight into and the unlearning of idiosyncratic behavior which is socially disruptive. Permissiveness is rooted in the lack of publicity and the lack of symbols of power. But it stems, too, from the immediacy of the hearing, the locus of investigatory initiative with the parties, and the wide range of relevance.

Permissiveness in therapy is impossible without the denial of reciprocity. This refers to the fact that the therapist will not respond in kind when the patient acts in a hostile manner or with inappropriate affection. It is a type of privileged indulgence which comes with being a patient. In the moot, the parties are treated in the same way and are allowed to hurl recriminations that, in the courtroom, might bring a few hours in jail as punishment for the equivalent of contempt of court. Even though inappropriate views are not responded to in kind, neither are they simply ignored. There is denial of *congruent* response, not denial of *any* response whatsoever. In the *bɛrei mu meni saa*, as in group psychotherapy, "private ideation and conceptualization are brought out into the open and all their facets or many of their facets exposed. The individual gets a 'reading' from different bearings on the compass, so to speak (Klapman 1959: 39), and perceptual patterns . . . are joggled out of their fixed positions. . . ."

Thus, Yua's outburst against Yokpo quoted above was not responded to with matching hostility, but its inappropriateness was clearly pointed out to her by the group. Some of them called her aside in a huddle and said to her:

> You are not right. If you don't like the woman, or she doesn't like you, don't be the first to say anything. Let her start and then say what you have to say. By speaking, if she heeds some of your words, the wives will scatter, and the blame will be on you. Then your husband will cry for your name that you have scattered his property.

In effect, Yua was being told that, in view of the previous testimony, her jealousy of her co-wife was not justified. In reality testing, she discovered that her view of the situation was not shared by the others and, hence, was inappropriate. Noting how the others responded, she could see why her treatment of her co-wife had caused so much dissension. Her interpretation of her new co-wife's actions and resulting premises were not shared by the co-wife, nor by the others hearing a description of what had happened. Like psychotherapy, the moot is gently corrective of behavior rooted in such misunderstandings.

Similarly, Wama Nya, the husband, learned that others did not view as reasonable his accusing his wife of having a lover and urging her to go off and drink with the suspected paramour when he passed their house and wished them all a good evening. Reality testing for him taught him that the group did not view this type of mildly paranoid sarcasm as conducive to stable marital relationships.

The reaction of the moot to Yua's outburst indicates that permissiveness in this case was certainly not complete, but only relative, being much greater than that in the courtroom. But without this moderated immunity the airing of grievances would be limited, and the chance for social relearning lessened. Permissiveness in the moot is incomplete because, even there, prudence is not thrown to the winds. Note that Yua was not told not to express her feelings at all, but to express them only after the co-wife had spoken so that, if the moot failed, she would not be in an untenable position. In court there would be objection to her blunt speaking out. In the moot the objection was, in effect, to her speaking *out of turn*. In other cases the moot sometimes fails, foundering on this very point, because the parties are *too* prudent, all waiting for the others to make the first move in admitting fault.

The manipulation of rewards is the last dimension of therapy treated by Parsons. In this final phase of therapy the patient is coaxed to conformity by the granting of rewards. In the moot one of the most important rewards is the group approval which goes to the wronged person who accepts an apology and to the person who is magnanimous enough to make one.

In the Case of the Ousted Wife, Kɔlɔ Waa, the mediator, and the others attending decided that the husband and the co-wife, Yua, had wronged Yokpo. Kɔlɔ Waa said to the husband:

> From now on, we don't want to hear of your fighting. You should live in peace with these women. If your wife accepts the things which the people have brought, you should pay four chickens and ten bottles of rum as your contribution.

The husband's brother and sister also brought gifts of apology, although the moot did not explicitly hold them at fault.

By giving these prestations, the wrongdoer is restored to good grace and is once again acting like an 'upright Kpelle' (although, if he wishes, he may refuse to accept the decision of the moot). He is eased into this position by being grouped with others to whom blame is also allocated, for, typically, he is not singled out and isolated in being labelled deviant. Thus, in the Case of the Ousted Wife the children of Yokpo were held to be at fault in 'being mean' to their stepfather, so that blame was not only shared by one 'side,' but ascribed to the other also.

Moreover, the prestations which the losing party is asked to hand over are not expensive. They are significant enough to touch the pocketbook a little; for the Kpelle say that if an apology does not cost something other than words, the wrongdoer is more likely to repeat the offending action. At the same time, as we noted above, the tokens are not so costly as to give the loser additional reason for anger directed at the other party which can undermine the decision.

All in all, the rewards for conformity to group expectations and for following out a new behavior pattern are kept within the deviant's sight. These rewards are positive, in contrast to the negative sanctions of the courtroom. Besides the institutionalized apology, praise and acts of concern and affection replace fines and jail sentences. The mediator, speaking to Yokpo as the wronged party, said:

> You have found the best of the dispute. Your husband has wronged you. All the people have wronged you. You are the only one who can take care of them because you are the oldest. Accept the things they have given to you.

The moot in its procedural features and procedural sequences is, then, strongly analogous to psychotherapy. It is analogous to therapy in the structuring of the role of the mediator also. Parsons has indicated that, to do his job well, the therapist must be a member of two social systems: one containing himself and his patient; and the other, society at large (1951: 314). He must not be seduced into thinking that he belongs only to the therapeutic dyad, but must gradually pull the deviant back into a relationship with the wider group. It is significant, then, that the mediator of a moot is a kinsman who is also a chief of some sort. He thus represents both the group involved in the dispute and the wider community. His task is to utilize his position as kinsman as a lever to manipulate the parties into living up to the normative requirements of the wider society, which, as chief, he upholds. His major orientation must be to the wider collectivity, not to the particular goals of his kinsmen.

When successful, the moot stops the process of alienation which drives two spouses so far apart that they are immune to ordinary social-control measures such as a smile, a frown, or a pointed aside. A moot is not always successful, however. Both parties must have a genuine willingness to cooperate and a real concern about their discord. Each party must be willing to list his grievances, to admit his guilt, and make an open apology. The moot, like psychotherapy, is impotent without well-motivated clients.

The fact that the Kpelle court is basically coercive and the moot therapeutic does not imply that one is dysfunctional while the other is eufunctional. The court and informal dispute-settlement procedures have separate but complementary functions. In marital disputes the moot is oriented to a couple as a dyadic social system and serves to reconcile them wherever possible. This is eufunctional from the point of view of the couple, to whom divorce would be dysfunctional. Kpelle courts customarily treat matrimonial matters by granting a divorce. While this may be dysfunctional from the point of view of the couple, because it ends their marriage, it may be eufunctional from the point of view of society. Some marriages, if forced to continue, would result in adultery or physical violence at best, and improper socialization of children at worst. It is clear that the Kpelle moot is to the Kpelle court as the domestic and family relations courts (or commercial and labor arbitration boards) are to ordinary courts in our own society. The essential point is that both formal and informal dispute-settlement procedures serve significant functions in Kpelle society and neither can be fully understood if studied alone.

DISPUTE SETTLEMENT IN
AN AMERICAN SUPERMARKET
A Preliminary View

Spencer MacCallum

A<small>N</small> IMPRESSIVE development in modern American land tenure has been the postwar rise of professional property management. Besides this, there has been a proliferation of new forms and functions of the multiple-tenant income property. Types of the latter that have become familiar in the landscape since the War include shopping centers, marinas, industrial and research parks, medical clinics, professional and office centers, mobile-home parks, real-estate complexes for which Rockefeller Center was an early prototype, and some of the new "planned communities."

As a landlord-tenant arrangement, the multiple-tenant income property represents a land-tenure pattern of a kind we are used to thinking of in terms of peasants and feudal institutions and of absentee aristocracy battening on the land. But in the present case, the landlords are modern, efficient firms specializing in property management for income on invested capital. From a structural viewpoint, nevertheless, these organizations are indeed akin to the landed estates and manorial organizations of antiquity, in which the internal public authority derived mainly from the proprietary land authority. They are truly "little communities" in modern garb, for to some extent they are modern counterparts

This paper is based on research by the writer which included a preliminary field survey of 35 shopping centers in California in 1962 under an NIH grant through the Department of Anthropology of the University of Chicago. The appended cases are taken from a group of 45 cases collected at the time.

also of village communities organized on the kinship tie, in which the land-distributive function was an attribute of the public authority, such as there was, vested in the chief or headman of the group.

The point I wish to make in this paper is simply that the multiple-tenant income property can be viewed in its internal organization as a community of landlord and tenants. Of the many forms, the shopping center is sociologically most interesting because of the complex relations among its members. This complexity derives especially, but not by any means solely, from the need for joint promotions on which the center characteristically depends because of its locations away from downtown where there is sufficient "natural traffic" to sustain the stores. While neighborhood centers are narrowly specialized, the larger shopping centers—containing from 50 to 200 merchant tenants and a mixed composition of land uses, including professional and office buildings and even motels and apartments in the same plan of development—begin to resemble communities as we are accustomed to thinking of them.

Pospisil (1958: 274) has pointed out that we need not think of there being one system of law in a given society, but that each subgroup has its own.[1] Following this idea and inquiring into the law of the shopping center as a community of landlord and merchant tenants, we find an intriguing situation: The legal system of a shopping center is composed of two parts, a written part and an unwritten part. For the totality of the leases in effect at any given moment in time is the written, formal law which defines the respective rights and duties of all parties, merchants and landlord alike. The employed personnel of the individual busi-

---

[1] "Many ethnographers assume that a given society has a single legal system. They either neglect legal phenomena on the subgroup levels or project these phenomena into the top society level and make them consistent with it. Instead of accepting this smoothed-out picture of a single legal system in a society, the writer suggests recognition of the fact that there are as many such systems as there are functional groups. The legal systems of families, clans, and communities, for example, form a hierarchy of what we may call legal levels, according to the inclusiveness of the respective groups."

ness firms within the center do not come directly under this jurisdiction, but are subject to the rules of their respective organizations. They belong to the shopping center community not in their
own right, but through their respective employers, as the members
of the domestic groups making up a village community might be
related to the polity through their respective "patresfamilias" and
not in their individual rights. Case 3 below illustrates an appeal
to lease law, and Case 4, the hierarchy of legal levels in the
center.

The informal law on the other hand develops outside of the
leases and consists of a body of rules and understandings, bylaws
as it were, governing behavior in the center. Case 5 suggests one
of the ways in which such law may develop, as does Case 4.

An important problem of shopping-center administration is
writing effective leases. One of the requirements of an effective
lease is that it consist with the existing leases—the rest of the
body of written law—and also with the unwritten law of the center.
A general development in the shopping-center lease has been a
movement away from the traditional form of lease which defined
a narrow dyadic relationship, specifying what the two parties
would do for one another and leaving it at that, toward the lease
becoming a conscious instrument of social policy in the shopping
center as a community of merchants. Increasingly, it has been developing lateral extensions, as it were, citing positive obligations
of the lessee not only to the landlord but also to the other
merchants in the center. Clauses requiring tenants to participate
in the merchants' council, spend a minimum percentage of gross
income on advertising and a portion of this in council-sponsored
media, coordinate his minimum opening hours with those of other
merchants, enforce the center parking rules among his own employees, and so forth, are becoming standard items in shopping-
center leases.

If the shopping center is thought of in this way as an autonomous community of landlord and merchant tenants, then many
suggestive parallels come to mind between its law and the law of
primitive communities. The emphasis in both is toward resolving

differences and preserving social relations, and neither is fundamentally concerned with rules and penalties.

One of the most fruitful areas for study, however, may be the problem of writing effective leases, since it is here that we confront the problem of the relation between written and unwritten law, and perhaps also the problem of boundaries between law and custom, on a manageable scale and, incidentally, without a language barrier. Moreover, the recent growth of these new forms of organization on the land—truly estate forms of urban land tenure —appearing *de novo* in the bare space of twenty years, affords unusual conditions for studying institutional emergence and change. For the anthropologist, moreover, it offers a natural opening to the study of contemporary society.

CASES

CASE 1   THE CASE THAT TURNED AROUND

Informants: Shopping-center manager; former promotion director; succeeding promotion director; consultant from an outside promotion firm who attended meetings of the board of directors of the merchants' council after the resignation of the promotion director.

Facts: Each year the baker had made a 500-pound cake for the center's Birthday Anniversary Sale. The new promotion director thought the baker charged the merchants' council too much for his cake. He told the baker that and asked for a specific bid on the following year's cake. When the baker failed to give a price, the promotion director obtained a cake at a low price from a baker firm in another city that operated a chain outlet for ready-baked goods as a concession in the supermarket in the center. At a council meeting after the Anniversary Sale, the baker was irate. He said the arrangement had been "rigged" and that he had been unjustly accused of charging too much for his cake. He said his cake was better quality. He charged that the promotion director had been disloyal to the merchants in the center by going "off the mall."

Outcome: The promotion director publicly asked the baker for his friendship and was refused. The baker withdrew from the council and stopped paying dues. Within a year, the promotion director had resigned under diffuse pressure from the council. The baker still did not return. Shortly afterward, the council directors decided to feature a cake again at the next Birthday Anniversary Sale and to ask the baker to provide it.

Comment: The former promotion director's account differed from the other accounts on the point of whether he had "gone off the mall" or whether there were, as he recounted it, "two bakers in the center." (E.g., the center manager's story: "We went outside and got another baker . . .") He thus contrived to avoid the issue of disloyalty on a technicality and cited more fundamental reasons for his inability to get along with the merchants, of which he said the baker's withdrawal and refusal to pay dues was only a symptom and a further aggravation. Among his reasons, he cited (1) tension in the center over a leveling off of volume gains over the past year due to new discount stores in the area and a natural tendency for a center's growth to slow around its seventh year, (2) the structural problem of his being employed directly by the council instead of by the landlord, so that every merchant felt he "owned a piece of" the promotion director, and (3) that he was not temperamentally suited to the job.

He predicted the problem with the baker would be settled by a delegation from the promotion committee of the council going to him and saying, "Frank, we like your cake best and want to have it, to hell with the cost. Will you make it?" And Frank would say, "Well, I'll think it over." Two months later, just prior to the writer leaving the field, this seemed to be the way events were developing; the promotion committee had decided to ask the baker to bake the cake, without making a point of price.

The succeeding promotion director suggested a further element in the baker's stand may have been that it gave him a chance not to pay dues. He quoted the baker as once having said to him, "Promotions don't help bakers."

295

CASE 2   THE CASE OF THE SHOPPING CARTS

Informant: Shopping center manager.

Facts: A supermarket's checkout area faced onto an arcade of
shops. On more than one occasion, boys bringing in shopping
carts from the parking lots made up lines of carts that partly
blocked access to shops in the arcade. Several of the merchants
spoke to the manager of the center about it.

Outcome: The manager took the problem to the food-store
manager and questioned him in detail about what could be done.
Together, they worked out a different system of stacking the carts
and decided upon various areas of the store where excess carts
would be stored when not in use. The manager of the center then
spoke to the other merchants, telling them something had been
worked out, and suggesting they be lenient with the food-store
manager, pointing out that often it is not the manager but employees who make the difficulties.

Comment: The center manager emphasized that problems are
handled in a face-to-face manner when they are still small. He
said the management could do this because they spent so much
time with the tenants that they learned the characteristics of each
person. He said, "Just so they know you're doing something, it
doesn't matter what you do. The merchants have got to feel that
their interests are being looked out for."

CASE 3   THE CASE OF THE WINDOW FULL OF SLIPPERS

Informants: Shopping-center manager; promotion director.

Facts: A shoe store had an exclusive to sell shoes in the center.
The ready-to-wear shop therefore had an express clause in its
lease forbidding sale of shoes. The shop bought a lot of colorful,
mule-type slippers of many different kinds and filled a window full
of them. The shoe-store man did not make a point of going to the
manager of the center, but he met him on the street, walking

casually, and said, "I see they're selling shoes next door. I didn't think they were supposed to do that." The manager said, "I'll chase the lease up and see what I can find out." He talked to the manager of the ready-to-wear shop, who said, "Oh no, these aren't shoes. They're boutique." The center manager went to his office and "let it cool off a bit . . . probably it was two hours." In the meantime, he looked for *boutique* in the dictionary and did not find it. He went to the shoe store, then back once more to the ready-to-wear shop, talking the thing down, rather than inflaming it. The ready-to-wear man, appealing to the professionalism that is stressed in the shoe business, said it really was not a shoe because it did not have to be fitted. It was not customized. He said, moreover, that he had a tremendous stock.

Outcome: The center manager went to his office, and then, after a while, went back to the manager of the ready-to-wear shop and "just sat down with him." He said, "This is a borderline case; you're asking me to define something the dictionary hasn't defined. I think the thing to do on this is to compromise. Instead of filling the window and making a specialty item of it, just put two or three pairs in the window as you would an accessory. Then you won't look like a shoe store." He allowed him to keep his stock and sell it.

Comment: The center manager said, "We don't let those things go quickly. We let them cool, go slowly on them." Commenting further on how cases usually come to his attention, he said, "The grapevine is faster than your ears . . . I'm one of the last people that ever gets a complaint. About 90 percent of the complaints I get are indirect. Somebody says, 'So-and-so's been beefing about that.' "

CASE 4   THE CASE OF THE OBSTINATE NURSE

Informant: Promotion director.

Facts: Despite warnings placed on the car by the security guard, the nurse employed in a doctor's office in the center continued to

take up valuable parking space, parking at the curb only twenty
feet from the doctor's office instead of in the parking area designated for tenants and personnel. The nurse told the center manager and the council of merchants that it was none of their concern.
The landlord advised the doctor by letter that if further violations
occurred, he would have to leave the center. The doctor spoke to
his nurse. She continued parking at the curb.

Outcome: When she had received three more warnings, the
center manager sent a letter to the doctor requesting the premises
at the end of the month. The doctor asked if he could stay if he
dismissed his nurse, and was told he could. He dismissed her reluctantly. He said she was a good nurse.

Comment: The promotion director said it thereafter became
the unwritten rule in that center that any employee who accumu-
lated three parking warnings (I did not think to ask over what
period of time) would be dismissed.

CASE 5   THE CASE OF THE MANIPULATED MERCHANTS

Informant: Shopping-center manager.

Facts: The manager of a major store in the center, while not a
director on the merchants' council, was active on its advertising
committee. He proposed at a weekly meeting that all the merchants hold a five-day flower show on the mall, during which they
could put out "throwaways" advertising the specials they would
run during that week only. The other merchants liked the idea
and began to develop the plan. Just before the flower show was
scheduled to open, a small merchant learned from a newspaper
space salesman that the major was coming out with a big newspaper section at the same time as the show. The small merchant
went to the center manager with this information. The center
manager called the large merchant, who confirmed it. On the day
that the "throwaways" on the flower show were put out announcing the individual merchants' specials, the big store announced

a major, week-long sales event that overshadowed the merchandising of the rest of the stores in the center.

Outcome: Everybody talked about the incident, but it was never brought into the open. The consensus was that the big store had conceived the idea of the flower show only to augment its own major promotional effort with advertising monies and specials put out by the other stores. All the merchants felt bad about it. They recognized there had been no lease violation and that all the stores were free to spend their own money for promotion as they liked, but they objected that the major had not told them about his plans so they could have geared their activity to his. Fortunately, everybody did a good business that week.

While the incident was never brought up in any kind of meeting, the informant said an understanding was arrived at with the merchants that the center management would assume responsibility in the future for knowing what promotions were being planned by the major stores, so that this could not happen again. Asked how he could do this, the informant said he and his staff ask the major merchants what they are planning, when they are coming out with circulars, and so forth.

"Do you ask them this in meetings?"

"No, just when we see them. We make it our business to keep informed about their advertising and promotion plans." The manager is able to do this because he is continually in touch with his tenants. He reported a Rotary Club organized entirely within the center; 52 merchants meet together every week.

"We're very close here. It's just like a little town. Now, at lunch today I talked to seven of my tenants . . ."

Part III | FEUDS, RAIDS, AND WARS

BLOOD REVENGE AND WAR
AMONG THE JIBARO INDIANS OF
EASTERN ECUADOR

Rafael Karsten

THE JIBARO INDIANS, who in their own language are called
Shuāra, inhabit the virgin forests around the great rivers Pastaza, Morona, Upano-Santiago and their affluents, regions politically divided between the Republics of Ecuador and Peru. Their
present total number can without exaggeration be estimated at
fifteen or twenty thousand. The Jibaros are divided into a number
of smaller tribes which are generally hostile to each other. They
have no uniform tribal organization and do not recognize any
common political authority. This division also stamps their social
institutions and customs, which are somewhat different among different tribes. Against the whites the Jibaros have, in critical times,
been able to maintain themselves as a united and homogeneous
nation. The best proof of this is the general insurrection which, on
account of the oppression of the Spaniards, was carried out in
1599 by all tribes living on the Upano, Paute, Santiago, and
Morona, and at which the majority of the white population in the
flourishing villages Sevilla de Oro, Logroño, and Mendoza were
massacred by the Indians. Since that time the whites have, on the
whole, left the Jibaros unmolested, but between themselves they
have continued those destructive wars which more than anything
else have contributed to the diminution of the Jibaro race.

The Jibaros no doubt at present are the most warlike of all In-

Extracted from *Blood Revenge, War, and Victory Feasts among the Jibaro
Indians of Eastern Ecuador.* Smithsonian Institution, Bureau of American
Ethnology, Bulletin 79, 1923. Extracted pages: 1–32. Reprinted by permis-
sion of the Bureau of American Ethnology.

dian tribes in South America. The wars, the blood feuds within the tribes, and the wars of extermination between the different tribes are continuous, being nourished by their superstitious belief in witchcraft. These wars are the greatest curse of the Jibaros and are felt to be so even by themselves, at least so far as the feuds within the tribes are concerned. On the other hand, the wars are to such a degree one with their whole life and essence that only powerful pressure from outside or a radical change of their whole character and moral views could make them abstain from them. This one may judge even from the fact that from a victory over his enemies the Jibaro warrior not only expects honor and fame in the ordinary sense of the word but also certain material benefits. The head trophy which he takes from his slain enemy is not merely a token of victory, but becomes a fetish charged with supernatural power, and the great victory feast itself with its many mysterious ceremonies, in fact, forms a part of the practical religion or cult of the Jibaros.

The education of the boys among the Jibaros first of all aims at making them brave and skillful warriors. When a Jibaro has enemies on whom he wants to take revenge for offenses and outrages, perhaps committed long ago, but despairs of being able to do it himself, he systematically tries to awaken and maintain hatred against them in his young sons. When a Jibaro chief goes on a war expedition he often takes his young sons with him in order that they may early learn the art of war and get accustomed to the bloody scenes which take place.

When a boy reaches the age of puberty and is to be received among the full-grown men, a feast is made in his honor which is called *kusúpani* and which chiefly consists in ceremonies with tobacco. After the feast, which lasts three or four days, he is obliged to take a narcotic drink, called *maikoa,* prepared from the rind of the bush *Datura arborea*. This drink has the power of completely narcotizing the Indian as well as awakening within him peculiar visions and hallucinations which are ascribed to certain spirits. The most important of these spirits are the so-called *arútama* ("the old ones") which are in their nature the souls of the ancestors. These appear in all sorts of terrible shapes, as tigers, eagles, giant snakes, and other wild animals, or reveal their presence in stupendous phenomena of nature, in the lightning, in the rainbow, in meteors, etc. They speak to the young Jibaro and advise and teach him in all kinds of manly businesses, but first of all in warlike deeds. Only the Jibaro youth who has seen the *arútama* in the dream and has been spoken to by them can expect to become a valiant and successful warrior, to kill many enemies, and himself secure long life.

Even older warriors who want to know who their enemies are and whether in a war against them they will be victorious are in the habit of drinking *maikoa*. If one asks a Jibaro why he drinks *maikoa* he generally answers: "I do it in order to kill my enemies." The Jibaro warrior generally receives the revelations of the spirits while sleeping alone in the virgin forest in a small ranch made of palm leaves, usually situated many miles away from the habitations of the Indians.

MEANS OF DEFENSE

That the Jibaros are professional warriors also appears from the way in which they construct their houses and from the defensive measures to which they have recourse when particularly threatened by their enemies. The Jibaros, like other Indian tribes inhabiting the virgin forests of Amazonas, do not live in villages but in sundry large communal houses in which several families of near relations may find room. Such a house (called *hēa*) is generally situated on a high hill from which it is easy to dominate the surrounding country, or in the angle of a river, which protects it from two or three sides.

Not only the houses themselves but also the manioc and banana plantations situated close by are protected in a similar way by high fences of strong chonta poles. The aim of this arrangement is to prevent the enemy from approaching the house through the plantations.

Formerly, before the use of firearms was so general among the

Jibaros as it is now, the chiefs especially were in the habit of constructing a sort of war tower at one end of their houses. These towers were of quadratic form and sometimes 30 or 40 meters in height. On the top of it there was a small room about 4 meters in quadrate and with walls about 1 meter in height, made of strong chonta poles, which protected the defender against the lances of the enemies. After the Jibaros began to make use of firearms in their wars these measures of defense proved less fit for the purpose, and consequently were no longer used.

It is still common among the Jibaros to arrange a kind of trap on the way which leads to the house and where one expects the enemy will try to approach it. One such trap consists of a round hole in the ground, about 1½ meters deep and large enough for a full-grown man to fall into it. At the bottom of the hole three pointed sticks of chonta, resembling points of lances, are arranged in an erect position. The part which sticks out from the earth has a length of about half a meter. At the surface of the earth the opening of the hole is covered with small sticks and leaves which makes it difficult or impossible for the enemy, creeping along in the darkness, to discover its presence before he falls into it. When he falls his feet are transfixed by the pointed sticks and he is not able to get out. Besides, the defenders of the house are often keeping watch at these holes, ready to dispatch the enemy when he is caught in them. The Jibaros call these traps "a hole of death."

Another kind of trap, which likewise is arranged on the narrow path leading to the house, consists of a small tree, growing close to the path, which is bent down, or of a big branch of a tree, one end of which is fixed in the ground so that with the latter it forms an angle of about 30°. To the upper end of this branch eight pointed chonta sticks are attached in such a way that they form as it were a comb. The branch is bent back like a bow against a couple of poles fixed in the ground for the purpose, to which it is attached by means of a strong liana. Across the path a few inches over the ground another liana is stretched and tied at one of the poles. Between this liana and the liana holding the bent branch there is such a connection that when the foot of the enemy touches the former, the bow is released, and the comb with the pointed chonta sticks will strike him with terrible force in the face or the chest.

The following defensive measure is of modern origin: Ac oss the path along which the enemy is expected to come a blacl ned string is stretched at such a height that it reaches a man t the chest. At the tree where one end of the string is fastened a charged and cocked rifle is tied, with the barrel fixed in the direction of the string. The end of the string is brought in such a connection with the trigger of the rifle that when the enemy, coming along in the darkness, gives it a push, the shot is discharged and is likely to hit him in the chest. Even if he should escape from being hit, the shot would warn the inhabitants of the house that enemies were approaching.

The principal weapons of war of the Jibaros are the lance and the shield, the former being used for attack, the latter for defense. Nowadays the Jibaros, besides these weapons, also commonly use firearms received from the whites, generally in exchange for a human head. The lance should be made of the hard wood of the chonta palm. The head is of prismatic shape and with the shaft forms a single piece. A special power is ascribed to the chonta lance, owing to the belief that the spiny chonta palm itself is a demoniac tree, the seat of a spirit. The chonta lance therefore inspires not only men but also the spirits and demons with fear.

The shield is made of a special kind of wood which the Jibaros call *kamáka,* and which has the property of being at once light and strong. It is always round and wrought of one single piece, although the shields are sometimes very large.

As soon as the shield is made it is often painted on the outside with the black dye obtained from the genipa fruit. The patterns represent spirits, giant snakes, butterflies, and other animals. These patterns are supposed to inspire the enemy with fear and to give strength and courage to the warrior himself.

The Jibaros never use blowpipes and poisoned arrows in their wars, but only for hunting. They believe that if they kill a man with a poisoned arrow that poison will no longer do for killing an animal or bird of the forest. Besides, it seems that the poisoned arrows are not regarded as a sufficiently effective weapon to fight men with. The Indian, when killing his enemy, desires to inflict as large wounds and to shed as much blood as possible, a fact that explains his predilection for the lance as a weapon of war.

CHIEFS AND WARS

Among the Jibaros each family father is theoretically absolute ruler over his house people, and in times of peace there is no recognized common chief even within the tribe, and still less any exercising authority over several tribes. The Jibaros have not even a proper name for a chief. The word *capitu,* which is sometimes used, is borrowed from the Spanish and is used principally to denote a white man of importance. It is only in times of war that a chieftainship exists; that is to say, during those great wars of extermination which are carried out against other Jibaro tribes. Such a temporary chief of war is generally only called *unta,* "the old one," because the chiefs are nearly always old, experienced men who have killed many enemies and captured many heads.

No Jibaro is selected as a chief if he has not killed at least one enemy. The Jibaros have absolute faith in the heritability of prominent qualities, and ascribe an extraordinary importance to education and the power of example. The son of a great chief, they say, must necessarily also become an able warrior because he is, as it were, a direct continuation of his father, has received a careful education for the deeds of war, and has always had the good example of his great father before his eyes.

The authority of the chief elected for a war is very great. It is he alone who disposes everything for the expedition planned, who decides about the time for and the mode of making the attack, and the younger warriors oblige themselves to obey him in everything. But as soon as a war has been carried to a successful end the power of the chief ceases, and he has, in spite of the great repute he always enjoys, no more authority or right to decide over the doings of his tribesmen than any other family father among the Jibaros.

CAUSES OF THE WARS

The Jibaros are by nature impulsive and choleric, qualities that among them frequently give rise to disputes and quarrels which may degenerate into sanguinary feuds. Their unbounded sense of liberty and their desire to be independent, not only of the whites but also of each other, is one of the reasons why they do not live in villages but each family separately, for in this way conflicts are more easily avoided. It may, for instance, happen that the swine, the most important domestic animals, who during the day are allowed to roam about freely in the forest, penetrate into the plantations of a neighboring family and devastate the crops. The owner gets angry and claims compensation for the damage done. In this way quarrels easily arise which may develop into bloody fights; at any rate there enters general discord and distrust between the two families. Some time later it may happen that one or more members of either family fall ill with some of the diseases which the Jibaros ascribe to witchcraft. When trying to find out the author of the evil the head of that family is most likely to attribute it to the malicious art of a neighbor with whom he has had such a quarrel. If the patient dies he has recourse to divination by means of the narcotic *natéma,* which generally leads to his suspicions against the neighbor being confirmed. The family's sense of justice as well as the duty to the deceased now require that revenge shall be taken, and the supposed wizard is assassinated. This murder naturally awakes the desire for blood revenge on the part of the family thus outraged, and so a blood feud is begun which, as is easily understood, has a tendency to make itself permanent.

Not seldom bloody feuds arise among the Jibaros for the sake of the women. The Jibaros live in polygamy and hold their wives in high estimation. The women, as a matter of fact, have much to say in Jibaro society and are generally treated well. The men, however, are very jealous of their wives and adultery is severely punished, the husband maltreating his unfaithful wife with the lance or a knife so as to sometimes cause her death. In such cases, however, the relatives of the woman frequently take her part, alleging that she is innocent. If in their opinion she has been punished wrongfully or with undue severity, they try to take a corresponding revenge upon her husband. Under such circumstances more than one Jibaro has been killed by his father-in-law or his brothers-in-law. Thus on the Rio Upáno a young Jibaro had once taken the life of his wife on account of unfaithfulness, real or supposed, on her part. Some time afterwards the cruelly mutilated dead body of the Indian was found in the forest. He had been murdered by the relatives of his former wife. Ordinary captures of women, which frequently take place among the Jibaros, also give rise to blood feuds. A Jibaro carries off the wife of another Indian or takes her with her own consent. The offended husband summons his friends and starts to persecute the seducer to kill him. If under such circumstances a murder has been committed, this usually causes a new murder from the party offended, and so on, until either all grown-up members of one family have been exterminated or, what happens more generally, each party gets tired of the feud and they decide to leave one another in peace. Sometimes the affair is settled by a formal agreement.

The Jibaro Indian is wholly penetrated by the idea of retaliation; his desire for revenge is an expression of his sense of justice. This principle is eye for eye, tooth for tooth, life for life. If one reprehends a Jibaro because he has killed an enemy, his answer is generally: "He has killed himself." But blood revenge among these Indians is not merely owing to moral or ethical, but also to religious reasons. The soul of the murdered Indian requires that his relatives shall avenge his death. The errant spirit, which gets no rest, visits his sons, his brothers, his father, in the dream, and, weeping, conjures them not to let the slayer escape but to wreak vengeance upon him for the life he has taken. If they omit to fulfill this duty the anger of the vengeful spirit may turn against themselves. To avenge the blood of a murdered father, brother, or son, is therefore looked upon as one of the most sacred duties of a Jibaro Indian.

Among the Jibaros blood revenge is not strictly individualized in the sense that it always directs itself exclusively against the slayer. The Jibaro certainly first of all wants to take revenge on the person who committed the crime, but if he cannot be caught it may instead be directed against some one of his relatives—his brother, his father, even his mother or sister. To understand this we have to consider that the conception of individual personality and consequently of individual responsibility does not exist among the Indians in the same sense as among civilized peoples. The individual forms an inseparable part of a whole; the members of the same family are regarded as, so to speak, organically coherent with each other, so that one part stands for all and all for one. What happens to one member of that social unit happens to all, and for the deed of one member the rest are held equally responsible. How the Jibaros conceive this connection appears from certain of their social customs. For instance, custom requires that after a child is born the parents shall fast and observe other rules of abstinence for a couple of years, or until the child is named. This is due to the idea that something of the souls or essence of the parents inheres in the child, so that all three in one way form a single organism, a single personality. But this mystic connection between the parents and the child also subsists after the child has grown up, although perhaps less intimately. Similarly, the tie which unites brothers and sisters in a family is so intimate that they may be said together to form one organic whole. When one member of the family is sick the rest have to diet in the same way as the patient himself, for if they eat unsuitable food it would be the same as if the patient ate that food, and his condition would grow worse. From the same point of view we have to explain the custom prevailing among the Jibaros that when a man dies his brother must marry the widow. The departed husband, who is still jealous of the wife he left behind, does not cede her to any other man than his brother, who with himself forms one personality and represents him in the most real sense of the word. When a younger Jibaro is murdered by his enemies the duty of revenging his death is also first of all incumbent on his brothers.

The Jibaro cannot even distinguish his own personality from his material belongings; at least not from things he has made himself. When he fabricates a shield, a drum, a blowpipe, or some other delicate object, he has to diet and observe abstinence in other ways; for, according to his own idea, he actually puts something of his own personality, his own soul, into the object he is making. His own properties, both the essential and habitual ones and those occasionally acquired through eating a certain food, etc., will therefore be transferred to that object.

Such a view prevailing among the Indians, it is easy to understand that a Jibaro, with regard to the murder of one of his relatives, asks not so much which individual has committed the deed, but rather reasons in the following way: "A member of that family has murdered my relative; consequently, in revenge, some member of that family must die."

When a murder committed by an own tribesman is to be avenged, the social morals of the Jibaros require that the punishment shall be meted out with justice, insofar that for one life which has been taken only one life should be taken in retaliation. Thereupon, the blood guilt is atoned and the offended family is satisfied. Consequently, if a Jibaro Indian wishes to revenge a murder of his brother, it may well happen that he, in case the slayer himself cannot be caught and punished, will assassinate his brother or father instead of him, but he does not take the life of more than one member of the family, even if he has an opportunity of killing more. If he, for instance, killed not only the murderer himself but also some one of his brothers, this would awaken indignation in the whole tribe, and it would be considered righteous that the family thus offended in its turn should take revenge. The blood guilt in such a case has passed to the original avenger. This principle, which requires that there shall be justice in the retaliation so that life is weighed against life, of course, in itself has a tendency to limit blood revenge. It happens, however, in many cases, and especially with regard to supposed witchery, that the person accused of the crime does not admit the guilt but asserts that he and his family are innocently persecuted by the relatives of the dead. If, then, he or a member of his family is murdered, his relatives try, in their turn, to take revenge, and so on, in which case the blood feud tends to become prolonged indefinitely.

If thus, as we have seen, among the Jibaros blood revenge takes place even with regard to members of the same tribe, it fails when such a crime is committed within the family. Among these Indians it sometimes occurs that a man kills his brother, if the latter, for instance, has seduced his wife or bewitched one of his children. But in this case blood revenge generally fails, inasmuch as the natural avengers—that is, the father and the remaining brothers—abstain from carrying it out. "It is enough that one member of our family has died," they say. "Why should we deprive ourselves of one more?"

That the blood feuds which take place within the tribe have an entirely different character from the wars of extermination waged against foreign tribes also appears from the fact that only in the latter case, but not in the former, the victors make trophies (*tsantsa*) of the heads of their slain enemies. Such trophies are prepared only of the heads of enemies belonging to a wholly different tribe, with whom the victors do not reckon blood relationship.

Between the different tribes in the regions inhabited by the Jibaros there exists almost perpetual enmity, and destructive wars are often carried out, especially between neighboring tribes. It is not easy to state what originally has been the cause of this enmity. Generally speaking, one may say that it has originated in the jealousy and rivalry existing between the different tribes, a rivalry personalized in the proud and ambitious chiefs who stand at the head of the different tribes. One chief tries to surpass another one in warlike deeds and cannot endure seeing his rival increase in wealth, power, and influence.

Often the hostility between two tribes is only latent, becoming suddenly active through some occasional incident, when a war ensues. Thus, a series of deaths, which are attributed to the evil art of the treacherous enemy, may occasion a war. It also occurs that an Indian, traveling through the territory of a foreign tribe, with which his own stands on no friendly terms, is assassinated by these secret enemies of his own people, who cannot abstain from taking the opportunity. Such an occasional assassination may be the signal for a general war of extermination between the two tribes.

Whereas the small feuds within the tribes have the character of a private blood revenge, based on the principle of just retaliation, the wars between the different tribes are in principle wars of extermination. In these there is no question about weighing life against life; the aim is to completely annihilate the inimical tribe, all members of which form one organic whole and are animated by the same feelings and mode of thought.

Although the wars of the Jibaro Indians are in their nature nothing but wars of revenge, they never aim at territorial conquests. The Jibaros, on the contrary, fear and detest the country of their enemies, where secret supernatural dangers may threaten them even after they have conquered their natural enemies. The sorcerers of the hostile tribe may have left their witching arrows everywhere, on the road, in the forest, in the houses, with the result that the invading enemies may be hit by them when they least expect it. The land of the enemy is therefore abandoned as soon as possible. Besides, the Jibaros, who inhabit endless virgin forests, where they can make new settlements almost anywhere, have no need of conquering the territory of other tribes.

When a family father, especially a chief or a great warrior, dies, and a medicine man, by drinking *natéma,* has established not only that death has been caused by witchcraft but also who the wizard is, it is incumbent on his nearest male relations, and first of all on his sons, to take revenge on the supposed assassin.

At the deathbed of the father they make a solemn promise to fulfill this duty.

Those preparing for the feud never omit to consult the spirits, who will let them know whether the planned attack will be successful or not. This divination, as already mentioned, is carried out through drinking the narcotic *maikoa*. The Indian for this purpose retires to the forest, where he remains for three days and three nights, fasting strictly and sleeping in a small "dreaming ranch." If the dreams are good, among other spirits the *arútama* appear to the warrior, speaking to him and telling him whether he will be able to kill the enemy or whether he will perhaps be killed himself. If the answer is favorable, he with his followers make the last preparations for the attack.

Such an attack is sometimes planned and carried out in greatest secrecy. Sometimes, and more frequently, the victim is threatened beforehand, the avenger letting him know what fate is awaiting him. He may then save himself by quickly flying to another part of the country. But it also happens that he sends his enemies the following menacing challenge: "I have been told that you intend to assault and kill me. All right, you may come if you have valor. I do not fear you, and I am ready to receive you." Such resolute behavior may cause the enemy to desist from the planned attack or to postpone it to another, more opportune time.

The attack is carried out in different ways. Sometimes the victim is attacked in his house at night, sometimes while he is working outside or traveling. In the former case the assault is made a little before dawn, at 4 or 5 o'clock in the morning. The Jibaros begin their day very early, and the family father is the first who gets up. Since it is difficult or impossible to force the entrance, the enemies generally avail themselves of the opportunity when he opens the door to perform his necessary duties. At this moment they rush upon him and kill him with their lances.

It is, however, easier to kill the enemy while he is outside the house, working or occasionally wandering in the forest. The conspirators beforehand carefully inquire about the movements of the intended victim, and ambush at a place along the path where he has to pass. This place is generally one where appears some natural obstacle, consisting of a small rivulet which the sorcerer has to wade across, or of a swamp where he is obliged to go slowly. Sometimes they also put up along the path some of the secret signs which the Jibaros use as road marks, or to give friends indications as to the direction they ought to take. When the sorcerer arrives here, he stops to examine what the mark means. At this moment the enemies rush forward and pierce him with their lances or shoot him to death. The dead body is left lying on the path or is thrown into the forest.

On the return from such a feud the avengers have for some time to observe certain rules of precaution with regard to their mode of life. The restrictions laid upon them are, however, much milder than those a Jibaro has to observe after he has killed an enemy of a foreign tribe, and essentially consist in fasting and sexual abstinence.

Whereas this blood revenge within the tribe is most often carried out simply through assassinations, the feuds fought out between the different tribes are naturally on a larger scale and with more reason deserve the name of "wars." In all his feuds, however, the Indian, if possible, avoids open fights, having recourse to treachery, assassinations, and sudden, generally night, attacks. But if a real combat and hand-to-hand fighting ensue, the Jibaro warrior often displays both valor and contempt of death. Not to take flight, not to abandon his comrades in such a situation, but gallantly to meet the enemy with lance and shield, is the ambition of every real Jibaro warrior, and, as we have seen, the education of the boys from the beginning aims at imparting to them the qualities necessary for such behavior.

When a whole tribe, or eventually several tribes in union, prepare a war against one or more other tribes, the first thing done is to elect a common chief. He should be an elderly, experienced man, who has taken part in several wars, killed many enemies, and celebrated at least one *tsantsa* feast.

During the time the expedition is planned and the preparations are made, the warriors, and especially the chief, repeatedly drink *maikoa* or *natéma* to consult the spirits. They pay great attention to their dreams, even to those not produced under the direct influence of the narcotic drinks, tell them to each other, and discuss their possible significations. Only in case they believe that they have received favorable answers and all omens are good are measures taken to carry out the war plan conceived. Meanwhile they try, through spies, to acquire as accurate a knowledge as possible about everything concerning the enemy: how many houses there are in the tract, how many fighting men in each house, if the houses are fortified, if the men are well armed, and especially if they have firearms. All these and similar details the spies investigate by making trips into the country of the enemy and by stealing at night to the houses. Everything is prepared with the greatest secrecy possible, so that the enemy is caught unprepared.

About a week before the warriors start for the expedition they assemble every night in the house of the chief, who develops the plan of the war, gives his men the necessary instructions, exhorts them to take courage, not to fear the enemy, not to abandon their comrades, etc. Part of these instructions are given during the war dance or exercise with the lance, which is called *enéma*. *Enéma* is a dialogue between two warriors. It takes place not only as a preparation for a war, but also, for instance, when two Indians, who are unknown to each other, suddenly meet while traveling in the forest or when unknown guests arrive at a house. The conversation all through has a ceremonial character, and menacing movements with the lance accompany each word or phrase.

The dialogue at the *enéma* is rather stereotyped, the words being always about the same and being repeated several times.

> Let us speak loudly!
> Let us speak words!
> What are we going to say?
> Let us quickly assemble!
> Let us avenge the blood guilt!
> Tomorrow we will sleep far away.
> Let us quickly take our enemy!

Quickly, before he is told about it!
So says the Old One (the chief).
Let us go, to return quickly, youths!
Quickly, quickly!
We have been fighting!
We have killed!
We have revenged the blood.
Let us cut off the head (of the enemy)!
Let us carry it with us.

Each phrase is strongly contracted in the pronunciation, so as to consist only of two to four syllables, which naturally makes the conversation entirely unintelligible to one who does not know the words. The phrase thus contracted is repeated twice, corresponding to the movements of the body.

At the beginning of the conversation the two warriors face each other, each having the lance resting on the right shoulder. They speak by turn. The Indian speaking pronounces the phrase in a loud voice, holding the hand over the mouth. With the right arm, upon which the lance rests, he simultaneously makes a movement as if to give emphasis to the words, but he does not, in the beginning, swing the lance and does not move from the spot. Again, in the second repetition or the latter part of the conversation the Indian who has the word takes one step toward his opponent, beginning with the left foot, simultaneously raises the right arm with the lance and lets it fall vibrating down on the shoulder; immediately thereafter he goes back to the original position, at the same time again swinging the lance over his shoulder. This whole series of movements is performed quickly and at one time. One of the conversing Indians having several times repeated this movement with its corresponding phrases, he stops and stands still, the other one then speaking.

When a war expedition is prepared in which many Indians take part, *enéma* is performed on a large scale. The warriors arrange themselves in two rows, one against the other, so that at the ceremony they converse two and two.

The *enéma* conversation implies a mutual exhortation for war and the future course of the combat is passed through, whereat naturally a successful issue of it is anticipated. The whole thing is a magical ceremony by which the Jibaros believe themselves to be able to conjure forth victory over the enemy.

About 1 o'clock in the night, when the new day is supposed to begin, the warriors assembled in the house of the chief start to perform *enéma,* which they continue until the break of day. This is repeated every night during one week.

The warriors, moreover, prepare for the expedition by drinking much manioc beer (*nihamánchi*), as they do for all big travels, without, however, getting too drunk. They likewise take much tobacco, partly in the form of tobacco water, which is drawn in through the nose, partly in the form of cigars, which are smoked.

The Jibaro chief Nayapi, on the Rio Pastaza, told me that among his people the warrior starting for an expedition takes tender leave of his wife, embracing her and consoling her, but at the same time preparing her for the eventuality that he, perhaps, will never return and never see her again.

Among the Jibaros of the Pastaza it is also customary for the women during the whole time the men are absent on the warpath to assemble every night in one house and perform a special dance with rattles of snail shells around the waist and chanting conjurations. This war dance of the women is supposed to have the power of protecting their fathers, husbands, and sons against the lances and bullets of the enemy, of lulling the latter into security so that he will not apprehend the danger before it is too late, and lastly of preventing him from taking revenge for the defeat inflicted upon him.

During the whole journey to the scene of the war, a journey that takes several days, sometimes even weeks, the warriors are allowed to speak only when necessary, and even then not in a loud voice but in a whisper. Only the chief has the right to speak in a loud voice when at the camping places he gives his men the necessary instructions. As soon as the warriors arrive at the place where they propose to camp that night they arrange themselves in two rows, keeping silence. The chief walks along the rows and gives his instructions, exposes the details of the attack planned and, above all, tries to dispel fear of the young warriors and to inspire them with courage. Although on the march to the war the chief no longer drinks *maikoa* or *natéma,* he still pays great attention to his dreams and from them tries to derive favorable presages. Thus he may with the following words try to inspire his people with courage and confidence: "Take courage and don't fear, for I dreamed this night that I saw the great eagle and the toucan. They told me that we are going to take a *wakáni* (a soul). You are not going to die; you are going to be victors and to kill your enemies."

On the eve of the day fixed for the attack the warriors arrange their dress. The Jibaro always pays great attention to his dress and his ornaments, which form a part of his personality, and at the feasts the dressing has a ceremonial character. The dress of the Jibaro Indian normally consists of a loincloth which is attached to the waist by means of a cincture of human hair, and of another small square cloth, called *awangéama,* which covers the shoulders, with a hole in the middle to pass the head through. The long hair, which is carefully washed and attended every day, is divided into three pigtails, a large one at the neck and two small ones at the temples. In the ears the Jibaro always carries ear tubes 20 to 30 centimeters long, the ends of which are frequently ornamented with incised figures.

When the Jibaro warrior prepares for an attack against an enemy, he puts on his head a sort of cap made of monkey's skin, which he prefers to the ordinary head ornament made of parrot or toucan feathers. The ear tubes ought to be as large as possible so that their ends nearly reach the shoulders. Around the neck the warrior wears a necklace of jaguar's teeth, and around the waist the usual cincture of human hair. Old warriors, however, for an attack prefer to cincture themselves with a broad belt of skin of the great boa. The uncovered part of the body, the face, the breast, the back, the arms, and legs, are finally painted black with genipa.

The Jibaros say that for a combat they paint themselves black in order to resemble the *iguanchi* (demons), which implies that the body painting is believed to impart to them something of the savage ferocity and strength of these supernatural beings. Besides, even in semidarkness it is possible to distinguish the black-painted Indian from one who does not wear that mark of recognition. To impart strength and valor to the warrior is also the object of the ear tubes, the necklaces of jaguar's teeth, and the belt of the boa serpent. The power which the Jibaros attribute to the cincture made of human hair depends on the supernatural properties ascribed to the hair, which is regarded as the seat of the soul or the vital energy.

Having arrived at the tract inhabited by the hostile tribe, the warriors try to surprise and kill particular persons belonging to the tribe, who, unaware of the danger, happen to be outside the houses, working in the plantations or walking in the forest. The proper attacks are, however, according to the general custom of the Indians, made at night or early in the morning, a little before dawn. Keeping strict silence, the enemies surround the house on all sides and ambush in the immediate neighborhood of it, expecting that someone will go out and open the door. That person is then instantly killed by a lance or a rifle shot, whereupon the enemies speedily penetrate into the house and massacre the rest of its inhabitants. In case it proves impossible to penetrate into the house by treachery, the enemies set fire to it by firebrands thrown upon its roofing, obliging the inhabitants to leave it and killing them during the confusion that follows. If in this way the assailants have been able to kill all the people in one house, and there is no fear of other Indians coming to the rescue, they may go to the next house and continue the massacre, for, as already pointed out, the wars carried out against foreign tribes always aim at completely exterminating the enemy if possible.

However, the enemy is not always in this way surprised and unprepared, and is not always annihilated without resistance. Not seldom the inhabitants of the house, through the dogs and the chickens, or in some other way, get knowledge of the presence of the enemy, and the latter may then to his disappointment suddenly hear the beats of the great signal drums in the fast time, which is a sure sign for the friends that the people of the house are in danger. However, if the enemy has already surrounded the house, there is little hope for those shut up in it to be saved through the intervention of friends. Their possibility of salvation then consists almost solely in breaking through the besieging ring and speedily fleeing to another house or into the forest.

It is, however, only in case the attacked people have been surprised unprepared and know they are absolutely inferior to the enemy that they try in this way to save themselves by flight. In other cases it happens that the attacking enemy is received by a number of well-prepared and well-armed warriors who, after having in a hurry performed the *enéma,* gallantly go out to meet the assailants.

The victorious enemy without mercy wreaks his savage vengeance not only upon the fighting men, but also on old people, women, and small children, nay, sometimes even on the domestic animals. The younger women are, however, often spared and carried off as prisoners of war, their fate being later to add to the number of their victors', and especially the chief's, wives. There are also numerous instances of small children being spared to be brought up as members of the victorious tribe. For the rest, the Indian does not content himself with merely killing his enemy. He wants to shed as much blood as possible and delights in mutilating the body of the slain enemy, being especially anxious to secure his head.

THE HEAD TROPHY (TSANTSA) AND ITS PREPARATION

As pointed out before, the Jibaros never make trophies of the heads of such enemies as belong to their own tribe—that is, with whom they reckon blood relationship. On the other hand, it is the rule that when a victory has been attained over a foreign tribe, the heads of the slain enemies are taken.

A warrior who has captured a head (*tsantsa*) should celebrate a feast. The head feast opens the road to honor and fame, to material wealth, to new victories over enemies, and a long life.

It is the great mystery feast of the Jibaro Indians; it in part has a purely religious significance, inasmuch as the Jibaro through the ceremonies thereby performed believes he acquires the same benefits as most other savage peoples try to acquire by cult actions of different kinds.

The warrior who has cut off the head is the "lord of the head" and the first who, when the victors are many, has the right to celebrate a feast with it. When several Indians in union have killed one enemy it is customary for each of them in turn to celebrate a victory feast with the trophy, which in this case is taken from one house to another.

During the speedy return which generally follows upon a successful attack, there is not always time for the victors to at once begin with the preparation of the trophy. They at first have to put themselves in safety from the eventually pursuing enemy. Thus, it occurs that they carry the bloody head with them during a couple of days before they get an opportunity to "skin" it. In this work only those warriors engage who have taken part in the killing of the enemy.

At first the following small ceremony takes place: The head is placed upon a large leaf on the ground. Upon the head there is placed another leaf of the forest which the Jibaros call *pingi nuka* and to which certain magical virtues are ascribed. The warrior who cuts off the head now seats himself on this "seat" and receives juice of tobacco mixed with saliva from the chief, who blows it in through his nose. Then another of the slayers takes his seat on the head and receives juice of tobacco through the nose, etc., until all have partaken. This is the first of a series of ceremonies which have for their object the protection of the slayers against the revengeful spirit of the killed enemy.

The *tsantsa* is now prepared in the following way: Along the back side of the head, from the apex downward, a long cut is made with a knife, whereupon the scalp and the skin of the face is slowly and carefully drawn off from the skull, in much the same way as is done with the hides of animals for stuffing. The skinning of the face is said to be the most difficult part of this work, for here the skin does not loosen by merely drawing it off, but has to be cut from the flesh with a sharp knife. The skull and all fleshy parts that adhere to it are thrown away and the scalp obtained is further prepared. It is attached to a vine and immersed in a pot of boiling water, where it is left for a while. It is then taken out of the pot and put on the top of a stick, fixed in the ground, where it is left until it has cooled.

By means of a needle and a thread consisting of a chambira fiber, that part of the scalp which had been cut open, is sewn together. The reduction of the trophy now should begin.

The proper reduction is brought about by means of hot sand. Some fine sand, heated at the fire in a piece of broken clay pot, is poured into the head so as to more than half fill it. The head is kept in motion so that the sand acts uniformly to remove the flesh still attached to the skin, to make the scalp thinner, and to reduce the whole trophy. As soon as the sand has cooled it is taken out of the head, reheated at the fire in the broken clay pot, and again poured into the head. Each time, after taking out the sand from the head, the scalp is scraped inside with a knife in order to remove from it what the sand has burned off. As the trophy dries and shrinks through this treatment the head, and especially the face, is cleverly molded with the fingers, so that it retains its human features. This work is continued during the whole return from the war, eventually even at home, consequently during several days or even weeks, the same sand and the same broken clay vessel being always used. These things are always kept and carried on the march by the first slayer, whose duty it is, as soon as the party arrives at a camping place, to collocate the clay pot on the fire and heat sand for the molding of the trophy.

By this treatment the Jibaros are able to gradually reduce the head to such an extent that it is no larger than an orange, or about one-fourth of its normal size, becoming at the same time completely hard and dry. Through both lips, shrunk in proportion to the rest of the head, three small chonta pins, about 5 centimeters in length and painted red with *achiote,* are passed parallel with each other, and around these pins a fine cotton string, which is also painted red, is wound. At the great feast both the chonta pins and the cotton string are removed and replaced by three twined and red-painted cotton strings. Lastly, the whole trophy, even the face, is dyed black with charcoal.

During the whole work particular attention has been paid to the hair, which is the most essential part of the trophy. The hair, according to the idea of the Indians, is the seat of the soul or the vital power.

The stronger the killed enemy had been in life, the more valiantly he had fought, the more difficult it had been to deprive him of life, the greater is the honor the victor earns by his deed, the greater is the power of the trophy made of his head.

BLACKFOOT RAIDING
FOR HORSES AND SCALPS

John C. Ewers

THE BLACKFOOT tribes were at the height of their power in the middle of the nineteenth century. Their Indian enemies and the white fur traders knew them as the most formidable and warlike people on the northwestern plains. Edwin T. Denig, able trader at Fort Union, who knew all of the tribes of the region, called the Blackfeet "the most numerous and bloodthirsty nation on the upper Missouri" (1930: 470). Certainly they were the most aggressive.

Their theater of warfare was a vast area which included the valley of the Saskatchewan and the upper tributaries of the Columbia, as well as the upper Missouri. Of the surrounding tribes, only the Sarsis and Gros Ventres, their lesser allies, were safe from Blackfoot attacks. They raided eastward down the Saskatchewan into Cree country and down the Missouri past the mouth of Milk River into Assiniboin country. They raided southward into the land of the Crow Indians beyond the Yellowstone. Blackfoot war parties crossed the Rockies to attack the Flatheads, Pend d'Oreilles, Kutenais, and Shoshonis in their own country.

In 1854, James Doty learned that Blackfoot war parties frequently raided the Shoshonis "by way of a pass on or near the headwaters of the Yellowstone River. The Blackfeet seem to entertain an inveterate hostility toward the Snakes and it is difficult

Chapter 7 of John C. Ewers, *The Blackfeet.* Copyright 1958 by the University of Oklahoma Press. Reprinted by permission of the author and of the University of Oklahoma Press.

to say how far removed these Indians must be to prevent the Blackfeet from reaching them" (Letter to Isaac Stevens 1854). Doty's word "inveterate" certainly applied to this warfare. The Blackfoot tribes had been fighting the Shoshonis for at least a century and a quarter.

Eight years earlier Father De Smet found the gallant little Flathead tribe "greatly reduced by the continual attacks of the Blackfeet" (1905: 992). These relentless attacks, coupled with the demoralization of the Flatheads, forced the Jesuits to abandon their mission of St. Mary's in the Bitterroot Valley in 1850.

Four years later Denig observed that the Assiniboins "have had the worst of it" in their wars with the Blackfeet. That same year the agent for the Crow Indians reported:

> Scarcely a day passes but the Crow country is infested with more or less parties of Blackfeet, who murder indiscriminately anyone who comes within their reach. At Fort Sarpy [the principal trading post among the Crows] so great is the danger that no one ventures over a few yards from his own door without company and being well-armed.

So relentless were the Blackfoot attacks that the American Fur Company abandoned Fort Sarpy the following spring. For two years prior to 1856 the Crow Indians preferred to go without the annuities to which they were entitled under the terms of the Fort Laramie Treaty of 1851, "rather than run the risk of passing through a country beset by their deadliest enemies, the Blackfeet and Blood Indians of the north." Denig feared that the Crows, caught between the Blackfeet on the north and the powerful Sioux on the east, might be exterminated.

It is doubtful that any other western tribes were so genuinely feared by so many other tribes as were the Blackfeet in the middle of the nineteenth century. The Assiniboins, the western bands of Crees, the Crows, Shoshonis, Flatheads, Pend d'Oreilles, and Kutenais all looked upon them as their greatest enemies.

Nevertheless, Blackfoot warfare was aimed at neither the systematic extermination of enemy tribes nor the acquisition of their territory. It was not organized and directed by a central military authority, nor was it prosecuted by large, disciplined armies. Rather, Blackfoot warfare was carried on primarily by numerous small parties of volunteers who banded together to capture horses from enemy tribes. Each raiding party was hastily organized before departure and disbanded immediately after its return home. It might never see action again as a military unit. Its members were motivated much less by tribal patriotism than by hope of personal gain—the economic security and social prestige that possession of a goodly number of horses would bring them. The killing of enemy tribesmen and the taking of scalps were not major objectives of these raids.

Many of the most active Blackfoot horse raiders were members of poor families who were ambitious to better their lot. They were inclined to take the most desperate chances. Some acquired horses, settled down, and became respected members of the middle class. A few became wealthy. Many lost their lives in actions with the enemy. Most sons of middle-class families needed more horses than their fathers could give them if they were to marry and set up their own households. A few cowardly fellows and some sons of wealthy men never went on horse raids. But there were also rich young men who loved the excitement of these raids and coveted the prestige that could be gained through success in war.

The raiding party itself offered the best training ground for the would-be warrior. Boys in their middle teens joined these parties to learn the arts of war. More than a century ago Doty observed:

> In one of these parties are generally found three or four young men, or mere boys, who are apprentices. They go without the expectation of receiving a horse, carry extra moccasins and tobacco for the party, do all the camp drudgery, and consider themselves amply repaid in being permitted to learn the science of horse stealing from such experienced hands.

Sometimes a childless wife, who preferred to share her husband's dangers rather than to stay home anxiously awaiting his return, accompanied a raiding party.

The seasoned Blackfoot raider was a courageous, alert, resourceful fighting man. Nevertheless, he did not attribute his success in war to these qualities. Rather he attributed it to the power of his war medicine. No leader or active member of a war party took the field without his war medicine. It would both protect him from harm and insure his success in his hazardous adventure. A young man might obtain war medicine in a dream in which a kindly spirit appeared, took pity on him, and gave him some of its supernatural power, together with complete instructions for making the sacred symbol of this power and for its use. However, it was more common for a young man to obtain his war medicine from an elderly man who had been a war hero in his youth and whose own war medicine had proved its potency by bringing him safely through many dangerous raids.

Before a young man embarked on a raid, he might take a pipe and other gifts to a noted old veteran and ask him for help. This older man might be his own father. Usually he was a relative. The young fellow made a sweat lodge for the older man, who prayed for him and who transferred to him some of his power and the sacred symbols thereof—a war song, face paints, a sacred object to be worn in action; and instructions for their use.

Of more than fifty Blackfoot war medicines known to me, the great majority were single feathers or bunches of feathers worn in the hair. Perhaps feathers were favored because they were light and compact—practical articles for carrying on long journeys afoot. But there were other war medicines—necklaces, bandoleers, headdresses, shirts, knives, and lances. Running Wolf's war medicine was a moon-shaped brass necklace with pendant feathers. The figure of a horse was incised on the brass ornament. Before going into an enemy camp to capture horses, Running Wolf sprinkled water on his necklace. "In a short time clouds would gather and cover the moon, making it easier to take horses from the enemy without being seen."

The horse-raiding party was led by an experienced man whose war record and good judgment inspired confidence in his ability to lead a group of men to an enemy camp, capture a goodly number of horses, and return home without losing any member of his party. The leader (or partisan, as the fur traders often referred to him) might invite others to join him on a raid, or several young men might come to him and ask him to be their leader. No one was compelled to go on these raids. All participants were volunteers. Although the leader might be a mature man in his thirties (rarely more than forty years of age), most of his followers were young men in their late teens or early twenties. Often two young men who were close friends joined a war party together. As partners they would look after one another in the field.

Spring and summer were favorite seasons for horse raids. Rarely did the Blackfeet try to raid the tribes west of the Rockies in winter, when deep snows clogged the familiar mountain passes. However, some raiders preferred to take horses from neighboring plains tribes in winter because their enemies were less vigilant in winter and falling snow would quickly obliterate the tracks of captured horses, making it impossible for their enemies to follow them after they started for home.

Before setting out on a raid, the party was supposed to obtain permission of the band chief, who was thus informed of their destination and objective. They would not do it, however, if they believed he might object to their venture. On the evening before departure the prospective raiders walked around camp drumming on a piece of buffalo rawhide and singing their wolf (war) songs. Their friends and relatives gave them food and extra moccasins to take on their journey. Other young men, upon hearing their drumming, might ask to join the party. The leader would refuse their requests if he thought they were unreliable or if he believed his party was large enough. Most horse-raiding parties were small, comprising less than a dozen men. Many leaders did not want large parties, for they were too difficult to command and to conceal from enemy eyes. Occasionally, parties of fifty or more men did raid for horses. Rarely, too, two or three men set out on one of these perilous quests.

After drumming around the camp, members of the party agreed upon a location at some distance outside the village where they would muster later that night or in the morning. Because they did not want to attract a host of brash young neophytes or uninvited incompetents, they kept the time and place of their meeting secret.

The objective of the horse raid was neither to kill enemies nor to take scalps but to capture horses. Like the World War II Commando raid, it was a stealthy operation in which the little attacking group tried to take the enemy by complete surprise, to strike quickly and quietly, in darkness or at dawn, achieve its limited objective, and be off before the enemy learned of its loss.

The raiders' dress and equipment were limited to the bare essentials. Because a group of footmen could conceal themselves easier than could horsemen on the outward journey, they usually set out on foot. In warmer weather they wore plain buckskin shirts and leggings, breechclouts, and moccasins. In winter they preferred Hudson's Bay blanket coats with white backgrounds, which provided a practical camouflage against snow-covered ground and overcast skies. Hair-lined moccasins and mittens and a fur cap with earflaps protected their extremities from the cold.

Each man carried a light pack containing several pairs of moccasins, one or more rawhide ropes for catching, riding, or leading horses, an awl and sinew for repairing moccasins, a small pipe with a short willow stem and some tobacco for an occasional smoke en route, and the raider's personal war medicine. These things were wrapped in a blanket roll carried on the back by a rawhide strap over the chest. Each man also carried his food for the early stages of the journey—some dried meat or pemmican in a rawhide case suspended by a shoulder strap or tied on top of his pack. Each also carried a sharp, heavy-bladed knife in a rawhide sheath at his belt. It served both as a tool and as a weapon. With it he cut firewood and timbers for temporary shelters, butchered animals killed for food, and, if the need arose, silently killed an enemy and lifted his scalp. Each also carried another weapon— either a short bow and quiver of arrows or a muzzle-loading flintlock with shot pouch and powder horn.

The raider's complete equipment probably weighed less than twenty pounds, including a gun weighing a little over four pounds. With this light load he set out on an expedition that might take him six hundred or more miles, at least half that distance on foot. In the early part of the outward journey, when danger from the enemy was not great, the raiders traveled in daylight. Moving at a steady pace and stopping now and then to rest and smoke, they made about twenty-five miles a day. But as they neared the enemy country, they traveled at night and hid during the day.

On approaching enemy territory, the raiders stopped to kill enough game to provide food for the remainder of their journey. Usually they built a war lodge in a heavily timbered bottom or on a thickly wooded height, or repaired an old one built by some earlier party. If a new lodge was needed, all set to work gathering fallen timbers or cutting new ones to erect a conical framework of poles. This they covered with bark or brush. They then laid heavy logs around the base and built an angled, covered entrance way. Working industriously, a war party could complete the lodge, large enough to sleep a dozen men, in two hours. It was built well inside the edge of timber, where it could not be seen from the open plains. But it was on dangerous ground. All hands were needed to speed the work.

The war lodge not only provided shelter from rain, snow, and cold, but concealed the fire of relatively smokeless willow branches built inside and served as a fortress in case of enemy attack. It was a base of supplies, where some food could be left to be picked up on the return journey, and a base for scouting operations.

From the war lodge the leader sent several picked men ahead to locate the enemy camp. Thus he avoided the danger that could arise from the entire party's searching for a nomadic foe in enemy country. The scouts moved with utmost caution, fearful of encountering enemy war or hunting parties. Wearing wolfskin disguises, they surveyed the surrounding country from high ground to make sure they could proceed with safety. They examined burned-out campfires and horse tracks, as well as tracks made by travois and footmen, to determine their recency and direction of movement. They were alert to any sudden movement of birds or animals that might indicate the nearness of other humans.

Meanwhile, the other members of the raiding party left at the war lodge hunted buffalo, deer, elk, or any other game that might provide dried meat for the remainder of their journey. They butchered the animals, dried the meat, and filled the men's provision bags. Sometimes they prepared an additional meat packet —a small rawhide container that could be fastened to the belt, holding enough concentrated dried meat to provide an occasional mouthful for the raider hastening homeward with captured horses. One of these packets was made for each man. It was called "war lunch."

When the scouts located the enemy camp, they watched it from a concealed position long enough to determine its size, the number of men, and the number and quality of horses. They then returned to the war lodge as rapidly as they could. As they came in sight of their waiting comrades, they approached in a zigzag course, signifying that they had found the enemy. While the leader went to meet them, the others set up a pile of sticks near the lodge. Returning with the scouts the leader kicked over this pile of sticks, and all the men scrambled for them. Each stick a fellow retrieved was considered a prophecy of a horse he would take from the enemy.

Guided by their scouts, the party then moved toward the enemy village, traveling by night and hiding during the day, until they reached a concealed spot overlooking or in sight of the enemy. The leader closely observed how the enemy picketed their choice horses near their lodges and where they drove their less valuable horses for night pasture. Then he explained his plan of attack.

As the zero hour approached, each party member opened his pack, prayed for success, sang his war song, painted himself, and donned his war medicine. Usually his prayers were addressed to the sun or the moon (who in Blackfoot belief was sun's wife) and consisted of a simple, direct appeal for help in taking horses and reaching home safely. These long moments before going into action were tense, even terrifying ones for the inexperienced younger fellows. One of them might ask a more experienced comrade for some of his medicine. Or a young man might make a solemn vow to give a feast for the owner of some sacred bundle back home or to undergo the agonizing self-torture in the sun dance of his tribe if he accomplished his mission.

The attack usually was scheduled for daybreak. Then the leader and a few of his bravest and most experienced men walked noiselessly into the enemy camp. If dogs barked, they threw bits of meat to them, waited, circled the camp, and approached it from another direction. Sometimes these men rubbed cottonwood sap on their hands and bodies. Its odor tended to quiet the horses and make them more willing to follow strangers. Quickly they approached the best horses, which were picketed in front of the lodges of their sleeping enemies, cut the picket lines with their sharp knives, and led the prized animals away. If there was no noise within the camp, no indication that any of the enemy had been roused, these adept horse thieves left the horses they had taken with a boy or inexperienced member of their party outside the camp and returned for more picketed animals. Sometimes the other members of the raiding party drove off some of the range herds while their leader and his most able men were after the picketed animals.

Whether or not the raiders' movements woke their enemies, it was important that they make a quick getaway in order to get as much head start on their pursuers as possible. Sometimes, in their haste to get away, a member of the party was left behind without a horse to ride. He had to shift for himself—find a hiding place in the brush until the next evening and get home alone as best he could.

It was always dangerous for a raiding party to be too greedy. To stay too long in the enemy camp or to try to run off too many horses was asking for trouble. Driving loose horses at a fast pace over uneven country, through timber and across streams for hundreds of miles, was a difficult task. Sometimes loose horses had to be abandoned to prevent the party from being overtaken by the enemy. Not infrequently an overambitious raiding party was overtaken and its men had to fight for their lives. My older Blackfoot informants, men who had raided for horses, could not recall that any Blackfoot party had brought home as many as one hundred horses, although they knew of parties that had driven off more than that number from enemy camps. Forty to sixty horses was considered a very good haul.

On the first leg of the homeward journey the raiders set a fast pace. For two or three days the men rode day and night, changing from one mount to another as the horses tired. Then the men stopped for a good overnight rest. Next morning they divided the captured horses. Unless the party had decided upon an equal distribution of the animals taken, each man could claim the horses he had led out of camp or the range stock he had run off. Bitter arguments over the ownership of range horses jointly run off by several Indians sometimes followed. It was the leader's duty to settle these disputes as equitably as possible. Some leaders gave fine horses they themselves had taken to members of their parties who could claim none. A leader's generosity helped him to maintain a reputation as a popular leader who would not want for followers in the future.

From this point the raiders rode homeward at a more leisurely pace. When near their camp, they stopped to paint their faces and decorate their horses. Then they rode triumphantly toward camp, firing their guns in the air to signal their return. After they were welcomed home, successful raiders gave horses to their relatives, most commonly to their fathers-in-law or brothers-in-law. Nor did the young warrior forget the old man who had prayed for him and given him his war medicine. He invited his benefactor to his lodge, fed him well, and gave him one or more of the animals he had taken on the raid.

This was the pattern of the successful Blackfoot horse raid—one which accomplished its limited objective without loss from action with the enemy. Many parties were not so lucky. The artist Paul Kane, in 1847, learned of an outward-bound horse-raiding party of seven men, led by the Blackfoot Big Horn, which had the misfortune of meeting a formidable Cree force.

> This small band, seeing their inferiority to their enemies, attempted flight; but finding escape impossible, they instantly dug holes sufficiently deep to entrench themselves from which they kept up a constant fire with guns and arrows, and for nearly twelve hours held

at bay this large war party, bringing down every man who ventured within shot, until their ammunition and arrows were entirely exhausted, when of course they fell an easy prey to their enemies, thirty of whom had fallen before their fire. This so enraged the Crees that they cut them in pieces, and mangled the dead bodies in a most brutal manner, and carried their scalps back as trophies. It is said that Big Horn frequently sprang out from his entrenchment, and tried to irritate his foes by recounting the numbers of them he had destroyed, and boasting his many war exploits, and the Cree scalps that then hung in his lodge. So exasperated were they against him that they tore out his heart from his quivering body, and savagely devoured it amongst them (Kane 284–85).

Alexander Culbertson told of three Blood warriors and a woman who were en route to a Crow Indian camp to capture horses. While they were stopping to smoke, they were attacked by thirty mounted Crow fighting men. Two of the Blood men were killed instantly. The third, though wounded, knocked one of the horsemen from his saddle, jumped on the horse, and escaped to Fort McKenzie. The lone woman was taken prisoner, stripped of her clothes, and kept under constant watch. One stormy night her captors relaxed their vigilance, and she escaped. Five days later she was seen by Culbertson in the bushes near Fort McKenzie. Naked, barefoot, and without food, she had made her way to the fort.

> She was in a sad plight, being entirely naked except for the little protection afforded by bunches of sagebrush tied about her person, with feet lacerated by days of travel over stones and prickly pear, and worn down with exposure, fatigue and starvation . . . She was at once clothed and fed, and speedily recovered from the effects of her painful experience.

Such were the hazards of horse raiding and the courageous ways in which the Blackfeet faced them. It is not possible to estimate the number of these small-scale actions in which the Blackfeet were involved. But the testimony of veteran horse raiders indicates that they were not uncommon. The first impulse of a small raiding party on sighting a superior enemy force seems to have been to run for shelter in timber or thickets if such refuge was near. The enemy was loath to approach wooded areas in which their opponents could not be seen. In woods or brush a gallant little group of men might hold off a much larger enemy force until nightfall and escape under cover of darkness.

If they were overtaken on the open plains at a distance from timber, the smaller party hastily dug foxholes with their knives and prepared to sell their lives dearly. The attacking force, if it was on foot, moved forward, keeping constantly in motion, jumping from side to side to prevent the men in the foxholes from taking careful aim. Those men who had the greatest confidence in the protective powers of their war medicines led the attack. They might storm the fortification and wipe out the defenders, but not without heavy losses among their own men.

The killing of one or more of their beloved leaders or of a number of their warriors roused the Blackfeet to seek revenge not only upon the killers but upon their entire tribe. On such an occasion they organized an expedition in force with the avowed object of taking enemy scalps. Sometimes presents of tobacco were sent to other tribes of the Blackfoot group accompanied by a request for assistance in raising a large war party.

This large-scale scalp raid differed markedly from the much more common horse raid in many ways. Prior to its departure, all the warriors who volunteered to participate rode for a distance outside the camp, where they mustered, dismounted, donned their war clothes and face paint, and decorated their horses, then mounted and converged upon the camp, carrying their weapons. While the mounted warriors circled the camp, several old men and women stood in the center of it, drumming and singing a lively song. The riders shouted, dismounted, and danced on foot beside their horses, imitating the prancing of spirited horses. This "riding big dance" was an impressive show of tribal solidarity and determination. It roused the fighting spirit of the entire group and sent the warriors off on their mission with the encouragement of those who remained behind. It might be likened to a modern football pep rally before a football team departs for a crucial game on the opponent's field.

Usually the raiding party was led by a prominent chief whose war experience and success in battle qualified him for leadership in the eyes of his followers. Its members rode ordinary saddle horses and led their prize buffalo horses to save their strength for the battle ahead. The warriors set out wearing their ordinary clothes, but carried their war medicines and fancy war clothes (if they were prosperous enough to own them) in bundles tied to their saddles. They carried their fire weapons (flintlocks or bows and arrows), shock weapons (war clubs and knives), and defensive shields of rawhide. Scouts were sent ahead to search for enemy camps and wandering enemy war parties.

If the scouts were lucky enough to find an inferior force, the Blackfeet lost little time in changing to their war clothes, putting on their war medicines, mounting their best horses, and attacking. Thus, in the year 1849, a large Blackfoot party (estimated, perhaps too highly, at eight hundred men) fell upon a party of fifty-two Assiniboin horse raiders and annihilated them.

When seeking revenge for earlier losses at the hands of the enemy, the Blackfeet wreaked terrible revenge upon their victims. A Blackfoot warrior whose father, brother, or best friend had been killed by the tribe he was fighting was not content merely to take the scalp of a fallen enemy. He mutilated the body of his foe —cut off his hands, feet, and head, or even literally hacked him to pieces.

In 1848, Paul Kane heard a report of a Blackfoot massacre of a party of Crees. Among "the slain was a pipe-stem carrier, whom they skinned and stuffed with grass; the figure was then placed in a trail which the Crees were accustomed to pass in their hunting excursions" (1925: 289).

If these actions on the part of Blackfoot warriors appear bloodthirsty, it is well to remember that they received no softer treatment from their enemies when the tables were reversed. Cruelty bred more cruelty. The reliable reporter Edwin T. Denig recorded this incident in the year 1854 (1930: 492):

> . . . some Blackfeet stole horses from the Cree camp, were pursued and 11 out of 12 of which the party consisted were killed. The remaining one was taken, scalped, his right hand cut off, and thus started back to his own nation to tell the news. Now as this man was

leaving the camp he met a Cree boy whom he managed to kill with his remaining hand, was pursued and taken the second time, and was tortured to death by slow mutilation.

In the spring of 1853 the Crow Indians pursued five Blackfoot warriors who stole horses from their camp near Fort Union.

> The Crows surrounded them and by constant firing killed all except one who was shot through the leg. This man they took out alive, scalped, and cut his hands off, gathered their boys around and shot into his body with powder, striking him in his face with his own scalp, and knocking on his head with stones and tomahawks, until he died. Afterwards the five bodies were carried to the camp, the heads, hands, feet and privates cut off, paraded on poles, and thrown around the camp, some of which found their way to the fort and were presented to the Cree Indians then there (Denig 1930: 491–92).

Scalping an enemy, so elderly Blackfoot Indians who performed this feat in their youth have told me, was quickly accomplished by leaning over the victim who was lying on the ground face down, grasping his hair with the left hand, using the right hand to cut around his crown with a sharp knife, and jerking off the hair with skin attached, removing a section of the scalp about three inches in diameter. Some warriors who had been scalped alive recovered and lived to fight again.

The Blackfoot Indians graded war honors on the basis of the degree of courage displayed in winning them. They recognized that a man might scalp an enemy who had been killed by another and that a man might kill an enemy from a considerable distance with bullet or arrow. Their term for war honor, *"namachkani,"* meant literally "a gun taken." The capture of an enemy's gun ranked as the highest war honor. The capture of a bow, shield, war bonnet, war shirt, or ceremonial pipe was also a coup of high rank. The taking of a scalp ranked below these deeds, but ahead of the capture of a horse from the enemy. The capture of a horse was too common an accomplishment to receive a higher rating.

After collecting their trophies, the successful scalp raiders rode homeward. As they neared their camp, they began to sing and proudly display their trophies. The wife or other female relative of each man who had brought home a trophy carried it in the post-raid scalp dance. The hands, feet, scalps, or even the heads of fallen enemies were raised on poles borne by the women as they danced in a circle. These gruesome trophies proved to the entire camp that Blackfoot warriors had revenged their past losses at the hands of their enemy. Usually they were thrown away after the scalp dance. They had served their purpose.

Battles between large Blackfoot forces and sizable enemy ones were rare. However, during the 1840s and 1850s, the Blackfoot tribes repeatedly attacked the small Flathead, Pend d'Oreille, and Kutenai tribes when they crossed the Rockies to hunt buffalo on the plains. The Jesuit missionary Father Gregory Mengarini (n.d.: 17), who accompanied the Flatheads to the plains in the spring of 1846, graphically described one of these actions:

> When the enemy is sighted, word flies from mouth to mouth, and all is hurry and bustle for a few minutes. Some strip themselves naked. These are poor men from whom the enemy can expect little. Others clothe themselves in calicos of flaming colors to show their riches and invite the attack of such as dare to face them. One thing remained to be done; the women and children and the missionary must be taken to a place of safety.
> Firing had already begun on both sides, and the plain was covered with horsemen curvetting and striving to get a chance to kill some one of the enemy. An Indian battle consists of a multitude of single combats. There are no ranks, no battalions, no united efforts. Every man for himself is the ruling principle, and victory depends on personal bravery and good horsemanship. There is no random shooting; every Flathead or Blackfoot always aims for the waist.

Although this battle lasted nearly all day, only four Flathead Indians were killed. They claimed the Blackfeet lost twenty-four men. However, Indians commonly exaggerated both the numbers and the casualties of their opponents.

In large-scale battles, when the size of the opposing forces was nearly equal, Blackfoot tactics suffered from weakness of organization and command and the relative independence of the individual warriors. Blackfoot fighting men were not soldiers but gladiators. True, they sometimes formed a line and charged the enemy on horseback, bending low over their horses' necks and weaving their bodies from side to side. A boy learned the difficult feat of protecting his body by hanging on the side of his horse, but men in combat rarely employed this trick-riding technique. It was too dangerous to expose the entire side of one's horse to enemy fire.

If their enemies were afoot, the Blackfeet tried to ride them down. Upon overtaking a mounted enemy, the rider tried to unhorse him with his war club. Then he dismounted and tried to finish him off with his war club or knife. A favorite shock weapon was a broad, sharp, double-edged knife known to the Blackfeet as a "stabber" or "beaver-tail knife." Grasping the handle so that the steel blade protruded from the heel of his fist, the warrior employed a powerful downward motion to strike his opponent above the clavicle, or a sidewise sweep to stab him between the ribs or in the stomach. This knife was useful in finishing off a wounded or disabled enemy and for taking his scalp.

If the initial ferocious charge was repulsed, the warriors were apt to fall back and continue the battle from a distance of one hundred yards or more with their fire weapons. The muzzle-loading flintlock, which had been so frightening to their enemies in the early years of its use, proved a relatively ineffective weapon after both sides became armed with these guns. Because it was difficult to reload on a running horse, riders commonly dismounted to employ it. Their well-trained horses stood nearby. To speed the loading process the warriors held the bullets in their mouths. They quickly measured two fingers of powder from the horn into the barrel, lifted the barrel to the mouth and dropped a ball into it, gave the stock a couple of hard blows with the hand to settle the charge and eject some powder into the pan, lifted the gun, aimed, and fired. But without wadding, both range and velocity of fire were impaired.

Governor Isaac I. Stevens called the Indians' firearm "an inferior kind of shot-gun." He regarded the bow and arrow as "a much more efficient weapon in the hands of an Indian than a gun." This was one good reason why many of the Blackfeet continued to fight with bow and arrow. Some poor young men could not afford a gun. Others carried both gun and bow and arrows to war.

In the intertribal warfare on the northwestern plains a century ago, the accent was placed upon offensive operations. The Blackfeet suffered almost as much as their neighbors from repeated thefts of valuable horses by small raiding parties. Nevertheless, they normally went to bed without posting night guards. Only when they discovered signs during the day that led them to believe enemy raiders were in the neighborhood did they take special precautions to protect their horses. Then they might build a crude corral of cottonwood posts connected by crossrails lashed to the posts with rawhide rope, and place a guard nearby. Some nights the men and women of a lodge took turns staying awake listening for any unusual restlessness among the picketed horses or any sound that might indicate the presence of an enemy horse thief in their camp. More rarely, when they believed an enemy horse raid was imminent, young men set a trap by concealing themselves in the tall grass surrounding the camp, lying flat on their stomachs with their loaded guns beside them. When the unsuspecting enemy approached they jumped up and opened fire at close range. Sometimes the men lying in ambush picketed a handsome horse near them, hoping to lure a horse-crazy enemy into their trap.

Older men and chiefs tired of incessant warfare with neighboring tribes and the terrible losses suffered in numerous engagements both large and small. Sometimes they managed to negotiate a peace with like-minded chiefs of an enemy tribe. But their peace usually proved to be only a short breather between hostilities. Their efforts were nullified by their own ambitious young men who needed enemy horses and war honors to gain economic and social status.

Father De Smet learned of a Crow attempt to make peace with their old Blackfoot enemies. The principal Crow chief sent twenty-five warriors, guided by a Blackfoot captive who had been offered his freedom, to present a pipe of peace to the Blackfeet. As they neared the large Blackfoot camp on the Marias River, they met two Blackfoot hunters. Two men of the Crow party, whose brothers had been killed by the Blackfeet a month before, killed them and hid their scalps in their bullet pouches.

When they reached the Blackfoot encampment, they found the leaders willing to accept the Crow peace offer. That night a curious Blackfoot woman found one of the scalps in a Crow bullet pouch and took it to her chief. He recognized the hair as that of one of the young hunters who had failed to return. After telling her to keep quiet about her find, the chief ordered his best warriors to be armed and ready at daybreak.

The following morning the chief showed the Crow delegation the scalp and asked who among them had taken it. When no one claimed it, the woman who had found it pointed out the man in whose pouch it was. He then manfully acknowledged it.

Unwilling to commit murder on the ground where they had smoked the peace pipe with the Crow delegates only the day before, the Blackfoot chief offered the Crow warriors a chance to start for home—as far as a nearby hill. When they reached it, the Blackfoot warriors went after them. The Crows hid in a deep ravine and fought off several sporadic Blackfoot advances. From their protected position they killed a number of the Blackfoot attackers without loss to themselves.

The Blackfoot chief then appealed to his men to follow him in a mass assault. They rushed into the ravine and killed every man of the Crow delegation with knives and war clubs. Angered by the treacherous actions of this Crow group, as well as by the killing of members of their own avenging party, the Blackfoot women cut the bodies of the slain enemies into small pieces and carried them on poles around the camp, amid "chants of victory, yells of rage, and howling and vociferations against their enemies. There was also a general mourning caused by the loss of so many warriors fallen in this horrible engagement" (De Smet 1905: 1037–43).

So the war with the Crow Indians continued. And at the same time the Blackfoot tribes fought the Crees and Assiniboins and the many small tribes from west of the Rockies who dared to hunt buffalo on the plains.

AN ANALYSIS OF
IROQUOIS MILITARY TACTICS[1]

Keith F. Otterbein

IROQUOIS military success has been attributed to several factors. These include, a strategic position between the western fur supply and the eastern market, a political organization superior to those of their neighbors, access to guns and ammunition, and high morale (Trelease 1962: 51). In recognizing the importance of these factors, scholars have overlooked the fact that the Iroquois achieved victory at critical times during the seventeenth century through the use of superior tactics. An explanation of why the Iroquois were a military success will be provided by analyzing their tactics in terms of three variables—weapons, armor, and mobility—which are commonly used by military analysts.

The approach used in this paper is based upon Tom Wintringham's study of the evolution of European battle tactics from ancient to modern times (Wintringham 1943). The development of European military methods is characterized by alternating periods of unarmored warfare. The shifts from one period to another were caused by changes in either the striking power of weapons, the protection of armor, or the mobility of the armies. When weapons became so powerful that they could penetrate armor, protection was abandoned and mobility became an important element. Until armament improved or tactics based on high mobility

Reprinted from *Ethnohistory*, Volume 11, No. 1, Winter, 1964, pp. 56–63, by permission of the author and of the editor of *Ethnohistory*.
[1] This paper was delivered at the American Anthropological Association meetings in San Francisco on November 22, 1963. I am indebted to Allen W. Trelease of Wells College for critically reading an earlier draft.

were devised, the side with the most effective weapons would be the victor. Eventually the pendulum would swing back when armor once again could efficiently stop the firepower of weapons. Wintringham's analysis is useful in studying the military system of the Iroquois because it provides a means of determining which side had tactical superiority at a given time.

The Iroquois possessed superior weapons and tactics at various times in their intertribal conflicts, a point which has not been made by scholars of Iroquois warfare. In fact they take an opposing point of view. George T. Hunt argues that they had little superiority in firearms (Hunt 1940: 9–10; 165–75). George S. Snyderman states that "in the formation of the war party, so in the war journey and encounter, the practices of the Iroquois were virtually identical with those of their neighbors" (Snyderman 1948: 56). Raymond Scheele also draws the same conclusions: "The instruments and weapons of war used by all the tribes were similar . . . Actual fighting tactics were the same for all the tribes . . ." (Scheele 1950: 83–84). If attention is focused on differences in weapons and tactics at various points in time, it will be apparent that the Iroquois did have superiority during certain periods. The following analysis pertains primarily to the Mohawk, the easternmost Iroquois nation, because the sources for the early part of the seventeenth century deal mainly with this tribe.

Prior to 1609, the Mohawks and their enemies wore body armor, carried shields, and fought with bows and arrows. The opposing sides formed two lines in the open and discharged arrows at each other. Champlain put an end to these tactics when he introduced the matchlock to the Algonquins in 1609 (Russel 1957: 2–3). For the next twenty-five years the Iroquois were at a great disadvantage because they possessed no firearms (Hunt 1940: 167). The Algonquins, on the other hand, were reasonably well equipped with matchlocks. This gave them such confidence that they began to increase their attacks upon the Iroquois. In order to cope with the enemy, small war parties of Mohawks would pretend to retreat and thus draw the advancing Algonquins into ambushes (Colden 1958: 7–9). The dissected Allegheny Plateau and the Adirondack Mountains of upper New York State are ideally suited for hiding war parties and staging ambushes. Tactics consisted of rushing upon the enemy and engaging in hand-to-hand combat before the Algonquins could do much damage with their matchlocks and bows and arrows. In these attacks the Mohawks discarded their shields, but not their body armor; thrusting spears and war clubs replaced their bows and arrows (Wood 1865: 65–67). However, shields and bows were still carried on the march, but were not used in a charge. The enemy were probably still wearing body armor and would perhaps have chosen to fight in a battle line if possible. Although the Iroquois were on the defensive during this period, they were able to maintain control of their hunting area through what is today known as guerrilla warfare (Scheele 1950: 15–17). Wiping out enemy raiding parties was undoubtedly a means of obtaining needed weapons.

By 1641 the Iroquois began to acquire muskets in limited quantity from the Dutch (Hunt 1940). These arquebuses—flint guns with better firing mechanisms than the earlier matchlocks—were adopted to the existing tactics. In 1642 the Iroquois attacked a French fort at Quebec; their tactics consisted of charging up to the walls of the fort and firing through the loopholes (Thwaites 1896–1901: Vol. 22, 277–79). In the open field the arquebuses were likewise used as assault or shock weapons. The Iroquois would charge the enemy battle line, fire their muskets at close range, and fall upon the fleeing enemy who had been dislodged from their position by the onslaught. By 1647 the Hurons had developed tactics for coping with such an attack. The Huron warriors would form a crescent; just before the Iroquois would fire their guns, the Hurons would drop to the ground; after the Iroquois had discharged their weapons, they would rise, fire their own guns, and countercharge the enemy (Thwaites 1896–1901: Vol. 32, 181). The more effective use, however, of the arquebuses by the Iroquois was in laying ambushes along the banks of rivers for canoe convoys laden with furs (Thwaites 1896–1901: Vol. 20, 269, 307). Guns loaded with chain-shot could sink canoes whose crews consequently had little chance for defense and none for counterattack (Colden 1958: 9). The captured furs were used to purchase more arquebuses. By 1649 the Iroquois were better armed than the Indians who were allies of the French (Hunt 1940: 174–75).

The extensive use of firearms resulted in the abandonment of body armor and the scattered deployment of warriors. Armor was useless against bullets; and if men were close together, one discharge of a musket loaded with several balls could kill more than one warrior. When the English took over New Netherlands in 1664, they supplied the Iroquois "with still more arms in order to prevent their defection to the French" (Trelease 1960: 24). By 1666, Iroquois warriors went into action only wearing a loincloth and moccasins, for in this manner greater mobility could be achieved (Snyderman 1948: 64). Before the end of the seventeenth century, Iroquois fighting tactics had changed so much that they were no longer efficient in the use of tomahawks and clubs. Sole reliance was placed upon the sniper who fired from behind any conceivable cover. Their enemies, who were not as well armed, had to continue relying upon war clubs and in-fighting, which gave them some advantage in meadows and open fields, but left them greatly outclassed in the forests (La Hontan 1905: 497–501). The Iroquois battle line was extended as much as possible: "They separate themselves, as far as each can hear the other's traveling signal . . ." (Snyderman 1948: 49). When the battle line advanced, each wing tried to envelop the enemy forces. In order to carry out such tactics, it was necessary to put as many armed men as possible into the field.

The Iroquois were able to put into the field more and larger "armies" than many of the neighboring tribes because they were well supplied with agricultural produce. The Montagnis and certain neighboring peoples depended entirely upon hunting. Other Algonquin groups had some agriculture (Hadlock 1947: 210). The Iroquois, however, were primarily an agricultural people. Each Iroquois warrior carried a bag of parched corn flour when he went on an expedition (Snyderman 1948: 49). "The agricultural people prepared food to take with them on battle forays, whereas the hunters did not" (Scheele 1950: 82). Not only were they well supplied when traveling in enemy territory, but when operating in Iroquoia they were able to draw upon the agricultural produce of any one of the Iroquois nations (Quain 1937: 254). Another important factor in maintaining large bodies of warriors in the field was the practice of adopting prisoners into the tribe. Incorporation of captives replaced the casualties in the ranks of the Iroquois army and maintained its size at an average figure of 2000 warriors for the seventeenth century (Snyderman 1948: 41).

In summary, an analysis of Iroquois tactics as compared with those of their enemies indicates three periods in time when the discrepancy between weapons and tactics gave an advantage to the Iroquois. The first period was in the early 1630s when the Mohawks were using armor and shock weapons in conjunction with guerrilla warfare, against archers and musketeers. The second period was in the 1640s. Although the arquebus proved to be an excellent weapon for charges only for a few years, it was the decisive arm in ambushing and destroying Huron trade canoes. The third period began in the 1660s and lasted for several decades. Since nearly every Iroquois warrior had a musket by this time, tactics were adapted to the weapon. In-fighting was abandoned and long battle lines of snipers were employed. The enemy of necessity persisted in, using war clubs—a weapon which required in-fighting tactics. Thus it appears that the Iroquois were often several years more advanced in the use of weapons and tactics than their enemies. Consequently, victory was more frequently theirs, particularly in the latter half of the seventeenth century. The first period in which the Iroquois held an advantage was an armored phase; the second period was a transitional phase; the third period was an unarmored phase.

In conclusion, the above analysis of the evolution of Iroquois military practices has demonstrated the feasibility of using concepts, variables, and theories derived from the analysis of Western military history, for an understanding of the military success of a so-called primitive people.

THE EVOLUTION OF ZULU WARFARE

Keith F. Otterbein

ALTHOUGH anthropological literature is replete with references to Zulu warfare and to Shaka, the famous Zulu warrior-king, there is no brief, analytic treatment of the development of Zulu warfare prior to and during Shaka's reign.[1] This study uses both qualitative and quantitative data on Zulu wars to graphically show the trends and changes which occurred during this thirty-year period (1798–1828). In particular, this study focuses on the factors which produced changes in the casualty rates of Zulu wars. The following factors are selected for treatment as independent variables: type of weapons, type of formations or tactics, type of military organization, and goals or reasons for war. Changes in one or more of these variables led to changes in casualty rates.

For approximately 300 years prior to 1800, Nguni tribes had been migrating into southeast Africa, now Zululand and Natal, from the northwest. Rivalry between the sons of the tribal leader frequently led to fission of the royal patrilineage. Such splitting kept the tribes small and scattered. The economy, which was based on shifting cultivation and cattle raising, also contributed to this

Reprinted from the *Kansas Journal of Sociology*, No. 1 (1964, Winter), by permission of the author.

[1] The major source drawn upon for quantitative data is Ritter (1957). It should be noted that Ritter, who was born in 1890, grew up among the Zulu. This account contains information on military affairs not found in the basic sources on the Zulu, such as Bryant (1927), Gibson (1911), or Krige (1936). This information was gathered by an army officer who campaigned in South Africa in the latter half of the nineteenth century: "The tactical and strategical details of the principal battle descriptions were supplied by the author's father, Captain C. L. A. Ritter" (Ritter 1957: 377).

dispersion by requiring tribes to constantly seek better land (Gluckman 1958: 28–29). When conflict arose between tribes, a day and a place were arranged for settling the dispute by combat. On that day the rival tribes marched to battle, the warriors drawing up in lines at a distance of about 100 yards apart. Behind the lines stood the remaining members of each tribe, who during the battle cheered their kinsmen on to greater efforts. The warriors carried five-foot tall, oval shields and two or three light javelins. These rawhide shields, when hardened by dipping in water, could not be penetrated by the missiles. Chosen warriors, who would advance to within 50 yards of each other and shout insults, opened the combat by hurling their spears. Eventually, more and more warriors would be drawn into the battle until one side ceased fighting and fled, "whereupon a rush would follow for male and female prisoners and enemy cattle, the former to be subsequently ransomed [for cattle], the latter to be permanently retained" (Ritter 1957: 10). If the pursued dropped their spears, it was a sign of surrender and no more blood would be shed. Since wounds were seldom fatal, the number of casualties was low.

By 1800 the increase in population and the dwindling of unoccupied land created a situation in which fission could no longer solve the problem of dynastic disputes. According to Gluckman (1958: 31):

> As far as one can understand the process from the almost contemporary records, under the distribution of population then prevailing it became more difficult for tribes to divide and dissident sections to escape to independence; as the Nguni cultural stress on seniority of descent and the relatively great inheritance of the main heir caused strong tensions in the tribes, chiefs began to press their dominion not only on their subordinate tribal sections, but also on their neighbors. The development of this trend was possibly facilitated by the unequal strength of the tribes.

There emerged from this situation a leader of the Mtetwa tribe called Dingiswayo, who was able to achieve military success by organizing the age grades of young warriors into regiments of soldiers (Bryant 1929: 98). Without altering weapons or tactics, but simply by increasing organizational efficiency and hence the discipline and size of his forces, he was able from 1806 to 1809 to defeat over thirty tribes and establish for himself a chiefdom. "After subduing a tribe with as little slaughter as possible, he left it under its own chiefly family, perhaps choosing from it a favorite of his own to rule, though the young men of the tribe had to serve in his army" (Gluckman 1960: 162).

Shaka, the illegitimate son of a Zulu chief, while he was an officer in Dingiswayo's army, invented, in approximately 1810, a new technique of fighting. He replaced his javelins with a short, broad-bladed stabbing spear; he retained his shield, but discarded his sandals in order to gain greater mobility. By rushing upon his opponent he was able to use his shield to hook away his enemy's shield, thus exposing the warrior's left side to a spear thrust. Shaka also changed military tactics by arranging the soldier in his command—a company of about 100 men—into "a close-order, shield-to-shield formation with two 'horns' designed to encircle the enemy or to feint at his flanks, the main body of troops at the center and the reserves in the rear ready to exploit the opportunities of battle" (Gluckman 1960: 162). Dingiswayo, however, always refused to use the formation and to adopt the short spear, because it meant high casualties for both sides.

In 1816, when Shaka's father died, Dingiswayo helped him to become chief of the Zulu. Shaka immediately outfitted his army of 500 soldiers with the short spear and taught them the new tactics. Although he remained within Dingiswayo's chiefdom, he began to conquer tribes on his own. Early in 1818 Shaka prepared to join with Dingiswayo in a campaign against the Ndwandwe tribe ruled by Zwide. Dingiswayo foolishly left the army without an escort and was captured and killed by Zwide before the regiments of Shaka and Dingiswayo could join forces. Shaka was forced to retreat and establish a defensive position on Qokli Hill, from which he defeated Zwide. After the battle the Mtetwa and several small tribes joined Shaka. The following year (1819) the Ndwandwe again invaded Shaka's domain and were defeated at the Battle of Umhlatuze. Statistical data on these and other battles are listed in Table 1.

Following the consolidation of his kingdom, Shaka launched forth on a series of wars for the next three years which resulted in expanding the kingdom into an empire of 80,000 square miles. Table 2 shows the increase in the size of territory, in the number of tribes in the kingdom, and in the size of the army for the period 1816 to 1822. However, once the empire was secure the army—which by then totaled 30,000 men—had few military duties. Shaka's answer to the question of what a nation does with a large army that is only necessary for defensive purposes (although the soldiers herded Shaka's cattle and worked his fields) was to send it on long-range campaigns; usually the army returned with plunder, which consisted primarily of cattle. These campaigns occurred during the last four years of Shaka's reign, until he was assassinated by his brothers in 1828.

The idea of organizing armies into regiments and the use of new weapons and tactics diffused rapidly to neighboring tribes. In 1817 and 1818 Dingiswayo faced tribes that had organized their armies around age-grade regiments. In 1818 the Ndwandwes seemed to be familiar with enveloping tactics; they certainly were in 1819 (Ritter 1957: 175–76). In 1818 the invading Ndwandwes carried javelins; in 1819 they carried one heavy spear and two throwing spears, but still wore sandals (Ritter 1957: 167). Thus it took only three years from the time Shaka became the Zulu chieftain for the innovations in weapons and tactics to diffuse to enemy tribes.

The evolution of Zulu warfare can be analyzed in terms of a progression of types of wars, the types being named for the goals of war (see Table 3). The first type can be characterized as "dueling battles" between small tribes whose warriors agreed upon the time and place of battle. Since spears were used only as projectile weapons, casualties were slight. The nature of war changed when Dingiswayo created—for the purpose of conquering other tribes—a more efficient military force by organizing his warriors into age-grade regiments. Thus he created a new concept of war by using his newly formed army as an instrument of political expansion. These "battles of subjugation," in which there were still few casualties, constitute the second type of war. Shortly after the establishment of Dingiswayo's chiefdom, Shaka invented a short stabbing spear and enveloping tactics which he had no opportunity to use until he became leader of the Zulu. Upon the death of Dingiswayo and the breakup of his domain, Shaka was forced to defend Zululand from invasion. The use of these new weapons and tactics and new motives for fighting resulted in a third type of war in which casualties were very high. The defense of Zululand was followed by a series of successful offensive battles in which casualty rates remained high; these "battles of conquest" resulted in the creation of an empire. The fourth type of war was the long-range "campaigns" into enemy territory, the aim of which was to keep the army busy rather than conquering new peoples. Casualty rates became low again, as they had been prior to 1816. It should be noted that each of these four types of war corresponds to a different level of sociopolitical development. In terms of Service's taxonomy (1962), "dueling battles" occurred on the *tribal* level, "battles of subjugation" led to the development of *chiefdoms,* "battles of conquest" brought about the emergence of the *state,* and with the eventual development of *empires* long-range "campaigns" became the dominant form of war.

In conclusion, the development of a new type of military organization (age-grade regiments) and a change in the goals of war from settling disputes to subjugation of other tribes led to a slight increase in casualty rates. This is described as a change from "dueling battles" to "battles of subjugation." The introduction of shock weapons and enveloping tactics combined with new reasons for war—namely conquest, rather than subjugation, of neighboring peoples—greatly accelerated casualty rates. This has been described as a shift from "battles of subjugation" to "battles of conquest." With a change in the goals of war from conquest to plunder, casualty rates once again became low. This was a shift from "battles of conquest" to "campaigns."

356

TABLE 1

SIX ZULU BATTLES

Year and name of battle	Tribes involved	Size of armies	Number killed	Average number killed	Average percentage killed
1 1810	Butelezi	600	50	35	3
	Mtetwa	1,800	20		
2 1813 Um Mona	Ndwandwe	2,500	500	325	15
	Mtetwa	1,800	150		
3 1816	Butelezi	600	550	300	44
	Zulu	750	50		
4 1818 Qokli Hill	Ndwandwe	11,000	7,500	4,550	60
	Zulu	4,300	1,600		
5 1819 Umhlatuze	Ndwandwe	18,000	17,000	11,000	80
	Zulu	10,000	5,000		
6 1826 Ndololwane	Ndwandwe	20,000	19,000	12,000(?)	42(?)
	Zulu	40,000	6,000(?)		

TABLE 2

EXPANSION OF THE ZULU EMPIRE

Year	Size of territory in square miles	Number of tribes in the kingdom	Size of army
1822	80,000	300	20,000
1819[a]	11,500	46	10,000
1818[b]	7,000	30	8,000
1817[c]	400	6	2,000
1816[d]	200	2	1,000
1816	100	1	500

[a] After battle of Umhlatuze [c] After second battle with Butelezi
[b] After battle of Qokli Hill [d] After incorporation of one tribe

TABLE 3

Types of Zulu Wars

1806	1808	1810	1812	1814	1816	1818	1820	1822	1824	1826	1828
		1	2	2	3	4 5		3		6	4
		B	B	B B	B	B B	B	B	B	C C	C C

1 Dueling battles (not shown)
2 Battles of subjugation
3 Battles of conquest
4 Campaigns

B = battle
C = campaign

Arabic numerals above battles identify the battle as one of the six in Table 1

Categories of Comparison	Dueling Battles	Battles of Subjugation	Battles of Conquest	Campaigns
1 Type of weapon	projectile	projectile	shock	shock
2 Type of formation	lines	lines	envelopment	envelopment
3 Type of military organization	patrilineage	age-grade regiment	age-grade regiment	age-grade regiment
4 Goals of war	settling disputes	subjugation	conquest	plunder
5 Casualty rate	very low	low	high	low
6 Socio-political system	tribe	chiefdom	state	empire

MAORI WARFARE

Andrew P. Vayda

Objectives and procedures

THIS STUDY represents an attempt to organize the data on Maori warfare and to see them in relation to other parts of Maori culture and in relation to the New Zealand environment in which the Maori people worked and fought.

Maori warfare had certain general characteristics which may serve as the criteria for distinguishing a type, or pattern, of warfare found in various parts of the primitive world. The characteristics include smallness in the scale and shortness in the duration of active hostilities, the poor development of command and discipline, the great reliance upon surprise attacks, and the importance of the village community or local group in the organization of war parties.

The attempt has been made therefore to describe Maori warfare primarily (although not exclusively) as it was in the latter part of the eighteenth and the early part of the nineteenth centuries. In other words, the attempt was to describe Maori warfare in its last stage of evolution before its character was greatly altered by European weapons and ways.

Some descriptions of European-influenced Maori warfare have been included, but this was done with an emphasis upon features likely to have persisted from earlier times or else upon features

Extracted from A. P. Vayda, *Maori Warfare*, Wellington, New Zealand, Polynesian Society Maori Monographs, No. 2, 1960. The original pages are 1–2, 10–27, 29–32, 46–48, 53, 65–66, 80–81, 90, 94–97, 102–7, 109–11, 113–16. Reprinted by permission of the author and of the Polynesian Society.

whose development could reasonably be attributed to European influences. Emphasizing these two types of features was valuable for reconstructing the native pattern.

Fortifications

Defensive works in New Zealand were more elaborate than anywhere else in Polynesia. For our study, it will be sufficient briefly to state, as Firth (1927: 66–67) has done, only the main characteristics of the Maori *pa* or fortified village.

The Maori *pa,* as distinct from the open, unfortified villages called *kainga,* were usually built upon hills, spurs, or craggy headlands, or upon islands in lakes, swamps, or off the coast. Natural features thus assisted the massive defensive works, which were commonly in the form of rampart and trench. Each of the several lines of defense constructed was normally surmounted by a stockade which had the defenders stationed immediately behind it so as to be able to fight off an attack. Overtopping the stockade there sometimes were fighting stages from which the defenders could more easily throw spears and stones down upon the enemy. These weapons might be kept upon the stages so as to be ready in case of an attack. Each line of fortification had a narrow gateway, while the larger *pa* had auxiliary entrances as well. A blind of palisading protected the gateway by laying the enemy open to flank attack if he attempted to enter. Dwelling houses and food-storage huts were within the lines of defense, while on the highest ground behind the innermost fortification was the stronghold's citadel, which was both the rallying point for all the people and the site of the houses of the principal chief and his relatives (Firth 1927: 66–69). Sometimes part of the population resided outside the *pa* and retired to the defenses, with what property and supplies were handy, only when threatened by an attack (Best 1924a: II, 305, 311). The *pa*-dwellers themselves did not stay permanently in their fortified villages. Sometimes they moved away to live at their fishing, hunting, or cultivation grounds (Best 1927: 19). Even the seasonal camps of fishers or cultivators, however, were often protected by fences or light stockades, and there were several transitional forms between the heavily fortified *pa* and the unfortified *kainga* (Lewthwaite 1949: 20–21).

Pa were very common only in Iwitini,[1] the northernmost of late eighteenth-century New Zealand's three geographic regions. *Pa* varied in type and size within Iwitini. Ramparts and trenches were not important in the huge forts that occupied the stumps of extinct volcanoes on the Tamaki isthmus and in the vicinities of Auckland and the Bay of Islands. These defensive works consisted of tier upon tier of scarped terraces, each separately protected by palisades, although connected perhaps by "crude wooden ladders or sunken pathways" (Lewthwaite 1949: 18–19). Such *pa* could accommodate thousands of Maoris (Lewthwaite 1949: 19). The forts of the Taranaki, the Bay of Plenty, and the Waikato districts were smaller and seem to have been characterized mainly by the rampart and trench, although equipped sometimes also with terraces (Firth 1927: 69). Many of the Taranaki *pa* are said to have had a high wooden watchtower erected near the main entrance (Skinner 1911: 76).

Approaching to fight

Maori war parties sometimes avoided arduous journeys on foot by using war canoes, which were made from the stoutest and largest timber available. Of course, paddling the canoes was arduous too. On the average, the canoes accommodated seventy people and were some seventy feet long. They were manned by a

---

[1] In 1949, two New Zealand geographers, Cumberland (in a short published article) and Lewthwaite (in a fuller but unpublished Master's thesis), distinguished (and invented names for) three main regions in eighteenth-century Maori New Zealand: Iwitini ("many people" or "a host of tribes"), a predominantly coastal northern region with a warm climate, a relatively gentle surface configuration, varied soils, flourishing vegetation, and a close association of land and water; Waenganui ("central," "in between," "transitional"), a centrally located transitional region which, compared to Iwitini, had a colder climate, a more frequently rugged surface configuration, a lesser intricacy of coast lines, and a less close association of land and water; and, finally, Te Wahi Pounamu ("the place of greenstone") in the south, a region with a dour climate, frosty and unsheltered grasslands, the unsocial *Nothofagus* forest, and a snowy alpine interior.

double row of warriors who plied their paddles in time to the chants and gestures of one or two leaders standing amidships (Buller 1878: 246; Colenso 1880a: 57; Henderson 1948: 11 ff; Hochstetter 1867: 297; Wilson 1907: 231). The canoes carried war parties not only along the coast, but also up and down the larger rivers and across lakes. However, difficult portages, together with the frequent roughness of many of New Zealand's waters, severely restricted the amount of traveling that could be done by canoes.

The Maori foottracks were narrow paths worn smooth by the repeated pressure of bare feet and kept open by travelers' breaking off of encroaching bush. There was some preference for paths that ran along the tops of ridges, from where the approach of hostile war parties could be observed. Other paths, however, had their course along valley bottoms. The beach also served as a road at times.

Some war parties' advance along the beach was timed so as to have high tide wash out all their traces. Except in the immediate vicinity of villages, all the regular Maori tracks were only a few inches wide and thus were suited to traveling only in single file. This form of column was, according to S. P. Smith (Smith 1910a: 11), the order which all Maori war parties employed on the march. Large war parties, therefore, were usually strung out for considerable distances along the track. When the scouts in advance gave an alarm, the party is supposed to have gathered together around the chiefs to await the arrival of the rearguard of warriors, who sometimes marched behind any supply-carriers accompanying the force (Smith 1910a: 11). Sometimes, however, the spread-out apparently was so great that the men either could not be led by a chief or else could not give one another mutual support and protection. A column thus thinned out could be routed by the concerted action of a smaller force lying in ambush.

When attacking fortified villages, war parties tried to advance unseen, whether on foot or by canoe, and then to camp at some distance from the *pa,* while sending scouts forward to reconnoiter. The scouts would approach the fort under cover of night and try to find some point at which the war party could get inside and surprise the inmates (Best 1927: 115).

At times a war party approaching its objective avoided all paths for fear that they had been "mined" by the enemy with supernaturally lethal objects. However, apparently not all approaching war parties conceded the efficacy of such charms.

Tactics in fighting

In open fighting but, according to W. E. Gudgeon, "only on desperate occasions" a wedge-shaped formation appears to have been employed (Gudgeon 1907a: 41; Maning 1876: 213). A compact body of men charging in the wedge-shaped formation could break through outer screens of defenders and reach the main position quickly. The anticipated results of such a charge were quick victory or death, since the attackers would immediately close with the foe. Buck says that the dangerous single position forming the point of the wedge and the two positions in the second row were places of honor to be occupied by the leading warriors (Buck 1949: 394).

A Wairarapa Maori quoted by Best says that a war party attacking a *pa* sometimes split up and, by simultaneous false attacks at several places, would draw the bulk of the defenders away from some spot where the real effort to gain entry would be concentrated (Best 1927: 120). Commonly, a part of a fighting force made a feint assault upon a *pa* and then retired with loss in order to tempt the enemy into pursuit to some prearranged place where the main body of the war party lay ready to attack. Sometimes the defenders left the fort and themselves used the feint attack and ambuscade so as to precipitate an engagement while the invaders were not yet prepared (Buck 1949: 394–95). In general, the mock retreat was a favorite Maori maneuver.

Best says that sometimes, usually during the night, an attacking force laid several ambushes at short distances from one another. Early in the morning a small party was sent forward, and, if successful in starting a fight with the enemy garrison, it retreated to decoy the enemy into pursuit past the ambushes. The furthest

ambush would be the first to rise from concealment and give battle to the pursuers, whereupon the other ambushes would attack
in the rear. At times, an attacking force laid only a single ambush
(Best 1902: 226). In some withdrawals, the fugitives, pretended
or real, scattered right and left to hide in the fern and the scrub
and managed to reappear simultaneously on the flanks, rear, and
front of the pursuing adversaries so as to give them the impression
of being surrounded (Gudgeon 1885: 34). The stratagem is said
to have been effectively employed against European troops. The
extent of its utilization before the advent of the Pakehas (Europeans) is, however, not clear.

Kinship and locality in Maori warfare

Like other Maori occupations, war was organized on the bases of
kinship and loyalty. The everyday life of the Maoris was lived in
village communities. As Firth has pointed out, the nature and
size of these varied according to the environment, especially according to the available food supply (Firth 1929: 76). The average village community may be very roughly estimated to have
contained a few hundred people. The people of a village were
divided into extended family groups called *whanau*. The members
of a *whanau* lived together in one house or perhaps two neighboring houses, shared the usufruct of small eel-weirs, fishing
grounds, etc., worked agricultural plots in common, and, in
general, united their efforts in those tasks which Firth describes
as "requiring a small body of workers and cooperation of a not
very complex order" (Firth 1929: 125). But the major communal
activities, war as well as subsistence tasks, were performed by a
larger group, of which the core was, as a rule, a single *hapu* or
subtribe. This was a named group of blood relatives, tracing
their descent from a common ancestor several generations back.
Marriages between members of a *hapu* were frequent and were
considered desirable (Best 1903a: 20). A single *hapu* usually
held an entire village, but occasionally several related *hapu* occupied a single village, or else one *hapu* occupied several small
villages. In any case, a group of kinsmen was the core of the vil-

lage population, and this population cooperated in major economic and military undertakings.

The largest kinship group among the Maoris was the *iwi,* or tribe. The members of each of the related *hapu* constituting a tribe could trace back their descent to a single ancestor of all the tribesmen. Pre-European New Zealand's 100 to 300 thousand Maoris were distributed among roughly forty tribes, most of which were subdivided into numerous *hapu.* The lands of related *hapu* were contiguous and together constituted the land of the entire tribe. In resisting invasions of the tribal land, the related *hapu* sometimes acted together. Otherwise, the tribe as a unit had no important functions. Indeed, when not engaged in extratribal warfare, different *hapu* of the same tribe not uncommonly turned upon one another and fought fiercely among themselves (Best 1903b: 40). The Maori lands were exploited effectively by the individual *hapu,* and no advantage would have accrued from bringing the different *hapu* together over long and difficult distances (Cockayne 1928: 155).

Within the *hapu* itself, there were no organized group-sanctioned hostilities. The *hapu* was as a rule the smallest unit from which war parties were mustered, and the men of the *hapu* were a unit in fighting. The organization of war parties was based upon the ties between *hapu* members to such an extent that the Maoris first coming into contact with British troops thought that soldiers and sailors were from two separate *hapu,* although both belonging to the *iwi* or tribe called England (Maning 1876: 207).

The *hapu* as a fighting unit is said to have been favored because its members, the relatives and immediate followers of one chief, were actuated by emotions and opinions that they had in common (Gudgeon 1907b: 78; Tregear 1904: 334).

Unfortunately there are no early and reliable estimates of the fighting strength of *hapu,* but there probably were not many (if any) *hapu* having more than several hundred fighting men.

When their village was attacked, all the warriors of the *hapu* probably had no option but to fight. However, for certain missions against the enemy, less than the full fighting strength of the *hapu* provided sufficient and practicable numbers.

Moreover, although, as Thompson remarks, all male persons capable of bearing arms were "morally obliged" to join the ranks, the Maoris had no formal sanctions to compel individuals in the *hapu* to join a war party. The check on shirking was provided by public opinion rather than by force.

Leadership and discipline

Visualizing any Maori kinship group as branches of a genealogical tree, we may identify the hereditary leader of the group as a first-born son on the senior branch in the male line. Such was the hereditary leader of a *hapu*. However, if he was lacking in military prowess or was otherwise physically or mentally deficient, then a younger brother or somebody from a junior branch might assume the role of leader, although the first-born son on the senior branch did retain seniority of rank. In Maori society, hereditary rank was determined by proximity to the senior branch. Those on it or near it were chiefs or *rangatira* of the *hapu,* while those far away from it were supposed to be *ware* or *tutua* and were regarded as lesser persons, although they themselves did not always acknowledge the fact. Best, who met a great many Maoris, says he never met one who admitted being a *ware* or *tutua* (Best 1924a: I, 346). *"Turanga tangata rite,"* says a Maori proverb, meaning that all people are equal (Gudgeon 1907a: 34). *Rangatira* and *ware* persons freely married each other, and they were all members of the same kinship group.

"Toa" was the name that the Maoris gave to warriors of extraordinary courage and good fortune—warriors who had survived dangers which would have overwhelmed ordinary beings (Gudgeon 1904c: 238). The principal chief had to be a *toa* in order to hold his position on the field of war (Best 1903b: 82). The usual leaders of war parties were high-born chiefs, since their training and their rank and *mana* through seniority of birth were supposed to make them brave men and good leaders in war.

In war as in peace, a Maori chief was more a leader than a commander.

The fact that in war (as in general) the chiefs could not effectually command made their presence as leaders all the more necessary. As leaders, they used words, gestures, and exemplary action to urge the men onward.

The general absence of military discipline among the Maoris and the importance of the mere presence of the chiefs, although not as commanders or disciplinarians, is brought out by the fact that it was common, perhaps very common, for Maori fighting men to flee if the chiefs leading them were slain. Even when on the verge of victory, an attacking force might withdraw because of the loss of a leader.

A hostile expedition might be given up if the leader died in the course of it.

Successful defense of a *pa* also is said to have required the presence of leaders. Maori oldtimers informed Best that a *pa* was lost if its outer defenses were captured and there was no influential chief to rally the defenders on the summit or citadel (Best 1903b: 209). The Maoris in the Bay of Islands *pa* assaulted by Roux ceased resisting when the last of their leaders fell (Roux 1914: 430 ff).

In peace as in war, leadership through exemplary action was present and regular authority was absent.

In general, the Maoris' tactics in fighting were such that they could be executed by a relatively small unit under the personal leadership of a chief, i.e., they were adjusted to the absence of regular authority. Even in the reputedly uncommon wedge-shaped formation, once the wedge had been arranged, the men had only to follow the chief who formed the apex of the wedge. Definitely more common than the use of the wedge-shaped formation was the Maoris' use of ambuscades and surprise attacks. For these, the leader had but to give the signal, whether by word or by action, for the warriors to arise or turn and to start fighting. However, the fighting unit had to be a compact one if the leader's signal was to be effectively conveyed to all members.

Small war parties

The *hapu,* or rather its men, was so practicable a fighting unit
for the Maoris that often it constituted an entire war party
(Tregear 1904: 334). Again and again, Maori accounts refer to
war parties as having been comprised of 140 men (*hokowhitu*),
or, perhaps less frequently, 340 men (*kotahi ma whitu, te rau ma
whitu,* or *rau hokowhitu*). However, as Best says, the Maoris
often did not aim at precision when they mentioned such things
as the size of war parties (Best 1942: 309). The caution must
be noted that the regularities might be in the Maori words or
phrases rather than in the actual size of war parties.

Large war parties

Numerical superiority alone was not always enough to offset the
disadvantages of large war parties among the Maoris. Numbers
are an advantage if their force can be concentrated or used in
concerted effort against the enemy. In Maori war parties, the
men from different *hapu* often could not get together for united
action. Each *hapu,* says Best, did as it pleased and remained
under its own chief (Best 1903b: 40). W. E. Gudgeon, a military
man as well as a student of Maori history, mentions that 300 of
Ngati Hau defeated the united strength of Ngati Ruanui at Te
Puia on the Patea River—"simply because each *hapu* of the last-
named tribe had decided to fight a little apart from the others,
with the result that they were beaten in detail, the rout of one
hapu involving another" (Gudgeon 1907b: 78).

Stratagems to conceal attacks

Anyone reading the traditional accounts of Maori warfare must
agree with Firth and Best that the annals are filled with instances
of ambuscades, stratagems, and treachery (Firth 1927: 77; Best
1902: 160). Best refers to the many recorded cases of the killing
of guests at feasts (Best 1902: 160). There was no telling when
something might happen; so guests went to feasts fully armed
and prepared for war; to have gone unarmed would have been to
ask for trouble from their hosts (McDonnell 1887b: 591). Ac-

cording to Best, even a party escorting a woman to her marriage feast always carried arms in former times (Best 1903a: 49). Probably this was often for aggressive as well as for defensive purposes.

Sometimes an attack was made suddenly at the *uhunga,* or wake. S. P. Smith relates that Tumu-Pakihi, an important Ngati Whatua chief, died around the middle of the eighteenth century. Neighboring tribes connected in any way with the deceased were invited, as was customary, to come to cry over the dead and to feast. Kiwi, a principal chief of the Wai o Hua tribe on the Auckland isthmus, accepted the invitation and went to Kaipara with a number of his people, all armed. At a signal, the Wai o Hua massacred many of their Ngati Whatua hosts (Smith 1896–97: 84).

The Maoris resorted to a variety of masquerades in order to effect a surprise by concealing intended attacks. Sometimes they pretended to be warriors of the village to be attacked. Best relates that about a dozen generations ago the Nga Potiki or Tuhoe went to attack a Whakatane *pa.* Just before getting there, they halted and prepared bundles of fern and rubbish made up to resemble swags of human flesh. Then they advanced to the *pa* slowly and with bended backs so as to appear oppressed by the weight of the packs. Finally they halted and were seen by Te Whakatane. The garrison, mistaking the men for their own returning warriors laden with the flesh of the enemy slain, marched out of the fort in column formation so as to welcome their supposed friends. Too late did Te Whakatane realize their mistake. Upon their heads there crashed the weapons of the wily sons of Potiki (Best 1904: 6–7; Best 1925: I, 46–47).

The traditions record that war parties sometimes pretended to be peaceful cultivators or fern diggers and then used their sharpened digging tools to stab unwary foes. Or they might pretend to be wood gatherers and conceal their clubs by tying them to the legs. More than one tradition tells of war parties playing the part of friendly fishermen (Best 1925: I, 96; Gudgeon 1895: 32; Smith 1910a: 241–42; White 1887–90: III, 156; V, 92–93).

It is said that sometimes they entrapped their unsuspecting enemies in fishnets before dispatching them. There even are accounts of intending assailants masquerading under black mats as large fish or seals; when the inmates of a *pa* rushed to the beach in anticipation of a fine catch, the mats were thrown off and the would-be fish-catchers themselves became the fish that were caught.

It is appropriate to consider how the Maori armory was adapted to safeguarding the element of surprise. Two main points may very briefly be noted. The first point is that by not using slings and by making very limited use of other projectile weapons, the Maoris avoided alerting a foe before the advantage of surprise was fully exploited. The second point is that the Maori short clubs or *patu,* handy and deadly weapons which could be kept concealed, were well suited to ambuscades or attacks by stealth.

Single combats

When two hostile forces did meet in the open, a tried warrior might step forth and challenge someone on the other side to single combat. Buck suggests that the single combats were fought by champion warriors who vied with one another for fame (Buck 1949: 399). Sometimes the principals, it seems, were attended by one or two seconds, called *piki.* They might join in the fray if their principal was getting the worst of the duel or if the opposite seconds were interfering. Apparently the issue of a single combat could virtually terminate an engagement between opposing parties. However, when this happened, it resulted ordinarily not from some prior agreement or understanding but rather from the flight of one of the parties when its fallen champion had been its leader. Flight as a result of the leader's fall, whether in single combat or otherwise, was, as previously noted, not uncommon among the Maoris.

Maori single combats are supposed to have been characterized by some degree of chivalry. Downes states, for example, that etiquette required the challenger to give his adversary the choice of weapons (Downes 1929: 164). On the other hand, Best says that each warrior pleased himself in single combats and used his favorite weapon (Best 1903b: 37 ff).

In any case, it seems clear from the traditional accounts that Maori single combats were not all chivalry. Kelly tells of a single combat in which the first move that one of the principals made was to throw sand into a nonplussed opponent's eyes (Kelly 1949: 157–58). Best describes a single combat said to have occurred around the beginning of the nineteenth century at Wai-Hora in Waikohu County (Gisborne district). Sallying forth one day, Poriro, a member of a besieged garrison, engaged in single combat with Mou, chief of the attacking force. Mou caught his antagonist by his long hair and proceeded to take him away. But a sister of Poriro attacked Mou and struck him down with a stone (Best 1904: 75). In another single combat referred to by Best, one of the principals, a famed warrior of Ruatoki (Whaka-tane County), got tired of receiving spear wounds and therefore called on his men to close in battle (Best 1903b: 38; Best 1925: I, 334–35).

Duration and frequency of military activities

In general, military activities among the Maoris seem to have been of short duration. The issue could be, and often was, decided in a matter of minutes both in the case of open fighting and in the case of surprise attacks or ambuscades. No fight, says Best, lasted long (Best 1924b: 157). Among the longest may be mentioned the battle of Ngai-tai-pari-rua in 1815. This is said to have been fought on the beach during two floodtides before the Ngati Maniapoto finally obliged the Ngati Tama to retreat (Smith 1910a: 279–80). Another battle, supposedly fought around 1700, is said not to have been decided until the third day (Kelly 1949: 238). This may have been exceptional. Thompson says of open battles in general that they did not last a minute before one party gave way and fled (Thompson 1859: I, 128).

Thompson also states that such a single battle generally terminated a campaign (Thompson 1859: I, 129), but this statement is to some degree open to question. Some accounts of fighting in premusket days tell of war parties making a successful attack, using the enemy's flesh and provisions for revictualing, and then going on to attack elsewhere.

Reference has already been made to the Maori practice of keeping debtor and creditor statements of encounters with enemies. Best points out that when one side deemed an account squared, the other side probably held that it was more than squared and would set about to equalize it (Best 1924a: II, 232). The result was a seesaw record of military exploits extending often for generations. Hostility between two groups thus could be of very long duration, although actual fighting between them would be only intermittent. If war periods are to be defined at all by the student of Maori warfare, they are probably best defined as those periods during which any given groups were hostile continuously and were actively belligerent, at least intermittently. From the standpoint of this definition, numerous examples of war periods lasting many years, even generations, may be found.

Pursuit and mortality

Ordinarily any of the enemy taken alive were either killed on the spot or else held as prisoners for future slaughter or, perhaps more rarely, enslavement. The old Nga Puhi cannibal, Toenga Pou, who had been with some of Hongi Hika's war parties, said to McDonnell: /

> "You ask . . . if it is not better to save the life of an enemy, when you have rendered him helpless, than to kill him? No, it is not better; neither is it wise. What is the use of getting a man down, if you are fighting with him during wartime, or wounding him, unless you finish your work by killing him? Never, even, let him get up again; that would be wrong, and wasting all the advantage your strength and education had given to you, a wasteful expenditure of strength and *matauranga* (science), and a future source of trouble; think, too, of your cartridges wasted. For your enemy will not cease to remember that you once got him down (but refrained from killing him because it was not worth it) until he has either killed you, or somebody else, even if only remotely your relative. Then, as it will have been entirely your own fault, you will have to kill someone else

in payment, and no end of trouble ensues. When you go to fish for *whapuku* (cod), and catch a big fish, you secure him and eat him, or give him to the tribe to eat; you do not let him go again, to laugh at you; that would be foolish. So always kill your enemy, if you once get him under, and make him fit for food. If ever you go to fight," continued old Pou, "fight for results; if not, stay at home and do not make a fool of yourself. Unless you are brave, and brave enough to let others know you are brave, you will be no better than a *tutua* (common fellow), and you will soon cease to live. Be really brave, then, so that you may remain long on the earth, and kill your enemies whenever and wherever you meet them. Be first, or they will kill you" (McDonnell 1889: 478).

Treatment of the enemy slain

Sometimes when revenge was not satisfied by eating the flesh of an enemy, his bones were saved for uses which the Maoris thought degrading. The victorious party might make from the bones such things as flutes, the heads of bird spears, the barbs of fishhooks, sconces to hold baskets of food, rings for the legs of captive parrots, pins for eating periwinkles, pins for holding dress mats together, and needles for sewing dogskin mats. For the skull there might be reserved the indignity of carrying water for the ovens. In 1770, Parkinson saw a skull used as a canoe baler (Parkinson 1773: 116).

But after a cannibal feast, many were the bones that were simply broken up and burned in the fire (Tregear 1904: 359). According to a Maori account cited by Best, the purpose of the burning was to prevent tribesmen of the slain from collecting the bones and depositing them in the sacred places of the tribe.

Sometimes the heads of detested enemy chiefs were preserved and taken home, where they were reviled and insulted. They were occasionally exposed, being impaled on sticks or else on the defensive stockade of the *pa* (Best 1924a: II, 61).

The technique of preserving the heads has been described by various writers in various ways. Buck's description is brief:

> The Maori technique of preserving consisted of removing the eyes and tongue, extracting the brain by enlarging the *foramen magnum* at the base of the cranium, stretching and stitching the skin of the neck to a small supple-jack hoop, steaming the leaf-wrapped head

in an earth oven and smoke-drying it. That the method of preserving
was effective is shown by the number in museums being still in a
good state of preservation (Buck 1949: 300).

It is clear that the number of enemy heads taken and preserved
increased very greatly after the Maoris found that they could trade
them for firearms and other European goods. Apparently by
1820, tattooed Maori heads were a not uncommon article of trade
in Sydney. For a while, some chiefs killed their slaves in order to
satisfy the demand.

Treatment of enemy goods

Difficulties in logistics made it impracticable to take back large
numbers of heads, especially when an expedition returned over-
land. These same difficulties probably operated also as a check
on the amount of plunder that warriors returned with, although
the smallness of the amount available no doubt was a check too.
But a war party capturing a *pa* did seize as much of the movable
property as possible. In addition to human flesh and other food,
the loot of war parties included weapons, mats, ear pendants,
fishhooks, lines, small baskets and calabashes, etc.

Prisoners and slaves

Apparently a custom of appropriation prior to the attack applied
to the persons, as well as to the goods, of the enemy.

But when the enemies were numerous, no more than a few
of them—and those the most notable ones—seem to have been
claimed as slaves beforehand. What was to become of most of
the captives was not decided until after the attack. In his account
of the fall of a *pa*, White says that warriors might be seen disputing for a woman, girl, or child, and the dispute would be
ended when one of them would deal a heavy blow with his *mere*
on the head of the already half-dead creature, who had been
nearly torn limb from limb in the dispute, and, releasing his hold
he would say, "Take our food now" (White 1874: 122–23). In
a similar vein, Polack says that many inferior chiefs met a hasty

death as a result of rough treatment by warriors trying to capture them (Polack 1840: II, 24).

Apart from such regular sharing or apportionment, a chief could secure a slave by throwing his mat over one of the enemy or by some similar means. These means are further examples of the isolation of things for a chief's use through their being brought into association with the chief or with some part of his body. Sometimes a chief's daughter saved a prisoner from death by throwing her mat over him. A man who had been thus saved was pointed out to Polack and was identified as the sole survivor of his tribe. He had become first his deliverer's slave, then her husband (Polack 1838: I, 215). Of Billy Bundy, one of the Europeans at Nga-Motu *pa* in 1832, it is said that he once was on the point of being killed and cast into the oven by a group of Maoris when their chief's daughter rushed forward and cast her mat or mantle over him. Bundy soon after became her husband (Smith 1910b: 472).

Sometimes the prisoners taken were tied up. Davis, describing nineteenth-century Nga Puhi expeditions, says that the mode of securing prisoners was by tying their hands behind their backs with cords and putting ropes around their necks. Not infrequently another method was employed. This consisted of interweaving the hair of the prisoner's head with a rope, of which the end was tied to the master's wrist at night so that by a slight movement of the hand he could ascertain if he still possessed his captive (Davis 1855: 11).

Occasionally some of the prisoners not escaping were killed for food before the war party got back home. Francis Hall, a Bay of Islands missionary, wrote in 1821:

> We hear, that, among the slaves who were taken . . . yesterday, one of them, a woman, becoming tired or lame, could not keep up with the rest: she was, in consequence, killed and eaten—this being the custom in New Zealand! (Hall 1823: 506).

When the victorious warriors reached home, the widows and other female relatives of those of their comrades who had been slain in the expedition might kill some prisoners in order to avenge the deaths of the men.

Prisoners surviving such scenes became slaves who did menial work for their captors. As slaves, they were individually owned, mainly by the leading chiefs, and their masters had the power of life and death over them. The slaves were liable to be killed in order to serve as a human sacrifice or as the relish in a feast.

Yet the condition of Maori slaves was not a severe one physically. As a general rule, they ate well, were forthright in their speech, were kindly treated, and were not expected to overwork themselves. Their work, including *tapu*-less tasks connected with cooking and burden-bearing, helped the chiefs to accumulate the supplies necessary both for the entertainment of travelers and for the initiation of major economic and military undertakings.

But in pre-European times, the population size of Maori communities depended not upon the extent of foreign demand for goods and services but rather upon local food supply. Not many slaves could be added to the numbers of a community which already was, as Maning says, "never far removed from necessity or scarcity of food" (Maning 1863: 208).

Conquests

Throughout the preceding discussion, captives have been spoken of as being taken away to the enemy's territory. It was not a usual aftermath of Maori fighting that the captives' territory became the enemy's. A successful campaign among the Maoris might be confined to victories over the inmates of a single *pa* or perhaps several *pa*. As a rule, such victories did not put the successful warriors in an effective position for occupation of the captured forts and adjacent food areas, because all the surrounding country was likely to belong to enemies, i.e., to friends and tribesmen of the defeated garrisons.

Yet a succession of victories against not just one *hapu* but against a single enemy tribe, whether in one campaign or over a period of many years, could enable a group to take over the enemy tribe's land. In former days, as Firth notes, large areas of land did indeed change hands as the result of conquest from the original owners (Firth 1929: 377).

Broadly speaking, two sets of conditions made some lands more desirable than others to the Maoris, and the more desirable lands were fought over. The two sets of conditions were differences in the actual or potential productivity of land and differences in the vegetation cover.

The pertinent differences in vegetation cover were the differences between primary forests and second-growth areas. To the Maoris, equipped with only primitive wooden and stone tools, the primary forests were very much harder to clear than the second-growth areas, and therefore were less desirable for exploitation.

Many times in the course of Maori prehistory, a group might have been increasing in numbers or it might have temporarily exhausted its existing land (Taylor 1870: 494; Lewthwaite 1949: 40). It now becomes clear what were the viable alternatives confronting such a group. It could undertake either to expand into the virgin rain-forest or to get previously used land from other groups. Because the labor involved in clearing the primary forest was so great, the preferred alternative probably was to get previously used land from other groups—by force if necessary. If the time and effort required for either clearing virgin land in order to make room for cultivations or breaking ground for the first time in order to dig fern root were considerably more than were necessary for the operations of both conquest and the preparation of previously used land, it follows that conquests would have added more efficiently to the prosperity of particular groups than would peaceful dispersion.

When an area such as Tamaki, or any other area, was conquered by a group, the conquerors could maintain their claim to the new land only by occupying and using it and by excluding the former owners. It is said that at times the exclusion of the defeated from conquered territory was achieved by extermination of them. Actually it may be doubted if literal extermination ever

took place. Best states as fact that tribes were not totally destroyed in Maori warfare (Best 1925: I, 132).

Most significant are two conclusions: (1) that individual survivors could flee to unoccupied land and form a new group; and
(2) that survivors persisting as a group might simply be driven
off to other land. Examples of conquests involving displacement
of the vanquished from their land but not their extermination are
numerous. If the survivors among the vanquished persisted as a
group, they might, like Te Rauparaha's Ngati Toa, invade the
territory of some even weaker group, and this latter group might
be driven off to yet other land—probably to virgin forest which
the group would then have no option but to clear. In any case,
an end result would be the occupation and exploiting of previously unexploited (or underexploited) land, and, in all likelihood, an increase in the extent of New Zealand's area covered by
second-growth rather than by virgin forest. Since those conquests
which were effective—i.e., those which the conquerors followed
up by exclusive occupation and use of the defeated tribe's territory—could have the result of forcing the survivors among the
vanquished to occupy and exploit new parts of the New Zealand
environment, it seems reasonable to identify the conquests as an
agency whereby more and more of the New Zealand environment
was settled and exploited by the Maori people.

Some other results

Some students of primitive warfare have written as if no practical
advantages could conceivably accrue from war if a victorious
war party did not take land or some other property from the
enemy. The Maoris of course did occasionally take land from the
enemy, and they also took human bone material for implements,
human flesh for food, other plunder, plus the small number of
slaves which could be useful to the community even in the absence of means for their systematic exploiting and control. But
Maori warfare had other results too. Some advantages, conducive
to the survival and success of the group, are discernible in those

features of Maori warfare which may be described as retaliation for injuries to the village community or the kinship group.

Regular forms of public justice in the relations between Maori communities were virtually absent. There were no intercommunity mechanisms of authority. In the absence of such mechanisms, war was advantageous as a redress for accomplished offenses and a deterrent to further offenses against the group by another *hapu* or tribe. The kinds of offenses for which a group sooner or later took some sort of retaliatory action included insults to the group or (amounting to the same thing) to *rangatira* members of it, poaching on food preserves claimed by the group, and homicide or other violence, whether by physical or fancied magical means, against members of the group. Just how the retaliation for these kinds of offenses helped Maori social groups to maintain themselves may be indicated briefly.

Fighting against trespassers on preserves of birds, fish, rats, berries, or fern root (as well as pigs in European times) was fairly frequent. The advantage accruing to the group through the prevention of outsiders from depleting its sources of subsistence is so evident as to require no further discussion.

The prevention and punishment of the physical loss of any member of the group at the hands of outsiders was advantageous because it served to keep the group together and to maintain the numbers upon which it depended for cooperation and success in the tasks of subsistence and defense. Among the Maoris, the murder of a member of the group was a *take nui,* a great cause for war.

In retaliating for curses, degradation of the bones of the dead, and other insults to the group or to its chiefly representatives, the Maoris redeemed the honor of the group and maintained its prestige in the eyes of other groups. Thereby the other groups were deterred from further offenses, which might consist of not only insults but also acts of trespass, homicide, and even attempted conquest.

Besides serving as a deterrent to further injuries, the retaliatory fighting probably functioned to maintain the group's integrity in other ways. For example, it may have strengthened or reaffirmed the bonds of union among those participating in the fighting. Social anthropologists writing about primitive warfare stress such functions, and it is a plausible view that they were not absent from Maori warfare. Johansen comments upon the hopelessness of examining all the available cases in which a Maori group stood united for revenging any injury. After noting that Maori traditional history teems with instances, Johansen remarks that kinship solidarity in war was so obvious a thing to the Maoris that the narrators of the traditions rarely dwell on the point. Instead they tell how the group loses a member through homicide or suffers some other injury which must be revenged. The next thing that is told is that there is a war party, and the account at once passes on to a description of the fighting (Johansen 1954: 31). Johansen notes that a means whereby the Maoris resolved dissensions *within* the group was for some member of the group to commit an act of violence against another tribe. The solidarity of the group would be restored in resisting any warlike retaliations by the offended tribe (Johansen 1954: 76). It was, above all, in its external relations that the group was a unity.

THE ALBANIAN BLOOD FEUD

Margaret Hasluck

FAMILY VENGEANCE AND COLLECTIVE VENGEANCE

TILL AFTER THE 1914–18 war communications in Albania were so bad, government centers so few and the gendarmerie so ill-organized that communities were largely self-governing. These communities consisted in the narrower sense of the family, and in the wider sense of the tribe. If a person was injured, the family in most cases, and the tribe in a few cases, by the law of self-government punished the wrongdoer. Since the individual was almost completely submerged in his family, an injury to him was an injury to the whole family and might be punished by any of its members. When the tribal community was involved, the injury might again be avenged by any of its members. When the injury took the form of murder, vengeance generally took the Mosaic form of a life for a life, but sometimes was achieved by the exaction of blood money or the imposition of exile.

When the family of a murdered man, in default of government action, took the punishment of the murderer into its own hands and killed him or one of his male relatives, the head of his family might admit that both sides were equal and make peace. On the other hand, while still admitting that both sides were equal he might prefer to continue the feud by killing a second male from the avenging family; that done, a second life was forfeit on his side. In this way the feud might rage backwards and forwards for years or even generations, each family being in turn murderer

Extracted from Margaret Hasluck, *The Unwritten Law in Albania,* edited by J. H. Hutton, Cambridge University Press, 1954, pp. 219–60. Reprinted by permission of Cambridge University Press.

and victim, hunter and hunted. 'To take vengeance' was 'to take the blood' (that is, of the man already killed, not of him who was to make atonement); the criminal was called 'the bloodstained,' and avenger and criminal thought of each other as the 'enemy.' In north Albania the criminal was also called the 'agent' and the avenger the 'master of the blood of the victim,' i.e. the master of the house in which the victim lived. 'To incur a feud' was 'to fall into blood' or 'enmity.'

A murdered man found his most natural avenger in his brother, especially if they had not separated. If his father was not too old, and his son too young, to bear arms, they shared the brother's obligation. In slightly less degree so did his father's brother and cousin in the male line, and their sons and grandsons, that is to say, all the other males who were in the collective sense his 'father,' 'brother' and 'son,' through being at the time, or having recently been, members of his household. If his son was in the cradle, the child's mother and the neighbors told him of the crime as he grew up and urged him, failing another avenger, not to rest till he had done his duty. No matter which of these relatives took revenge, his 'rifle could be hung up' and 'go to sleep,' to quote the picturesque phrases of Dibër and the North. The lawful representative of his murdered kinsman because he belonged to the same household, he had only made the two sides equal, with one of two results; either peace could be made or the feud continued between the same two families.

A man might kill his enemy where and when he could—in a chance encounter, in a meeting deliberately sought or in a carefully laid ambush. If he was 'strong' with plenty of good shots in his house, he and his family went alone on set expeditions. If he was weak he was probably accompanied by friends, who included friends in the ordinary sense, relatives by marriage, dependents, and servants. They came, not for pay, but on his invitation or of their own accord. Invitations, always verbal, requested the recipients to come with so many rifles to such-and-such a place by such-and-such a day and hour. Those invited were bound to come; those who volunteered were praised by the public for their bravery and devotion, a much coveted distinction. The distance from which they came was immaterial; a feud had no geographical limits.

If the enemy fell to the rifle of a friend, the shot was always credited to the 'master,' who was expected to assume responsibility for it. The enemy accepted the kill as a bout in the feud and either made peace or continued the feud with his original antagonist. The friend who fired the fatal shot could 'hang up his rifle' and let it 'go to sleep'; he did not need its protection for he was quit of the affair. If he had been alone when he killed the man, he would have 'brought the feud home,' i.e. involved himself in a separate feud with the victim's family while leaving his friend's feud unaffected.

In a few cases vengeance was lawfully taken by men who were not, strictly speaking, members of the victim's family. Theoretically, the man who had 'drunk blood' with the victim[1] and so had become his foster-brother could not go alone to avenge him, for he had not been an actual member of his household. In Lumë and Labinot such a man was held to the letter of the law, and could take vengeance only when accompanied by the victim's 'brother'; taking it when alone involved him in a separate feud with the murderer, with no benefit to the victim's family. In many other districts it was recognized that great love must have existed between the two men before they swore blood-brotherhood, and in virtue of that love one could, even when alone, lawfully avenge the other. In Dibër, indeed, he had no choice but to do so, and often outstripped a brother by birth. In Shkrel such vengeance has been taken 'five hundred times.' On the other hand, a compromise was the rule in western Mat. Solitary vengeance by a foster-brother was theoretically as unlawful as in Lumë, but in practice it was generally legalized by the 'master' of the feud, who sent the foster-brother a cartridge and so recognized him after the event as his emissary. Wherever foster-brothers had the right to take solitary vengeance, they seem to have derived it from

---

[1] I.e., had sworn blood-brotherhood with him.

their community of blood with the victim. For only those united by the drinking of blood possessed the right; those united by any other ceremony, by hair-cutting, for instance, were denied it. And in districts where they had the right, one could not go alone to avenge any relative of the other's. During their lifetime each regarded the other's relatives as father, brother, etc., and was regarded by them as son and brother, but when one was killed, the other ranked as an alien by blood and household and could only avenge his foster-brother by joining an expedition led by their 'master.' And almost everywhere, blood-brotherhood was recognized as a complete bar to marriage between the two families.

Relations on the female side could always avenge a murdered man by joining an expedition led by his 'master.' Opinions differed about their right to avenge him when alone. Shkrel, the Malësi e Madhe generally, and Labinot held to the view that a sister's son belonged to his father's family and was an outsider in his mother's. He had, therefore, no right, joint expeditions apart, to avenge or to be avenged by the males in his mother's family. The two men belonged to different households, and if one attempted independently to avenge the other, he meddled in business that was no concern of his and so could only involve himself in a separate feud.

On the other hand, in central and east Albania—in Çermenikë, Dibër, Kurbin, Lumë and Martanesh—it was held that a man could not avenge his maternal 'uncle' but could be avenged by him. The confused practice is locally explained as follows: A man could not avenge his maternal 'uncle' because he was the son of his mother and she as a woman had no rifle, presumably to hand on to him with all its offensive and defensive possibilities; the rifle he carried came to him as a member of his father's family. On the other hand, he could be avenged by his maternal 'uncle' for the same reason that the latter was entitled, when his 'sister's' daughter was married, to receive a 'maternal uncle's fee' at the time of the wedding and, if she was afterwards killed, to avenge her.

'Women do not have rifles' ran the Kanùn. As a corollary, 'Women do not have blood feuds,' it continued. One result of these Kanùns was that women could not properly avenge their murdered relatives. It was also recognized that they were generally too timorous to do so. A few 'strong characters,' however, had been known to lay aside their feminine fears and to kill an enemy. Thus the virgin Emin of Orenjë in Çermenikë avenged her father. When he was killed she was still in the cradle and as she grew up she became aware that her four cousins, the only males left in the family, did not show too much zeal in avenging him. When she was fifteen, she secretly bought a rifle and, seeing the enemy one day come within range of the windows of her home, she fired at him and killed him with the third shot. Then her cousins were trebly annoyed. She, a woman, had proved herself their superior in courage; for her crime one of their lives was forfeit; and they had hoped to compound the feud without further bloodshed, a hope she had destroyed. In fact, she had embittered the feud by putting the enemy to the shame of losing a relative at a woman's hands. Again, a woman from Tërbaç, near Elbasan, hearing that her son had been killed at a third person's instigation, took his revolver and killed the instigator. Unfortunately for her, the date was about 1923 when a modern government was already functioning; she was arrested and tried for murder, but in view of the circumstances she was condemned to no more than a year and a half's imprisonment. The public were astonished to find that the government had punished a woman on much the same terms as a man.

In certain cases both the avenger and the expiator of a murder might be drawn from outside the household directly concerned. For instance, if a murderer and his brother were separated, the avenger might kill the latter while his blood was boiling, a period estimated in Dibër at one hour and in Mirditë and elsewhere at twenty-four hours. When his blood had cooled he must not molest the separated brother, and might be required to find a guarantor that he would not do so. Conversely, a man separated from his murdered brother might avenge him during the regulation period, but not afterwards.

Sometimes the rule of 'boiling blood' was extended to larger units. For twenty-four hours after a murder in Lumë, a district peopled by little groups of kinsmen, any man of the victim's kin might avenge him on any man of the criminal's kin. So long as members of this group survived no other would move. If they were killed off, other groups, beginning with the nearest neighbors, might seek vengeance. Within living memory this license found dreadful expression in Theth, the beautiful northern part of Shalë. About 1890 a man who lost a lamb promised to give a cartridge to a shepherd if he found it. When the shepherd succeeded, the man went back on his promise saying he would 'give him five' (*sc.* fingers on the trigger) instead. For the moment the shepherd let the matter drop, but later met the man and asked once more for his promised reward. Again the man refused it, not too courteously, and was immediately killed by the incensed shepherd. Unfortunately, it was Easter Sunday and the murder took place in a meadow where all the men of Theth were gathered for the festival. Immediately the dead man's *vllazni* (brotherhood), comprising all the males descended from the same ancestor, sought vengeance on the murderer's brotherhood. These were not backward in replying, and within an hour fourteen men lay dead for the sake of one cartridge.

Whole tribes might be affected by the rule of 'boiling blood.' In the Malësi e Madhe if a Kastrati tribesman killed a Koplik man, any member of the latter tribe had license for twenty-four hours to kill any man from Kastrati. The murderer was, therefore, bound to announce his crime at once so that his fellow-tribesmen might take cover. The time limit elapsed, vengeance lay as usual between the two households. In such cases of intertribal aggression each tribe became temporarily a single family in which each member represented the whole.

In Çermenikë, kinsfolk were sometimes fused into one family, not by boiling blood as described above, but by a particularly atrocious murder such as that of a guest by his host, when 'circle after circle' was the rule. The guest's 'circle,' consisting of his own household, his kinsmen in separate homes, his neighbors and the sons of the married daughters of his family, wherever these last might live, tried to kill the murderer, and failing to find him or other members of his household, they might kill one of his 'circle.' On succeeding, they held that they had avenged their relative's death, and their victim's family agreed. In other districts they would have found themselves involved in a new feud with the household of the man they had killed, but by the local rule of 'circle after circle' he died as proxy for the real criminal and no new feud entered into the question. There seems to have been no time limit to their extended vengeance.

National solidarity was recognized in the debatable borderlands where Slav and Albanian lived side by side. If an Albanian was killed by a Slav, any Albanian would kill any Slav in revenge. The crime, it was felt, had pitted the Albanian family against the Slav family. This national sentiment was so strong that though there has never been any love lost between Gegs (north Albanians) and Tosks (south Albanians), no Geg would allow a Slav to kill a Tosk without seeking in return to kill any Slav he could find. The less warlike Tosks did not feel a similar impulse. If one of their number or a Geg were killed by their Bulgarian or Greek neighbors, they left vengeance to the victim's family.

The community also acted as a single family when certain public servants were killed. If the victim were a Roman Catholic priest, he might lawfully be avenged by his parish, the tribe in which the parish lay, and his own family. If action were taken by the parish or tribe, the matter ended. The avenger's act closed the feud, and, fearing no retribution, he could hang up his rifle. If the priest's family afterwards killed another of the murderer's men, they began a new feud. Generally the family did not wait for the parish or the tribe to act. When a Mohammedan or an Orthodox priest was killed, it fell to his relatives to avenge the crime; the feeling that sacrilege had been committed was too slight to drive their parishioners into action.

If a field-guard of Lumë were killed, he was publicly avenged.

If the murderer was from another village, any of the field-guard's fellow-villagers could lawfully kill any man from the murderer's village during the first twenty-four hours, and afterwards he could kill the murderer or any other man in his household. In either case he could hang up his rifle. If the field-guard were killed by a fellow-villager, the village expelled the murderer. On the other hand, if a miller were killed, vengeance rested with his family; the village could not act. A field-guard was a public necessity; without his services the village economy would suffer, and he must be given public protection. A miller had taken up his work for the sake of private gain and was not a public necessity; if he were not at the mill, the villagers themselves could work it; the miller was therefore not entitled to public protection. The village black-smith, with few exceptions a gypsy, was in even worse case than the miller. He was a public necessity, since Albanian peasants will not make horse shoes or farm implements, but he was only a gypsy, and no Albanian community would trouble about so low-class a creature. If he was murdered, only his family would avenge him, and they probably lacked the spirit to do so.

COURSE OF THE FEUD

The fatal shot fired, a murderer's life was in such instant danger from the avenger that it behooved him to fly with all speed. But often his 'blood seized him' so that 'his legs gave way under him' and he was rooted to the spot from shock. Custom therefore prescribed in Shkodër, Lumë and Godolesh that he must drop on the ground a cartridge or an article of clothing such as his fez, sash, or handkerchief; in Elbasan, Shpat and Çermenikë that he must lick the muzzle of his rifle or pistol; alternatively, in Elbasan that he must inhale the smoke of the gunpowder or let his comrades slap his face; in Labinot that he must hold the cartridge case in his mouth and bite his little finger and suck the blood, and in Mat that he must eat a little gunpowder. That done success-fully, 'his blood was set free,' 'the seizure passed,' and he was able to run away.

When an article of clothing was left behind, it served to identify the murderer; where none was left, word had to be sent to the victim's family. It was everywhere 'held dishonorable' to kill and not to tell.

In the early days of a feud the father or brother of the victim might in his furious rage kill the murderer and shoot a second time at the lifeless corpse. When the feud was older, it was not permitted to kill and shoot again. A murderer seldom looked at the corpse, a fact which gave men quick-witted enough to feign death a chance to escape. In some places, such as Mirditë, the murderer was expected to turn the dead man in the right direction for one of his religion—with his head towards the east if Christian, whether Catholic or Orthodox, towards Mecca if Mohammedan, and to rest his rifle against his head; if unable to touch him, he had to tell the first man he met to attend to those matters. In Shpat the murderer left the cartridge case by his victim, allegedly not to 'set his own blood free,' as in Lumë, but to avoid carrying away a thing that was unlucky because stained with blood and sin. In Mat and the Malësi e Madhe, the murderer's own life being in grave danger from the avenger, it was thought 'brave' to tread in the victim's blood as a last insult.

A murderer must not rob his victim; he had killed him only to defend his honor and not to enrich himself. As was popularly said, 'low-class fellows' take a man's rifle, watch, money or clothes; 'good-class men' take only vengeance. Certain exceptions to the rule were admitted. A murderer could everywhere, except in Mirditë, take his victim's rifle to prove that he 'had really trodden in his blood,' but he must afterwards send the weapon to the family. On similar terms he might take the dead man's watch also. When the murderer was a hired assassin, he commonly took a token from his victim, usually his cap, to prove to his paymaster that he had earned his money.

A murderer usually announced his crime to the victim's family by a crude message to fetch him from such-and-such a place and bury him. He was always expected to surrender the body, but if a feud was unusually bitter, the murderer might forbid the body

to be buried in the cemetery in the ordinary way. If he was backed
by enough men to make his ban effective, the body was buried
in the secrecy of night. Sometimes he forbade it to be taken even
at night to the cemetery; in that event it had to be buried elsewhere. A story comes from Sopot in Dibër. About 1893 Abas
Kamber's enemy killed one of his men and forbade him to carry
the body to the cemetery. Abas, strong though he was, could do
nothing but bury it in the courtyard of his house. Just before it
was lowered into the grave, the enemy repented and sent him
leave to bury it in the cemetery. To show that he was not always
prepared to do the enemy's bidding, Abas sent back the message that he would not dig up the body again and concluded that
burial as it had begun.

By rights a man was never buried where he was killed. Even if
the spot were two days distant, or if, like Kol Mali's victim, he
had lain three weeks undiscovered, he was carried home for
burial. 'He had been theirs,' his relatives said, and neither distance
nor a natural repugnance could prevent them from doing their
duty by him.

The ideal was to take vengeance as soon as possible. In Kurbin
the piled stones [at the site of the murder] served to make the
dead man's kinsmen hasten to take vengeance, reminding them
of his death and so 'heating their blood.' For the same purpose
the Catholics of the north frequently buried the man in his bloodstained clothes; the Mohammedans, however, obedient to the
dictum that all who profess their faith must go to the grave in
a clean winding sheet, discarded this custom. A still stranger re-
minder of the need to take vengeance, a little bottle filled with
the dead man's blood, was used all over north Albania and in
Kosovë. This bottle the relatives looked at day and night. As
soon as the blood 'boiled,' i.e. fermented, they seized their rifles,
cocked their skullcaps over one ear to show their determination,
and rushed forth to kill the murderer. If the blood did not 'boil,'
they might accept a money indemnity instead of taking a life.

Public opinion also spurred the avenger on. A man slow to kill
his enemy was thought 'disgraced' and was described as 'low

class' and 'bad.' Among the Highlanders he risked finding that other men had contemptuously come to sleep with his wife, his daughter could not marry into a 'good' family and his son must marry a 'bad' girl. As far south as Godolesh on the outskirts of Elbasan, he paid visits at his peril; his coffee cup was only half-filled, and before being handed to him it was passed under the host's left arm, or even his left leg, to remind him of his disgrace. He was often mocked openly.

All over north Albania it was permissible for the victim's kin to burn down the murderer's house. In hot blood an avenger might in some places do as much material damage as possible to the murderer, burning his hay as well as his house, scything his ripening grain and harrowing over his growing maize. For fear of reprisals in kind he could nowhere harm his children or animals.

With poverty as general and murder as frequent as they used to be, it is obvious that if burning the murderer's stone house and destroying his crops had been freely permitted, the life of the tribe could not have gone on. To restrict the attacks on property, sanctions were introduced. In Dibër an avenger guilty of incendiarism was banished in perpetuity by the community. In Krujë the crime was deprecated as doubly unwise; it might cause further deaths, so involving the avenger in further feuds, and women and children might be among the victims, in which case the avenger would be covered with disgrace. In Shpat an avenger who burned his enemy's house found the whole community against him as a man willing to burn women and children to death and to harm property; in Shpat property was so sacrosanct that one must not touch even 'the leaf of the leek' belonging to one's enemy.

When an avenger burned down the murderer's house in hot blood, his motive was to do the murderer as much damage as possible. When he burned it down in cold blood, his motive was to drive the murderer into the open to be shot at. A murderer not infrequently shut himself up in his house during the daytime and stirred outside only at night, so remaining beyond the avenger's reach. When his house was set on fire, he knew that if he remained inside the blazing building, his death was certain, and that if he came out, he had a sporting chance of escaping the avenger's bullets. He had, therefore, no choice but to leave the burning house.

EXPIATOR AND EXPIATION

In most cases of murder one life only was forfeit to the avenger; 'one for one' was the formula. This was irrespective of the social standing or the character of the victim.

The formula of 'one for one' was disregarded only in a few cases. In Lumë, a district which prided itself on its 'spirit,' 'two for one' was the rule when a man killed his social superior; nothing less would content his victim's injured pride. In most districts a man who suffered the more grievous forms of bereavement, losing his wife, guest or child at a murderer's hands, took double or even triple vengeance. In the Malësi e Madhe the victim's family, if 'strong' with all the pride that the epithet denotes, might kill two of the murderer's relatives if they found them together, though not otherwise. Spiro Toli of Shënjon, near Elbasan, a man as proud as any Lumjan of his 'spirit,' felt so degraded when his brother was killed by a hireling at another's bidding, and that hireling a gypsy, that he killed both the instigator and the hireling. Pride, of course, was the ruling motive in every blood feud. By his successful crime the murderer had proved himself the better man, and the victim could not endure this inferiority and was bound to strike back in kind.

The person of the expiator seems to have undergone an historical development. Long ago, 'blood feuds went by the finger,' that is to say, only the actual murderer, the man whose finger had pulled the trigger, was made to expiate his crime. In modern times the merging of the individual in his family was stressed as in the case of the avenger, and expiation might be made by any male who lived in the same house as the murderer and was in either the actual or classificatory sense his 'father,' 'brother' or 'son.'

This rule was subject to several important reservations. The man killed in the murderer's stead must not be too old, feeble-minded, or physically frail to carry arms, for such men were counted women, and women could not be killed in blood feuds. If the avenger killed such a man, he lost caste, was publicly branded as 'low class' and made it certain that the feud would not be closed. It was also illegal to kill boys who were still too young to carry arms, that is to say, under fifteen or in some cases twenty. In the Malësi e Madhe, however, it was held that one must take vengeance where one could, and that in default of an adult enemy one might kill a boy. Even in that region such a crime was not committed except by a very bad man or one who was frenzied with rage at the recent murder of a relative or other-wise. For instance, in 1933 a subaltern of the Alije family, whose wife had been carried off by another Dibran, refrained for some years from avenging the insult in the way demanded by mountain law. Taunted with this restraint at a chance meeting in a café, he put aside the civilization acquired during his military education in Albania and in Italy and rushed for his revolver. As he was unable to find the man who had taunted him, he lay in wait for the latter's schoolboy son, aged fourteen, and shot him dead.

A particularly nasty case was reported about 1932 from Shalë, one of the most backward regions of Albania. While two families were quarreling about a piece of land, the wife of Grimës one day voiced her opinions so volubly in Gjelosh's house that he lost his temper and pushed her out. She fell down some steps by the door and bruised her hip. She showed the bruise to the gendarmerie, who were sympathetic enough to arrest Gjelosh and to imprison him for three months. The woman, who cared more for the viola-tion of her honor by the push than for the bruise, was not satisfied and instigated her son, a boy of twelve or thirteen, to vindicate her honor by killing Gjelosh's son, who was of the same age. Since the boys habitually herded their goats together, her son found an opportunity of pushing the other boy over a rock and, as he lay there helpless he stoned him till he died. Then Gjelosh, still in prison, paid a man to kill the little murderer. Grimës retorted by killing Gjelosh's remaining son and dooming Gjelosh's family to extinction.

Two instances, both from Beshkash in western Mat, in which a child was killed by a woman in revenge for the death of a relative, are recorded. In the first (about 1918) the only son of Pushko Zefi of Beshkash had been killed, and the cousins, who were his natural avengers, did not seem inclined to do their duty. Maddened by their inaction, the victim's sister, who was married in Perlat, took the opportunity provided by a visit to her old home and called at the enemy's house. On being left alone for a moment with a small boy in the kitchen, she cut his throat. Another woman in Beshkash, crazed by the murder of her grown-up son by Pal Dede Hajo, went to Pal's house and cut off the head of a little boy she found asleep in his cradle.

Since women do not have rifles or blood feuds according to the Kanùn, a woman could not possibly be killed to avenge a murder. It follows that when a woman avenged a murdered relative, she could not be killed in return, and indeed this did not happen very often. The tabu on killing a woman in any circumstances was reinforced by all the forces of public opinion and superstition. Killing a woman save when taken in adultery or incorrigible pilfering was the most disgraceful thing that an Albanian could do. Only one who came from 'a low-class family' would do it, he never again had any luck with his rifle and he could not hope to have his crime pardoned, but must wash away his crime with his blood. He need pay with only one life, but if his victim was a married woman, he could hardly hope to save it, for two or even three families sought to take it. The dead woman's husband wished to avenge his wife, her father his daughter, and, in Martanesh, her maternal uncle his niece. At Shënjon, near Elbasan, the father asked the husband if he meant to kill the enemy; if from cowardice or weakness he said no, the father at once set about tracking down the enemy. Since 'rifles can't weigh'—that is, discriminate—a woman was sometimes shot accidentally in a man's stead in spite of the tabu. In that unhappy event in Kurbin a woman in the murderer's family might be killed in return. If, too, a feud was unusually bitter, as was, for instance, the Kaloshi family one in Dibër, all barriers of law and disgrace were thrown down; 'kill at all costs' was the order of the day, and in its execution women and children were as likely as men to suffer.

One more class of expiator remains to be considered. It sometimes happened that a man hired an outsider to kill his enemy. In the Breg i Matit some held that such a man was a 'witch,' and since witches could not have blood feuds, he must go scotfree and his hireling suffer, like any other murderer. In most places, if the instigator could not be discovered, or if time was passing without vengeance being taken on him, the hireling was killed. These practices were exceptional, and in general the feud was credited to the principal rather than to the subordinate who fired the fatal shot.

Vanity as well as justice came into the question, for the instigator was usually a more important person than his instrument, and killing him brought the avenger more glory.

If expiation took the form of blood money, no distinction was made for age; the payment for a worn-out man of eighty or an able-bodied man of thirty was the same as for a boy of five or an infant of a few weeks. As when a life was taken for a life, no distinction was made for social standing or moral character; the payment for a bajraktar was the same as for a laborer. A female's 'blood,' however, cost only half a male's. In the early days when these payments were determined, money was so distributed that the rich had a great deal, while the poor, who formed the bulk of the population, were all but penniless. The fear of having to pay a large sum in blood money was therefore a considerable deterrent against murder.

Blood money was accepted only in Mirditë and north Albania. Elsewhere it was scorned. Neither lived up to its pretensions, the north being more truculent and the other districts less truculent than they claimed. In the Malësi e Madhe, only weak, low-class families would accept blood money; if other families did so, they were held to have 'disgraced themselves.'

Given the stigma attached to blood money, it was seldom paid except in lighter cases. After an accidental murder, for instance, honor was in most places satisfied by a money payment. For example, two men of Krujë were examining a revolver together, not knowing it was loaded, when it went off suddenly and killed one of them. The other was held guilty of murder, but in view of the circumstances escaped with a payment of twenty-five napoleons, the conventional six purses.

Accidental though a murder might be, the murderer could not rely on saving his life with blood money. Especially while the crime was fresh, he was well advised to lie low until responsible men had weighed the case and confirmed its accidental character. After paying the money he was not absolutely safe unless he found a guarantor.

In Mirditë when blood money was accepted the murderer had also to pay fines of 100 rams and one ox to the tribe and of 500 grosh (piastres, i.e. one purse) to the family of the Hereditary Captain of Mirditë; the animals were eaten at a public banquet by the tribe. These fines were imposed on the murderer for disturbing the public peace. In cases of accidental murder, however, no fine was payable; the formula ran: 'The rifle which kills accidentally entails blood (really blood money) for blood, but not a fine or pursuit.'

The payment of blood money also solved the difficulties in certain cases of murder within the family where atonement had to be made, yet could not properly be exacted in the form of a life for a life. For instance, if two brothers in Shkrel had separate households, when one killed the other's wife for any but a question of honor, the victim's husband could not kill his own brother for her sake but had the right to exact blood money; after all, he had been unjustly deprived of his wife's services and must buy another wife. If a married woman in Shkrel were killed, again unreservedly, by some member of her husband's family, her son, if fifteen years of age or more, could not kill the murderer, his own relative, but exacted blood money. In Shalë another principle came into play. If the dead man's relatives did not succeed in killing the murderer within seven years, they accepted blood money.

A murderer might also expiate his crime, voluntarily or involuntarily, by exile. If voluntarily, he ran away fearing for his life, but only a weak man who was personally a coward, or had few adult males in his family to keep the enemy at bay, consented to show the white feather. Voluntary exile might be temporary or permanent.

A normal exile's hope of ending his feud lay in several directions. The victim's family might become so weakened by other blood feuds that they knew themselves to be no longer formidable and sank their pride enough to accept blood money in full payment. They might even become poor enough to be tempted by the offer of money. Or they might consider an absence of ten or twenty years' duration as part atonement and for the rest content themselves with blood money. They might even, on the intervention of friends, forgive the crime outright.

Voluntary exile might become premanent for several reasons. It might, for instance, be so protracted that the murderer grew used to his new surroundings and, ceasing to hanker for his old home, settled down where he was. Again, an exiled murderer sometimes prospered so much that he found it to his interest to stay away permanently. If he found the climate or the soil of his new home kindlier, he might sell his paternal holding through an intermediary and with the proceeds buy land in his new home. Sometimes an exiled murderer set up a small business, selling cigarettes and cleaning shoes, and made money as he could never have done in his mountain village. Sometimes, too, he entered the service of a rich man and in return for his devotion was given a grant of land.

The emergence of a central government which punished murder tended to increase the number of permanent exiles and to make the strong as well as the weak run away. An Albanian would face boldly enough the vengeance of his victim's relatives, but he detested being imprisoned by the government. A man of Bashabun, near Elbasan, killed a neighbor years ago. Blood money was

paid, and so far as his victim's family was concerned, he was free
to return home. Unwilling, however, to serve the short term of
imprisonment to which the government would condemn him, he
remained in exile in Bosnia.

Sometimes a murderer did not run away of his own accord, but
was forcibly expelled by the community. Although when murder
was not punished by government, only the weak ran away voluntarily, the community expelled a strong man as readily as a weak
one. In tribal districts like Mirditë which contained several villages, the murderer's village could not expel him without the
other villages' consent and help. If the village resisted the expulsion, the tribe as a whole had the right to 'proclaim' the village
or to call in other tribes to bring it to reason. In small tribes like
Nikaj the murderer's kinsmen could expel him independently of
the tribe. In nontribal districts like Shpat, where each village was a
self-contained unit, it needed to ask no one before expelling a
murderer.

A man sentenced to communal expulsion was always one
whose crime struck at the roots of society as understood in the
mountains. Perhaps he had violated the acknowledged sanctity of
the 'pledged word' by killing his enemy during a public truce or
even after making peace with him. Perhaps he had infringed the
sacred laws of hospitality by killing his host or guest. Perhaps he
threatened family solidarity by killing a cousin to get his land.
Perhaps he had killed a man to steal his rifle and thereby as good
as robbed him of his manhood, for a man without a rifle is as
nothing, no better than a woman. Perhaps he had committed
sacrilege by killing someone, possibly the priest himself, inside
the territory of church or mosque, or by breaking into the church
to steal.

For any such antisocial murder no ordinary vengeance, no
pardon, was possible. The community assembled and passed judgment in the time-honored formula that so-and-so 'is burned,
roasted, cut down and expelled from the tribe.' Without loss of
time—probably immediately after passing sentence—they burned
the man's house, killed, roasted and ate his sheep, goats and

cows, cut down his trees, and drove him into exile. They further required him to make public confession of his guilt by himself applying the burning brand to his house. In Mirditë and elsewhere he had at the same time to make himself a public scapegoat, saying as he lit the fire, 'On my head be the ill luck of the village and the tribe.' If he and the other men in the house who were qualified to represent him refused to set the house alight, the head of his clan bade his next nearest relative do so. The fire once started, the whole village or tribe kept it going until its work was done, for it was essential that the whole community should take part in executing the communal sentence. But they could not touch the fire until the criminal had lighted it. In the same way, the murderer had to be the first to apply the ax to his trees and vines; if he jibbed, his nearest relative took his place and the work was completed by the whole community. If he had a vegetable garden it was destroyed in the same fashion. On the same day all his edible livestock was roasted and consumed by the community at a public banquet. This was by way of a fine. He himself, with his wife and children, was escorted to the tribal frontier to make sure that he was not killed on the way. At the frontier he was ordered never to return again. In Shpat he was literally drummed out of the village; the community hired gypsies to lead the way beating drums, and all the men sang to mark their joy at getting rid of a bad character.

The community destroyed the murderer's house, fruit trees, and livestock not to punish him directly for his crime, but to make it impossible for him to defy the sentence of exile by remaining in his home. For the essential feature of their sentence was the condemnation to exile, the expulsion of an undesirable, of one whose act had dishonored the whole tribe and must be repudiated by the whole tribe. Since robbery was not their motive, the murderer was free to take his money with him; in any case, it could not be seen, securely hidden as it was in a purse in his armpit.

If the murderer did not choose to go into exile of his own accord, he was condemned by the avenger to virtual imprisonment in his house. Sometimes he shut himself up voluntarily; more often, especially in north Albania, he was peremptorily ordered to do so by the avenger. For the period of his 'imprisonment' fear that the avenger was lurking near prevented him from stirring outside during the daytime and restricted his movements to the night hours. If he left home, he had by dawn to find shelter under a friend's roof, and he could not continue his travels until the next night fell. These disabilities were his so long as he eluded the avenger, and he might do so for years, as in the case of a native of Sheshaj who had been shut up by his enemy for twenty-five years. At Belsh in Dumre, as a result of this confinement, two men who had been shut up for twelve years were 'waxen and yellow as the dead.' They longed to walk in the sunlight and were bored indoors, where they could do nothing to pass the time except strip maize and knit (knitting is one of the staple occupations of the men, but not the women, in Dumre). But they could not help themselves, since it was certain death to step outside during the daytime.

Just as the murderer's house could not be burned down in case women and children perished in the conflagration, so his 'imprisonment' could not be allowed to stop the work of the family in case women and children died of starvation. There were several provisions for carrying on the work. The first was the law that women, children, servants and domestic animals must not be shut up. So in comparative security the able-bodied women, on whom fell the heaviest burden, tilled the fields, went to market, ground corn at the mill and fetched water from the spring and firewood from the forest. The boys and aged women herded the cows, sheep and goats. The servants took part in any or all of these tasks, but few households could afford the luxury of servants.

When an avenger felt too bitter to release indefinitely one or more men in the imprisoned murderer's household, he was sometimes induced to make a minor concession. When all the men were shut up, women were able to hoe, to carry manure, to sow seed, to reap wheat and to harvest maize successfully, but they could not plough—so it was believed in north, though not in south, Albania, where the wives of many emigrants must to this day plough if they and their children are to eat. There was therefore danger in north Albania that if all the men were shut up during the ploughing season, the family would, in spite of the women's efforts, starve. This led to a ticket-of-leave system, called *besë,* literally 'pledged word,' 'truce,' or *kuvend,* 'agreement.' At the instance of a mutual friend the avenger granted the murderer leave for one or more men in his household to come out and work his land for a stipulated period, varying from three to twelve months. As so often, the forces of public opinion reinforced the friend's urgings; indeed, it was said of an avenger who refused his enemy leave to plough that he 'was not to be entered in the register,' i.e. could not be classed as a man, and of one who did not that he was both brave and honorable.

In Dukagjin the kanun of murder was so stern that neither the murderer nor his womenfolk were allowed to work his land if the avenger was strong. Indeed, the avenger often worked it and carried home the produce, leaving the murderer's household dependent on charity. At best the elders fixed a sum to be paid by the murderer for leave to work his own land: the money paid, the avenger gave his word not to molest him; or a 'strong' friend guaranteed his safety as he tilled his fields. This arrangement continued until he was killed elsewhere or the avenger consented to make peace.

Various devices were tried to outwit an avenger too venomous to make the smallest concession to his 'imprisoned' enemy. The commonest was for the murderer to let his land to a neutral on the usual Albanian terms of 'halves.' Once some men of Lurë, trusting to the prevailing immunity of women from attack, dressed in their wives' clothes and went out to work. They were soon discovered and compelled to return home. Frequently a woman was made to work alongside the men, the assumption being that from fear of accidentally hitting the women and so disgracing himself the avenger would not fire on the party. The man who murdered the brother of Kodhel Dede of Nezhar in Shpat be-

longed to a large family, the members of which went to work with
a woman between every two men. Kodhel thus found it impossible
to kill one of them and after a long period of years made peace.
Sometimes a man's wife kept watch while he worked; if she
signaled the enemy's approach, he seized his rifle and prepared
to defend himself. During Kodhel Dede's feud with the Trepsani-
shti family he found himself long balked by the vigilance of his
enemy's wife. At last his chance came on the eve of 15 August.
The wife had her mind set on making *melata* (sacrificial foods)
for distribution on the festival, and, forgetting her husband who
was at work on the threshing floor, she went home to make them.
Kodhel, who had crept up through a maize field, shot her husband
as soon as her back was turned. In the hilly landscape of Fulqet
in west Mat a different sort of watch was kept. The 'imprisoned'
men, aided by friends, dug a hole on top of a hill commanding
a wide view. One of their best shots, rifle in hand, settled down
in this hole ready to snipe the avenger if he tried to kill any of
the men at work.

Work in the fields apart, an 'imprisoned' murderer might for
short periods leave his house under escort of a friend. This friend
had to be 'strong,' otherwise the murderer might be killed by his
enemy, a lasting disgrace to the man whose protégé he was for
the time being. Sometimes murderer and avenger had a common
friend who took the former out; in that case the friend ran less
risk of losing his protégé, but even so he had to be fairly 'strong.'
In Mat such a friend might take the murderer out three times with
impunity. Afterwards he was sure to receive a message from the
avenger which ran, 'Don't stir out again. Stay indoors. It was for
your sake that I didn't fire.'

In the majority of cases the murderer neither ran away nor
was shut up, but went about his normal business, taking certain
precautions. An Albanian never despised his enemy; the strongest
man will say, 'I am stronger than he is, but a rifle doesn't care for
bravery, a rifle kills.' He remembers also that an enemy is ever
on the watch: 'A wooden stake rots, but an enemy doesn't.'

The first precaution a hunted man had to take at home was

never to answer the door himself. Another precaution commonly taken by a 'wanted' man was to live in a house of more than one story. Such a house never had more than slits for windows in the ground floor, and those in the upper room were square holes without glass, across which stone shutters were drawn at night. In Çermenikë the outside staircase that led down to the stables on the ground floor was always fenced in carefully with wood. For greater security the women lived on the ground floor protecting the men who lived above. If a man were rich enough, he built a high wall round the house; this gave him the freedom of his courtyard. In this case all the windows looked inwards on the court; the outer walls were blank save for the loopholes. A still richer man, or one with many enemies, had several doors in his courtyard wall and watchtowers at strategic points. (The turrets at each corner and in the middle of the long walls effectually commanded these entrances, and many loopholes in the walls provided space for many defenders to shoot from.) Shevqet Bey Verlaci of Elbasan had several posterns in his garden wall, each commanded by a watchtower and each providing him in case of need with a possible means of escape.

Failing armed attendants, a hunted man was not without protectors on his journey. In districts where women were immune, a woman's company, on a journey as at work, was sufficient. In Mat it was a protection to have a foreigner in front of you, for a foreigner was as sacred as a woman. This held for most districts of Albania.

The principle of the guest's sacrosanctity was often invoked. If a guest of an important man in Dibër had an enemy and was traveling alone, his host would give him an attendant when he left. This attendant must see him safely to his next destination; should any harm befall him on the way his powerful host would avenge him. The protection, and with it the obligation, of his host ended by nightfall, for he would by then have either reached home or become the guest of another man. His journey being thus limited to a day's duration, the mere fact of his being accompanied by the attendant would generally suffice to keep him safe, for within the radius of a day's journey, on foot, everybody knew everybody else, and on his being seen in the company of the attendant, it was at once recognized whose guest he had been and who his avenger would be.

It sometimes happened that a hunted man, when paying a visit to a friend, found his enemy was his fellow guest. This was natural enough, for especially where both belonged to the same village, hunter and hunted always had a number of mutual friends. All over Albania the two enemies, being fellow guests, did not molest each other, but rather, out of courtesy to their host, talked together as if nothing divided them. In the old days they would in Çermenikë even shoot at a target together without turning their rifles on each other. In Çermenikë the hunted man's immunity was not quite complete, varying according to his behavior. If he cocked his fez to one side and held his head high, his enemy might kill him even at their common host's in his exasperation at his effrontery. If, on the other hand, the murderer pushed his fez straight to the back of his head and kept his head down, his enemy would almost certainly not touch him till both had left the house. Sometimes hunter and hunted were invited to the same wedding or funeral feast. Then the same rules of courtesy came into play. The enemies sat at one table, ate out of the common dish, passed each other their tobacco boxes and drank coffee side by side. If toasts were drunk among the Highlanders, they would not drink to each other's health nor would they willingly address each other, but otherwise they gave little sign of their enmity.

PEACE-MAKING

Peace was seldom made until the same number had been killed on both sides. If the first man was only wounded, and in revenge killed his enemy, the elders made the first pay wound money, half a blood, so as to make it 'one for one.' In the same way if three, say, were killed on one side and two killed and one wounded on the other, peace was made on condition that the latter side should pay one wound money; then two killed, one wounded, and one wound money paid made the equivalent of the three killed on the enemy's side.

Peace was always made through an intermediary. If it were directly solicited by the hunted, the enemy's triumph would know no bounds, and he would arrogantly refuse to grant the other's request. But he could not indefinitely turn a deaf ear to the pleadings of friends; to do so risked quarreling with them. 'You've shot enough,' they said, as though to convince him that he had vindicated his honor. 'Forgive him, we beg you,' they added. At length he replied, 'All right, I've forgiven him.' Sometimes not private friends, but a whole tribe, through their spokesman, intervened.

The ceremony of ratifying the promise of forgiveness varied from place to place. In Shpat the original criminal must take the initiative and go to his enemy's house, escorted for safety's sake by at least one friend. The enemy came to meet him in the open air, but did not offer him his hand, for a man reserves his hand for his friends. Then both went into the house, the coffee, the all-essential to a peacemaking, was soon served, followed perhaps by a meal with meat. Both coffee and meal were 'like a funeral,' enlivened by next to no conversation and with little cordiality of mien. A day or two later the enemy must go to the original criminal's house, and the same ceremonies were gone through. Alternate visits had to be paid for some time, until at last the original enemy declared that he had forgiven the other. A marriage very often cemented the peacemaking.

New elements were introduced farther north, for example, in Krasniqë. Accompanied by six to eight men, the man originally at fault, with his hands tied behind his back, went unexpectedly on a festive evening to his enemy's house. The host, as in duty bound, said, 'Come in!' and invited them to sit down. They refused to do so until in sign of forgiveness he untied his enemy's hands. He never refused, for he said, 'Better forgive and forget one dead man than quarrel with ten living ones.' If he had not granted their request, the murderer's escort would never have visited his house again. That night the uninvited guest ate a meal

at the involuntary host's house, and the next day the man forgiven carried them all off to his house, where he provided a meal
with meat pasty and sweets.

In Lumë the murderer was thrust into his enemy's house before dawn so that his enemy might not see him coming; no notice
of his coming was given beforehand. If the host did not untie his
hands, the friends who accompanied him refused to drink coffee;
the host always yielded to the threat of this disgrace.

In Kurbin peace was made by the same methods as in Lumë
and Krasniqë. The murderer, who had the sailor collar of his
jacket thrown over his head, a sign of mourning and penitence,
as well as his hands tied behind his back, a sign of helplessness,
remained standing near the door, while his friends sat down
round the hearth. The host gave coffee to them, but not to him;
his forgiveness was not yet assured, and without such assurance
he could not drink his coffee. The friends pleaded with the host to
untie his hands; they threatened as well as pleaded saying, 'If
you like, forgive him—otherwise kill us along with him.' At length
one of two things happened. The host consented to pardon the
murderer, got up to throw down his collar and to untie his hands,
and bade him sit down and drink coffee, saying, 'You are pardoned, friend.' More frequently, he said he could not at once
pardon the man, but would give him a truce of six months, a
year, or more; in sign of his mollification he probably gave him
coffee, though he sent him away with his hands still tied behind
his back and his collar over his head.

Friends were not the only interveners. Occasionally the Turk-
ish Government took a hand, declaring on penalty of imprisonment, internment and burning out that all feuds more than seven
years old were to be compounded by a money payment and not
reopened. When during the 1914–18 war Austria-Hungary was in
occupation of all north Albania, she also ordered blood feuds
to be ended with a money payment; the resentment of Çermenikë
at this attempt to force them to make peace on northern terms
is still hot. Sometimes a whole community itself interfered. The
procedure of west Mat was typical. When a man had been killed

on either side and the feud was 'one for one,' the neighbors took effective steps to prevent its continuance. They each forbade the avenger to come on his land to kill his enemy; if he did so, he would be considered a trespasser and would have a feud with the owner. If, after this warning, the neighbor saw the avenger trying to kill his enemy on his land, he shot at him, and if he killed him, he had no feud, for he had forbidden him to raise his rifle on his land.

Religious influences were also brought to bear on the two enemies. The Bojdani sheikh of Bicaj in Lumë often intervened when there was shooting, both before and after the murder was committed; telling both parties they were in the wrong, he induced them to make peace. There is no record known to the author of an Orthodox priest acquiring influence enough to end a feud, and a Roman Catholic parish priest, though not ridiculed by his flock as his Orthodox brother too often was, had no power to curse people who kept up blood feuds, and without such power he could not compose a feud. Even a bishop was powerless in such cases. Jesuits, on the other hand, had the power and on occasion exercised it; it is commonly believed to this day that they are sent by the Pope and they are correspondingly feared. Every ten years or so, summoned by the archbishop or the priest in charge, at the instance of the village, they toured the Roman Catholic districts, their main object being to compose blood feuds. In 1932 three priests went to Shkrel for the best part of a week. Due warning of their advent had been given, and all devout Roman Catholics were bidden to attend church every day. Banners depicting the flames of hell and the crimes which earned them were hung round the church and the sermons were in the same strain. On the second day these placed emphasis on the privileged position of Roman Catholics; in return for this good Catholics should settle their blood feuds rather than risk losing the blessing of the church for themselves and their families during their lifetime and after it burial in consecrated ground. On the third day the priests inveighed against keeping up grudges; those who cherished their blood feuds risked the curse of God. This meant that nothing would go right for them. They would be shunned by everyone—an engaged girl could not marry with the blessing of the Church, but only by civil marriage—if indeed her betrothed did not prefer to give her up, although this meant losing her bride-price. On this occasion in Shkrel the vehemence of the priests' exhortations and the fear of the consequences of the curse resulted in the termination of several outstanding feuds.

BIBLIOGRAPHY

Barton, R. F.
  1919 *Ifugao Law.* University of California Publications in Archaeology and Ethnology, Vol. 15.
Best, Elsdon
  1902 "Notes on the Art of War as Conducted by the Maori of New Zealand," *Journal of the Polynesian Society,* XI.
  1903a "Maori Marriage Customs," *Transactions and Proceedings of the New Zealand Institute,* XXXVI, 14–67.
  1903b "Notes on the Art of War as Conducted by the Maori of New Zealand," *Journal of the Polynesian Society,* XII.
  1904 "Notes on the Art of War as Conducted by the Maori of New Zealand," *Journal of the Polynesian Society,* XIII.
  1924a *The Maori.* Polynesian Society Memoir No. 5, 2 vols. Wellington: Board of Maori Ethnological Research.
  1924b *The Maori as He Was.* N.Z. Board of Sciences and Art Manual No. 4. Wellington: Dominion Museum.
  1925 *Tuhoe, the Children of the Mist.* Polynesian Society Memoir No. 6, 2 vols. New Plymouth: Avery.
  1927 *The Pa Maori.* Dominion Museum Bulletin No. 6. Wellington: Dominion Museum.
  1942 *Forest Lore of the Maori.* Polynesian Society Memoir No. 19. Wellington: Polynesian Society.
Bohannan, Paul
  1957 *Justice and Judgment Among the Tiv.* London: Oxford University Press.
  1963 *Social Anthropology.* New York: Holt, Rinehart and Winston.
Bryant, Alfred T.
  1929 *Olden Times in Zululand and Natal, containing earlier history of the Eastern-Nguni clans.* London: Longmans, Green and Co.
Buck, Peter H.
  1949 *The Coming of the Maori.* Wellington: Whitcombe and Tombs.
Buller, James
  1878 *Forty Years in New Zealand.* London: Hodder and Stoughton.
Bunzel, Ruth
  1932 *Introduction to Zuni Ceremonialism.* Bureau of American Ethnology Forty-seventh Annual Report (1929–30). Washington, D.C.

Burridge, Kenelm O. L.
1957 "Friendship in Tangu," *Oceania*, XXVII, No. 3, March, pp. 177–89.
Carstairs, Robert
1912 *The Little World of an Indian District Officer*. London: Macmillan.
Cockayne, L.
1928 *The Vegetation of New Zealand*. Vol. XIV of *Die Vegetation der Erde*. Leipzig: Engelmann.
Colden, Cadwallader
1958 *The History of the Five Indian Nations: Depending on the Province of New-York in America*. Ithaca: Great Seal Books.
Colenso, W.
1880 "Historical Incidents and Traditions of the Olden Times, pertaining to the Maoris of the North Island (East Coast), New Zealand," *Transactions and Proceedings of the New Zealand Institute*, XIII, 38–57.
Commons, J. R.
1901 "A New Way of Settling Labor Disputes," *American Review of Reviews*, Vol. 23.
Davis, C. O. B.
1855 *The Renowned Chief Kawiti and Other New Zealand Warriors*. Auckland: Lambert.
Denig, Edwin T.
1930 *Indian Tribes of the Upper Missouri*. Ed. by J. N. B. Hewitt. Bureau of American Ethnology *Forty-sixth Annual Report* (1928–29). Washington, D.C.
De Smet, Pierre Jean
1905 *Life, Letters and Travels of Father Pierre Jean De Smet*. Ed. by H. M. Chittenden and A. T. Richardson. 4 vols. New York: F. P. Harper.
Doty, James
1853 *Reports on the Indian Tribes of the Blackfoot Nation*. Pacific Railroad Reports, Vol. I.
Downes, T. W.
1929 "Maori Etiquette," *Journal of the Polynesian Society*, XXXVIII, 148–68.
Evans-Pritchard, E. E.
1940 *The Nuer*. Oxford: The Clarendon Press.
Firth, Raymond
1927 "Maori Hill-forts," *Antiquity*, I, 66–78.
1929 *Primitive Economics of the New Zealand Maori*. London: Routledge.
Frank, Jerome D.
1955 "Group Methods in Psychotherapy," in *Mental Health and Mental Disorder: A Sociological Approach*, Arnold Rose, ed. New York: W. W. Norton and Company.
Gibbs, James L., Jr.
1962 "Poro Values and Courtroom Procedures in a Kpelle Chiefdom," *Southwestern Journal of Anthropology*, Vol. 18.

Gibson, James Young
  1911 *The Story of the Zulus*. London: Longmans, Green and Co.
Gluckman, Max
  1955 *The Judicial Process among the Barotse of Northern Rhodesia*. Manchester: Manchester University Press; Glencoe, Illinois: The Free Press.
  1958 *Analysis of a Social Situation in Modern Zululand*. The Rhodes-Livingstone Papers 28. Manchester: Manchester University Press.
  1960 "The Rise of the Zulu Empire," *Scientific American* 202 April 1960, 157–68.
Gomme, George Lawrence
  1880 *Primitive Folkmoots: Open-Air Assemblies in Britain*. London: S. Low, Marston, Searle and Rivington.
Grinnell, George Bird
  1910 "Coup and Scalp among the Plains Indians," *American Anthropologist*, Vol. 12.
Gudgeon, T. W.
  1885 *The History and Doings of the Maoris*. Auckland: Brett.
Gudgeon, W. E.
  1895 "The Maori Tribes of the East Coast of New Zealand," *Journal of the Polynesian Society*, III, 208–19.
  1904 "The Toa Taua or Warrior," *Journal of the Polynesian Society*, XIII, 238–64.
  1907a "Maori Wars," *Journal of the Polynesian Society*, XVI, 13–42.
  1907b "The Tohunga Maori," *Journal of the Polynesian Society*, XVI, 69–91.
Gurvitch, Georges
  1947 *Sociology of Law*. London: Kegan Paul, Trench, Trubner and Co., Ltd.
Gusinde, M.
  1937 *Die Feuerland Indianer—Die Yamana* (vol. 2, Mödling bei Wien: Publikation Anthropos).
Hadlock, Wendell S.
  1947 "War among the Northeastern Woodland Indians," *American Anthropologist*, Vol. 49, 204–21.
Hall, Francis
  1823 "Extracts from the Journal of Mr. Francis Hall," in *Missionary Register for MDCCCXXIII*. London: Seeley.
Hart, H. L. A.
  1954 "Definition and Theory in Jurisprudence," *Law Quarterly Review*, 70:37.
Henderson, G. M.
  1948 *The Antecedents and Early Life of Valentine Savage, Known as Taina*. Wellington: Wingfield Press.
Hobley, Charles W.
  1910 *Ethnology of the A-Kamba and other East African Tribes*. Cambridge: Cambridge University Press.

Hochstetter, Ferdinand von
   1867 *New Zealand*. Stuttgart: Cotta.
Hoebel, E. Adamson
   1936 "Associations and the State in the Plains," *American Anthropologist*,
      Vol. 38, 433–38.
   1939 "Comanche and Hekandkika Shoshone Relationship Systems,"
      American Anthropologist, Vol. 41.
   1940 *The Political Organization and Law-Ways of the Comanche Indi-
      ans*. Memoirs of the American Anthropological Association No. 54.
      Menasha.
   1954 *The Law of Primitive Man: A Study in Comparative Legal Dy-
      namics*. Cambridge: Harvard University Press.
Hohfeld, W. N.
   1923 *Fundamental Legal Conceptions as Applied in Judicial Reasoning
      and Other Essays*. Edited by W. W. Cook. New Haven: Yale University
      Press.
Holm, G.
   1914 *Ethnological Sketch of the Angmagssalik Eskimo*. Medelelser om
      Grønland, Vol. 39.
Howell, P. P.
   1954 *A Handbook of Nuer Law*. London: Oxford University Press.
Howitt, Alfred W.
   1904 *The Native Tribes of South-east Australia*. New York: Macmillan.
Hunt, George T.
   1940 *The Wars of the Iroquois: A Study in Intertribal Trade Relations*.
      Madison: University of Wisconsin Press.
Johansen, J. Prytz
   1954 *The Maori and His Religion in Its Non-Ritualistic Aspects*. Copen-
      hagen: Ejnar Munksgaard.
Jones, Harry W.
   1962 "Law and the Idea of Mankind," *Columbia Law Review* 62:
      752–72.
Kane, Paul (ed. J. W. Garvin)
   1925 *Wanderings of an Artist Among the Indians of North America*.
      Toronto: The Radisson Society of Canada.
Kantorowicz, Herman
   1958 *The Definition of Law*. Cambridge: University Press.
Kelly, Leslie G.
   1949 *Tainui*. Polynesian Society Memoir No. 25. Wellington: Polynesian
      Society.
Kennedy, Raymond
   1937 "The Ethnology of the Greater Sunda Islands," MS, as quoted in
      Thomas, W. I., *Primitive Behavior*. New York: McGraw-Hill Book Co.
Klapman, J. W.
   1959 *Group Psychotherapy: Theory and Practice*. New York: Grune and
      Stratton.

König, H.
1927 "Das Recht der Polar Völker," *Anthropos* 22: 689–746.
Krige, Eileen J.
1936 *The Social System of the Zulus.* London: Longmans, Green and Co.
Kroeber, A.
1925 *Handbook of the Indians of California.* Washington, D.C.: Government Printing Office.
La Hontan, Baron de
1905 *New Voyages to North America,* ed. by R. G. Thwaites. Chicago: A. C. McClurg and Co.
Lewthwaite, Gordon R.
1949 "Human Geography of Aotearoa about 1790." Unpublished Master's Thesis, University of New Zealand.
Lindblom
1916 *The Akamba in British East Africa.* Uppsala: K. W. Appelbergs.
Lips, Julius
1938 "Government," in Boas *et al, General Anthropology.* Chicago: D. C. Heath and Co.
Llewellyn, K. N. and E. Adamson Hoebel
1941 *The Cheyenne Way.* Norman, Oklahoma: University of Oklahoma Press.
Llewellyn, K. N.
1930 "A Realistic Jurisprudence—The Next Step," *Columbia Law Review,* Vol. 30.
Lowie, R. H.
1927 *The Origin of the State.* New York: Harcourt, Brace and Co.
McDonnell, Thomas
1887 "Tales of the Maori," in *The Defenders of New Zealand* by T. W. Gudgeon. Auckland: Brett.
1889 "Personal Courage of the Maori," *Monthly Review* (Wellington) I, 472–80.
Malinowski, B.
1926 *Crime and Custom in Savage Society.* London: Routledge and Kegan Paul.
1934 *Introduction* in H. Ian Hogbin, *Law and Order in Polynesia.* New York: Harcourt, Brace and Co.
1945 *The Dynamics of Culture Change.* New Haven: Yale University Press.
Maning, F. E.
1863 *Old New Zealand.* Auckland: Creighton and Scales.
1876 *Old New Zealand, A Tale of the Good Old Times; and a History of the War in the North Against the Chief Heke, in the Year 1845.* London: Bentley.
Mengarini, Gregory
1738 *Mengarini's Narrative of the Rockies.* Ed. by Albert J. Partoll. Montana State University *Sources of Northwest History No. 25.* Missoula: Montana State University.

Moon, Penderal
1945 *Strangers in India.* London: Faber and Faber, Ltd.
Mooney, James
1898 *Calendar History of the Kiowa.* Bureau of American Ethnology Report, Vol. 17. Washington, D.C.: United States Bureau of American Ethnology.
1928 "The Aboriginal Population of America North of Mexico," Smithsonian Institution *Miscellaneous Collections,* Vol. 80.
Murdock, George Peter
1949 *Social Structure.* New York: Macmillan.
Nader, Laura
1964a "Talea and Juquila: A Comparison of Zapotec Social Organization," *University of California Publications in American Archaeology and Ethnology* 48: 195–296.
1964b "Variations in Rincón Zapotec Legal Procedure," *Homenaje Ingeniero Roberto J. Weitlaner.* Mexico: in press.
Nader, Laura and Duane Metzger
1963 "The Distribution of Conflict Resolution in Two Mexican Communities," *American Anthropologist* 65: 584–92.
Oberg, Kalervo
1934 "Crime and Punishment in Tlingit Society," *American Anthropologist* 36.
Opler, Marvin K.
1959 "Values in Group Psychotherapy," *International Journal of Social Psychiatry,* Vol. IV.
Opler, Morris E.
1956 "Factors of Tradition and Change in a Local Election in Rural India," *Leadership and Political Institutions in India, Paper No. 28.* Berkeley: mimeo.
Opler, Morris E. and Rudra Datt Singh
1948 "The Division of Labor in an Indian Village," in Carleton S. Coon, ed., *A Reader in General Anthropology.* New York: Henry Holt and Co.
1952a "Two Villages of Eastern Uttar Pradesh (U.P.), India: An Analysis of Similarities and Differences," *American Anthropologist,* Vol. 54, 464–96.
1952b "Economic, Political, and Social Change in a Village of North Central India," *Human Organization,* Vol. 11, No. 2, Summer.
Parkinson, Sydney
1773 *A Journal of a Voyage to the South Seas, in His Majesty's Ship, The Endeavour.* London: Stanfield Parkinson.
Parsons, Elsie Clews
1917 *Notes on Zuni, Part II.* Memoirs of the American Anthropological Association, No. 4.
Parsons, Talcott
1951 *The Social System.* Glencoe, Illinois: The Free Press.

Polack, J. S.
  1838 *New Zealand.* 2 vols. London: Bentley.
  1840 *Manners and Customs of the New Zealanders.* 2 vols. London: Madden.
Pospisil, Leopold
  1958 "The Kapauku Papuans and Their Law," *Yale University Publications in Anthropology,* No. 54. New Haven: Yale University Press.
Pound, Roscoe
  1930 "The Call for a Realistic Jurisprudence," *Harvard Law Review,* Vol. 44.
Quain, Buell H.
  1937 "The Iroquois" in *Cooperation and Competition Among Primitive Peoples,* ed. by Margaret Mead. New York: McGraw-Hill.
Radcliffe-Brown, A.
  1922 *The Andaman Islanders.* Cambridge: The University Press.
  1933 "Law, Primitive," in *Encyclopaedia of the Social Sciences,* Vol. 9.
  1952 *Structure and Function in Primitive Society.* Glencoe, Illinois: The Free Press.
Rasmussen, Knud
  1929 *Intellectual Culture of the Igulik Eskimo.* Reports of the Fifth Thule Expedition, 1921–24, Vol. 7.
Rattray, R. S.
  1929 *Ashanti Law and Constitution.* Oxford: Clarendon Press.
Ritter, E. A.
  1957 *Shaka Zulu: The Rise of the Zulu Empire.* New York: G. P. Putnam's Sons.
Roscoe
  1909 "Notes on the Bageshu," *Journal of the Royal Anthropological Society,* 39:181.
Roux, M. Le St. Jean
  1914 "Journal of the *Mascarin,*" in *Historical Records of New Zealand,* ed. by Robert McNab. Vol. II. Wellington: Government Printer.
Russel, Carl P.
  1957 *Guns on the Early Frontier.* Berkeley: University of California Press.
Scheele, Raymond
  1950 "Warfare of the Iroquois and their Northern Neighbors," Unpublished Ph.D. dissertation, Columbia University.
Seagle, William
  1937 "Primitive Law and Professor Malinowski," *American Anthropologist.* Vol. 39, 275–90.
Service, Elman R.
  1962 *Primitive Social Organization.* New York: Random House.
Sherif, Muzafer
  1947 "Group Influence upon the Formation of Norms and Attitudes," in *Readings in Social Psychology,* ed. Theodor Newcomb and Eugene L. Hartley. New York: Henry Holt and Co.

Skinner, W. H.

    1911 "The Ancient Fortified *Pa*," *Journal of the Polynesian Society*, XX, 71–77.

Smith, S. Percy

    1896–97 "The Peopling of the North," *Journal of the Polynesian Society*, V–VI, Supplement.

    1910a *History and Traditions of the Maoris of the West Coast, North Island of New Zealand Prior to 1840*. Polynesian Society Memoir No. 1. New Plymouth: Polynesian Society.

    1910b *Maori Wars of the Nineteenth Century*. Christchurch: Whitcombe and Tombs.

Snyderman, George S.

    1948 *Behind the Tree of Peace: A Sociological Analysis of Iroquois Warfare*. Philadelphia: Unpublished thesis, University of Pennsylvania.

Spear, Percival

    1951 *Twilight of the Mughals*. Cambridge, and India Office Library, Home Miscellaneous Series, Vols. 714, 715.

Stevenson

    1901–2 *The Zuni Indians*. Bureau of American Ethnology Annual Report, Vol. 23.

Stone, Julius

    1964 *Legal Systems and Lawyer's Reasoning*. Stanford: Stanford University Press.

    1965 *Social Dimension of Law and Justice*. Stanford: Stanford University Press.

Strong, W. Duncan

    1933 "Plains Culture in the Light of Archaeology," *American Anthropologist*, Vol. 35.

Sumner, W. G.

    1907 *Folkways*. Boston: Ginn and Co.

Taylor, Richard

    1870 *Te Ika a Maui, or New Zealand and Its Inhabitants*. London: Macintosh.

Thalbitzer, William Carl

    1923 *The Ammassalik Eskimo*. Mendelelser om Grønland: 40. Copenhagen: B. Luno.

Thomason, James

    n.d. "Report on the Settlement of the Ceded Portion of the District of Azimgurh, Commonly Called Chuklah Asimgurh," *Journal of the Asiatic Society of Bengal*, Vol. VIII, 77–136.

Thompson, Arthur S.

    1859 *The Story of New Zealand*. 2 vols. London: Murray.

Thwaites, Reuben G., ed.

    1896–1901 *The Jesuit Relations and Allied Documents . . . 1610–1791*. 73 vols. Cleveland: The Burrows Brothers Company.

Timasheff, Nicholas S.
 1938 "Law as a Social Phenomenon," in *Readings in Jurisprudence* ed.
  J. Hall, pp. 868–72. Indianapolis: The Bobbs-Merrill Co.
Tregear, Edward
 1904 *The Maori Race*. Wanganui: Willis.
Trelease, Allen W.
 1960 *Indian Affairs in Colonial New York: The Seventeenth Century*.
  Ithaca: Cornell University Press.
 1962 "The Iroquois and the Western Fur Trade: A Problem in Interpretation," *The Mississippi Valley Historical Review*, Vol. 49, 32–51.
Turney-High, Harry H.
 1949 *Primitive War*. Columbia: University of South Carolina Press.
Walsh, Cecil
 1912 *Indian Village Crimes*. London: E. Benn Ltd.
Weyer, E. M.
 1932 *The Eskimo*. New Haven: Yale University Press.
White, John
 1874 *Te Rou; or the Maori at Home*. London: Low.
 1887–90 *The Ancient History of the Maori*. 6 vols. Wellington: Government Printer.
Williams, Francis Edgar
 1930 *Orokaiva Society*. London: Oxford University Press.
Williams, Glanville
 1945–46 "Language and the Law," *Law Quarterly Review*, 61–62.
Wilson, John Alexander
 1907 *The Story of Te Waharoa*. Christchurch: Whitcombe and Tombs.
Wintringham, Tom
 1943 *The Story of Weapons and Tactics: From Troy to Stalingrad*. Boston:
  Houghton Mifflin Co.
Wood, William
 1865 *Wood's New England's Prospect, 1634*. Boston: Prince Society.
Yang, Martin C.
 1945 *A Chinese Village*. New York: Columbia University Press.
Yate, William
 1835 *An Account of New Zealand*. London: Seeley and Burnside.

INDEX

Other Texas Press Sourcebooks in Anthropology

ANTHROPOLOGY AND ART
Readings in Cross-Cultural Aesthetics
Edited by Charlotte M. Otten

BETWEEN FIELD AND COOKING POT
The Political Economy of Marketwomen in Peru
By Florence E. Babb

ENVIRONMENT AND CULTURAL BEHAVIOR
Ecological Studies in Cultural Anthropology
Edited by Andrew P. Vayda

GODS AND RITUALS
Readings in Religious Beliefs and Practices
Edited by John Middleton

KINSHIP TO KINGSHIP
Gender Hierarchy and State Formation
in the Tongan Islands
By Christine Ward Gailey

MAGIC, WITCHCRAFT, AND CURING
Edited by John Middleton

MYTH AND COSMOS
Readings in Mythology and Symbolism
Edited by John Middleton

PERSONALITIES AND CULTURES
Readings in Psychological Anthropology
Edited by Robert Hunt

RITUAL HUMOR IN HIGHLAND CHIAPAS
By Victoria Reifler Bricker

THE WAY OF THE DEAD INDIANS
Guajiro Myths and Symbols
By Michel Perrin

WOMEN OF VALUE, MEN OF RENOWN
New Perspectives in Trobriand Exchange
By Annette B. Weiner

Law and Welfare examines the resolution of conflict from the anthropological—that it is to say, comparative—point of view. There are basically two forms of conflict resolution: administrative rules and fighting; law and war.

Here are brought together the best anthropological reports on conflict around the world. The book's three sections examine the nature of legal phenomena; institutions and means of conflict resolution (courts and moots, compromise and decision, self-help and ordeals); and war (feud, riots and raids, outlaws and police, warriors and armies).

Paul Bohannan is professor of anthropology at the University of California, Santa Barbara.

Write for our complete anthropology catalog.

UNIVERSITY OF TEXAS PRESS

Post Office Box 7819   Austin, Texas 78713-7819

Printed in U.S.A.   ISBN 0-292-74617-2